# Shards of Memory:
# Messages from the
# Lost Shtetl of Antopol, Belarus

## Translation of the Yizkor (Memorial) Book
## of the Jewish Community of Antopol

### Edited by Alicia Esther Goldberg

### Translated by Nathan Snyder

**Published by JewishGen**

**An Affiliate of the Museum of Jewish Heritage - A Living Memorial to the Holocaust
New York**

Shards of Memory: Messages from the Lost Shtetl of Antopol, Belarus
Translation of the Yizkor (Memorial) Book of the Jewish Community of Antopol

Editor: Alicia Esther Goldberg
Translator: Nathan Snyder
Layout: Joel Alpert
Cover Design: Jan R. Fine
Publicity: Sandra Hirschhorn

Published by JewishGen, Inc.
An Affiliate of the Museum of Jewish Heritage
A Living Memorial to the Holocaust
36 Battery Place, New York, NY 10280

"JewishGen, Inc., the editor and any participants in the production of this edition, are not responsible for inaccuracies or omissions in the original work and makes no representations regarding the accuracy of this translation. Digital images of the original book's contents can be seen online at the New York Public Library Web site."

The mission of the JewishGen organization is to produce a translation of the original work and we cannot verify the accuracy of statements or alter facts cited.

Printed in the United States of America by Lightning Source, Inc.

Library of Congress Control Number (LCCN): 2013948543
ISBN: 978-1-939561-11-4  (hard cover: 484 pages, alk. paper)

Cover photographs: Artwork from the original Yizkor book.
Front cover note: The synagogue was called "The Cold Shul"  because it was unheated and was not used in winter.

# JewishGen and the Yizkor Books in Print Project

This book has been published by the **Yizkor Books in Print Project,** as part of the **Yizkor Book Project** of **JewishGen, Inc.**

**JewishGen, Inc.** is a non-profit organization founded in 1987 as a resource for Jewish genealogy. Its website [www.jewishgen.org] serves as an international clearinghouse and resource center to assist individuals who are researching the history of their Jewish families and the places where they lived. JewishGen provides databases, facilitates discussion groups, and coordinates projects relating to Jewish genealogy and the history of the Jewish people. In 2003, JewishGen became an affiliate of the **Museum of Jewish Heritage - A Living Memorial to the Holocaust** in New York.

The **JewishGen Yizkor Book Project** was organized to make more widely known the existence of Yizkor (Memorial) Books written by survivors and former residents of various Jewish communities throughout the world. Later, volunteers connected to the different destroyed communities began cooperating to have these books translated from the original language—usually Hebrew or Yiddish—into English, thus enabling a wider audience to have access to the valuable information contained within them. As each chapter of these books was translated, it was posted on the JewishGen website and made available to the general public.

The **Yizkor Books in Print Project** began in 2011 as an initiative to print and publish Yizkor Books that had been fully translated, so that hard copies would be available for purchase by the descendants of these communities and also by scholars, universities, synagogues, libraries, and museums.

These Yizkor books have been produced almost entirely through the volunteer effort of researchers from around the world, assisted by donations from private individuals. The books are printed and sold at near cost, so as to make them as affordable as possible. Our goal is to make this important genre of Jewish literature and history available in English in book form, so that people can have the personal histories of their ancestral towns on their bookshelves for themselves and for their children and grandchildren.

A list of all published translated Yizkor Books and how to order can be found at:
http://www.jewishgen.org/Yizkor/ybip.html

*Lance Ackerfeld, Yizkor Book Project Manager*

*Joel Alpert, Yizkor Book in Print Project Coordinator*

# JewishGen
# Yizkor Book Project

This book is presented by the
Yizkor Books in Print Project
Project Coordinator: Joel Alpert

Part of the
Yizkor Books Project of JewishGen, Inc.
Project Manager: Lance Ackerfeld

These books have been produced solely through volunteer effort
of individuals from around the world.  The books are printed and
sold at near cost, so as to make them as affordable as possible.

Our goal is to make this history and important genre of Jewish
literature available in English in book form so that people can have
the near-personal histories of their ancestral towns on their bookshelves for themselves and for their children and grandchildren.

Any donations to the Yizkor Books Project are appreciated.

Please send donations to:
Yizkor Book Project
JewishGen
36 Battery Place
New York, NY 10280

JewishGen, Inc. is an affiliate of the
Museum of Jewish Heritage
A Living Memorial to the Holocaust

Title Page of Original Yiddish and Hebrew Yizkor Book

# א נ ט ו פ ו ל

(אנטיפאליע)

## ס פ ר ־ י ז כ ו ר

ערוך בידי

בן־ציון ח. אילון

„ארון קודש" מעשי ידי האמן יהושע וואראשא

בהוצאת ארגון יוצאי אנטופול בישראל ובאמריקה

תל־אביב. תשל"ב — 1972

# A N T O P O L

## (ANTEPOLIE)

## YIZKOR BOOK

EDITED BY

### BENZION H. AYALON

"Kalte Shul" — Drawing by A. Warsaw

Published by
Antopol Committee in Israel, Actively Assisted by
The Antepoller Yizkor Book Committee in the U.S.A.
Tel-Aviv, Israel, 1972

# Dedication

This book is dedicated to the Antopol survivors and the memory of the 3,000 martyrs, whose names and stories fill these pages.

# Survivors

Professor P. Czerniak, with his wife and daughter
Ita Wolinetz
Shoshe Wolowelsky
Itka Mazurski
Reizl Kagan

# Acknowledgements

I must acknowledge the significant effort of the Memorial Book Committee of Tel Aviv, who first published this book in 1972, as well as the American landsleit organization, which generously supported the work of the original publication. I apologize for any errors present in the translation and editing of this noble work.

This edition would not be possible without the dedication and translation expertise of Nathan Snyder, a professional librarian in the Hebrew and Yiddish Studies Program at the University of Texas at Austin.

For inspiration and editorial insight on the Yiddish messages, I recognize my father, Professor Jack Otis, and his wife, Patricia Folmar Otis. Leanne Hunt and Bonnie Glendinning were invaluable in providing encouragement as well as editing and designing this work.

Finally, I pay homage to all of the descendents of Antopol, who have created new lives of freedom and prosperity for themselves and future generations.

May these messages reach our hearts and remind us of the strength of our heritage.

Alicia Goldberg Funk

Our sincere appreciation to Alicia Goldberg Funk who has kindly donated this book to the Yizkor-Books-in-Print Project of JewishGen, Inc.

Joel Alpert, Coordinator of the Yizkor-Books-in-Print Project

# I want to say Kadish today

## By Pintshe Berman
## (Resident of Antopol)

I want to say kadish* today
for the "ten lost tribes" --
the destroyed of my beloved home.

I want to say kadish
for my world, which is vanished,
and which lies under ashes and clay.

I want to say kadish today
for the garden of my youth
for the world of my dreams, which is gone.

The forest there is burnt,
and the garden: a cemetery.
And every beaten path and way abandoned.

Woe is me! I have sat in the shade of poplars,
and the wind has fondled and embraced me.

And there the storm,
like a wild animal, wildly tore
and destroyed, without mercy, my world.

I want to say kadish today,
and place myself before the cantor's desk,
in a prayer shawl, woven from ashes and smoke.

I want to say kadish today,
to call God to a minyan.**
He should come.
He should also say, Amen!

*prayer for the dead
**prayer quorum

# Map of Antopol, Belarus Today

ESTONIA

LATVIA

RUSSIA

| | 2012 Border |
| | 1940 Border |

**BELARUS**

0  25  50  75  km

0  25  50  75 miles

LITHUANIA

RUSSIA

VILNIUS •

**BELARUS**

1940 Border

• MINSK

• ANTOPOL

POLAND

UKRAINE

Antopol, Belarus is located at
52°12' North Latitude and 24°47' East Longitude

# Second Edition Notes:

This book represents a translation and editing of the complete Hebrew, Yiddish and English sections of the book <u>Yizkor (Memorial) Book of the Jewish Community of Antopol (1972)</u>. In some cases, stories were duplicated in several languages and in this edition they appear only one time. In many instances, a story appears in the original edition only Hebrew or Yiddish and in this edition it is available to read in English.

Within the text the reader will note that the words like *[Page 34]* standing ahead of a paragraph. This indicates that the material translated below was on page 34, for instance, of the original book. However, when a paragraph was split between two pages in the original book, the marker is placed in this book after the end of the paragraph for ease of reading.

All references within the text of the book to page numbers refer to the page numbers of the Hebrew and Yiddish original Yizkor Book edition, available online, at: http://yizkor.nypl.org/index.php?id=1729

## Geopolitical Locations and Names

|  | Town | District | Province | Country |
|---|---|---|---|---|
| Before WWI (c. 1900): | Antopol | Kobrin | Grodno | Russian Empire |
| Between the wars (c. 1930): | Antopol | Kobryń | Polesie | Poland |
| After WWII (c. 1950): | Antopol' |  |  | Soviet Union |
| Today (c. 2000): | Antopol' |  |  | Belarus |

Antopol is know as Antopol [Russian and Polish], Antapoli [Yiddish], Antopal [Belarussian], Antepolye, Antipolye, Antopole.

Antopol sits in the Polesian Plain, near Kobryn and Brest (Brest-Litowski), near the river Pripyat, a tributary of the Dnieper River.

# TABLE OF CONTENTS

## Photographs

# Hebrew Messages

# People and Families of Antopol

## Antopol Martyrs of the Holocaust

# Family Notes

*[Page 1]*

# Preface

Everything I've done to bring this book into existence I've done for my father, Professor Jack Otis. My grandfather, Abraham Osipowitz, came here from Antopol, and my grandmother, Esther Goldberg Osipowitz, came from a nearby region. They came here as immigrants, speaking little English, and raised my father to be a success in America. He became dean of the school of social work at the University of Texas, fought hard for the rights of people suffering from poverty and injustice, and accomplished more than they could have ever hoped for.

My grandfather died before I was born, and my grandmother died when I was five years old. I can't say that I really knew them well or understood anything of my family's past until my mid-20s, when I began incessantly asking my father questions about where we came from.

Part of becoming a successful American meant forgetting the past. He couldn't answer my questions, and out of his love for me, took me to Israel, to meet my grandmother's sister and the family members who had never known America. They welcomed us with a warmth that eased the distance, the lingering questions, and the stories untold.

Finding this book happened during our trip to Israel. We met a first cousin, Chaim Ossip, who had actively participated in the creation of the Yizkor Memorial Book, published in 1972 by the Antopol Committee in Israel. We took a copy of the book back to the United States, sensing somehow that we had discovered a key to understanding our past, and consequently, our present.

My father arranged for the translation of the Hebrew and Yiddish sections, by a modest, dedicated Yiddish scholar at the University of Texas by the name of Nathan Snyder. He spent over five years working on the translation, sending us typewritten pieces of the past, two or three pages at a time.

Due to prejudice and social pressure in the 1940s, even in the land of the free, my father felt compelled to change his last name to Otis. My fervent desire to embrace our heritage forced me to change my name back to my grandmother's maiden name of Goldberg.

Although our names have changed and somewhere along the way our identity became indistinguishable from other Americans, our hearts are forever linked to the Jewish people scattered around the globe and especially to the individuals who closely hold the fragments of our forgotten past.

This Memorial book was written in English, Yiddish, and Hebrew by gathering the stories of numerous individuals originally from Antopol, now residing in Israel, Canada, and the United States. It offers a glimpse into the lives of the Jews of Antopol. May the strength of their stories encourage us to speak the truth and stand up for what is right, regardless of the consequences.

Alicia Esther Goldberg

February 13, 2003

For my father's 80th birthday, in respect of all that he has taught me.

*[Page 3]*

# At the Gates

## Introduction

With a heavy heart and spirit, full with sorrow, I am writing in memory of our beloved Jewish community, which was annihilated, in our town Antopol, where I was born and where I spent my youth – the spring of my life. Ben I left our town Antopol in the year 1921 in order to immigrate to Israel, I parted from all my dear and beloved and from a town in which dear and fine Jews were living, satisfied with their fate, productive artisans, decently educated in Jewish tradition and spirit, a town which was renowned by its Rabbis and scholars and by the very old and nice synagogue and numerous Batei-Mdrashim. Also the hard-working Jews used to spend there every day, early in the morning as well as till late in the evening in learning Torah and in doing charity and aid to those in need, thus symbolizing the splendor of human nature which was found throughout all generations in Antopol for over 500 years.

Much to our regret and sorrow, the bitter and cruel destiny cut off the life of the whole dear Jewish community, and all our good and bright hopes entertained by us and by them for the future, disappeared with their souls into the high heavens in Sanctification of the Holy Name, and their blood was shed by the Nazi and Polish murderers and their heirs, may their name be blotted out, Amen!

We the Antopol landsleit, the bereaved orphans, who left Antopol more than 50 years ago and immigrated to far countries overseas, with the ardent wish and aim to extend relief to our parents and families, who were left behind in the old home, and numerous families did get relief at the end of the first world war by their children, husbands and relatives who remitted the first aid through delegates, and since them many families and youths, with the help of American relatives, did immigrate to all States of America as well as to Eretz-Israel, with the desire and hope to send relief for their families and take them out of the Polish anti-Semitic regime and people.

Alas, to our deep regret we were too late and had not the privilege to let our beloved join us, so that it has just been left to us – the orphans – to set up monuments in their memory. We have already erected many monuments, and now, with the publishing of the nice Antopol Memorial Book we have set up a really great and magnificent monument. The erection of this monument has taken many years, since I met the first rescued remnant from Antopol who arrived in Israel, from whom I became aware of the heavy disaster which had befallen us with the annihilation of the whole beloved Jewish community of Antopol, of blessed memory. Since then I started outlining the Antopol plan, marking all houses, just as I recalled them to my mind from the eve of the first world war, having contributed to the Book many articles which I had taken out of my memorial book, as I noted many years ago.

I have also been active in demanding and collecting some material from local and American landsleit, who have very warmly responded in contributing plenty of material, pictures and money towards the publishing of this nice and monumental book. Following our ardent wish and tendency that our Antopol Book should include contributions of our landsleit who knew Antopol, the writers and poets, who are capable of perpetuating the memory of destroyed Antopol, in eulogy and lamentation over the ruin and destruction of the Jewish Antopol community of blessed memory, and in this way publish the Memorial Book, in its proper form and appearance. We shall, however, refrain from being arrogant and giving compliments to ourselves.

We did it because this is our ardent duty and devotion for the memory and honor of our perished families of our dear townlet Antopol. I highly appreciate the activities of all devoted landsleit of all the America Committees, with respect and gratitude for their nice and gigantic help and assistance, which continues already for over 50 years, and for their great help extended to our institutions, that all of us, of the Antopol landsleit in Israel highly appraise and appreciate with innermost gratitude, all that they have done for us and for Israel, and especially for the magnificent Antopol Book. I express my special thanks to our devoted friends; Max Futerman, Leizer Volynieta, Israel Pernik and to all those who assisted us in publishing the Book.

Your sincere and grateful Antopoler,
YOSHE POLLACK

*Note: This is the only edition that includes all three sections in English. Since the "English Messages" were originally extracted from the Yiddish and Hebrew sections, some stories will be told twice.*

*[Page 7]*

# English Messages

## Antopol History
### By Prof. P. Czerniak

## Physical Geography

Antopol is one of about 30 similar little towns in Polesia, the greatest area marshes in Europe. The district lies 150 meters above sea level, at 52 degrees 11'N and 24 degrees 42'E. The town is situated between Kobrin, Drohichin, Radostov, Zafrod, near the great marshes which extend south, east and north-east, and occupy about 56% of Polesia. Antopol, like other similar settlements, lies on a small elevation of land, but in its immediate vicinity we find already the beginning of marshes, especially to the east.

## Hydrograph

There is no river near Antopol, but 7 miles from the town lies the Karolevski Canal, 50 miles long, 20- 30 meters wide, and two meters deep. As long back as 1795 the Poles began the project, which was finished by the Russians during the Czarist regime. The Soviets in 1941-42 deepened and extended it in order to adapt it to the shipment of vessels carrying wheat to Nazi Germany, and bringing back coal and metal ores. These were the times after the treaty between the German and Soviet foreign ministers. In the winter of 1941-42 they brought to Antopol about 5,000 prisoners from Russian concentration camps, who extended the canal and also built an airport for military use. The zone, in which Antopol is situated, belongs to the border of the plateau separating the Baltic basin from the Black Sea basin. A smaller canal, named after Oginski, 30 miles long, 12 meters wide was dug in the eighteenth century. A total length of 1,250 miles of other canals was counted in 1935. The ground water is very high in Antopol. Many wells were dug in the backyards in town, especially in the years 1930-1940, when cement pipes were manufactured by a local citizen, Podorewski.

## Climate and Precipitation

The climatology of Antopol is affected by its being situated in an enclosed area, low and marshy, in a continent extending from the Ural to the Atlantic, from the Black Sea to the Baltic Sea. The summer lasts from the end of May till the middle of September, and the temperature is about 17.6°C. In the summer there are western and north-western winds, sometimes also storms with rains. After the hot day come nights with heavy fogs rising from the marshes. The winter is severe, full of snow which lasts three months, and the frozen water, especially in the marshes, serve for transportation. Spring is short, and this is the time when the marshes melt again. Autumn is usually a rainy season. Precipitation reaches 600mm per annum.

## Soil

Geologically the soil has a granite basis with varying layers of lime and sand. During the Diluvial period the whole area was covered with huge glaziers. The granite hills prevented them from moving, and thus were formed the Polesian marshes. In these marshes began to grow layers of Torf, which occupy about a third of the area. In other zones we find layers of Kaolin and Black Soil. Around the 16th century, after beginning to dry the marshes, they began to till the land in an orderly manner. Most of the good land belonged to different princes. In the 20th century, with the abolition of servitudes the land was parcelled and colonization began in 1927-33. After World War II the soviets established two agricultural groups (Kolhoz): Pervomaiski and Gubemia.

*[Page 8]*

## Flora

Wild flora abounds in the region, especially in the marshy region. Large areas are covered with forests, which occupy 25% of the region, with 65% pine trees, as well as other indigenous species. These forests are full with mushrooms and berries. The agrarian flora includes: Wheat, barley, flax, as well as potatoes, onions, cabbage, garlic etc. In Antopol itself there were many plots tilled by both Jews and non-Jews. The Jews perfected their production of industrial crops, mainly two: pickles and ganders for export.

## Fauna

The region boasts of riches in fauna. Forest animals include all the known varieties, from bears and wolves to rabbits and beavers. Hunting was therefore very popular in the area. Also fowl is abundant, and there is a variety of 40 different species of fish, as well as insects indigenous to marshy areas.

# Population

The population numbered up to 3,000 in good times, but epidemics, pogroms and immigration did not allow it to grow. The majority were Jews, and the others were: Polishuks, Belorussians, Russians and Poles. The inhabitants lived in primitive huts, wore hand made clothes, until manufactured goods arrived. Their countenance is pale, long oval faces, wide foreheads, straight noses, auburn hair. Quiet people, calculated, patient, conservative, not industrious, and in spite of availability of water – unclean. The adults often sleep on the furnace. The prevailing religion is Pravoslavic, but the peasants believe in many superstitions. Poles began swarming into the area in the 16th century. In various periods their immigration increased or decreased. After World War I, immigration increased and with this wave came also the postman Chrominsky, the cursed hangman of Jewish Antopol.

# Our town
## By A. Ben-Ezra

## Location and Origin

Antopol (Antipolie, in the Jewish slang) is situated near the railway Pinsk-Kobrin, 8 kilometers east of Horodetz and 28 kilometers west of Drochichin, in the subdistrict of Kobrin, district of Grodno.

The town is part of Polesia, known for its vast marshes and forests. Antopol is therefore known by its nickname "marshes of Antopol". Near Antopol, on the west side, there used to be a large forest beginning from the road to Kobrin. To the south, on the road leading to the village Rusheve, there was another dense forest.

It seems that ancient Antopol began to develop from the Kobrin road; where the forest ended, and stretched until the site of the old cemetery, which by religious law was outside the town limits. When was Antopol founded? When did Jewish settlement begin there? There is little documentation, which can be relied upon, and we must contend ourselves with assumptions that Jewish settlement in Antopol began about 1604. According to documents in Polish, the town is mentioned in relation to the building of a monastery around 1718. In the same documents it is mentioned that the good lady Antonina Zamoiska built the monastery, and the town was named after her – Antopol, Antonina's town (=polis in Greek).

## Changes in Government

The region of Polesia has undergone many occupations, following revolutions and counterrevolutions. In 1315-1341, Polesia was conquered by the Lithuanian Archduke Gdimin.

After the unification of Poland and Lithuania in 1386, the Lithuanian archduchy opened its gates to Polish culture, and especially to its Roman Catholic religion. The Roman Catholic church extended its influence everywhere. Gradually and successfully it completed the Polanization of Polesia. This situation aroused the anger of the Cosacks and caused the famous Chmelnitzky Rebellion. The Cosacks looted the country for two years. Much Jewish blood was shed in those two years in Polesia, until the Polish army drove out the rebels. In the spring of 1706, the Swedes, led by Karol XII, declared war on Poland, but the marshes of Polesia caused them to withdraw in the same year. History does not give us details about the fate of Antopol Jews in those years, but in Jewish folklore there remained the saying "it remembers the Swedes" as signifying an old story. Poland was saved and remained intact until 1772, the year of its first partition.

*[Page 9]*

In 1793-1795 Russia annexed the-districts of Minsk, Vilno, and Grodno. The district of Grodno contained the following eight subdistricts: Grodno, Lidda. Novogrodsk, Slonim, Volkovisk, Prozhani, Brrsk, and Kobrin. Antopol was then part of the subdistrict of Kobrin.

In the 1812 Franco-Russian war, Antopol also took its share of misfortunes. During the battles in the town the inhabitants suffered much and the Jews most of all. The Polish residents were not happy under Russian rule, and tried twice to rebel against the foreigners, in 1830 and in 1863, but they failed in both attempts. These Jews supported the Poles. They provided them with food and shelter, even though the Poles in the Jewish shelter did not forget to shout at their saviors: Filthy Jew, take off your hat!

The Russians did not forgive the Jews for harboring the Poles, and punished them very hard for their support of their enemies. Punishing Jews was an easy undertaking under Czarist Russia. The land of Antopol and environs belonged to the squires, the noble landowners, and the Jews used to pay taxes.

In 1904 the Jews paid taxes to Lady Sofia Martina Voitosh. Her property in land was immense and her business manager was an Antopol Jew by the name of Mordechai Sheinboim, through whose initiative she did for the Jews of Antopol many favors.

The region had been resting from wars about 100 years when World War I broke out. In the summer of 1915 the Germans conquered Antopol. Many Jewish houses were burned down and the Jews settled in the houses of the gentiles who had fled to Russia. The few Jews who remained reorganized life in the little town but the German rule was very strict. The young people were hurt most of all. They were seized and sent to labor camps. The German conquerors began to establish German public schools to spread the German language and culture. Antopol was under German rule until November 1918, when the Germans began to return to Germany. Anarchy spread in town.

When eventually Antopol was annexed to the new Poland, "legal" terror began to reign. The Polish regime protected the terrorists who continued to loot and riot. Later Antopol became a zone of fighting between the Russians and the Poles.

In 1919, the Bolsheviks arrived in Antopol and they began to introduce their "new order". They did not stay long and the Poles returned to Antopol. Upon their return they avenged themselves on the Jews who suffered much during this period.

The region began to quiet down, and the population began to rehabilitate its life, when Poland and the Bolsheviks began fighting in July 1920. At first the Russians succeeded in getting to the gates of Warsaw, but finally the Poles repelled them. In the meantime the soldiers of General Belachovitz, leader of the White Russians, join forces with the Poles.

This union is written with blood and tears in Jewish history. In 1921, a truce was signed in Riga and Antopol was incorporated in Poland. The Polish government introduced strict laws against the Jewish people, including compulsory education in Polish schools and service in the army. In spite of that, many Jews excelled themselves in their army service.

When World War II broke out, the Bolsheviks took over Antopol and environs. The Soviet regime lasted, for better or for worse, until June 1941, when the Nazis crossed the Russian border and conquered all of Poland and the Ukraine, on their way to Moscow and Leningrad. Under the Nazis, the Jews of Antopol were persecuted, tortured, and imprisoned in a ghetto, but they did not surrender. They fought back, joined the partisans and took an active part in the underground. But eventually they were executed and murdered by the cursed Nazis. In July 1944, the Red Army reconquered Antopol, which is now incorporated in the district of Kobrin in White Russia, but her Jews, our dear families are no more. Thus came an end to Jewish life in Antopol.

*[Page 10]*

# Economic Life in Antopol

We do not know much about economic life in old Antopol. We also lack information about its Jewish population in those years. Nevertheless we know that the Jewish population was constantly increasing. About 200 years after its establishment in 1847 the Jewish population numbered 1,108 inhabitants. By 1860 they increased to 1,259 out of a general population of 1,563. If we take into account the fires in town which drove away many people, the net increase is remarkable. In 1897, the Jews were already in the majority, 3,137 out of 3,867. In 1904, when the total population numbered 5,235, the Jews accounted for at least half that number. During that period the town developed, roads were extended and the side streets were inhabited by Jews.

What did the Jews do for a living? What caused them to spread out? Most Antopol Jews tilled the land, grew potatoes, onions, carrots, cucumbers etc. Those agricultural workers were called Morgovniks and worked the land in the back of their houses, especially along the roads to Pinsk and Kobrin. Some worked by themselves and others employed gentile hired workers. The vegetables were loaded on wagons and sent to the markets in nearby towns. In the beginning of the 20th century an industrial crop came to the fore – pickled cucumbers, which were stored in cellars to protect them from the cold. Later they were sent as far as Warsaw.

The second agricultural industry was the goose trade. They used to import them from far away Russia, feed them and raise them in special "poshornies". When they became fat, they were transported to Lithuania or to Germany. Merchants and commercial agents from other towns used to come to Antopol, and Antopol merchants were also constantly going to Vilno (capital of Lithuania).

There were also other enterprises in town, such as mills, brick factories, lime factories etc. In the middle of the town stood the market place, numbering 42 stores. On Sundays, the inhabitants of the neighboring villages used to come to Antopol for the weekly fair to exchange goods in the local market which attracted also merchants from far away. There were also two yearly fairs which were famous all over the region. In 1840, when the Royal Canal was dug from Pinsk to Horodetz, a local Jewish contractor supplied workers for the project. In the 1880's, the Lifshitzes, famous forest traders, supplied lumber for a regional railway. Another large project was the road between Horodetz and Antopol in 1908-1910. This road gave Antopol access to the Horodetz railway station. A traders loan association began operating in Antopol in the beginning of the 20th century. Merchants were granted loans without interest from its bank. Its chief accountant was Peretz Gurewitz.

In the period between the two world wars, a Gmilus Hassodim Fund was established following the initial generous contribution of Mrs. Esther Cornblum from the U.S.A. This fund was a significant aid in the economic development in Antopol. About 1928 a bus line was inaugurated, connecting Antopol with Kobrin, thus helping also the trade of the town. In 1935 a small power station was constructed to supply electricity and power. The U.S.A. was an immense source of income for Antopol. Many men who had immigrated to America used to support the families left behind. After World War I, the amount of aid increased, especially when the Polish regime proclaimed restrictions on the Jews. Two waves of immigration began then: one to Israel and the other to South America. The Jews who immigrated from Antopol were the ones who remained alive to tell the world of the destruction of their birth town and the murder of their families by the Nazi inhumans.

*[Page 11]*

# Culture in Antopol

Antopol, like many other Jewish towns in Polesia, was a religious town. Religion was the framework for everyday life. The rabbis were the leaders in all walks of life, and everything went by religious law. Even some young people who "went astray" did so within the religious sphere. Such a man was Dr. Israel M. Rabinowitz, son of the rabbi Moshe-Hirsh, who went for secular studies, and became known as the translator of the Talmud into French.

The thirst for knowledge spread more and more, and the public demanded teachers for Hebrew, Russian, and mathematics, and when they were brought – they had an increasing number of students for these subjects.

The social movements during the Russian revolution had a great influence in Antopol. Antopol Jews tell about Fradel Stavsky, one of the organizers of subversive activities in town. She was exiled to Siberia. Zionist movements followed and many young people joined them. Young boys and girls learned also in Russian public schools and continued in high schools in Brick and other cities.

The traditional Heider was reformed by Reb Aharon Lifshitz (Lief). The reformed Heider was later followed by another one established by Reb Israel Wall-Wollowelsky, who introduced also a teacher for the Russian language. A private school for girls was conducted by Mrs. Teibe Shagan. Also private teachers were brought to teach languages and sciences. After World War I, a Hebrew School Tarbut was founded, in which Hebrew was the language used. There was also a library called "The I. L. Peretz library". Talmud Torah schools and Yeshivot were opened in town and Jewish studies gave the tone until the Soviets closed the schools and the Nazis executed the population.

# Colonies of Antopol Jews

Jews from Antopol spread also over Russia and Poland. Already in the 1880's there were famous branches in Kishinev and in Warsaw. An important center for Antopol immigrants was the U.S.A. Although it was far away – one had to prepare a passport, cross frontiers, and travel by boat 2-3 weeks, and upon arrival they could not observe religion as they used to back home – the desire to wider horizons overcame everything.

They used to come to New York and Chicago, and other metropolitan cities, where they could make a living and build a home, but people went also to Brownsville which was nicknamed "Jerusalem of America" on account of its Jewish population. There they established a union with immigrants from Kobrin and Horodetz called "Hevra Gmilus Hassodim Agudas Achim Anshei Kobrin, Horodetz and Antepolie". One helped another to settle in the new country, but some did not find their place and returned back to the old country. Many of Antopol immigrants in America advanced themselves in American industry, like the Farbers in silverware and Margolies in gas stations. In music we all know: Cantor David Putterman who was dean of the cantors association, and Roberta Peters (also a Putterman) star of the Metropolitan Opera in New-York. In science Antopol is represented by: Prof. P. Berman, who was director of the large hospital in Pasadena; Dr. M. Kletsky, for many years chief dentist of Arbieter Ring and contributor to professional magazines; and Prof. Herbert L. Henderson, who took an active part in the development of the first atom bomb. Antopol Jews have earned prominent places also in Chicago.

They established organizations and various associations. Their synagogue in Chicago was famous in the city. Rabbi Jacob Greenberg founded the "Beit Midrash LeTorah" in Chicago and presided over the institution all his life. In Argentina, there is an important chapter of Antopol landsleit, especially in Buenos Aires, and it is said that they were of the first immigrants there. In the building of the State of Israel the Jews from Antopol wrote (and are still writing) a brilliant chapter. The Holy Land was always the dream of the Jews in Antopol. Already 200 years ago they began coming to Israel. Seventy Hassidim of the followers of Hagra came to Zefat in 1808. Others came individually in the same century, like Reb Moshe Ben Akiva and Reb Moshe Zvi, Reb Benjamin Yahalom and Reb Jacob Benjamin, Reb Nathaniel Haim Pape and his family, and the whole Saharov family.

[Page 12]

# The End

In 1960, our dear brother, the late Prof. P. Berman, wrote a letter to the governor of Antopol. In his letter he inquired what had become of his birth town. After two years came the answer in the form of a newspaper article in the local paper published in Minsk, capital of White Russia. The reporter described a Jewish citizen named Isaac Berkovitz, who told him about the suffering of Belorussians, Jews and Poles. He did not point out that the ghetto imprisoned only Jews and that the Nazis killed all the Jews with the help of the local population. He tells happily about the progress which the Soviet regime brought to town. He tells about schools, libraries, bookstores etc. but no Hebrew or Yiddish is mentioned, because no Jews were left to enjoy it. There is a church in town. But where are the synagogues and the prayer houses? Why does he not mention any of them? And so, with this report we seal a 300 years chapter of the Jewish community in Antopol.

# The Synagogue Court
## By Dr. P. Berman (O.B.M.)

We called it in Yiddish, Shut-heyf (-court, plaza). It was a "court" in the center of the town, around which were grouped the religious and communal institutions of the Jewish community. This was probably the center of the first Jewish settlers in ancient times, and from here they gradually spread out to the other parts of the town of Antopol, extending pretty far out. I remember that, when I was a boy, the court was the only paved, or, rather, cobbled, area in town, and was therefore less severely affected by the large puddles of water in the fall and in the spring. The court was square-shaped and surrounded on its four sides, by: The "Cold Synagogue"; the two B'eiss Medresh (prayer house); one "new" and the other "old"; and the Beiss Horau (-rabbinical residence).

Behind the "old" Beiss Medresh stood the Bad (-communal bath-house) and the Hekdesh (-poorhouse, hostel). There, too, began the old Jewish cemetery. The Cold Synagogue was the tallest building in town, excepting the Greek-Orthodox church, which stood in the market place, a distance away from the. Jewish synagogues. The architecture of the Cold Synagogue was of the well-known type of the Jewish synagogues of Poland and Lithuania, as depicted in literature, and I have seen pictures of such synagogues which looked to me like copies of our own.

I do not know how old that synagogue was. It must have undergone many repairs and thorough rebuilding in olden times. I remember it as a solid edifice, clean-looking, devoid of any external ornaments and, in my boyish eyes, the greatest and most beautiful building in town. There was a Polesh (-lobby) in the synagogue, and to its right there was a chapel which served as a classroom for one of the classes of the Talmud-Torah (-Jewish early public school). The main classrooms were located in the "Old Prayerhouse". The chapel was also used for daily prayers on weekdays. To the left of the lobby there was a room, which was used as the center of the Hevrah Kadisho (-burial society), for there were to be found the Tohoroh-Bret (-cleansing board) and the Mittoh (-couch for the dead) as well as other utensils. As boys we used to avoid getting near that place, being afraid of the assortment of burial utensils. The tall Gothic windows were situated about two floors above the ground, right under the ceiling, and therefore permanent darkness reigned inside the synagogue. Even the walls were painted dark grey. A small, metal frame hung on one of the walls, containing unleavened bread.

*[Page 13]*

The ceiling was a dome, resting on a single rafter, which was etched out with designs like a pleated Halla (-Sabbath loaf). It was painted in whiteand- gold and extended from wall to wall. The domed ceiling itself was decorated with figures of animals – deer, lions and even, as I recall, the mythological unicorn.

Underneath the animals were painted the twelve planets, with Hebrew legend. Hebrew captions were painted also under the animals, quoting verses or idioms like Mighty as a Lion. As a child, I was strongly attracted to the pictures described above, and I could never have my fill of contemplating them, whenever I had the opportunity. In the center of the synagogue, nearer to the doorway, stood the Bimah (-pulpit), while at the Eastern Wall, as usual, was the Ark containing the Sifrei Thorah (-Holy Scrolls), and on top of it – over the various designs – were drawn two hands in the position of the priestly benediction. In a corner of the synagogue stood the Chair of Elijah, on which used to sit the Sandak (the man who holds the male child on his knees during the ceremony of circumcision). Nearby there was a large copper vessel on a stand, filled with sand, into which were thrown the foreskins.

The women's section was on the second floor, over the lobby and the chapel. This section was fairly large. Its Eastern Wall was built up only to half its height, and protruded into the main synagogue like a gallery with grillwork, through which the womenfolk could look into the men section and follow the reading of the prayers. The Cold Synagogue was used for services on Sabbaths and holidays. Unlike the prayer study houses, it was used only for prayer and the recitation of psalms.

Many legends circulated in town about the Cold Synagogue. It was said that a great rabbi once blessed it and it would never be consummated by fire. As a result, the synagogue survived the numerous fires which had happened in Antopol.

Another legend related that one of the Poreiches (-curtain of the Ark) had been bought from a Cossack who had it salvaged from a synagogue pillaged in the time of Bogdan Khmelnitzky's massacres of the Jews.

One of the earlier sextons of the Cold Synagogue was a man by the name of Avreml, a small old man, who used to find enough strength to come to the market place every Friday at eventide to call the people to finish their business and trade and go to the synagogue.

The sexton in my days was Elyeh, a handsome man with a wide red beard. He also served as teacher in the Talmud Torah classes, which took place in the chapel of the Cold Synagogue.

The New Beiss Medresh was not really new. The "old" one was a much newer building, but it was erected in place of the older prayer house which had been destroyed by fire and therefore kept the name. The New Beiss Medresh consisted of two large rooms, divided by a long brick stove which separated the men's section from the women's section, Here worshipped some of the leading Jews of Antopol, such as Reb Hersch – one of the three rabbis who reigned in Antopol after the demise of the religious leader of the prayer-house, Reb Pinchas Michael, of blessed memory, who won great fame among the leading rabbis of that time. Other notables were: Efraim Lifshitz – the richest man in town, and his family; Shmuel Sborschik – the sturosta (-mayor, elder) of the town. He was also the Reader of the Scrolls and on High Holidays, the leader of the services.

Chaim the hunchback was one of the important storekeepers in the market place, owner of the only two-story brick structure in Antopol in which the town's pharmacy was located. Reb Hatzkel the Rushever – an impressive looking man, a great scholar and so much engrossed in his studies that he was hardly conscious of the world around him. He used to read and interpret for the congregants the Book of Ein-Yuukov, a collection of stories, parables and homilies selected from the Talmud and Talmudic literature.

*[Page 14]*

RebYaakev Chaim, the sheyhet – ritual slaughterer – was a shrewd man who took an interest in many communal affairs, and was one of the main leaders in the welfare societies in our town, which occupied themselves with charitable and other communal activities. Leizer, the sexton of the "new" Beiss Medresh, was a tall, powerfully built man, with a long beard and nimble in his motions.

I recall how, on Friday evenings before sundown, he used to walk with vigorous strides from bench to bench, lighting the numerous candles of the large candelabras. The function which he performed in the prayer-house was his secondary occupation. He drew most of his livelihood from bookbinding. At his place I always found many books in different languages which were entrusted to him by the Polish and Russian nobility of the manors around our town Antopol. At that time there was no general public library in town, and Reb Leizer's bookbinding establishment was thus the only place where one could find so many old and new books.

I believe that that was where I first acquired my urge for reading books. I used to spend a great deal of my time there, because Leizer's son, Ahron, was my close friend.

The Old Beiss Medresh had new walls, although – as mentioned above – it was called "old." As a matter of fact, even after the rebuilding of the prayerhouse, they left a few wooden pieces of the old edifice in their place, follows the instruction of Reb Pinchas Michael, of blessed memory. The path between the Old Beiss bledresh and the rabbinical residence was paved with several wooden planks, to enable the rabbi to walk the path without stepping into the mud and soiling his shoes. The Old Beiss Medresh was a much larger and much more modem structure than the new one. The entrance faced directly the entrance to the rabbinical residence. There was much room for worshippers and students. The long tile stove occupied nearly all of the Western Wall, behind the pulpit. Long tables stood along all the walls in the prayerhouse. Here, too, was a chapel in which there were classes of the Talmud Torah.

The women's section was on the second floor and had a separate entrance. As mentioned above, the prayer houses were used also as houses of study, in which young men spent their whole days at the folios of the Talmud or the codes. One of these students was Yaakev Shleyme Henech's. The father, Shleyme Henech, ran a coach service which brought each week goods from Brest-Litovsk for the Antopol traders, but he, too, like the others, dedicated much time to study. My father used to spend most of his time in the Old Beiss Medresh.

I, as a child, used the place as part of my home. On coming back from the Heider (Hebrew religious school) during weekdays, or on Saturdays and holidays, when there was little homework to be prepared, I would stop off at the prayerhouse. When I grew up, I used the place of study for learning under my father's supervision. Some of the many congregants who worshipped at the prayerhouse, left interesting impressions in my memory: There was Yekussiel, Beile Chanke's, who used to sit at the comer of the Eastern Wall near the Ark. His wife, Beile Chanke, was the provider who carried on the business for the whole family.

Reb**Error! Bookmark not defined.** Yekussiel spent all of his time in the prayerhouse. He was a short man whose beard and earlocks were dark black, and he had a quiet somewhat hoarse voice. He was always studying, and took little interest in worldly matters. His two sons were the only young men in my memory of the Beiss Medresh, who had long black beards.

Then there was Bezalel Troika, who owned a dry goods store in the market place. I remember him as the Reader, the man who used to read the portion of the week, or of the day, from the Scrolls, on the Sabbath and on holidays. He was a very learned man, but very naive in respect to many things. In matters concerning every day life he displayed childish simplicity.

Here worshipped another mayor-elder, Reb Avigdor Sirota. He was one of the leading Budei Batim (-house holders) in Antopol. Because of his official position in town he was involved in all relations between the Jewish community and the Russian authorities, as well as taking part in all communal and philanthropic activities. In the Old Beiss Medresh he occupied a prominent pew.

*[Page 15]*

Reb Binyomen, the Rosh Yeshiva (Dean of the Yeshiva) was a fine-looking elderly man with a flowing white beard. His title had nothing to do with his occupation, at the time Yeshiva Students from Antopol that I knew him. He lived near the synagogue court and had a soda-water business. Another one of the regular worshippers in this prayerhouse was Shmuel the Scribe, a miniature man with a dusky face, who was always busying himself with communal affairs. You could often see him in the midst of a crowd discussing local politics, especially on late Saturday afternoons, before the evening services. He was honest, honorable, and devoted, and did nothing but good for all the inhabitants of Antopol.

Avreml Shmuel Farber, was one of the leading butchers in our town, an ardent follower of my father's. I often used to see him early in the morning already busy with the Mishna study group of the congregation, the Hevra Mishnayess.

Yankl the Healer, was one of the most attractive personalities. He was indeed an expert in the medical sciences of the day, so far as general practice went, and was called for help, much more than the Polish doctor. Thus it was that the state of health of the town depended very largely on Reb Yankl. He also took an active interest in all leading local institutions. He was honest, honorable, and devoted, and did nothing but good for all the inhabitants of Antopol.

Avrom Aron, the old man, used to spend the whole day in the prayerhouse, studying. I do not know what he did in his youth. In his old age he took his meals at the houses of charitable. People took weekly turns donating his daily meal. It was called "eating days". He spent his days near the large tile stove, bent over a folio of the Talmud or some other book. As a child, I always marveled at his spectacles: one frame had a tin-piece instead of a glass lens, and the other frame was hollow. He did use a lens when reading, but that he held in his hand over the text. He would explain that one of his eyes did not function at all, and the other could see better through the empty frame.

The Old Beiss Medresh had two sextons: Gedaliah, the chief sexton, and Yankl Menkes, his assistant. Yankl Menkes used to do all the hard tasks; such as sweeping, heating, and cleaning the building. His ritual functions, so to speak, consisted of reciting the Psalms and the Slihos (-prayers of penitence) during the weeks before the High Holidays. He was also one of the grave-diggers of the burial society. Naturally, he was a very poor man and his wife supplemented the income of the family by working for the more prosperous households.

Gedaliah himself, the chief sexton, was also the general manager of the congregation. He handled the accounts, looked after the collections, etc.

During the services he called the man for attending the reading of the Torah, and he also made the Mi Shebeirah (-blessing after reading the portion of the Torah). Frequently he also led services or read from the Torah, substituting for others. Outside his functions at the prayerhouse, he was a master of all trades: He could build a house, a brick-stove, do carpentry work, and other skills.

Once, when he was carving an inscription on a stone monument, his hand was injured as a result of an explosion of the material and he was confined to the hospital for a time. When he came out he had a stiff arm which he could not use. Nevertheless he continued to work with one arm. Gedaliah was killed in the war between the Poles and the Bolsheviks in 1920. In the evenings the prayerhouse housed study groups seated at the lit tables: Talmud-study group, Mishna-study-group, Ein Yaacov study group, and individuals, usually young men, who spent their time studying for themselves. The chanting of the scholars filled the house day and night, except during services.

*[Page 16]*

Sometimes the prayerhouse would be lit up all night, when young Talmud students "kept watch" all night over their studies. This all night study was known as Mishmar (-watch). It was usually from sundown on Thursday till sunrise on Friday. The Betis Horau (rabbinical residence) was a fairly large house which was probably built in the days of Reb Pinchas Michael. It had five large rooms and a kitchen, and a built-in succah (tabernacle) which was used most of the year as a pantry, and on the Succoth Holiday – for its original ritual purpose. The large baking oven and the long heating stove which obtruded into every room keeping the whole house warm in the winter, occupied a substantial portion of the house. The large dining room served also as a waiting room for the many people who came to see the rabbi, and as a "sales-room" for yeast every Thursday, since this was the major source of the rabbi's income. The many shelves which filled the room from the floor to the ceiling, were lined up with old books.

A few years after the demise of Reb Pinchas Michael, his eldest son, Avrom Meyshe, took the books to his home in Brest- Litovsk, where they were destroyed by fire a short time later. In my memory, I see this room with the unpainted spot right above the rabbi's seat. This unpainted spot was "In Memory of the Destruction". The second large room in the rabbinical residence was the court-room, where the rabbi presided over rabbinical tribunal hearings, where questions of Kashrut (dietary laws) were answered and decided, and where disputes between individuals were arbitrated. There was a small cupboard in that room, built into the wall, about which my father told me an interesting anecdote relating to Reb Pinchas Michael.

The old rabbi once invited the members of the congregation to come to his house on Purim- Day, after the service, promising to treat them to "wine out of the wall". The guests were somewhat disappointed, when the rabbi took out a small flask out of the small cupboard, and good-naturedly drank "Lehayim" with his guests.

In front of the rabbi's residence, near the entrance, stood a long bench, where we used to sit in the evenings, enjoying the fresh air and listening to the familiar sounds of prayer and study in the house of worship. The town-bath stood a short distance behind the Old Beiss Medresh, while its windows gave out on the Old Cemetery. Men went to the bathhouse every Friday. To accommodate the women, the bath-house was heated on the other days of the week. The Mikve (pool for ritual bathing), was used every day, not only for women but for men as well, who performed immersions of purification whenever necessary.

There was a whistle fixed on top of the steam boiler, which could be heard all over town. On Fridays the whistle blew twice – once, to summon the people to come to the bath-house, and the second time – to announce the time for lighting the Sabbath candles. The attendant of the bath-house lived in a house nearby, half of which was taken up by the Hekdesh (traditional poor men's hospital). I remember also the assisting attendant, David-Ber the madman, one of the number of demented people who were taken care of by the community. Dovid-Ber used to come to our house, where he kept his Tefillin (philacteries). He never wore a Tallis (prayer shawl), presumably because he was never married. I remember him as a middle-aged man, short of stature, with a black beard. He spoke very little, but often complained that "Man is done for", This phrase of his was known in town, and served as an object of jokes usually at the expense of anybody complaining of his health.

The Old Cemetery extended for a fairly long stretch as far as the Rusheva highway. It is difficult to tell how old the old cemetery was. It was probably as old as the town itself. There were altogether three cemeteries in my time. There was the "new" cemetery, at the other end of town, in which Reb Pinchas Michael was buried, and a third cemetery was opened beyond the fields, a good distance away from town.

*[Page 17]*

In my childhood, the proximity of the Old Cemetery to our house, the many funerals which I saw and the horror stories about the dead, had a profound effect on my mind and soul. I retained, through the years, a strong hatred for death and a great respect for human life. These attitudes were later reflected in my make-up when, in ensuing years, I became the medical superintendent of a large municipal hospital. It was a place where many births and deaths took place daily, and my greatest concern was always the possibility of a medical error which might cost a human life. In my frequent lectures to young physicians and nurses I never missed an opportunity to speak of the absolute sanctity of life and the importance of applying every possible means to avert a death and to prolong life under all circumstances.

The Synagogue courtyard was the nerve center, as well as the barometer, of the inner life of the community. Here started the meetings and assemblies of various organizations where resolutions and general regulations were adopted, which not infrequently affected the life of the whole community. The joys and the sorrows of Antopol Jews found their echoes in the synagogue courtyard. Most wedding ceremonies were performed here. The canopy would be put up in the yard for the bride and groom from the farthest parts of town. First the groom was brought here, accompanied by musicians walking through the streets, and then the same band would go back to bring the bride while the groom stood alone waiting under the canopy, his face turned towards the synagogue.

While waiting, the groom was not allowed to move, and we, the urchins, hanging around the yard, would sneak up to stick a pin into his pants and laugh at his helplessness. The ceremony itself always impressed me deeply. The many lighted candles, the long pleated wax tapers (at the rich people's weddings), in the hands of happy, festively dressed men and women, the flames moving in the breeze; the familiar standard tune of the benedictions and the festal pleasing voice of the cleric performing the ceremony with a flair of pomp, all these remained indelibly stamped in my memory. When returning from the wedding canopy, the band would strike up a sorrowful march, which used to evoke the jocular comment that the music sounded like "Bagroben dem Kop" ("Ruined for life...").

Deep sorrow would descend on the synagogue courtyard each time a funeral procession passed. When the deceased was an important member of the community, the procession would stop at the plaza for a eulogy.

Every misfortune that happened in our town was reflected in the synagogue court. Epidemics sometimes struck Antopol, especially during the winter months, and many children fell ill with Diphtheria or scarlet fever. Those were occasions for the reciting of psalms in the synagogue courtyard. Now and then a loud wail would be heard and a woman would rush into one of the prayerhouses to come before the Ark and, wringing her hands and weeping loudly, would pray for the life of her child, who had been stricken ill.

On Saturdays and holidays the courtyard was full of worshippers and students dressed in their finest clothes. A festive mood reigned in every corner. Also on an ordinary weekday, crowds were sometimes attracted when a well-known Maggid (itinerant preacher) came to speak in one of the prayer houses. Some preachers could draw a large crowd in a winter evening when the windows were shut and the air was close and the flames in the lamps flickered, But the audience was thirsty for "a good word," especially for the fiery preachments of the Zionist propagandists. They were ready to stand for a long time, tightly packed like herring in a barrel and listen.

The all-pervading joyousness of Simhut-Torah, the sacred grief of The Ninth of Ab, the solemn melancholy soul-searching of The Day of Atonement, all these are associated in my memory with the Synagogue Courtyard of Antopol of fifty years ago.

*[Page 18]*

There was a small pool of water in the plaza, which would spread out during the rainy season as far as Reb Hersh's house. The pool was useful on occasions. In the first place, it provided water for putting out fires – which broke out frequently in Antopol. In the second place, it was convenient for Tashlich (the ritual of shedding one's sins into the water on the day of Rosh Hashana. Before Passover the townspeople would throw the unleavened bread and the wooden utensils of non-Passover use into the pool. In the wintertime, when it froze over, the boys would skate on the frozen pool. In the summertime the water would dry up and the air would be filled with microbes spreading diseases. Finally the city fathers decided that the pool served no useful purpose and filled it with earth and branches. In the end only a memory remained of the pool.

# R. Pinchas Michael
## (Of Blessed Memory)

There is an accepted premise among us: The "rebbe" status is one thing and the rabbinate is another, and one does not wear both crowns simultaneously. For the "rebbe" is a wonder worker, a performer of miracles and a guide to the common people. The rabbi, on their other hand, is a teacher of law, a father and a leader for scholars. One realm does not infringe on the other. Historical facts, however, contradict the above premise. There have been several great and revered personalities both who there were combined the traits of the rebbe, goodhearted and concerned with the problems of the individual and the community, as well as learned, the epitome of scholarship, building spiritual worlds and destroying them. These personalities come and rebuke our premise about the "rebbe" and the "rabbi". Even before the Baal Shem Tov, we had such luminaries as Rabbi Yehuda Hechassid, the Maharal of Prague and others who combined in themselves the fine traits enumerated in the "rebbe" and the rabbi.

After the spread of the influence of Baal Shem Tov, there were revealed here and there great crowns of a good name, such as R. Zekiel Leib Wormser (Baal Shem of Mitchaelstaadt), R. Joshua Gottmacher of Greiditz and others. A rabbi of this category was R. PinchasMichael O.B.M., who combined in himself the proficiency and keen analysis of the Talmud, and at the same time diffused through his noble personality light and warmth to everyone created in the image of G-d, drawing to himself thousands of people, Jews and Gentiles, who flocked to him to enjoy the light of his countenance and to receive his blessing.

R. Pinchas Michael was born in 1808 to his father R. Yitzhok Isaac and his mother Braina Henia, in the city of Shereshov (Grodno County). R. lsaac was a grandson of R. Joshua of Pinsk, a descendant of R. Elazar of Amsterdam, author of "Maasay Rokeach." On his mother's side he was a descendant of the author of "Ponim Meiros."

R. Pinchas Michael was an only son, but he did not behave like one. An only son tends to become spoiled and seek to escape the burden of Torah. But this was not the way of Pinchas Michael. From his earliest childhood he dedicated himself to Torah and good deeds. The ideals of his parents were not secular in nature, to increase wealth and material possessions, but to increase Torah and wisdom. They, therefore, exempted him from worries of a livelihood and the burdens of life. The boy Pinchas Michael spent day and night over the Torah and thirstily drank the words of the sages.

Of the teachers who impressed him we know only one whose influence was great. He was R. Asher Ha-Cohen, author of "Birchas Rosh." R. Pinchas Michael tried to go in the footsteps of this teacher in his humble behavior. From R. Asher he learned the trait of being content with little, and he refused to accept the crown of the rabbinate until he was close to fifty, as was the case with his teacher R. Asher. Also in authorship he followed the path of his teacher. The latter authored a commentary on tractate Nazir – so he also wrote a commentary on this tractate. Like his teacher, he attained the height of constancy in study and deprived himself of sleep, until his father used his paternal prerogative to get him to nap one hour in the afternoon. From his father, R. Yitzhok Isaac, he inherited his great love for Israel and his dedication to matters of charitableness.

*[Page 19]*

In accordance with the custom of those days, his parents married him off at an early age. He married Mushka, daughter of the well-to-do R. Yahiel Michal of Pavsal, a descendant of the author of "Seder HaDoros." His wife operated a store and managed the household, and thus removed from him the burden of livelihood so that he could devote himself to Torah. Even in those days, when he was still a youth, R. Pinchas Michael became renowned as one of the great negotiators of the sea of the Talmud.

At that time he began to correspond with the luminaries of Torah in matters of law and the comments of the early and later sages. They all saw in him a keen mentality and an expert analyst in coming up with the correct conclusions. These innovations – in the Shas, Rashi, Tosefos, Rif, Rosh and Ran, he began to note down until they accumulated to a heavy tome. But all this he did with modesty and without fanfare. And not only in matters of jurisprudence did R. Pinchas Michael demonstrate his prowess, but he also favored matters of legendary nature.

Shereshev, the birthplace of R. Pinchas Michael was known for its rabbis, outstanding in Torah and wisdom. Among those who served there were R. David, author of the book "Ramparts of Jerusalem". It is said about this rabbi that he planned to appoint three days of Rosh Hodesh and that he also used to read the Megillah on Shushan-Purim as well. The rabbinical chair in this town was also occupied by R. Pinchas Halevi, son of Azriel of Amsterdam, author of the book Nachlas Azriel" on "Yoreh De'oh." Another who served there was R. Isaac HaCohen, author of the book "Shaaray Yitzhok." In this town also served R. Asher HaCohen, a pupil of R. Chayim of Wolosin, author of the book "Birchas Rosh" on the Tractate of Brochos and editing of the interpretations of Rashi and Tosephos, and "Birchas Rosh" on the Tractate Nazir and editing and commentaries on Rashi, Tosephos and Maimonides.

At first R. Asher HaCohen refused to make a livelihood from Torah. To his fiftieth year he was a merchant in Shereshev, and during his free time he sat and studied Torah. Finally at the insistence of the town's leaders he agreed to occupy the rabbinical post. He did not serve there long, for the leaders of the community of Ticktin (Grodno County) turned their attention to him, and in 1853 he was appointed Rabbi of Ticktin.

When R. Asher HaCohen became Rabbi of Ticktin the community leaders of Shereshev began to look for a rabbi who could continue the rabbinic tradition of Shereshev. Finally they selected R. Pinches Michael to fill the place of R. Asher HaCohen. They saw in him the counterpart of their rabbi greatly proficient in the Talmud, in the first and latter sages, a modest man of high virtue. When the crown of the rabbinate was placed on the head of R. Pinchas Michael he did not change his former behavior and he conducted himself with the same modesty as prior to his assumption of the rabbinate. As always he was a close friend of the masses. He gave heed to their conversation, he participated in their sorrow and helped them in their hour of trouble. He was particularly beloved by the children, whom he treated with respect and addressed as he did their elders.

Despite his democratic behavior, R. Pinchas Michael became renowned for his Torah knowledge and he became the cynosure of all eyes. On the one hand he received responses in theory and fact from famous rabbis, and on the other the masses flocked to him for advice in matters of daily living. His home was open wide to every pauper and misery stricken individual.

Thus he conducted his rabbinical post for six years in Shereshev until 1864. This year marked a milestone in the life of R. Pinchas Michael, for on that year he left his native town of Shereshev where he grew up and went to the town of Antipolia, (Antopol in Russian) in Kobryn County, in the State of Grodno.

*[Page 20]*

Antopol, or Antipolia as it was known among the Jews, was famous not only in the State of Grodno but outside its confines as well. It is true that this town had practically been overlooked by the Russian Government, but the Jews regarded it highly because of its rabbis, famous for Torah and Kabalah. In town lived the famous Kabalist R. Moshe Zvi for forty-four years, from 1818 to 1862. R. Moshe Zvi was known not only for his vast erudition in matters known as secret but also for his generous soul and for his sensitive heart. He was sought after in spiritual and mundane matters, in problems of livelihood as well as matters of healing body or soul.

Following the death of R. Moshe Zvi, the rabbinical post was occupied by R. Chayim Zalman of Breslav, a descendant of the illustrious R. Yosef David of Mir. Evidently there was some argument about this post and after two years R. Chayim Zalman was forced to leave Antipolia and settle in Mir. The post of Rabbi of Antipolia waited its rightful heir. Several rabbis, renowned in Torah and teaching, were candidates for the rabbinical post in this small town, but none satisfied its Jewish residents, for the rabbi who was to occupy the rabbinical post would also have to continue the tradition of Antipolia's rabbis and to be acceptable to all the segments of the people because of his paternal attitude everyone created in the image of G–d.

It was not an easy matter to be acceptable to the Jews of Antipolia, who at that time numbered more than a thousand souls, for almost all of them were scholars and men of erudition, instructors in Gemora, such as R. Yekusiel the blacksmith, etc. The heads of the community of Antipolia could not find a rabbi more suited to this post than R. Pinchas Michael, who was thoroughly imbued with Talmudic erudition and was also devoted to every human being in distress. The heads of the community paid no attention to the "fault" that he had, namely his impaired speech. They knew that this was not a physical imperfection but the result of the quick thinking and lightning-like grasp that R. Pinchas Michael had. They saw his simplicity, both in study and in daily life, and his broad heartedness and his tremendous knowledge in the Talmud. These virtues recommended R. Pinchas Michael as the occupant of the rabbinic post in Antipolia.

Before accepting the rabbinate in Antipolia, R. Pinchas Michael stipulated with the heads of the community that he would not gain anything materially from the rabbinate, and that he would live on the sale of yeast by his wife. On Rosh Hodesh Heshvan 5624, the residents of Antipolia were blessed with the arrival of R. Pinchas Michael. The entire town rejoiced in welcoming its new rabbi. At last Antipolia was privileged to a rabbi worthy of two crowns, the crown of Torah and the crown of good repute. Everyone was eager to hear his inaugural sermon, which would certainly be of the first magnitude, as was the custom of the Torah greats in those days. But R. Pinchas Michael's sermon was nothing like that. They heard not words of legalism but words of legendary and moralistic nature. Only as a matter of course did he add words of jurisprudence, for this was the way of the Holy One, who spoke naught to the children of Israel on the first day of their arrival at Mt. Sinai because of the toilsome way.

Such was also the course of the commandments that the Lord gave. First he gave the light commandments, such as Chalah and the Omer, and later offering tithe, seventh year and jubilee which are weightier, "When the Lord gave us His commandments He taught us the ways of righteousness gradually, how to behave in ways of grace". From legendary material he goes on to speak of moralistics. He repeatedly admonishes concerning the light commandments, such as praying on time and the value of Torah study. At this point he expanded his speech and almost his entire sermon centered on this theme.

*[Page 21]*

And these were his words: "Everyone, even if he is busy with his work or business, must set aside a definite time for study, more or less as he is able, or to listen to others, each according to his own mentality. The Holy One comes to no one with a demand that he study involved matters, only as G-d has endowed him. Only let him not go about idle. Let him also beware of idle conversation, especially in the Beth Hamisdrosh and the Synagogue. Great is the importance of Torah study and the woman who helps her husband and lightens his burden of livelihood, her reward is very great, as was the reward of Isaachor and Zebulun.

The first sermon that R. Pinchas Michael delivered in Antipolia set the program for his behavior during his stay in that town. In it he explained the principles of his procedure in Torah and general matters, for first and foremost in everything was the study of Torah. And these thoughts he would repeat in almost every sermon. The study of Torah had to be done simply without undue sophistry. One had to direct the heart in study, and to learn outwardly with the lips and every individual had to study according to his nature. "One may be able to study more before retiring and another may find it easier earlier in the morning when a persistent mind is more at rest."

In addition to the pillars of Torah there are two other pillars: prayer and acts of consideration. On these three pillars he would build his sermons and his private conversations. R. Pinchas Michael veered away from the accepted custom that the rabbi sermonized twice a year, on the Great Sabbath and the Sabbath of Repentance. He delivered a sermon on every holiday. On the Sabbath of Repentance he would ascend the pulpit, envelop himself in the Talit and burst into tears, and the congregation would follow. This was his "sermon," designed to awaken the hearts for repentance and good deeds. Most of his sermons were not studded with disputation and argument, but with words of moralism and admonitions about daily affairs, such as the observance of the Sabbath, act of consideration, provision of food for the poor and proper weights. These things he would stress every opportunity he had.

R. Pinchas Michael approved the method of explanation and kept away from disputation. In his reply to one individual he says: "Continue with your good method of study, my dear man, and see to it that you make your mark in Shas. And this you will not be able to achieve unless you drop the method of disputation and stick to proficiency." The study according to the elucidated text was his course.

He studied and taught others according to this method; in other words, to elucidate the hidden meaning without disputation and an overflow of words, but with logical explanation and the correct norm briefly stated. R. Pinchas Michael followed this course in his brief commentaries on the Tractates of Nazir, Temura, Meila and Tamid. And this is what he says: "I have seen that this tractate (of Nazir) is more hidden and impenetrable than all the other tractates in the Shas, in that even the commentary of Rashi is not like the Shas Rashi Commentaries, and it is likely that it is not Rashi's commentary at all, in that it is not his customary language – because of the paucity of interest in this tractate, the bulk of which does not apply to the present, it suffers from many errors of omission and superfluity – even though it has had many commentators who dwelled on it at great length, nevertheless many chapters are still obscure – and one must teach his pupils intensively because of the lack of time – I have set my goal to set forth the chapters of the Talmud explicitly – and to abandon disputation. I have not made the compilation for the luminaries of our age, but for people of my level."

Whoever peruses his "Leket Hakotzrim" sees that R. Pinchas Michael does not compile indiscriminately. This commentary though brief includes a great deal. He knew the secret of conciseness. He knew what to include and what to exclude.

He thus also acted with his commentary on Ternura, Meilah and little of the Tractate Tamid and in the case of his preface to "Nazir", so does he say apologetically in this commentary: "I appreciate the paucity of my attainment and of my intellect. I have other shortcomings no doubt of which I am not aware." Evidently, R. Pinchas Michael kept this manuscript with him for several years, probably because of the lack of funds, until he was notified "from above" (see the story of the dream) that he was duty bound to publish the manuscript in question. He then placed it for publication, and immediately his commentary on these tractates received wide circulation, because it was brief but outstanding.

*[Page 22]*

Directly and indirectly, R. Pinchas Michael influenced thousands of Jews, both those who were privileged to hear from him words of moralism and wisdom and those who merely knew him by reputation. When still among the living he became a legend which was passed on from father to son and from grandfather to grandson. All spoke about the righteous one, who lent his ear to every one who turned to him, and who did not differentiate between Jew and Gentile, for "a Gentile also has to live." He was a father and patron for every embittered soul and downhearted that came to him even from far away.

Among these, were scholars, merchants, artisans, women and children. If a tragedy occurred in a home, immediately they ran to the righteous one. If the "overlord" refused to renew the lease, R. Pinchas Michael was asked for advice. When an individual became seriously ill, they called on the righteous one for aid. And he would say: "I know not, but the Lord will bless you." Pinchas Michael became the emissary of whoever turned to him, and when he prayed the "Shmoneh Esreh" he added prayers for those who had handed in notes of supplication. He did not handle these notes like the Chassidic rabbis. He did not accept "redemption money." At most he accepted a few coins for the poor students. He had a purse tied about his neck into which he put these coins, which he spent for charity.

The act of charity is one of the foundations on which the Jewish world is built. He continually admonished about this commandment. He was concerned not only with problems which demanded immediate solution. His keen eye penetrated into the life of our people which had just began to take shape in distant America. At that time, when the Jewish community was yet small and Judaism there was weak, he would advise those who asked him about immigrating to America: "Go to America. You will make a living there." And he would add: "Observe the Sabbath."

Like his contemporary, R. Israel Salanter, his heart ached for the condition of his people, and he sided with the idea of immigration to America, for his vision foresaw the wave of pogroms about to inundate the Jews of Russia. As for himself, he yearned to go to the Land of Israel, but his townspeople would not let him go. With deep longing he would send off whoever went up to the Land, whether it was a tailor, a shoemaker or a merchant and an investor. He would accompany them on foot a mile outside the town. Settlement in the Holy land was very important in his eyes. Not only residence itself, but even he who desired to return to the land was entitled to redemption and thus he comments in the passage: "Because of these matters were our forefathers redeemed from Egypt – that they did not change their tongue and name." For he who intends to settle permanently in another land changes his language, name and attire and becomes accustomed to the ways of the land. But "he who intends to return to his father's house is the opposite. They therefore had this great merit, that during the entire harsh enslavement they did not lose their faith to return to their land, and therefore they emerged from slavery to redemption".

R. Pinchas Michael had a formula for redemption from the harshness of slavery and from all oppressors – the observance of the Sabbath. He would therefore ask his audience to hasten and inaugurate the Sabbath early. For instance, the artisans and their employees should leave their work benches early so that they may be through at the bath house in time. R. Pinchas Michael would himself take the trouble to be in the bath house a good hour before sunset every Friday eve, and in his hand he had a switch with which he prompted those who were late in leaving. This switching was one of affection, since R. Pinchas Michael objected to corporal punishment. Once he slapped a boy of fourteen – Meir Utenof, the Cantor's son – for having beaten his companion, and he regretted his act to such an extent that his prayer became confused. R. Pinchas Michael approached the stricken boy several times and asked his forgiveness. When the boy forgave him, he grasped his hand with great joy.

*[Page 23]*

By nature R. Pinchas Michael was forgiving, foregoing upon the honor and respect due to a man of his station. Many exploited this "weakness" of his and used it for their own ends. One instance of this sort is told by R. Pinchas Michael himself. One crook forged his signature and traveled about from town to town to collect funds for the Talmud Torah in Antipolia. R. Pinchas Michael reacted to this matter in the press and asked the rabbis in the towns where the crook might appear to take away the document and the forged letter and burn them. Evidently this crook perpetrated his act following the conflagration that took place in Antipolia in the summer of 1885. Some eighty houses went up in flames at that time.

On the 20th of Sivan of the same summer a second conflagration broke out and 120 homes burned down. The Jews of Antipolia became completely impoverished and emissaries went forth to gather contributions for the victims. This situation was fertile ground for acts of deception. Antipolia was "famous" for its conflagrations. The elders of the town used to tell about the first one, in 1860, as though it were an historic event in the life of the town, for at that time almost the entire town went up in flames. In that year R. Pinchas Michael together with R. Natanel Chayim Pappe, one of the foremost townspeople, went forth long distances in behalf of the victims. They went as far as St. Petersburg. Everywhere they were cordially received. Thanks to these distinguished men the town was rebuilt and Jewish life began to pulsate there again, with all its light and shadows.

R. Pinchas Michael returned to his town and its Jews. He cared not only for his congregation but also for the problems of the entire Jewish community. Once he said to R. Jekutiel, the husband of Beila Hannah "You are better off than I am, for the world is not upon you." From all corners of the earth people turned to him and gave him no rest, neither for the soul nor for the body. His wife, Mushks, would drive away those who besieged the rabbi's home saying, "He is not able and he does not know. Let him alone."

The more she drove them away, the more they came. And what about the study of the Torah? After all, one had to carry out, "thou shalt dwell on it day and night." He therefore followed the dictum of the Talmud "The night was not created but for study" (Erubin 55). He slept intermittently, and spent almost the entire night studying, and as a result his proficiency in Shas and Poskim was marvelous, "so that all his distinguished contemporaries had the greatest respect for him."

Lack of sleep, his innumerable burdens and his strong concentration on his studies begot R. Pinchas Michael a severe case of hemorrhoids, and on orders of his physicians he went to Berlin for an operation. On leaving for Berlin he prepared for a journey to the hereafter, for who knows what the next day might bring? One must issue his testament to his household. R. Pinchas Michael then wrote his will. Ostensibly the will was for his sons, but whoever reads it with open eyes would see that this will constituted R. Pinchas Michael's credo, and witness thereby his inner, higher world, one of harmony and equity for one and all. Here we see his democratic attitude and viewpoint towards the status of the poor and the artisans, for in his day the artisan was looked down upon. All important in his eyes was the Scholar. He therefore orders his sons to marry off their sons to the daughters of scholars "and do not seek out the wealthy – and for your daughters provide good and scholarly men, even from families of artisans. For this is no stigma at all, as the fools would have us believe. It is a greater stigma for those of wealthy families who lose other people's money. But the artisans who enjoy the fruits of their labor are precious in the eyes of the Lord." As it has been said, R. Pinchas Michael gave priority to scholars. He therefore orders his sons to purchase Shas and Poskim and all the other sacred books, for sometimes it is the lack of books that hampers study.

*[Page 24]*

R. Pinchas Michael also possessed a sense of the esthetic, for he asks them to bind the books handsomely, "for this brings glory to those who do so in this world and in the world to come." R. Pinchas Michael admonishes "let not any curse come from your lips, even against gentiles or animals – and raise your children gently, not by beatings, only goodly words – and beware of being inconsiderate toward anyone, especially the maid servants, for they like you are descendants of our forefathers. Be careful to earn their respect and you will merit much goodness. He also admonishes at great length about peace in the household. A man must be easy going with his spouse, even though she may at time embitter his spirit. He advises not to argue with her, since it is difficult to vanquish them, and they should be judged affirmatively and kindly. He also admonishes his daughters and daughters-in-law to be careful to respect their husbands and not to irritate them "even with slight speech." Concerning moodiness and anger he warns several times, "for with aggravation you will not in any way repair the matter" and "remove the traits of aggravation and anger, and trust in the Lord in all your dealings." He therefore cautions concerning the giving of tithe for the benefit of the poor and other sacred matters. Such funds should be kept in trust as though they did not belong to the giver. If conditions of livelihood are not so good, there should be no journeying for the aid of a tzaddik in another town for "in every town there are G-d-fearing people" who would intercede with the Lord for the needy.

The same applies to physical matters. One must ask the grace of the Lord for himself first and then turn to others to request grace for him. And as he was the emissary of every pauper and downhearted in his lifetime, so he promises to intercede for those who seek his help in the hereafter. Reading the admonitions of R. Pinchas Michael O.B.M., we are reminded of the admonitions of R. Asher of Stolin O.B.M., the son of R. Aaron of Karlin, founder of the Karlin Chassidism. He too cautions several times about the observance of the Sabbath and the extension of the secular into the sacred, about the appointment of time for Torah study, about the contribution of tithe, etc. And one asks, was R. Pinchas Michael influenced by the Baal Shem Tov Chassidism, was he inclined toward Chasidism? The latter question can be definitely answered in the negative. On the contrary, from the numerous tales told in his name we learn that he was a strong opponent of the ways of Chassidim and its leadership. How then can two extremes exist in one entity? In truth, both opinions are correct. In his youth, R. Pinchas Michael was a strong opponent of the system of Chassidim, especially where it concerned the belated hour of prayer. But during his last years he came near to Chassidism, and at times prayed in the Chapel of the Stolin Chassidim.

For more than twenty years, R. Pinchas Michael occupied the rabbinic chair of Antipolia. Not all of them were years of peace and serenity. More than once someone was offensive and R. Pinchas Michael passed over the insult in silence and in his heart he forgave the offender. And the truth must be said that not all the residents of Antipolia recognized the greatness of their rabbi. This is a psychological truth: the townspeople do not give their rabbi recognition. An anecdote told in the name of R. Pinchas Michael reflects the attitude of the Jews of Antipolia toward him. Once he was asked, "Why is he not as important in Antipolia as elsewhere?" R. Pinchas Michael replied, The sedra "Pinchas" in its place and season is not especially important since it is read during the season of depression. But when it is read outside its environment, as in the case of Maftir on the festivals, which is taken from "Pinchas", one pays a large sum for this "Aliyah." For Pinchas in its place is not so noteworthy, while Pinchas outside its place is more important.

*[Page 25]*

Only after his demise did people begin to recognize the great importance of their "Zaddick rabbi" who lived like a saint and left the world in holiness. It is said that in 1890 (Rosh Hodesh Adar 5650), R. Pinchas Michael was stricken with typhoid. For two weeks he did not leave his bed, but his mind was clear. When prayer time came he woke up and prayed. On the last Sabbath of his life he went up to the Torah, saying to his household, "I am a guest, and a guest must receive an Aliyah." On Sabbath night after Havdalah he sent a card by messenger to the Rabbi of Pinsk, informing him about his death and inviting him to his funeral, and in the same card he asked for his forgiveness. He also notified him that in the case of one place in the Rambam the law was according to the writer of the card.

On the eve of the 17th of Adar, his soul departed in purity. Immediately the entire town went into mourning. Messengers were dispatched to Horodetz and Kobrin to announce the bad tidings about the death of the Zaddik. Many inhabitants of these towns, Jews and gentile alike, came to the funeral. And these rabbis eulogized him: R. Joshua Jacob Rabinowitz, rabbi of Horodetz, Rabbi Zvi Hirsch Rabinowitz and R. Moshe Berman, son-in-law of R. Pinchas Michael, the later rabbi of Antipolia, eulogized him at the synagogue. At the Beth Hamedrash in Pinsk Street he was eulogized by the dayan of Antipolia, R. David Rushkin and R. Pinchas, son of R. Elijah of Lida, dayan of Kobrin. Then they went to the old Beth Hamedrash where the deceased used to pray and the eulogy was delivered by the Gaon R. Joseph Saul Epstein, Rabbi of Kobrin. Thus came to an end the history of R. Pinchas Michael O.B.M. With his passing there closed a bright chapter in the history of Antipolia, whose Jews participated in its writing.

# Rabbi Moshe Berman, O. B. M.
## By P. Licht

Rabbi Moshe Berman was born in 1864 in Razinoi, White Russia, where his father – Reb Feitl – had been Rosh-Yeshiva for many years. Both his parents having died when he was still a boy, young Moshe grew up at the house of the famous charitable woman Hodeske, who was related to him through her husband. This wonderful woman had an enormous influence on the boy, and contributed immensely to the formation of his moral and personal character. He learned at the Razinoi Yeshiva, and later at Volozin and Minsk. Finally he came to Antopol, where he studied under the guidance of Rabbi Pinchas Michael O.B.M. In Antopol he married Breine-Henie, granddaughter of Rabbi Pinchas Michael, and following the wedding he spent some time in Kobrin.When R. Pinchas Michael died, and following the Grand Dispute about his successor, Rabbi Moshe became Rabbi together with Rabbi Hersh. After that Rabbi Hersh passed away, and Rabbi Moshe continued as the only successor.

Rabbi Moshe was a quiet man, always at study with the interests of the community close to his heart. He was a Zionist and also alert to worldly affairs. He tried once a business partnership with Reb Avraham- Moshe, son of the R.P.M., but he used to return his profits to the customers, for he would not take "extra money" from them. Eventually he sent back the merchandise to his partner, and went out of business.

After the end of World War I, he was brought over to the U.S.A. by his devoted sons, who had long before preceded him: Dr. P. Berman, and Mr. P. Berman. In 1921, Rabbi Moshe was appointed Rabbi of the Agudath Achim Congregation in Los Angeles. He soon received recognition from most of the orthodox Jewry, and was elected to be Chief Justice of the orthodox rabbinical court of Los Angeles. Being aware of the special circumstances in keeping Judaism in America, he was an understanding judge in religious matters. He himself sat all day long studying in the synagogue, and upon coming back home he continued till late at night. Rabbi Moshe carried a continuous correspondence with many rabbis in the U.S.A. and was respected by all who knew him. Ten years he sat on the rabbinical chair in Los Angeles, until he was called to Heaven in 1930 (Heshvan 22, 5691).

*[Page 26]*

For many years after his death they used to hold a special mourning meeting in his honor on the day of his Yorzeit, even after the synagogue had moved to another suburb. His blessed memory will always be with us.

# The Belachovitzes
## By Abraham Warsaw

It was in the summer of 1920. Our little town was in ruins, after passing from hand to hand between Russians and Germans, Germans and Poles, Poles and Bolsheviks. The Jews suffered pogroms, looting, requisitions, hard labor etc. Eventually the Poles remained and the front moved away from Antopol. There remained only a bakery which supplied bread to the military. One evening when I was at the prayer house I was summoned to the military. On my way home I was met by Belachovitz soldiers who told me that their commander called for me. The town was in panic. Everybody knew that in a nearby town these Belachovitz soldiers took the rabbi as hostage until they received the contribution and supplies which they requisitioned, and in another town they killed everybody.

I came to the commander, who stood in the middle of the market place, surrounded by soldiers. He introduced himself as commander of those who killed in Kamin-Kashirsk over 300 Jews. His battalion camps not far away waiting for the fulfillment of their requisition. Otherwise they will come down to extinguish everything. I asked him for his requirements and he gave me a list of meat, corn, boots, salt, etc. which made me shiver.While we were thus talking he shouted: "Why are we talking like this in the middle of the market? let us go into my office." Upon arrival he sat down and added to his list more and more provisions. In his office we were joined by the town mayor and leaders of the community. He then demanded that the whole requisition should be in his office within 4 hours. We pleaded for more time but to no avail. In the meantime came in the owners of the cattle which he had confiscated and offered to replace them with meat. He finally' agreed to exchange them for an additional ransom of 60,000 marks. They asked my advice, and I told them that he would take both the money and the cattle. They did not listen to me and found out later that I was right. We collected the items which he demanded while realizing that we will have robbed ourselves of everything after the completion of this task.

It all ended unexpectedly. When the owners of the cattle came asking for their cattle, the Belachovitzes began shooting at them, and when the soldiers stationed at the bakery heard the shooting they started shooting at the robbers who fled and left town to our great relief.

# The Roof Corroded
## A. Warsaw

Winter was over early that year. The snow had already melted. Spring was coming from the warmer lands. The little town was still lying under the dirt of the heavy winter, which had kept the few alleys, as if under siege for full five months. Now it looked as if it has just started breathing again. The people themselves felt as if they had just grown a new skin, and accepted the deep marshes patiently.

In the prayer houses, Jews have been predicting an early spring, but the favorable predictions caused some of them to worry about provisions for the coming holidays Purim and Pesach, and they relied on the Almighty to help them solve their problems.

It was quite late after the third morning service. Shloime had participated in all three, after which he also took in a chapter of Psalms, and went home for breakfast. The street was quiet. The sun had just emerged, and was biting, mercilessly into every hiding piece of ice. Birds were singing in the clear air and Shloime was overwhelmed with the beauty of God's world.

*[Page 27]*

He was nearing the Kobriner Street, when he observed a cart approaching towards him out of the marshes. The man traveling in the cart was Mordche, who greeted Shloime wholeheartedly. Shloime returned the greeting, adding his own wishes for a happy good month, meanwhile indicating that he was not working these days. Mordche then spoke up, saying, "As a matter of fact, I wanted to call you, Shloime. You see, my roof is getting rusty."

"What did you say?", exclaimed Shloime as if s mitten with a club. "What did I hear you say? Only about two weeks ago I went by your house and saw your roof shining like a mirror. As a matter of fact I enjoyed seeing it, after that the weather and the sun had brought out its true color of shining copper."

"Yes, this is true about the front of the house," answered Mordche, "but it did corrode on the other side."

Shloime could not refuse the invitation to come and see what could be done to repair the roof, and the two men bade each other farewell. Continuing on his way home, Shloime became gloomy, on account of "his" roof needing repair. Coming home, he kissed the mezuza, greeted the family and waited for his wife to call him to breakfast. His wife came towards him right out of the kitchen, where she was preparing a special breakfast in honor of Rosh-Hodesh (First day of the month), cut herring, skinned potatoes and sweet chicory, plus a white pletzl from Raphael the baker. Noticing the breakfast table, Shloime praised the Lord for His kindness, and later told his wife about Mordche's roof. But Leine Feigl never claimed any understanding in mending roofs, and consequently Shloime put on his coat and left the house, on his way to examine the roof. Shloime was walking with sure steps, encouraged by his wife's farewell blessing.

While walking he remembered his childhood days when he and Mordche went to the same Cheiders and later to the same Russian school. Both of them stood up bravely against the Russian boys. He, Mordche, was of the Sheinboim family, and Shloime was himself known for being of a good family. Later in life they separated. Mordche traveled over the world, seeking his fortune, which he did not find neither in America, nor in Africa. His fortune turned out to be right at his door, and he became a millionaire. But Shloime neither pursued his fortune, nor did fortune seek him out. Still he thanked God for everything and did not begrudge Mordche and felt equal to him in this mundane world. Walking like this, deep in thought, he did not feel the road, or the deep marshes. He approached the gate of Mordche's courtyard, the dogs greeting him in a friendly manner. He remembered the saying: When dogs play in town, it is a good omen. He is thankful for the friendly welcome, and his eyes begin to examine the roof. He goes around once and twice. The roof smiles at its master. There is no sign of rust. The gardener sees Shloime and greets him wholeheartedly:

"Panie Shliomka, what brings you here ?

"Tell me, have you noticed any rust on the roof?" The gentile put away his gardening tools and gazed at Shloime:

"Who was kidding you?"

"The landlord himself told me about it."

"Oh! Panie Shliomka, you are a great friend of the landlord, and you drink tea with him. Don't you know that he is a kidder?"

Now the driver approached, and he remembered the meeting on the road between his landlord and Shloime. Although he did not understand Yiddish, he knew what they talked about.

"What do you say, Stepan Stepanowich, is the roof rusty?"

"I do not know what goes on the roof. You have to see for yourself–meaning, we all see there is no rust." Shloime came near the steps leading to the kitchen, cleaned his boots and entered the house. Somebody had told Mordche about Shloime's arrival, and he came towards his guest to greet him and invited him for a glass of tea.

*[Page 28]*

"Well, have you examined the roof?" A smile appeared on Shloime's face as he was staring at Mordche. But Mordche did not let up, waiting for a reply.

"Mt do you kid me? Do you think that I have enjoyed your kidding these last few hours?"

"Never mind. Listen to me. The roof did come out beautifully, and therefore, come summer, I want you to go over it for protection."

"Bless you," exclaimed Shloime in relief, "there is no need for it."

"But I am the landlord here, and I want to have it painted."

"It won't make it any better. You will throw away your money."

"Here, put some brandy in your tea, suggested Mordche."

"Well, in honor of Rosh-Hodesh it is nice to have a drink, but still I will not paint your roof."

"Listen, in order to be sure that you will paint the roof, here is an advance payment of 25 rubles."

"I won't take it. If you insist, I will paint your roof, but I won't take any payment in advance. I trust you."

"Today I have it, maybe tomorrow I won't."

"Leave me, go. I won't take it."

Mordche could not control himself any longer, and with a fraternal impulse stuffed the banknote into his friend's hand. At this gesture, Shloime froze, and like in a haze looked at Mordche as at an angel from heaven. He could not utter a single word of all he wanted to say. They both finished their tea and Shloime left the house with a mere, "Good day, Mordche". Upon leaving the house, and being a little further away from the aristocratic courtyard, Shloime envied his friend Mordche for the first time in his life.

*[Page 29]*

# The Holocaust

### By Prof. P. Czerniak
### (One of the seven Antopol survivors, from his diary)
### War Years in Antopol (1939-1944)

It is late August of 1939. The weather is hot. We hear the German radio thunder: "Poland must cede the corridor! We must have a thoroughfare to East Prussia ! Danzig must be German! The Germans in Poland want to join Germany!"

The diplomats are working desperately; the Polish Ambassador in Berlin, Mr. Lipski, seeks an audience with German Foreign Minister Ribbentrop to discuss the situation. Ribbentrop finally receives him late on August 31; when he knows already that several hours earlier Hitler ordered to start the march on Poland. What can Lipski accomplish?

The army is busy with preparations; Ridz- Smygly declares, over the Polish radio, that not a button from a Polish jacket will be lost. At the same time the generals are forming their divisions.

In Antopol, few people knew what was going on. Everyone had his own troubles with making a living, looking after the children, the house, and communal affairs. To be sure, they all had their faith in God. Some housewives were provident and stored up more groceries. In the drugstores they bought some aspirins and other medical supplies for the house. They prayed in the synagogues more ardently than usual. The Polish intellectual "elite" of the town was unnerved. Some had already been drafted and were leaving.

It was 4:45 in the morning of September 1, 1939. There was a report of an alleged attack by Polish soldiers reported over the German radio station in Glywic, Silesia. Other well-planned incidents between Poles and Germans were reported in other localities. Hitler "cannot endure Polish aggression. He has given the order, and the divisions are crossing the Polish border". That was reported in the early morning broadcast and was heard in the houses in Antopol. We were benumbed. I was ordered to prepare first aid stations in town. The main center was in Dom-Ludowy (Peoples' House) in the market-place. We were collecting medical supplies and were preparing to treat the wounded.

At night the town was dark. Windows were shaded, lights were shaded. Streets were vacant. Only soldiers on patrol duty moved about. It was war! Antopol was under military rule! The next day we eagerly sought out news reports and groceries to store up. Faces were grim and worried. Parents grieved for children who were gone; women grieved for menfolk. Some were stuck, since the whole governmental machinery had been quickly disorganized and nothing moved anymore.

We did not move from the radio. Why was Russia silent? What were the British doing, with whom we had concluded a pact? Why was France inactive? On the third day of the war German airplanes appeared over Antopol. They descended near the electric station behind town, looking for something important, and were off. We waited in the prepared dugouts in the nearby fields and imagined that a plane was throwing bombs precisely at our dugout. One morning, August 17 to be exact, we experienced a sense of relief. The radio announced that Russia had entered the war. We waited and hoped for the Russians to come to our town. It was now clear that Poland would be torn apart, and there was nothing to be done about it, Unfortunate Poland was fated for another partition as in the 18th century. We felt for the Polish patriots, who had so little time to enjoy the modem rebirth of their nation, only from 1919 to 1939! But what of us, Jews? What will happen to us?

The Russians advanced fast, and the Germans were also flying forward fast. They were racing towards each other, with Antopol between them. On the radio we heard reports from each side. Our young people stopped all daily work and were glued to the radios. They were our source of news. They told us that the Russians were quite close. The Germans were reported to have reached south of us, and turned towards Brest-Litovsk. Woe to us! We were in their clutches! They were already in Kobryn.

*[Page 30]*

The next day things looked brighter. The youngsters heard a report over the radio that the Germans were retreating to Brest-Litovsk, and the Russians were coming to our town, The people of Antopol were waiting anxiously while, in the meantime, the town got along without any constituted authority. Jews stayed at home, sat around in the prayer houses, in the stores and workshops, talking, praying, and hoping.

On September 20th, the Russians entered Antopol. The Soviet army passed in a long line far out into the distance; motor vehicles, men, armaments and amiability. Every spot was being occupied – vacant lots, large houses, orchards and fields. Temporary accommodations were sought out by infantry, artillery, tanks, communications and other services, in

Gorin's Park, in the market place, on the square facing the Hebrew school "Tarbut", in the old synagogue courtyard, and alongside the pavement. Some of the officers in the Soviet army were Jews. This was good news to us, Polish citizens. The arrivals were under strict orders not to talk much; they were busily at work. Antopol was now becoming part of Russia, White Russia (- Byelorussia) to be exact.

It was spring of 1940. Antopol had changed, having been transformed from a small community into a district center, the administrative capital of a segment of White Russia, with a population around it of some ten thousand people. The authorities had established their headquarters in the market place. The party secretary was staying in Mazurski's house. The drug store had been moved from there into Yudl Lifshitz's brick-house. At the other end of the brick-house they had installed a radio receiver, which had been connected by wires to the houses in town, where earphones were installed. The reception center functioned throughout the day and newscasts and music programs were heard in the houses. Lifshitz's other brickhouse had been taken over by the post office. The militia established itself in Greenberg's brick-house. Sirota's brickhouse was taken over by the military commission which registered the young people and mobilized them. Klorfine's brickhouse housed the State Bank, carrying on the financial business of the region. Sacharov's house became a courthouse. Polciuk's brick-house became a hotel for visiting dignitaries, and later it became the center of the komsomol. The stores were converted into warehouses for the military and for the administrative authorities. Some stores were used for the newly established state co-operative shops with a limited choice of merchandise. Lifshitz's long frame house was turned into a polyclinic. The brick-house across the street became the office for civil registration of births, weddings and deaths. A shoemakers' co-operative was established in Wysocki's house; a tailors' co-operative on Kobryn street, The Isplkom (Executive Committee) ensconced itself in the former Jewish Community House. Three schools functioned. The NKGB was in Saga's house. Telephone wires were strung between houses and everything was carried on in strict order, under punctilious control. Many new settlers arrived from White Russia and from Russia proper. Party Secretary Subatin occupied Bereh London's house on Pinsk street, and ruled together with Pastushenko of the Ispolkom.

Jews had to change their occupations. Instead of shopkeepers and middlemen they "became" clerks, administrators, members of cooperatives or artels (collective independent labor unions). On the side they did a little trading. They lived, listened to speeches, read Russian papers, heard the radio broadcasts. Young people went to the cinema; older people went to the prayer houses, especially for the evening services. Their numbers shrank as the atheists intensified their activities.

*[Page 31]*

To go back a few months to the end of 1939, great projects were being carried out in the Antopol region. The Bug Canal was being shortened, an airport was being built, apparently for military purposes, and several thousand deportees were brought from Russian labor camps to work on the projects. The Antopol Jews were organized into "Sabbath brigades" and "volunteered" to help in the digging. I well remember the trip out and the work. More than one of those "volunteers" returned ill with pneumonia or swollen legs, but the canal was finally completed.

Through the canal the Russians were able to send their barges laden with wheat to the Germans (it sounds like a bad joke, but that was a fact) and come back with other goods (seemingly gasoline). The airport was nearly ready but was not to be made use of. Life marched on. The number of sick people in town grew. It did not cost any money to get treatment. Anyone, if he so pleased, came into the polyclinic, registered, was examined, received a prescription, went to the drugstore and got what he needed. Others, to be sure, were in need of hospitalization, and so a hospital was set up in Antopol. There was the house of Jankiewicz at the foot of Kobryn street. One day I was brought there and was told to open up a hospital. Two weeks later, the first patients were admitted.

Two houses belonging to XuZuks (well-to-do peasants) were brought from a village and were converted into hospital wings, one for obstetrics, the other for patients stricken with contagious diseases. The Antopol hospital had 35 beds. Close to a hundred patients would apply each day for treatment in the dispensary of the hospital. Antopol became a medical center. A Jewish girl from Moscow and another from Bobruisk were brought to Antopol as physicians. Several nurses and apothecaries were from Homel. Our townspeople nearly stopped going to Kobryn and to Pinsk for medical treatment.

The Soviet occupational authorities ordered that "elections" be held in Antopol. A list of candidates was posted in Mazurski's house and everyone was "advised" to vote for the whole list. The citizens of Antopol went one rainy autumn day to the ballot boxes, into which they threw in printed pieces of paper with printed lists of candidates. Later there was a meeting of the so-called elected Soviet-council in the frame house of the Polish school on Pinsk street. It was a festive occasion. The "delegates" were allowed to buy chocolate, sausages and cigarettes. In other districts it was the same thing. The delegates then adopted a resolution to demand the incorporation of the district into the Soviet Union.

On October 29, 1939 the Supreme Soviet took cognizance of the resolution and voted to accede to its demand to have the Antopol region become an integral part of the U.S.S.R.. We were annexed to the

Byelorussian (White Russian) Republic of the Union. Minsk became our capital too, and from there we received decrees and officials, commissars and leaders. The new regime took to purging the atmosphere of reaction, kuhzks, ideological and economic opposition, etc. Among others, recent Polish settlers were carried off to the interior of Russia. At night the military authorities informed the victims to dress and pack, and they were loaded on motor cars to be taken to an assembly center.

It was a sunny morning June 7, 1941. I was about to take a short rest, but at seven a.m. my rest was disturbed: Yossl the tailor knocked on my door, all excited. At 6 a.m. he heard the German radio announcing that the Germans had attacked Russia. A train of coal cars arrived at the Brest-Litovsk station from the German side, as it had been every day. The sealed cars opened and German machine-gunners jumped out of them rushing straight into battle. Many Russian officers had spent Saturday night celebrating as usual. Now they were so treacherously attacked by their erstwhile allies, after the Ribbentrop-Molotov treaty.

The brigands were coming here. At dawn their planes bombarded Kharkov, Odessa, Homel, Minsk. There was a state of panic. What was to be done now? Although we were part of White Russia, we heard reports reaching us by word of mouth about brutalities across the Bug river: killings, and oppressions, evidently with the view of exterminating the Jews.

*[Page 32]*

We did not quite believe everything we heard. We did not want to believe that Man could descend to such bestiality/ After all, even Nazis are human beings, so we thought. The Jews of Antopol took to their feet. Everyone understood he had to flee. But where to? Russia? Leave everything and run! But one man was ill, another had small children. Besides, there was no transportation available. Could we advance as fast on our feet or by wagon as the Germans on vehicles? What if they overtook us on the road? That would be certain death! What was there to be done? What did other people do? What were the Russians doing?

What were the authorities doing? Four days passed, an unbearable four days, when life and death were on the scales, terror and impotence, decision and helplessness. The Soviet authorities threw everything they had onto the vehicles and rushed away, promising they would return. "Don't be afraid! We'll come back! We'll show the Germans what we can do." They offered to take me along. But how could I do it? What of my family? We now envied the kdaks who had been forcibly deported to the land beyond the Volga. They were sure of their lives.We remained here chained by lies of family and friendship, by human sentiments, and by an inner sense of responsibility. Whatever happened to others might very well happen to us.

The Germans entered Antopol. A new page was tuned in Jewish history, a page which degrades the word Man. This was a period of suffering unlimited, of appalling savagery and of very few miracles, including those which enabled myself and seven other people to survive. Small shreds of large beautiful flower-pots smashed to pieces. The German jackboot trampled over Europe, stepped over town and hamlets, among them our dear town Antopol, and destroyed them – how it destroyed them. So much brutality, and so much blood shed unjustly! Such degradation of human dignity and human spirit! Those were dark days, darker than black, years of history. Alas for the people who made them! Alas and alas for those who went through them.

I leaf through the diary of my ghetto days and I come up with the following:

1) There is deathly silence in Antopol. It is 2 p.m.; the second "hunt" has been completed. I quietly emerge from my hiding place in the house on Zaniew street, to which we have been driven by the Germans. I see, at a distance, a green two-legged swine walking. He passes by Appelbaum's house. The doors are open, the inhabitants already evacuated. Out of the left-hand side a small child crawls out, on all fours, advancing serenely, as if there were nothing to fear. Evidently his mother had hidden him away before being driven off by the Germans. Now the child is looking for its mother. The swinein- jackboots with their hobnailed soles sees the child. He approaches and raises his boot...I cannot look any more. Later they took away from there a bloody bundle with a smashed head for burial. Why did not a thunder strike the beast?

2) The tailor's son, also a tailor, has been arrested by the police on the charge of being a communist. But everybody knew he was a non-party man. He ran away. The police served notice that unless he surrendered, they would shoot his parents, his wife and child and ten Jewish notables of Antopol. Meanwhile, the young man's father and wife were placed under arrest. Ten notables were being picked as hostages. The "fugitive" was in the neighborhood. At night he would slip into his house, where he was told about the situation. Yet, no person was willing to betray him to what everybody knew was certain death. Everyone imagined what suffering this fine-looking young man endured and what his inner conflicts were. Should he give himself up, then he would be subjected first to torture and then to shooting. If he did not, his wife and child, his father and mother and the other hostages would be the victims. Thus he lived through forty-eight hours of anguish. When the time was up, he came and reported to the police. "Shoot me, but spare the others!" he told them. The murderers did just that. They paid no attention to the noble courage of the man. They did not even think of it. They placed him onto a truck going to Kobryn and there shot him on the high bridge over the Muchowiec river. There, on that

place of execution, many victims fell. We, who survived him, honored his memory as a hero.

*[Page 33]*

3) It is the last "hunt." The remaining 300 wrecks of human beings are surrounded by a chain of killers and machine-guns, lurking across the fence of the small ghetto. The Judenrut and "our own" police are no more. In another few minutes they will begin rounding up all of us, dragging us away and taking us to the sands to the left of the highway leading to Proszychwost. There we shall be ordered to strip and a bullet will put an end to life. More thoughts race through my brain like flashes. Some time ago, I was given a ride back to town by a colleague, the Ukrainian doctor, by the name of Niestruk, who had been brought to us from Kobryn to serve as Chief Physician of the district. He tried to comfort me with his philosophy: "Well, my dear Sir, what can we do? A prosecuting attorney has arisen, by the name of Hitler, and he issued a decree, a death. sentence against all the Jews, and there is no appeal. So you can't appeal. All you can do is wait in your cell until you are taken out for the execution!" I now thought, "Has the end now actually arrived?" But another flash comes, "What kind of a trial? What verdict? On what basis? By what right? What for?" I made a firm resolve not to let it happen! To save one's life by every possible means! Under all circumstances!

The sum total of our family was as follows: Our own child, a little girl of ten months, we had handed as a "gift" to a Gentile woman (Vera Okhritz) a month earlier; my sisters, Radia and Peshka with her husband and two wonderful little children, Rochele and Yudele, had been done in by the brutes some time earlier. My mother Shifra was hiding each time in a different place. My wife's mother Zivia and her brother Avromtze were still alive. This is all. What now? It is 6 a.m., October 15, 1948, past the High Holidays. Our fate had already been sealed up on high. The survivors, mere remains of human beings, had dressed quickly and were running around like shadows, like trapped birds or mice, silent, speechless, humbled, resigned, bewildered, pale and dried up.

I feel a welter of emotions which it is difficult to describe and difficult to understand, because they are emotions born in human beings living in bestial conditions. Short sights are dropped. What is one to do? Where is one to hide? Jews, save yourselves! I take a look at the nearest and dearest survivors. Zivia has gone to Yossl Sirota's secret hide-out, taking leave with profound grief in her eyes. I take my mother and wife...come, let's try to get away. I've go into the cabin at the end of the ghetto street, where there is a window out on the Gentile street. A last look in my mother's deep, dear, true, infinitely devoted and sad eyes. I leap through the window. My wife tries to draw me back. She has seen through the mist a German standing on the other side. But it is too late. My feet land on Gentile soil, outside the ghetto. An impudent act on my part. A German gun faces me, its bayonet pointed at me. "Halt!", I hear the command. It's a miracle that I haven't been stabbed. He takes me in. The dull-witted German has orders to shoot anyone who leaps from a window in the ghetto. The head does not think; the heart flutters; cut to pieces.

I left there my mother and wife. They won't leap; they saw the German take me in and must be sure it is all over with me. What will they do? What will become of me? I resolve again that so long as they haven't deprived me of my life, I will not submit! October 16, 1942. I lie on the rim of the cut rye in the granary of Ivan, whose cabin is the last in Antopol, on the road to Proszychwost, to the left of the cobbled highway. A few weeks earlier, I saved the housewife's life by stopping a hemorrhage. That day I left my home and my wife, with Ivan who had come to plead with me, at the risk of being killed by the Germans if they caught me. Now this woman, whose life I had saved, found me in the shed on an early morning when she came to milk the cow. The cow was on the other side. When she noticed me, she was frightened at first, as if she saw a ghost. Then she called out her husband, Ivan. They took me up to the top and hid me. But first they brought me a coat to cover me up. I was wet from the rain and shivering from cold. Then they brought me hot milk and pancakes. The sun has arisen, and so, I am alive, among sheaves of rye. For a whole day the head did not think was dulled. It was only the inertia and the instinct which were functioning. I clung like a dog to the ragged clothes to keep warm.

*[Page 34]*

Then gradually, the brain began to react. I see it clearly now: The German orders, "Forward." and I walk. He brings me to a group of brutes, among which were the German, the Landwirtsmann, the Chief of Police and their dog, the Buergermeister of Antopol, the former mail carrier Chrominski, who was a Pole and Volksdeutsche, the murderer of our dear ones, the fiend stained with the blood of his victims, whom he had dispatched with his own hands. I see his diabolical face with its pointed nose and frozen dead eyes, his hand on the revolver by his side. His swinish snout utters the command: "Zabrac Jego!" (*Take him away]*) and two policemen grab me and lead me into Sirota's gate, where the pasterunek (detention) was located. Four other people were there who had been seized earlier. A few minutes later they bring the midwife Weinstein and three young men. It was too early in the day to shoot. Every article we had on us had been taken away and we were told to sit on the floor. The verdict is unmistakable. The brain thinks only in one direction: Where does one find the strength to administer them such a blow that we could liberate all those who are scurrying about the fence looking for holes to hide in? The heart is full of hatred for the brutes, full of pain and worry. How long will it go on beating ? I picture the German with his revolver aimed, taking me about 8 a.m. Any split second he may press the trigger and pierce me with a bullet.

I walk quietly. He is leading me back into the ghetto to the assembly place. On all fours like a cat, I leap forward when the machine gunner leading us, bends down to light a cigarette. My heart beats even now when I think of the decision I made in a flash and carried out: I ran over to Eisenberg's stable. I am noticed at a distance by the old chief of the German constabulary. I am sure he sees me, but he pretends not to.

I am not afraid of him. I recall that after the second "hunt", when he stood at the well near Markiter's house in the ghetto, he was looking into the well and said to me quietly with a sigh, as I approached the well "What a misfortune." His voice trembled, and I thought that tears would come to his eyes. That was the only true sorrow which I noticed in a German in those days.

Here I lie in Eisenberg's stable, and I don't move. Pain, hunger, thirst – I don't feel them. I have covered myself with rotten hay and am waiting. Night is coming and I have to make use of it. I slide down the loft and begin wandering among the dark mute houses of the ghetto. I can still hear, on one side, the dead silence, and on the other – the voices of the sentries who make the rounds, and shoot into the air from time to time, to see that no one escapes. I stole out between Polciuk's and Sirota's houses, and am now crawling on my belly through the market place, A thin rain is falling; it is dark. I am already on the Zaniew street, and suddenly in the dark there is a gun facing me with the command, "Stoj! Kto idzie?" (*Stop! Who is going?*). I recognize the voice of the policeman Kostia, whom I know well. I used to give him some salve to irritate the sore on his finger, so that he would not be able to put on his boots and have an excuse to stay away from the raids. Kostia, it seems, also remembers and is grateful. He let me go through. This way I reached Ivan's stable. My body is trembling now, not from cold but from excitement, from impatience, from anger. What of the rest? What of my mother, my wife Gittel, my child? What of all the 300 survivors? I saw some of them being led away.

*[Page 35]*

Ivan crawls up to me in the afternoon and tells me that it is not good in the ghetto. He brings me a German newspaper and I read with pain of the Nazi victories at the front. Night falls, but how can one sleep?

April 1943. My wife and I are under the floor of a house not far from the railway station, between Antopol and Proszychwost. We were united three days after parting, when she came at night to the hiding place where Ivan kept me. Suddenly the order arrives to demolish the house under which we are hidden – the demolition was deemed necessary for security. Our hosts are faced with the dilemma what to do with us? Letting us go free is dangerous, because my wife would not be able to withstand the blows and would divulge her hiding place and our hosts would be executed. I hear them discuss the matter over our heads. The question is: should we be shot or poisoned? But there is no poison to be had anywhere, and the man, an acquaintance of mine, though he has a weapon, does not want to shoot me. I get an old iron bar ready and fix up a lock on the door. I will not surrender. I will fight for my life! Finally, a way out was found.

Arcyszewski learned that Dr. Czerniak and his wife were alive and came to take us. We came out to him. This wonderful man, the Polish patriot, burst into tears when he saw what was left of a Jewish community. We went to live with him. Our address as of the end of April: Antopol, Kobryn street No. 10, the loft of Arcyszewski's stable. We are buried in the hay, near the planks. There is a crack, which serves us as a window. Three times each day the doors of the stable open wide and the housekeeper, a kindly village spinster, comes in carrying a pail with food for the denizens of the stable: a couple of pigs, a cow, hens and a rooster, a horse and a Jewish doctor and his wife, the Jewish pharmacist. The food for the humans is hidden at the bottom of the pail under the fodder for the animals. She talks to the animals, climbs up the ladder, ostensibly to get some hay, and unloads the meal for the Jews. While on top of the ladder, she whispers a few words to us. Now and then the master himself would come for a chat, while the housekeeper waits underneath. He would give us some news and bewail the fate of Poland, of Polish Jews, of his relatives. He works for the Germans but he would always end his conversation with a curse: "Let the cholera seize them, the sooner the better!"

One night a pig became hungry. He grabbed a sleepy hen from the fence. The hen raised a cry. The other animals in the stable woke up and raised a din. The pig evidently became frightened, let go of the hen and the conflict in the stable was terminated, with no damage to anyone. I watched the struggle, thinking to myself that with humans it is not so simple. We the powerless, have been attacked by a ferocious beast, all of us, adults and children, old and young, well and sick. Our outcry reached up to the heavens and was loud enough and strong enough to move mountains. But it was of no avail. Here we are in the very heart of the once living Jewish town, where we had a community of some two thousand souls, and now it is all vacant, quiet, dead.

From Arcyszewski's we moved to the village Rushevo. The moving took place in a singular way. At 12 noon a cart drove in into the courtyard on Kobryn street, near the market place, right in front of the eyes of the arch-murderers. The cart was loaded with tall logs and some straw. Arcyszewski together with the tall young village blacksmith from Rushevo came into the stable. There were two full sacks tied up ready for them. They looked as if they were filled with potatoes. The two men took first one sack and threw it onto the cart, then the other. They put the sacks straight, covered them with some straw, then made an opening in them to enable us to breathe. The sacks contained me and my wife, of course. The two sat in the driver's seat, whipped the horses, drove up to Kobryn street and out of Antopol. We arrived in a farmstead in Rushevo, to an address which goes back to the ghetto......

*[Page 36]*

When the Jewish doctor had to visit a patient in the country, he had to get a permit from the burgomaster to leave the town limits. One day a Gentile woman brought me such a permit and asked me to come to see a gravelly ill woman. I went along and arrived at a farmstead to the right of the road. I was invited to sit down and wait. In about ten minutes the door opened and a Gentile entered, armed with an automatic and hand grenades. He was the "sick woman". I was brought there, so I was told, because they had confidence in me. The German invaders were hunting them as they were hunting me.

"I took ill," he told me. "When I get well, we'll go on fighting the enemy." I examined him and found out that he suffered from jaundice. The prescription was made out to the "peasant woman". Grateful and silent, dignified and proud, he pressed my hand and took me back to the ghetto.

In about three weeks, a man who did not look Jewish came to see me at the polyclinic, closed the door tight and told me the following story: "My name is Aliosha. I am a Jew, a pilot, a soviet wax-prisoner. My plane was shot down by the Germans at the battle of Brest-Litovsk. I was taken prisoner and handed over to a peasant to work for him. They thought I was a Gentile. Now I am being called to headquarters for investigation. I am afraid they will order me to undress to see if I am circumcised. Can you perform an operation over me to make me look uncircumcised?" "That I cannot," I said, "but I have another idea for you. Go to that farmstead at Rushevo and tell them who you are. They will take you in." Ten days later a peasant in sheepskin came to see me. It was that same Aliosha. Under his sheepskin he had a weapon and a slice of sausage for me with a promise, "We'll help you when you want help. We'll tell you when things are bad. We have people with us who know." Evidently they were late with their information and weren't able to warn me. But I had their address and this is how I found refuge in Rushevo.

At long last! The end has come to the accursed Germans. They look so ridiculous now, so broken up, so filthy: bloodied, humiliated and ruined! I have lived to see the day when justice triumphed. But what a colossal price we paid for it!

We enter Antopol again. It is empty. Last night it was evacuated by the monsters. The cur Chrominski fled along with his masters. On leaving they burned a few houses. It is a beautiful day in June. The first one to meet me is Ivan Baiduk. He falls on my neck and kisses me. What an outpouring of affection! A pity to mention it. My first steps are directed to the house where our little girl is supposed to be. The Lord be praised! She is here, in good health. But what about later? It is so difficult to breathe here! So difficult to watch everything around you. Here, in this place, we once lived and loved every spot of it. Four other girls came, who managed to save themselves, and that was all that was left of Antopol Jewry.

We have to get settled, carry out the orders of the new authorities – the soviet armed forces. I am told to organize the health services in town and also for the whole region. I ardently throw myself into the task. I look for work to keep me busy all day and through the sleepless nights. I don't want my brain to be free to think, to remember.

But we cannot remain here. For whom? We must leave, we must come among Jews, we must leave the diaspora and realize our old dream...

Our little daughter is over three years old now. Vera Ochritz still keeps her. She is holding onto her in order to "save her soul" for the "true faith." She refuses to give her up, feeling like a mother to her, the girl owing her her life. Vera says, "We shall wait until the girl is eighteen years of age. Then she will decide whom the wants." What is to be done? It is a difficult problem. The woman has become so attached to the child! Once the constabulary arrested the woman on suspicion that she was harboring a Jewish child. They had an idea that the girl was ours.

They were ready to shoot the girl. Vera held her in her arms for three days, saying: "If you are going to shoot, shoot both of us. Then both our souls will go up to Heaven together!" The local priest stepped in and saved them. He testified that Vera was a believing Christian and that the child was Christian (the priest knew the truth, however, from Vera's confession). She was entitled to the rights of a custodian. Yet the parents were alive. We gave her everything we could, we helped her a great deal, but we could not make her a gift of our child. There was a trial and the court ruled that the child belonged to its parents.

*[Page 37]*

We finally made it. We packed and left for Brest-Litovsk. There we boarded a train for Poland, as repatriates. First we went to Lodz and thence to Gorzub (Landsberg) and later to Wraclaw (Breslau). Here we found some survivors of Antopol Jews, namely Mazurski's daughter and Itke Wolinetz. Mazurski's daughter saved herself under extraordinarily difficult circumstances and lived to see freedom. Itke came with her husband Meyshe Helefantstein.

We take our seats in the carriage of the train leaving for Paris. Farewell, Poland. Farewell, land of exile. We are determined and we are able to realize our ideal – to come to the Land of Israel. Midway we linger a little in France. In the hotel, where the remnants of the escaped survivors are gathered from the larger and smaller towns of the now extinct Jewish communities, there is a great deal of talking, reporting, discussing. History is being recorded!

There are sick people, survivors of annihilated households, broken spirits, frustrated ambitions, melancholy neurasthenic people, unnerved individuals, undernourished, frostbitten, cut-up tortured bodies, arms tattooed with numbers; each one a world by himself, a history, a tragedy. What is to be done?

Our firm resolve is to shake off the dust of the exile from our feet, not to let ourselves be discouraged by the hard times in the Homeland (that was in the years 1949-1950). On the contrary we must now come there to help. But not everyone feels that way. Some have other ideas. The idealists are quietly ridiculed. It was we, the survivors, who have seen how little value human ideals have. Hitler has trampled them underfoot.

In Marseilles we embarked on the Israeli ship Artza. How well we feel among our own people! How precious that is!

On Wednesday, April 4, 1950, we greet the soil of Israel. We have become the citizens of our ancestral land!

# The Ghetto of Antopol
## By Prof. P. Czerniak, diary entry

I see before my eyes the town of Antopol, with its market place and its stores and other buildings. There are Greenberg's, Lifshitz's, Smolinker's, Sirota's, Polichuk's, Mazurski's, Rosenbaum's, Vissotsky's, Kaplan's etc. I can see the streets running through the town – the Zaniev, the Zhalove, the Greblie, the alley leading to the old synagogue, to Healer Yankel. Here are the prayer-houses, the schools, the bathhouse with the ice-cellar, the orphanage, the traditional Jewish schools, the drugstore, the post-office, the bank, the free loan society, the newspaper stands, the booths, the stores, the larger and smaller shops. Here is everything dear to memory and everything appears so beautiful.

In those early September days of 1939 faces changed. Everyone is anxious, worried. Bombs are falling over all of Poland. The treacherous Germans destroy everything in their way. They are coming closer to us.What is to be done? Where can one flee? We are drowning in a sea of hatred and hostility, we have nothing good to look forward to; we are powerless, poor and weak. Affection and loyalty in our own ranks can be of little avail in such days of fire and blood.

It is mid-September now. All night, only the noise of the Polish army vehicles can be heard, as they are leaving the front to flee towards the Rumanian border. Explosions are heard. On the Kobryn side the sky is reddening. The wounded are being brought in. In the morning information reaches us that the Russian army is approaching. The Jews of the town become alive. Finally there will come an end to the uncertainty and a new chapter will open. A new order of things, new joys and sorrows – but, the main thing, life will be secure. The Russians arrive. People adapt themselves, they work, they build. Months go by.

*[Page 38]*

It is 6 a.m. on June 22, 1941. A new conflagration is on. On the Bug, near Brest-Litovsk, the Hitler bands are moving forward. The Soviet forces are fleeing in great haste, abandoning large stores of supplies and ammunition. They managed to destroy only part of their archives; the remainder was to be made good use of by the Germans. On the fourth day of the German-Soviet hostilities, the last of the Russian soldiers left Antopol. The Jewish section is drained of all life. Already the sound of the German airplanes overhead is to be heard. The first motorcyclists arrive. The frightened Jewish population looks out through the curtains as the killers come in. The march of the German army took several weeks. As long as the Germans were marching, the power was in the hands of the gendarmerie (constabulary). After the gendarmerie came the Gestapo, which set up the civil police force, formed out of the local Polish and White Russian (Bielorussian) population. The first act of the police was to square accounts with those who collaborated with the Bolsheviks. They also handed over to the S.S. two Jewish men who had escaped from a German camp and returned to Antopol during the Soviet rule. The men were taken to the S.S. car which arrived from Kebryn, where one of the brutes first beat them and kicked them with his feet and finally shot them dead.

This opened the blood-stained chapter of the story. The police invented an amusement for itself consisting of whipping Jews. They made use of the time when an S.S. car would stop at the market place. They would then catch Jewish passers-by, who were already wearing the badges on their sleeves with the Star of David, and bring them into the police station to be whiplashed. The crying and weeping of the victims would freeze the blood in the veins of the listeners. Whenever an unfortunate, released from under the lash, was not quick in making a getaway – crawling away, for that was all he could do they would punish him by calling him back, pouring cold water over him and submitting him to new lashings. Some of the victims would be confined to bed for weeks as a result.

Another amusement the Germans had was to order the Jews to wash their cars and use the opportunity to whip them as they worked and to make them run up and down like dogs.

By employing these barbarian methods, the Germans succeeded in making the Jew hate his life and lose his self-respect and his sense of human dignity.

A short time after their entry into Antopol, the German rulers called together the Christian population of the town into the local church and enlightened them on the proper way of handling their Jewish townspeople. The lesson was quickly learned by the Ivans and the Marussias.

Thus began the systematic cold-blooded implementation of the anti-Jewish plan: a strongly armed monster pitted against a handful of helpless men, women and children. No one asks why or when. Placards are hung in the marketplace with shocking medieval anti-Semitic slogans.

Then evil decrees begin to crowd one another in quick succession. The Jews are ordered to sew on a yellow badge on the breast and on the back. All Jews living on the right hand side of the Pinsk street are ordered to move out of their homes.

The letter-carrier Khrominsky is appointed Chief of the town and the district. He orders the Jews to form a Judenrat consisting of a Chairman and five or six members. At first the demand was for the two Jewish physicians, Dr. Sunschein and myself, to enter into it. But they later realized that if the physicians devoted any time to the sessions of the Jewish Council, the sick of the town and the surrounding villages would be neglected and they rescinded the order. On a cold October morning, formations of armed bandits in German uniforms appear in the fields near Antopol, with their guns trained. They surround the town and the Judenrat is presented with two demands: 1) an indemnity of gold, silver, jewels, leather, various foods and Polish and Soviet currency; 2) all able-bodied men to gather in the marketplace for work.

*[Page 39]*

Men scurry away to places where they can hide. I was hidden by the Russian priest in his barn. To be seen are only women and members of the Judenrat. Everyone is carrying what he has to the collecting point, at the home of the late sainted Rabbi Wolkin. The gold, the silver and the money are taken into the house, the merchandise – to a store in the marketplace. Before the evening came, the Germans managed to capture about 140 men, including boys of 14 years of age and shut them all up in the Polish school on Pinsk street. At the very same time that the wives, mothers and sisters of the imprisoned men were collecting their indemnity to ransom their nearest and dearest – as they hoped – the peasants of the village Proshikhvost were digging their graves in a nearby wood. (Of that we learned much later).

The day is done, it is dark and a thin dreary rain is falling. Everyone is seated in his house. The curfew forbids to appear outside. But the hearts are with them over there, with the imprisoned fathers and brothers.

In the houses which are situated near the school they hear the sound of approaching automobiles. The innocent victims are being led out, loaded into the cars and taken to a "labor camp." But they don't get very far. Others had a story to tell about the dull sound of machine guns, which took the lives of the male members of the despoiled families. Hearts were beating fast, but the minds refused to believe that such things could happen in an era of culture and civilization in the twentieth century!

The next morning an automobile arrives and the brutes report that everyone taken away yesterday is now at work in a labor camp and is entitled to receive a parcel of five kilograms of foodstuffs. A new sport for the demons. But mothers and wives make up packages of the best that they have left, write the name of the addressee on each side of the parcel and hand the packages over to the messengers of mercy. An hour later, outside the town, the packages are opened, the best is taken out and consumed and the rest thrown away. In this vandal manner the assassins trample underfoot the dignity of Man and his culture.

A short time after the first liquidation, the first ghetto was set up. We were assigned to one half of the town, on the left hand side of the Pinsk and Kobryn streets. For a few weeks things were quiet. It was the quiet before a storm. Then came a new decree: there would be two ghettos now, Ghetto A and Ghetto B, the one for skilled workers, useful Jews, the other for the useless. No one wished to be counted among the useless. The Judenrat, together with the Labor Office, had to make up lists. There began the bargaining for places on the useful list, which was believed to involve the difference between life and death. People pleaded, begged, gave presents, and wept, anxious to be included in Ghetto A among the "useful" Jews, or to add to the roster an old father or mother. What next?

The Jews of the surrounding countryside were gathered into Antopol – from the villages and towns of the Pruzhan district and the Bielovezh Forest and other places. That resettlement had to be carried out within 24 hours. Often people were just driven from place to place. After a day's strain and tension in moving about, the newcomers begin to look for secret hiding places, potainiks, where to hide out from the hangmen. A great deal of ingenuity and technical skill had to be invested in that effort to discover or contrive them. The potainiks – a new term coined in those years – were within the walls, under the floors, behind cupboards, under screened or curtained-off entrances, double walls and various dark holes. Men ran into such holes like mice, hiding from the brutes human and canine (the Germans employed specially trained dogs to catch the Jews), who pursued us as a cat pursues a mouse. In those days we became the sympathizers of the mice.

*[Page 40]*

It is an early summer day in 1942. The murderers surround Ghetto B. Their task was to capture over 1,000 people. Whoever is caught is led to the market place. Old people and children are driven like sheep onto carts.

From the market place they are all driven to the railway station. They are met by another train arriving from Pinsk, Janowa and Drohichin, filled with Jews from those towns. The Jews of Antopol are driven into the same train. There are gruesome scenes, accompanied by outcries, wailing and shouting.

Subsequently it became known that near Kartuz- Bereza, in the woods of Bronie-Gura, mass graves had been made ready among the tall fir trees and the sandy hills. When the train arrived, one carload after another of human beings was thrown out into the graves while the machine guns fired on without cease.

A woman who was wounded managed to escape from that inferno to tell us what had taken place. Petrified, dumfounded, stunned, people listened to her story but even then a spark of hope glimmered in their hearts, and they thought the woman had gone off her mind. For how was such a thing possible?

After the second "operation" the ghetto became too large, and we were confined to a smaller ghetto, in the part of the town between the market place, on Kobryn, Zhalov and Grushev streets. A tall barbed-wire fence was put up around it and guards were posted before it. Here the inmates were suffocated and eaten up by various diseases and by hunger. Every morning a group of workmen was driven off to some labor under guard to be paid in beatings and curses. The vandals could not tolerate the few survivors and organized a third "operation".

One night the ghetto was surrounded again. People were dragged out of their hiding places. Four hundred people were gathered together. More human tragedies were played out. Families were broken up, but who took stock of such things? The monster did its work. At this point, they took the rabbi and beat him. We hid on the garret and watched through a crack what was going on. A young shoemaker ran by, crying, "Let me live. I can work well". The German fired and evidently hit the mark, for all we heard was a feeble groan.

Following this tragic day and its events, came other sad days. Wet with tears, drained of feeling, each one was busy with himself alone. Why have I remained alive? Why didn't I go with all the others? How long am I to suffer and "fight" for my life? Is it worth it?

About 300 fragments of families, fragments of human beings, remained. It was certain that the death sentence had already been pronounced over us, but we still wondered, when will the German bullet pierce us? We were isolated from the world and didn't know what was taking place outside. We hadn't even the small consolation that somewhere someone was thinking about us. Usually a condemned man is visited by a rabbi or a priest and sees a face with an expression of compassion, knows that his relatives grieve for him. But nothing of the kind reached us through the walls of our ghetto. Sometimes one has an ideal for whose sake one is ready to lay down one's life. A soldier is ready to die for his country. We had nothing. We were surrounded by the full grinning faces of our Russian neighbors, headed by the letter-carrier Khrominsky, together with the beasts from the Land on the Rhine and they are all waiting for the time they can carry away what is left of ours after our death. They did not have long to wait. Khrominsky had already promised them they would soon be able to take a walk through the ghetto. A Christian woman doctor came from Brest-Litovsk and took up a house in the ghetto. My former patient Vera from the Kobryn street warns me to hand over my 10 month old child to her as quickly as possible, because we are to be done away with pretty soon.

*[Page 41]*

It is early September 1942. I see shadows rather than living human beings in the ghetto. One has to search for a smile with a lantern. The sleepless nights are spent in prayer for a speedy end to the suffering by death or by some miracle. Some of the inmates consult with one another about building some hiding places outside its walls, where we could bide our time until the Germans left. But where can we obtain arms?

The bearer of the idea – the father of the project – was Markiter. As a capable electrical technician, he was often called by the Germans to repair their radio transmitters and thus had access to their arms. The day had already been fixed when Markiter would seize a few rifles and run into the woods. But we were afraid of the likely consequences in the ghetto and the plan was dropped.

One night, six Jews escaped from the ghetto. They roamed the countryside for a few days but no one would help them. Emaciated by hunger and cold, they came back. It was during that time that we placed our little daughter at the doorstep of the Christian woman. Other people had similar ideas but could not bring themselves to carry out such a daring deed. Lipshe Wolowelsky, the wife of Meyshe Hershenhorn, had handed over her daughter, several years old, to a Christian who had a farm near a village. But the children playing with the little girl used to call her zhidovka, so the Christian woman became frightened and brought the girl back to her parents. At the same time, Gittle Zeidel came to an understanding with a Christian woman in the vegetable patches on the road to Pinsk that she should hand her over her child of 7 or 8 months of age. But she found it difficult to part from her baby and she missed the opportunity. There were other such cases in which places had been arranged for the children, but the parents, unable to part with their offspring, were too late to save them.

On the night of October 15, the treacherous letter-carrier assembled the Jewish Council and the Jewish police and put them in prison. Simultaneously, the S.S. surrounded the ghetto. The Jews in the ghetto had no knowledge of what was happening. I remember that at 6 a.m. Abramchik knocked on the shutters of our room to let us know the ghetto had been cordoned off. Now everyone realized that the end had come. Our first reaction was that it is good that our child is not with us now. She may survive it all and remain as a living memory to us...Then a new feeling surged up. No, I will not let myself be done in! I leaped out of the ghetto. I am caught and led into the gendarmerie and then to the square from which the way leads to the grave. Is this the end?

I shall never forget that place. With me was the young barber, smoking one cigarette after another and saying: "Let those killers hurry up and finish it!" Here was also the dentist Shogan and his wife. He says to me, "What, you want to flee? It is of no use!" At a distance, I see the midwife Mrs. Weinstein and her son, the physician, who clings to her. When I ask him to join me in my escape, he answers, "My mother cannot run with us. I cannot leave her." Then a boy is driven up, his stomach shot up by a gun, with his entrails hanging out. I take my blood-soaked handkerchief from my forehead (bloodied by the rifle butt of a German after my first attempt to flee), and stuff up the boy's belly. Who could dream of a bandage? At least, let him have some relief from his pain. The automobile has arrived. Just then I jump up like a cat on all fours, run out and in a few seconds I am on the roof of a nearby stable.

Every one of the eight survivors of the two thousand Jews of Antopol has a similar story to tell. Mine is one of the eight.

A will of iron was needed to merely wish to be saved, and still more luck was needed later, to survive in the ocean of hate, which had overrun our fair countryside of Lithuanian Russia.

The final liquidation of the Antopol ghetto lasted about four days. It took four days and four nights for the bestial Nazis to hunt down the last unfortunate Jews with the aim of destroying them. After that there remained only empty pillaged broken down houses, filthy streets, a dead silence, polluted air but free of Jews, and the sun went on shedding its light on the place of destruction. Only eight emaciated and lonely creatures, deprived of all hope, were in the fields, woods, marshes and bunkers in order to remain alive and be able to tell at least a part of the bloody story, of the days of monstrous evil done by fiends compared to whom Pharaoh, Nebuchadnezzar, Nero, Khmelnitzky and many other wicked rulers in history appear like angels of mercy.

*[Page 42]*

Twenty-eight years have passed since those days. Time has somewhat healed the wounds. Memory has lost some of it. But this can be said of the community, of society, of our people. We, the individuals who lived through all that hell, can never forget it. We seek to dull our remembrances in work, to keep our minds busy so as to be able to sleep at night. A new generation is growing up, which has not witnessed it and will not be able to picture it or be willing to believe it. Let them at least read the record and keep in mind that the pen of an ordinary writer cannot describe everything. But the little that is poured out comes out of a bleeding heart. It is a mere drop of the anguish accumulated in two years of Inferno beyond the powers of a Dante to depict.

We, the survivors, are the mere small fragments that are left. Millions lie speechless in their graves or have gone up in smoke. Of those who are left among the living, some will never forgive or forget and wait for vengeance to come. They raise their fists to the skies and shout for the whole world to hear, "We remember, we will not forget what the wicked Amalek has done!" Others accept things as they are, nod their heads and make peace with fate. What can one do now to better things?

There are yet others who refuse to concern themselves with the brutes. They leave it to history to pass judgment. They bear too much of their own pain to have room for other people's worries. They know what mental anguish is, and they can appreciate the mental anguish of others. We have been broken by our ordeal. Let now our murderers be broken by their anguish. We must not help them become morally rehabilitated before the judgment of history. Let them suffer if indeed their conscience awakes!

# Memoirs of an Antopol Physician-Partisan
## By P. Czerniak, from a diary entry

The month of October of 1942 in the Western part of White Russia, the region between Bialystok, Brest-Litovsk and Pinsk, under the German. Remnants of Jews, who have so far escaped the massacres, are still living in the innumerable towns and townlets. Now comes the final act: the liquidation of the ghettos, including the ghetto of Antopol.

The operations are marked by unspeakable atrocity. The ghettoes are strongly guarded so that there was no chance to escape. The slightest attempt to get away brings a bullet in the head. The physicians were left to the last moment since they were still needed. So far there were no Aryan doctors to be found in the small out-of-the-way localities, and the Jewish physician was still in demand.

It so happened that in Horodec (Horodetz), where there was only one doctor, a fugitive from Brest-Litovsk, Dr. Sunschein, was tolerated for three months after not even a single Jew was left in town. He was placed under a strong guard day and night, and was ordered to treat the non-Jewish population of the region. But as soon as an Aryan doctor was found, the Jew was liquidated. A motorcyclist with black insignia came down from Brest-Litovsk and, with the help of his local flunkeys, the doctor, his wife and his child were taken outside the town limits, ordered to dig a grave and were covered with earth while still alive.

In Kobryn, Dr. Goldberg was to have a similar fate. But, unlike others, he prepared himself for it and decided to exact a high price for his life. He had succeeded in obtaining a few hand grenades and a loaded revolver. When they came to take him, he threw the hand grenades against the murderers, defended himself with his revolver and finally turned the last bullet on himself. Another fellow-physician, whose name I do not recall at the moment, threw upon his assassins a flask with sulphuric acid and leaped from the balcony.

*[Page 43]*

There were many such examples in our parts of quiet heroism mingled with tragic resignation in the part of Jewish physicians. These facts deserve to be recorded for posterity. For the present, I merely wish to dwell on some of my colleagues who, by some miraculous combination of favorable circumstances and their own courage, managed to break out of the claws of the brutes and become active in the ranks of the partisans. Each case is a miracle in itself. I knew six such fellow-physicians in our region who joined the existing partisan formations.

It was a long road from the ghetto walls to the freedom of the partisans in the woods and swamps; from the state of a hunted and condemned "fly" to the post of a physician or chief physician in the partisan units. In the environs of Antopol, the first partisan ranks began to form as early as 1941. In 1943, a whole corps was active and known as the Brest-Litovsk United Fighters. It consisted of a staff and brigades spread over the forests and the marshlands. Attached to staff headquarters was the Chief of the Partisans' Medical Service. He was one of the six Jewish doctors. The remaining five were attached to separate field units.

It is difficult to convey what each one of us did and under what conditions! We worked in the midst of battles, of thousands of dangers, in the woods, fields, marshes, caves, pits, under the open sky, under a tree, in a primitive tent, or in a rural cabin, at best. We were often under the hot sun or in a slashing rain, in a snowfall or hailstorm, here by day, there by night, and frequently under the hostile looks of not-too-friendly strangers. Not to mention the lack of medical installations and instruments, an operating table, cots, medicines or bandages! We always had to improvise, to create something out of nothing. Not only were we called upon to take care of the health of our fellow – partisans, but also to look after the local civilian population to receive their sick and wounded and to combat epidemics. How do I convey or describe all of this?! Here are some personal reminiscences.

Noontime of a sunny April day. A cart enters a courtyard on the Kobryn Street in Antopol. Two sacks are carried out of the stable and loaded onto the wagon. The sacks are covered with straw. Arcyszewski, who is under obligation to me for having saved the life of his wife, has taken pity on us – for it was my wife and myself who were in those sacks – and punctures an opening in the sacks to enable us to breathe. We travel for seven kilometers. Our hearts flutter, we hardly even wish to believe that we shall reach our destination. Night has fallen. We come to a threshing floor. Here, we are awaited by ten armed partisans. We experience our first friendly encounter with people at liberty after five months of hiding and constant fear of death. How good it is to breathe the free air of the forest! We walk. It is way past midnight when we reach a clearing not far from the village of Odrinke. That is our destination. For the time being, this will be my place of work, my new quarters.

On the morrow, the first personal meetings of acquaintance. The work begins. First of all, a general medical examination for everybody. Between two trees, overhead, they draw a coarse sheet for shelter, and the inspection begins. It turns out that more than 20% of my comrades suffer from scabies; the rest are sure to get the itch soon. It is a highly contagious ailment, especially under prevailing conditions of life. My first task is to relieve the suffering. I explain that since no medical supplies are available, it would help if they could secure some sulphur. Once animal fat is secured, the mixture would serve as an ointment. My wife prepares a pot with the ointment – 15-20% sulphur. For several days the odor of sulphur hung over the countryside. The laundry was boiled, clothes were changed, people bathed in the nearest swamp. Soon they were rid of that plague. There is no way to describe the gratitude of these people of the forest. That "partisans' ointment," as it was known, spread among all the detachments of the brigade and among the civilian population as well.

*[Page 44]*

But there were other ailments. Unfortunately, I had to do my work empty-handed. I had nothing in the way of medicines or instruments, bandaging material or syringes. At a meeting I proposed a plan and asked for general cooperation. I asked that they collect old, unused medicines in every house and village where the partisans went to carry out operations. I asked the staff to set aside some lard which could be bartered in the Antopol pharmacy for the necessary medical supplies; that they should search out medical instruments in the loot of the robbers of the ghetto. It was done. Thus we set up the partisans' dispensary in the woods. A syringe was found as well as some distilled water. The machinery used by the peasants to produce homebrew was put to work in distilling water. The work progressed.

June 20th. We play host to distinguished visitors. For the first time we were visited by the Chief of Staff of the United Partisans of Brest-Litovsk and w e discuss organizational problems. The Chief was accompanied by the head physician.

As we were seated on the ground, consulting with one another about sanitary problems, we were suddenly apprised of the arrival of a car with 15 German military personnel in Hruszewo, two kilometers from our camp. The Germans came to look for eggs, milk and fowl. The session was interrupted and we quickly formed a group, with the few arms at our disposal, to attack the enemy.

Before long we heard the loud reports of firing. Our men had ambushed the German party on their way back and showered them with a rain of bullets on all sides. Eight Germans were killed on the spot. Five were seriously wounded and two, defending themselves with their automatics, managed to escape. Their automobile was no longer fit to be used but we found in it several cans of benzine, and some arms and ammunition. This was quite a loot for us. We suffered two casualties, one of them wounded seriously, in the tip of his right leg. When he was brought to our station, I made use of the reserves I had built up. I gave him, instead of a transfusion, injections of a specially prepared physiological mixture. I used up the only ampule of morphine I had to relieve his pain. Taking care of the lightly wounded was a much easier task.

However, we were compelled to make a quick getaway, expecting as we did a retaliatory expedition by the Germans. We set out for the Juchon woods, winding our way through little known hidden paths. Carrying him on a hastily improvised stretcher, we took our seriously wounded comrade with us and everything we possessed. We later learned that two hours after we left, several German armored trucks appeared in the neighborhood, cruising it up and down and unable to find any trace of us.

Time moved forward and the number of partisans grew. The engagements with the Germans took place more and more often and the Germans stepped up their repressions against the civilian population. The latter increasingly demanded of us medical assistance. It was impossible to find auxiliary medical personnel, and I began to train some in my unit.

My colleagues, doctors in the neighboring partisan detachments, were in a similar position. They did not have a moment to breathe and, in addition, there was not a single nurse or attendant. I picked 16 women partisans and began to teach them how to handle a sick person, how to clean and bandage wounds. I trained them in the practice of first-aid. They were eager and capable and very devoted. They finally acquired the art and were assigned functions. Every small unit was allotted one nurse and two male attendants, chosen from among the partisans who had some idea about such work. This was the nucleus of each of the larger groups of first aid. The three members of the nucleus usually accompanied the group whenever there was a minor engagement in the area. The staff refused categorically to risk its only physician except in very important sorties.

*[Page 45]*

November of 1943. Our detachment, in agreement with several other smaller ones in the same area, undertook a joint attack on the town of Antopol. We concentrated our forces at night. According to the prearranged plan, each grouping was assigned its objective; to occupy this or that position, to carry out this or that act of sabotage. I went with my group to seize Gody's Mill. The new owners of the flourmill were shut up by us in the cellar, while we converted the rest of the premises into a field hospital. I established myself with my assistants, ready to receive the wounded. In this place, behind Gody's Mill, I used to romp and play as a child and play pranks as a boy. Now I was here again, to treat the wounded partisans who were fighting to avenge the destruction of a large Jewish community.

The longed-for moment had arrived. On all sides there was the din of machine guns, automatic rifles, guns and hand grenades. Next the houses were on fire. The first wounded arrived. I am assisted by a young Jewish physician from another unit and three trained nurses. One man has a bullet in his head, three have their legs wounded, a few have light wounds in various places, one has a broken leg. All of them receive first aid. Two return to the firing line immediately. Three will have to be carried on stretchers.

At daybreak all the fighters have reassembled worn out, but pleased with the job well done, courageous and inspired. The Germans and their collaborators were taught a good lesson, their "fortress" was destroyed and a large quantity of food and ammunition was taken to last a long period.

In October 1943, on the anniversary of a national holiday, we get an order from above to blow up the Brest-Pinsk railway line for a stretch of four kilometers. Our unit marches towards its objective through woods, fields and hamlets. I go along. We have arrived, spread out, laid out the bricks with the explosives. Here is the agreed signal, and then come scores of explosions. Chunks of iron soar up and fall down groaning to the ground. The German watchmen wake up suddenly in their booths and open a wild fusillade with tracer bullets. One of our men has been hit in the back by a piece of fallen iron. We take him along. I give him an injection of morphine to relieve his pains. I do what I can under the circumstances. But could he be saved under ideal conditions?!

Early in 1944. An epidemic of spotted typhus fever is raging in the region of Antopol. The partisans were infected and brought the disease to camp. There are over 20 sick. They make it difficult. We must be mobile and on the alert, because the Germans are lurking for our lives. The typhus patients are like lead on our feet while their absence from the battlefield is keenly felt. There is no time to lose in fighting the epidemic. The first thing to do is to exterminate the lice. Since there were no chemicals to do the job, I invented an abattoir for lice. I arranged one of the dugouts used for hanging the clothes in such a manner that it could be sealed hermetically and filled with hot steam; two hours of such treatment killed the lice. At the same time I ordered close-cropped haircuts and two baths in the open air for each partisan. The partisans were ordered not to spend a night in any strange house and to bathe and steam their clothes after every contact with civilians. I also ordered strict insulation for the sick and suspicious cases. The partisans carried out all my instructions with remarkable promptness. The success was amazing.

Among the duties of a physician in the partisan forces was one of rendering assistance to the civilian population when it asked for it or when it was forbidden, for security reasons, to go seek medical assistance in a town occupied by the Germans. We were constantly approached by sick civilians and we helped them.

One hour after we had entered the village Derevnoye, a young peasant came to me and told me his wife was bleeding. I see her: she had a miscarriage. Her womb must be scraped immediately or she would bleed to death. I took some of the pipes used by the peasants for making homebrew, the wiring used by the soldiers to clean the rifles and some other such obtainable materials and made my own instruments for the occasion, sterilized them together with the gynecological speculum and treated the woman. After half an hour the bleeding ceased.

*[Page 46]*

March 1944. Six thousand Germans are assembled around our unit, armed with tanks and cannon, in order to put an end to us. I am laid up with severe pneumonia, and 39 degrees fever. I contracted it a few days earlier traveling in rain and wind to a distant hamlet to see a patient. On account of my illness the staff had to alter its schedule, waiting for me to recover somewhat, perhaps following the crisis on the ninth day, But when the German noose began to tighten around us, waiting any further was impossible. I was placed on a wagon and, traveling during the night, by hidden byways, we managed to break through the ring. It was a long way but finally we arrived at the Sporow marshes, where we were out of danger. While on the way there, I was visited by the doctor of a neighboring unit who gave me some treatment and helped me to recuperate somewhat.

A "hospital" was hastily put together in the marshes: trees were cut and chopped down, and a structure arose with a wooden floor. We had a sickroom with cots for eight patients, one for the sick who could walk and a physician's office. Out of here issued sorties into evacuated localities and the men returned weary and some wounded. There was plenty to do.

In June of 1944 we emerged from the marshes and went over to the Russian army. On our way we engaged some of the retreating German units. My wife took gravely ill. I had to obey orders and leave her to her own devices. Fortunately, I managed to contact a Jewish woman physician of a neighboring unit and she looked after my wife until she got well. The last battle with the Germans took place south of Bereza Kartuzka. A larger unit of Germans took up some trenches and idled their time away, awaiting instructions. Meanwhile the Germans went out to pick berries in the nearby woods. Our woodsmen then attacked in full force. A strong fusillade ensued. Many Germans lost their heads and raised their arms, throwing away their weapons. Others defended themselves and ran for cover into the nearby distillery. None came out alive.

When the first elements of the Red Army appeared, the men continued to fight the remnants of the fanatic Germans, but the task was much lighter. On July 22, I returned to my "liberated" hometown, Antopol. It was a desolate place for Jews. Only seven Jewish souls were there. How could one bear it? How could I stay there for any length of time?

Before leaving Antopol I made two calculations. First, what did the partisan-doctor of Antopol do from April 1943 until July 1944? I received 7,320 sick partisans, treated while they could walk around, and 2,358 sick civilians spread over 46 different localities, which necessitated my making 152 trips. I treated 213 gravely ill partisans, requiring a total of 1,278 confinement days; treated 58 wounded partisans of whom only two were unable to return to the line; performed 35 complicated surgical operations; treated six wounded civilians, delivered seven children of civilian mothers, of which one had triplets; waged war on epidemics, lice and all sorts of plagues, and so on. I based the total on diaries kept during work.

Secondly, what did the German occupational authorities and their collaborators achieve in Antopol and its environs in the field of medicine and health? They murdered three physicians, one dentist, two pharmacists, two medical attendants, two midwives, two nurses and 39 male nurses along with 2,000 Jewish inhabitants of the town. They destroyed health centers (Detkowic, Torokan, Aniskowic, Berezno, Worotnic), the medical laboratory, the health department and the contagious diseases department in Antopol and more.

It remains for the world to compare our total to that of the murderers.

*[Page 47]*

# Verdict Without Appeal
## By P. Czerniak, from a diary entry

It is late summer of 1942. The day is warm, sunny and bright. A carriage comes to me from the hospital to the ghetto, with Dr. Smimov in it. "Kolezhka!", he addresses me affectionately, "come quick, I'd like to show you something!"

Smimov is now director of health services, and his wish is an order for me. I have known Smirnov our high school days in Kobryn, under different circumstances.

When I fist entered high school, Smirnov was one grade above me. When I was completing the final grade, the eighth, he was repeating his seventh grade. The poor fellow was a bad student and had difficulty even in memorizing the fact that water boiled at 100 degrees C. On my graduation from high school I was refused, as a Jew, admittance to a university in Poland. Smirnov, however, did manage, two years later, to enter the Vilno School of Higher Learning, and even to study at the Faculty of Medicine. Somehow he pulled through during the war years, when the Russian occupied Vilno.

When the Germans arrived, he became important – a man with Slavic Aryan blood in his veils and a diploma in his pocket. It did not matter much what he had, or did not have, in his brain. It was this Dr. Smirnov who was brought by the Germans from Kobryn to Antopol to be entrusted with all the functions which I, the accused Jew (verfluchte Jude) had been charged with before. This was the role of director of the health service for the region and of the hospital, which I had built in Antopol during the time of the Russian occupation, beginning in 1939 and continuing until the German invasion. Whenever something happened in the hospital which Dr. Smirnov did not know how to handle, he would come running out of breath to the ghetto to ask my help.

This time too, the carriage clattered loudly on the cobblestones of the Kobryn highway. In it were seated Dr. Smirnov, the director; I with my yellow badge, and the coachman, who when no one was looking, would take off his hat before me, as in olden times. The three of us drove out to Janyszewski's farm, at the end of the Kobryn Lots, where the hospital was situated. I found there a child, sick with whooping cough, suffering from strong attacks of coughing and eczema under the skin of the throat and on the upper part of the chest. Apparently the pressure created by the coughing caused a rupture in the windpipe, and air entered under the skin. The child was hurt by the pressure and looked terrible. I asked for a couple of coarse needles, pricked the skin and the air came out. The distended skin contracted and the suffocation was relieved. I administered some bromophorm to the child and he was saved.

Dr. Smimov accompanied me on my way home. There was no need to hurry, so we walked. I wanted to gain time and perhaps obtain some information from this stupid fellow about what was being planned for us, Jews in the ghetto. For several minutes my colleague kept tapping his forehead and muttering, "It is all so simple, why didn't I think of it? You prick the skin with a needle and you relieve the coughing. A puncture in the skin makes the air come out. Then you administer bromophorm to relieve the coughing." It looked, just as in olden times, when he used to rehearse to himself, "$H_2O$ is water, $H_2O$ is water."

I let him complete his course in the subject, thinking to myself: There he is, the Pan Direktor of today; the man who is superior to me, greater, more handsome, the more pureblooded specimen of the human race in this world. He rules and leads me as one leads a dog by a leash into its kennel – the ghetto. And here is the yellow badge on my back. That is the rope which stifles me and weighs me down. This dull-witted brain on two legs trudging like a bear, and carrying a living carcass shaped like a human being, this thing is my superior, the one who lords it over me, and I am the Jew, for which nothing will avail – neither science nor industry, nor talent, nor culture. I am the one that is not wanted, not needed. I am the hated and despised, the one to be destroyed. Why? Why did the Poles admit this total zero to the university in Vilno but would not admit me, the Jew? Why is this absolute nonentity now a free physician in control, event thought it is clear that the distance between him and the Jew-dog is the distance of long years of evolution of the human species on earth? Why, after all, is he sure of his life and is entitled to it, while I am sure of death and am not entitled to live?

*[Page 48]*

That beautiful, summer day, as it was nearing its send at twilight, while Smirnov and I were walking back to the ghetto, I received the answer to my query.

Dr. Smirnov began, "It is a pity that you are a Jew, a zhid. You understand, a great ruler arose in the world, a great judge. He issued a verdict which ordered all Jews to be destroyed. There is no appeal against this judgment. That is plain, no mistake about it. You've got no one to appeal to, no one to discuss it with. You cannot defend yourself, and I am sorry about you, because you have been helping me (the unassailable logic of a numbskull!)."

Smirnov went on, "It seems it won't be long now. Pan Chrominsky, the Mayor, told me: Just wait a short while and you will soon be able to take a walk with your lady, in the ghetto freely." (Pan Chrominsky is the postman turned German– a Volksdeutsche–whom the Germans appointed Mayor of Antopol).

Smirmov spoke some more. He offered to save my equipment by taking it for himself and hiding it. According to his way of thinking, that ought to make it easier for me to take my bullet in the head, or console me somehow, when my end comes, with the rest of the Jews, while my stupid companion will be able to stroll over the blood-drenched soil of the ghetto. He kept on talking and talking, but I kept quiet. Here I was given my verdict of death not subject to any appeal. I, my family, and all the remaining Jews of the ghetto were soon to be put to death. All of us knew about it or felt it, but none of us dared to formulate it so plainly, the way this descendant of the Khmelnitzky killers blurted it out. The cold bullet, eight grams of lead, already entered my brain and dazed it, killing the best that there is to be found in a human head and leaving an automatically propelling, numb body. This body took leave of the Pan Direktor of the hospital, who continued to mourn, "Too bad, panochku, that you are a zhid, because I need you. But a verdict is a verdict."

Time passed and, during the period still left for us to live, the wound made by Dr. Smirnov was healing. What is to be done? The first thing decided by myself, and all those to whom I repeated my conversation, was to make arrangements about the children. In a few days, we deposited our little girl Vera at the doorstep of a Christian household (our daughter was five months old at the time). She stayed with them in the Pinsk Lots. The woman saved her and took good care of her. After the war, following strenuous efforts, we got our child back.

A few weeks later they knocked at our door at 5:00 in the morning: "Get up! the Judenrat has been arrested, the ghetto police is disbanded and the Germans are guarding us." I jumped up from bed with the thought, Smirnov's prediction has come true. The 8 grams of lead will bring the end. It makes it so much easier that our baby is not with us, that we saved the Deutsche Wehrmacht the expense of three pfenning for a bullet. And immediately thereafter a new determination came into being. If there is no appeal, let there be a fight for life or death. This is a fight of a hunted against the hunter: he has the gun, but the animal has the swift legs, it has justice on its side, the right to live. We are such animals. We must flee, out of the ghetto, and then we shall see. The decision was taken and carried out...

*[Page 49]*

# The Story of a Martyr
## By P. Czerniak, from a diary entry

Taylor Yossi Friedman had a son named Meyshe, who was also a tailor. He was a fine good-looking young man. Meyshe got married a couple of years before the War. His young wife gave birth to a child, who grew to be a year and a half when the German horde brought darkness to Antopol.

A non-Jewish farmer denounced the young man to the Germans as a communist. He was arrested, though he was pretty far removed from communism. Meyshe managed to escape from the police station and hid in the Pahonie (a large marshy field), where cows had their night pasture. The enraged Nazis were furious. Two motorcyclists came from nearby Kobryn. They called up the Judenrat (Council of Jews) and announced that if "the communist" failed to appear within the coming 48 hours, they would shoot his wife and child, his parents and ten prominent Jews. The next day Meyshe's wife and child and his parents were shut up in a brick-built store, with a guard posted in front of the store. A warning was issued that the would wait 24 hours more. Ivan Baiduk, a representative of the local gentile burghers, a supposedly progressive man who was literate enough to be able to sign his name, met me in the market place and said, "Mister Doctor, it looks bad. Meyshe is not coming. The rulers are sure to take another ten Jewish notables. In that case, dear doctor, we may lose you. We have got to do something about it."

Life had already lost its value for us. No one dreamt of acting along the lines suggested by Ivan. We knew Meyshe would be put to death as soon as he fell into their hands. Would anyone betray him? Sell him out? Would any one do anything to please the Germans, give them cause to feel triumphant? And why should Meyshe get this? Is he a communist or any sort of an activist or communal leader? He is nothing but a nice, quiet, decent and hardworking man. And even if were some sort of a party-man who believes in his ideal, does he deserve to be shot without a trial, just because some peasant wanted to have him dead?

Everyone in town knew that at night Meyshe came from the Pahonie, and sneaked into his house. On the first night he saw his wife and child, his father and mother, and together they grieved. They wrung their hands, sought out friends to ask for advice, had no food and no sleep. What was there to be done? On the second night the house was empty, because his nearest and dearest were shut up in the store. In the dark of the night he knocked on the doors and windows of his friends, asking, "Dear friends, what can be done? My heart is about to break, my head is whirling, the air is tight and life is a curse!"

They quietly sighed with the unhappy man. They felt for him and were sorry for him. The young man had become transformed. He was no longer good looking and had aged. They quietly parted and Meyshe went back to the Pahonie. The next morning he reported at the police station. He put in his appearance before the killers, as if to say; "Here I am; hang me but I let my wife and child and parents go. They are innocent!"

He was put in chains, although there was no chance that he would try to escape again. He had made a decision to give his life for his family. That same day he was taken to Kobryn. Not far from the tall bridge over the river, several scaffolds had been prepared. Within a few hours the body of the innocent brave man was swinging off one of the nooses. May the memory of Meyshe Friedman live forever!

# Survival
## By Ita Wolinetz, one of the seven survivors

We were liberated in the summer of 1944. The handful of survivors had begun to come out of the woods and other hiding places. The sum total was very saddening. Very few Jews remained as living witnesses of the brutal murders. Only five Jews survived of such a large community as Brest-Litovsk. Even less remained in Kobryn. The number of women and' children survivors was proportionately smaller, because they. had not been readily admitted by the partisans to join in fighting the Germans.

*[Page 50]*

Fate willed it that only seven Jews were left of the residents in the ghetto of Antopol. Among them were Dr. Czerniak, his wife and child, and four other girls, namely: Shoshe Wolowelsky, of Grushev street; Itka Mazurski, the daughter of Itzl Mazurski; Reizl Kagan, Yankl Tebins daughter, of Kobryn street, and the writer of these lines, daughter of Naftoli Kaplaniker. How each one of us remained alive is a subject for a book about the period when we saw death before our eyes every day.

I lived in the ghetto of Antopol from its first day, together with my whole family. During the final operation, when the last remaining Jews in the ghetto were being driven to the railway station for shipment (in October of 1942), I managed to escape and hide with a Polish Christian acquaintance, Arcyszewski. To remain in Antopol was out of the question, since at that time there was not a single Jew left in town. Arcyszewski took me, a few days later, into the village of Novosolok, to a Christian family's home, where he had prepared for me a place in a pit under a cowshed in the backyard. It is difficult to imagine life in a pit in the cold and in the dark, isolated from the world, but yet this is how I was saved.

I was fed as it was customary to feed a cat or a similar animal in rural places. There were moments of fear, when drunken Germans visited the family, and I used to hear their wild voices from my hiding place. The unhygienic conditions for a long time caused my getting ill very often. There was no hope for medical care. It took great strength and endurance to bear all this. I had about six months of this tortured existence, until I could not remain in the village any longer. The man who shielded me feared for his life all the time, because he risked death for harboring a Jew. He told me that Dr. Czerniak and his wife lived in the nearby forest among a group of partisans, and advised me to seek a way to contact them and apply for joining them. We managed to make the contact, and one day a sleigh drove into the yard of my host, who hid me under a pile of straw and sent me with the driver into the forest.

A different type of life began for me in the forest. The partisans lived in primitive conditions, in tents and booths. They often had to be on the move, in order to escape the pursuing Germans. Spread out in the famous Pinsk marshes, the partisans had to endure unusual hardships in the wintertime, when they suffered from a shortage of clothes and footwear. It was my good fortune to get quarters in the same tent with Dr. Czerniak and his wife, who contributed so much to the cause of the partisans, and he enjoyed great respect and popularity with them. If it were not for him, they probably would not have admitted me, since they seldom agreed to admit women.

Dr. Czerniak and his wife looked after me as if I were their own child. We carried on in the marshes as best as we could until the summer of 1944. We took solace from the defeats which the Germans were beginning to suffer in the front, and we nursed the hope that we would live to see a better day. Finally liberation came. All of us returned to Antopol. It is difficult to describe the impression we had on coming back to our native town, and meeting the other survivors, namely: Itka Mazurski, Shoshe Wolowelski, and Reizl Kagan. After the end of the war, another dozen families returned to Antopol, coming from distant parts of Russia, where they served in the army, or through other circumstances which brought them there. We all nurtured the idea of building up connections with the outside world, and beginning a new life. In 1945, we left for Poland with the intention of proceeding thence to Israel.

Thus came to an end a long chapter of the Jewish community in Antopol.

[Page 51]

# Antopol in the Years 1957-1959
## By Prof. P. Czerniak

During the years 1945-1950 there were only three Jews to be found in Antopol: Avigdor Devinietz ("Nat"), Chaim-Leib Finkelstein, and Yitzchak Zacks. Even these three failed to strike permanent roots. Devinietz married and moved with his wife to Pinsk; Finkelstein moved to Brest-Litovsk, and thus Yitzchak Zack remained the only Jew in a town which once boasted a flourishing Jewish community.

No Jews are left in the whole neighborhood. There are no Jews in Horodetz, and there are only four Jewish households in Drohichin. The same picture is to be observed in Kobryn and all other towns in the region.

Finkelstein, until the 1950s, was manager of a Kom-Khoz (communal economy). He utilized his position to convert the large marketplace into a municipal park. He had trees and flower beds planted, and walks and benches installed. The old market-square was gone, the stores were hidden from view by the trees and the whole scenery changed.

Yitzchak Zack was at first a member of the party, but he was later expelled and he is content with being an official in the Regional Consumers Cooperative (Ray-potreb-soyuz). Now there are in Antopol three thousand Russians and Poles, some of whom are the former Gentile inhabitants of the town, while the others are newcomers from nearby villages in Russia and White Russia.

The Christian population presents a different story than that of the Jews. Two kolkhozes were established. Work groups (artels) were organized, as well as cooperatives and other such bodies. The former Jewish prayer house on Kobryn Street now houses an artel for combing wool. Other artels were formed to carry out various kinds of building jobs. Houses were built along the cobbled Drohichin highway as far as Pryschikhvost. A new street called "Niekrasov" was opened up at the right side of the highway.

At first the authorities planned to create in Antopol a "Regional Committee" (Raykom). In order to carry it out, they began building a two-story brick house on Feiwel Bendet's lot. Later it was decided that the town would become, administratively, a "Posielkov Selsoviet," or Village Council, attached to the Drohibitz Region. The new edifice was converted into a children's home. Kobryn, too, became a regional centre, including also Horodetz and Khadlin, under its jurisdiction.

The internal appearance of the town changed a great deal. Various institutions were built. The rabbi's house in the synagogue courtyard was confiscated. The same fate befell Feldstein's house on Pinsk Street, the Orphanage on Grushav Street, the Squire's prayer house, the ice-cellar and many other buildings. The Turbut Hebrew school building was converted into a dairy restaurant; Polchuk's brickhouse became a Soviet orphanage; the Talmud Torah building is being used for a secular school, the old frame prayer house now houses a cinema; and the new brick building of the synagogue was occupied by the offices of the Regional Union. Bales of flax are stored in the old large brick prayer house. The "Squire's" prayer house was moved to the village of Holovietz, where it was used to build a Church. The old school building on Pinsk street is used for a tenyear secondary school. The hospital on Kobryn street has been enlarged, with the addition of a Surgical department and a staff of four physicians.

The Gentile population of Antopol is still busy rummaging in the ruins of the Jewish houses, hoping to unearth some treasures. They did succeed in finding some valuables in the cellar of Itke Miriam's house. The police confiscated them.

That is what the once Jewish town of Antopol looks like after the brutal murder of the Jewish men, women and children by the Nazi horde. Where 2,000 innocent Jewish martyrs found their graves, there are now some 3,000 Christians, mostly newcomers, living a life free of Jews. Some of them remember the past and secretly yearn for it and for the Jews. But where are the forces that can bring back to life the souls which still live in the hearts of the few survivors scattered all over the world?

*[Page 52]*

The ever unanswered question arises, whence will come that moral force which can stir up the conscience of mankind which watched with equanimity the vandalism of the Nazi brutes, while now everyone seeks to obscure and forget and obliterate every trace of the perished Jewish population, or attempts to succeed to its heritage undisturbed?

But we cannot forget. "Remember what Amalek hath done to thee."

# In Fire
## By A. Warsaw

It seems that up there, Providence had predestined Reb Elie Mass to be a leader and a representative of his people.

Everybody knew Reb Elie, who lived opposite the old post office and had a glass porch, which served all the year as a veranda, and during Succoth – as a Succoh.

Reb Elie Mass enjoyed the respect of everybody, young and old, small and grown up. You got to like him from the first time that you saw his aristocratic-patriarchal countenance.

He used to pray in the Pritsishn Beis Medrosh, on Kobriner Street, and he was always on hand to answer queries and solve disputes. Always dressed neatly, on the Sabbath Reb Elie wore a top hat and a white collar shirt. He knew all about the big metropolitans of the world, and people said that he learned to wear a top hat in America.

Still he knew nothing of the neighboring villages around his home town, until one day a war broke out between Nikolai of Russia and Willhelm of Germany, and the Germans advanced as far as the other side of Pinsk. When the local farmers fled deep into Russia, the local Jews and Reb Elie among them harvested their crops in order to feed their own families, and thus they got to know all the villages around, and the fields surrounding them.

Then came a declaration, by U.S. President Wilson, famous for its fourteen points, followed by a war between Poland and Red Russia. This fire also swept Reb Elie's town. It came about in the month of Elul, when the sun usually celebrates its last days of summer. The air is clear, full of blossoms, and people feel fresh and prepared to pick all the ripe fruits to preserve them for the winter, when everything will be covered with snow and ice. In these very days the Jewish people were hiding in dug-outs, awaiting death any minute.

On the last day of Succoth, the air was filled with the noise of bullets, houses crumbled under fires, and the Poles were driving the Bolsheviks beyond the other side of town. While passing by, the Poles advised the hiding Jews to put out the fires. Reb Elie instinctively looked out to see the fires, when one of the soldiers asked him for the road to Sweklitch.

Reb Elie came out and, approaching the commanding officer and trying to give him directions. But the officer ordered him to lead them in person as a scout.

Night came, and they were still walking. When they approached the outskirts of the village, Reb Elie began to feel better. He outlined the place to the officer, who checked with his map and verified it. But now, after telling Reb Elie what would have been his fate if he had misled them, they ordered him to go into the village and re turn with information as to the possibility of the Bolsheviks still being there.

Reb Elie walked over, tired and exhausted, and came out reporting that the village was empty. But now they ordered him to continue to the next village. He had to go on. On the way he prayed the evening prayer which he had missed before, and it made him feel better until he reached the village. And then onward...by the time he reached the third village he knew what to do. In that village there lived a farmer named Mikita. Reb Elie woke him up and asked him about Bolsheviks, and the latter replied that he would not know for sure. Reb Elie came back and related what he had heard. Now they told him to walk ahead together with Mikita. The Batallion halted as the two went forward scouting. Suddenly: "Who goes there?" We start firing on them. Both armies began shooting while Mikita pulled Reb Elie down to the ground. Then he took him back with him through back roads until they reached the village, and then he sent him on his way to his hometown. Now Reb Rlie continued alone on his way until he reached his town, all dirty and exhausted.

*[Page 53]*

"Dear Papa," his children said to him, "where have you been?" He replied, "Hush children, we have a great God. If not for the war, I would not know the villages, and if I would not know the villages – what would be my end? I come from "no man's land" and I came out alive from the fire. Who would have thought that Mikita would earn himself a place in Paradise?!

*[Page 57]*

# Yiddish Messages

## Antopol, My Town
### By Aharon Gofer

It is hard to forget the town where I was born and passed my youth. This is where I went to Jewish school and spent days in joy and sadness. it is hard to forget the town in which I lived and where cruelly died my dearest and beloved. This is where there were small houses, sandy streets, and where the inhabitants perished.

I was away from Antopol for five years, war years in which the anti-Semite Hitler and his bandits murdered millions of innocent people, only because they were Jews. With them died the Jews of Antopol.

Then I returned to Antopol for a five-day vacation. I traveled from Breslau, Germany, living with hope that a miracle had happened and that Antopol remained everything it once had been. Only when I got to town did I realize I had been living an illusion. For a long while, I stood by the house of Aharon Shemuel, the hunchback. My heart filled with blood, and my eyes with bloody tears. While I was still standing there, a wagon drove up and a gentile climbed down.

He came up to me and said, "Aren't you Hyayim, the shoemaker's son?" And before I could answer him, he told me the news. The Germans had killed all the Jews of Antopol, including my parents, sisters, brothers, the entire family. Only Vigdor Dviniets remained, and he offered to take me to him.

Sitting on the wagon and traveling along Pinsk Street, I saw on the steps of Hayyim Betsalel Moses' house, Shoshke, the miller's daughter. I recognized her and she me. I jumped down from the wagon, and we ran to each other and embraced. We cried for our nearest and dearest loved ones.

# The Fires of Antopol
## By Y. Varsha and M. L. Ben David

Everyone in Antopol reckoned years and events according to the fires that took place. People would say, "That happened before the first fire."..."That happened after the second fire." And so forth.

In the years between 1870 and 1885, our town survived two big fires. In the first fire, half the town burned down, with the loss of one person's life.

On a pretty summer day, the big fire began at the house of Gedalya, the sexton, which was in the north part of town. The sexton's house was next to the Hasidic prayer house. Despite the fact the prayer house had a straw roof, the fire stopped without harming it.

On that day, it seemed, the lord of fire made a partnership with the lord of wind, and it led him to the south of town. There it seized the house of Yenkel Kovel, whose second name was Terah. One of his children saw that the house was on fire and was so frightened that he hid under the bed. When h i s parents could not find him, they thought that he had fled with the other children to the cornfields near the house. They always told the children to flee to the fields when they saw fire.

Afterwards, they found the child in the ashes of the house, burnt as black as coal in the place where the bed had been. Imagine the sadness and grief that overcame the parents. The father, a pious man, began to prepare a memorial, collecting money to buy a Torah scroll. Every Friday he collected money for that holy purpose. He would take with him one of the seminary students to write down the donations.

Getting back to the great fire, the wind led the fire to the south side, to the market. The house of Sender Moses, the cap maker, went up in flames. Then the fire burned the entire east side of the market and burned the whole stretch of Pinsk Street on which the study hall was located. Later, on the site of the study hall, they built a new bigger building, and they called it the "brick study hall."

Our little town, Antopol, survived a second fire 15 years later. However, in many details, this fire was different from the first. For one thing, fire broke out several times that summer, always in the morning.

*[Page 58]*

What caused these fires? It seemed that someone was trying to get revenge against a man who was rich and respectable. Everywhere this particular man moved, his apartment was set on fire. Many innocent people suffered. The first time his house was set on fire was a hot July morning.

Early that morning, when some men were driving cows to pasture, they suddenly saw black smoke coming from Abraham's house. A cry for help and a shout, "Fire! It's burning!" rang out.

Abraham's house was located on the west side of the market. Soon nearby houses caught fire. People began crawling out of windows, escaping with their lives in their nightclothes.

To add to the confusion, everyone in town, young and old, jumped out of bed and rushed to the fire brigade house in the middle of the market. Here was found the equipment with which to put out the fire: barrels of water on wheels which people harnessed to themselves or to horses and ran to the burning houses. There were also pumps to pump water from wells.

However, all the equipment was useless because of the wind. It blew pieces of burning wood around like rocketten. The fire was blown to the house of the black-bearded Hebrew teacher and then to Zanivier Street where the houses had roofs of straw.

Fleeing to safety, women wheeled trunks and bundles of bedclothes from the burning houses out to the open fields. Little children, gasping for breath, held on to their mothers' clothes in fear; some older children cried, begging their mother to take along the cat and small kittens. The mothers shouted to the children to keep close to them and not run off.

Then Yosl Shemuel Rosel's house caught fire. Here our experienced fire fighters – the Osipovitses, Aryeh and his brother, Shelomoh, the painter – threw themselves like lions on the house. These men were never afraid of fire! Each belted his clothes, stuck a hatchet on one side and a spear on the other, took a long sack soaked in water and covered his head like a prayer shawl, and went up on the burning roof. They dug in, chopped and cut to shreds the burning straw, and with other wet sacks put out the flames. When unburned pieces of straw fell off, the men threw water on them so they would not catch fire. Finally, they saved the house, and by much effort, prevented the fire from spreading farther.

After the fire, the burned-out Jews moved into the home of HayyimZelig, the carpenter, on Pinsk Street. This house was set on fire a short time later. Once again, our experienced fire fighters fell on the house from all sides and did not let the fire burn it.

However, the fires were set again. The city's rabbi, R. Duvid'l of blessed memory, spoke out and called for a kind of religious ban. He said that whoever knew something suspicious about the disasters should speak out and that those who set the fires would be punished by God.

At length, everything was rebuilt. Better houses and brick houses were built. First the bathhouse and the ritual bath were rebuilt because these related to modesty and family purity. An individual, a man who had returned from America and who had money, had been located. His name was Moshe, the tailor. He gave money to rebuild the bathhouse, and he became the bath keeper.

# The Beginning

Antopol, or as the Jews used to call it Antopolie, is located seven kilometers from Horodets and 32 kilometers from Drohitshin in the Kobrin District in the Province of Grodno.

The town is part of Polesye, which is famous for its marshes and forests. Richly reflective of its geographic region, Antopolye had not without cause the nickname mud. About 60 years ago, west of town on the road to Kobrin, was a thick pine forest, which stretched to Horodets. To the south, on the road to the village of Rusheve, was also a pine forest. The forests were not lacking in wolves, bears, and snakes. Apparently, the old town of Antopolye began at the edge of the forest at the Kobrin road and ended at the old cemetery, since religious laws decreed that a cemetery could not be inside town limits.

*[Page 59]*

When was Antopolye founded? When did the Jewish settlement begin there? Reliable historical documents are few, so we know little about how the town began. We assume that the Jewish settlement was founded around 1640. Polish documents, for Antopolye then was part of Poland, mention the town in connection with the building of a church in 1718. According to the documents, a rich landowner, the lady Antonina Zamoiska, founded the church and called the town Antopol in her name, that is the town of Antonina, pol or polis meaning town in Greek.

These facts are further documented by inscriptions on monuments in the old cemetery and by tablets in the synagogue bearing the date the synagogue was built, according to Y.A. Shulruf 's "Antopolye–Its Name and Age," Antopolye Aid Society, Fifteenth Yearly Jubilee Book. Shulruf discredits the belief held by some that the name Antopol comes from the fact that the town had many poplars (polye) in contrast with the surrounding fields.

# The Political Picture

The region of Polesie experienced various political changes and shake-ups. The Lithuanian Grand Prince Gedimin (elsewhere, Archduke Gdimin) conquered Polesie and ruled it from 1315-1341. Later, in 1385, Lithuania was united with Poland. The Lithuanian Grand Principality opened the doors to Polish culture and its institutions, especially the Roman Catholic Church.

The Church used all its means to extend its influence to every branch of life and was successful in this effort. Little by little, the entire region of Polesie was Polonized. This aroused the anger of the Cossacks, which resulted in the famous Chmelnitski Rebellion of 1648. The oppressed peasant masses joined the Cossacks who were in revolt for about two years. Not a little Jewish blood was spilled in Polesie before the Polish government put down the Cossacks.

In the spring of 1706, the Swedes under the leadership of Karl XII began a war against the Polish government. Thanks to the swamps of Polesie, however, the war was short-lived, and the Swedes withdrew from Poland the same year. We do not know the fate of the Jews of Antopol in those years. History is silent about this. But among the Jews of Antopol, there remained the saying, "He remembers the Swedes," used in reference to something that happened a long time ago.

Poland was saved and remained intact until 1772 when it was divided for the first time. Between 1793-1795, Russia annexed the provinces of Minsk, Vilna, and Grodno. In Grodno were eight subdistricts: Grodno, Lide, Novogorodek, Slonim, Volkovisk, Pruzshani, Brisk, and Kobrin. Antopol was part of the Kobrin subdistrict.

During the 1812 Franco-Russian War, it did not take long for Napoleon Bonaparte to attack Russia, and Antopolye was not excluded. During battles in the town, the inhabitants suffered much and the Jews most of all.

The Poles in the region were not happy under Russian rule and tried to rebel twice, in 1830 and in 1863. These rebellions or pavstanyes were harmful to the Jewish inhabitants, who suffered at the hands of both sides. Many Jews of Antopol supported the Poles, providing them with food and shelter. However, even when the Jews helped the Poles hide from the Russians, the Poles mistreated them. For example, when a Jew hid some Poles in the chicken coop with the hens, the Poles remembered to shout at their savior, "Filthy Jew, take off your hat!" Later the Russians did not forgive the Jews for harboring the Poles, and more than one Jew was severely punished. In Czarist Russia, punishing Jews was part of life, and all the decrees and persecutions the Russians devised for the Jews were faced by those in Antopol.

*[Page 60]*

In those days, the land in Antopol and the surrounding region belonged to the noblemen, and the Jews paid platsove, land tax. In 1904, they paid taxes to the noblewoman Sofia Dmitirevna Voytash who owned 4,500 acres of good land and 100 acres of poorer land. Lady Voytash did many good things for the Antopol Jews through her manager, Mordekhai Shaynboym, and the town and surroundings were free of war for about 100 years. Then, on April 9, 1914, World War I broke out and lasted until November 1918.

At the end of the summer of 1915, the Germans took Antopol, and a great many Jewish houses were burnt. The Jews settled in the houses of gentiles who had fled to Russia. The few Jews who remained in town began to organize and resume their daily lives; however, the German rule was extremely harsh, especially for the youth. Young men were seized and sent to work camps in other regions or enslaved in the town itself.

The Germans required their language in the elementary school, and Antopol Jews, young and old, began to study German and to try to fit into the German order. German rule lasted until November 1918 when the Germans began to withdraw. During the last days of 1918, anarchy spread in the town and terrorists took over. In the end, Antopol was integrated into the new Polish government. Then terror was legalized by the Polish government, which even protected the looters and murderers. The Pozniantshikes rebelled everywhere, tore Jewish beards, and established widespread pogroms.

Soon Antopol became a war zone in the conflict between the Russians and Poles. In 1919, the Bolsheviks arrived in Antopol and introduced their new order. Their rule did not last long, and the Polish legions returned to Antopol. Upon their arrival, much Jewish blood was shed and possessions and goods were confiscated.

Then, after a period of peace and recovery in the region, the Polish-Bolshevik war broke out in July 1920. In the beginning, the Russians were the victors and arrived at the gates of Warsaw. However, the wheel of fortune turned, and the Polish forces began to drive out the Russian army. Meanwhile, the volunteer army of General Belkhovitsh, the leader of the White Guard, undertook to help the Poles. The union of the White Russians and the Poles wrote a new period of blood and tears in Jewish history.

In 1921, a peace agreement was signed in Riga between Poland and the Soviet Union, and Antopol was declared a part of Poland. The Polish government imposed strict laws of cleanliness, mainly aimed at the Jews, and introduced compulsory education in Polish schools and general military service. Although the Jews resisted joining the Polish army, some who served distinguished themselves.

Then in September 1939, World War II broke out, and the Bolsheviks took over Antopol and the entire region. Conflicting reports exist about the years of Soviet rule in the town. Some state that the Russian army brought complete spiritual and material renewal. Other reports, written in disguised fashion, describe the Russian paradise as a hell. For better or worse, the Bolsheviks ruled until June 1941 when the Germans attacked the Russians and entirely occupied Poland and the Ukraine, advancing almost to the gates of Leningrad and Moscow.

Antopol came into the grip of the Nazis. The Jews of Antopol were enslaved, tortured, and put into a ghetto, and yet they did not give up. They rebelled, participated in sabotage, and fled to the partisans in the forests who gave the Germans a dose of their own medicine. However, Hitler, may his name be cursed, was stronger. He destroyed everything and everyone. The German murders of the bloody years from June 1941 to July 1944 will never be forgotten! We will always remember the bestiality that wiped out hundreds of Jewish communities, among them our beloved Antopol.

*[Page 61]*

In July 1944, Antopol was integrated into the District of Kobrin in Soviet Russia. Today a mist hangs over it. We know little about it and its inhabitants. Rarely breaks through a light from the Jewish town of Antopol, which had existed almost 300 years.

# Economic Conditions

We don't know much about the economic condition of Antopol in its early years of existence. In addition, we don't know much about the Jewish population during those years but we guess that it was increasing. We do know that over 200 years ago, in 1847, the Jewish population of the town consisted of 1,108 souls. It took only 13 more years for the Jewish population to reach 1,259; the total population was 1,563. During those 13 years, a number of great fires impoverished many Jews, and they left Antopol. Yet the Jewish population grew. In 1847, the Jews were a minority. However, 50 years later, in 1897, the Jews comprised the majority of the population. They numbered 3,137 souls out of 3,867. In 1904, Antopol had a total population of 5,235, with an estimated half of the inhabitants Jewish. At that time, as Antopol grew, Pinsk Street stretched almost to Prishikhvast and the side streets were full of Jews.

What did the Antopol Jews do? How did they earn a living? What brought them to spread out the length and breadth of the town? We can answer the first question. The Antopol Jews were farmers. They planted potatoes, onions, beetroots, cucumbers, radishes, etc. These Jews were called Margavnikes, and they farmed the land in back of their houses, mainly on Kobrin and Pinsk Streets. They either worked the land themselves or hired gentile help and took their vegetables to surrounding towns to sell. At the beginning of the Twentieth Century, a great trade developed for selling cucumbers in Warsaw and other cities. To keep the cucumbers fresh, the farmers laid them in barrels and then lowered the barrels down into deep wells. This kept the cucumbers from freezing in the winter. Until the outbreak of World War I, the cucumber business provided a livelihood to many Antopol households.

The second major business was the raising of geese, which Antopol Jews began in the 1890s. The geese, which were brought from deep inside Russia, were large and heavy and had long necks and a hump on their beaks. These qualities led to rabbis mentioning the geese in their response. The great rabbi Ben-Tsiyon Shternfeld devoted 18 pages to the Antopol geese.

The geese were raised in special buildings called Fasharnies where they were stuffed with oats and millet. When they became fat, they were sent to Vilna or Germany. According to the popular saying, "A goose should not live to hear the reading of the Scroll of Esther." Merchants from other towns came to Antopol, and geese merchants from Antopol traveled to Vilna, typically spending the Jewish New Year's and Day of Atonement there. They had their own prayer quorum in Vilna, and yellow-haired Hershel was their cantor.

A number of other businesses provided livelihood for the Jews of Antopol. For example, there were presses used to press oil and horse-driven and wind-driven mills to grind rye. In addition, masons at a brick factory made bricks for Antopol and the surrounding region. Another factory turned out Dutch tiles for ovens. An important business was provided by a linen press, which was used to smooth linen brought by the gentiles. The first person to establish a linen press was Efrayim Volyusher. The press was well known in the region, especially because of its factory whistle.

In the middle of town, between Kobrin and Pinsk Streets, was a market with a row of stores in the middle. In 1890, Jews sold wares from 42 stores to city and village customers. On Sundays, gentiles from the villages brought their products to the market and sold them to the Jews. With the money, the gentiles bought kerosene, salt, calico for clothing, etc. The largest sales to gentiles were made during the yearly fairs, Desiatikha and Traytse. Desiatrikha (from the word for ten) fell on Friday 10 weeks after Passover. During the Polish government, a fair was also held on the first day of each month of the civil calendar. The fairs were well known throughout the region. Out-of-town merchants came to Antopol to shop and Jews from surrounding towns came to trade and find bargains. During the fairs, Antopol was like a beehive, so bustling and noisy one could hardly walk through the market.

*[Page 62]*

In 1840, the digging of the Royal Canal from Pinsk to Horodets played an important role in the economic structure of Antopol. A local Jewish contractor, Yankel Shmulevitsh, supplied workers for the project. Later, in the 1880s, the building of the railroad between Zshabinke and Pinsk provided employment for many Antopol Jews and Christians. The Antopol forest merchants, the Lifshitses, provided the wood for the railroad ties. Another large construction job was the highway built between Horodets and Antopol during 1908-1910. The highway made life easier for cart drivers who used to go to the Horodets railway station to pick up passengers and merchandise.

At the beginning of the Twentieth Century, Antopol had a savings and loan bank, which made it possible for Antopol storekeepers to get loans without interest. The bank was located in Avigdor Sirota's house, and Perets Gurvits, who later became a dentist, was the bookkeeper. When World War I broke out, the bank ceased to function. In 1921, as the town began to recover, the bank was reopened, and by 1924 it had 190 members. Between the First and Second World Wars, a Free Loan Association was founded, thanks to Mrs. Esther Kornblum, a visitor from the United States. The Association did much to improve the economic situation of the Antopol Jews at that time.

Little by little Antopol began to recover from World War I. A train stop was built where trains stopped briefly and mail was delivered, instead of at Horodets. Around 1928, buses began to run between Kobrin and Antopol. These changes improved the commercial businesses in Antopol. Then, in 1935, the family Pomeraniets from Yaneve installed an electric generator, which gave Antopol electric light and provided electricity for the mill to grind groats.

Before World War I, the United States was a major source of income for Antopol. Many men who were working in the US sent their wives US dollars, which doubled in value when exchanged for rubles. Also parents, who had grown children in the States, often received a few rubles from them. After World War I, support from the US increased as those Jews who could escape Antopol immigrated. Under Economic Minister Grabski, the Polish authorities had begun to dry up sources of income for Jews.

However, where could a Jew flee? The United States had shut itself off from immigration. A stream of immigration began to the Land of Israel and a second stream to South American countries such as Argentina and Brazil and to Cuba, Mexico, etc. Thanks to these two streams of immigration, the Jews of Antopol survived to help build the countries to which they moved, especially the Land of Israel. The Antopol Jews in the Diaspora gave with an open hand to the rebuilding of the Jewish State. Those who saved themselves in Israel took an active part in the building and defense of the country.

# Cultural Change

Life in Antopol, as in other Jewish towns of Polesia, was dominated by the Jewish religion with the rabbis setting the tone for every walk of life and the Code of Jewish Law directing how one should live. Although it was often difficult to identify the specific text of the Code, the Jews of Antopol did not fail to live up to the letter of the law. For example, one story tells of how, over 100 years ago, the Jews of Antopol fulfilled religious law by cooperating with those of Drohotshin in the purchase of a piece of citron to celebrate the holiday of Tabernacles. Perhaps the Jews of Antopol did not have enough money to buy a citron for themselves. Every other day during the Tabernacles holiday, a horse and wagon were dispatched to take the citron to Drohotshin, a distance of 28 kilometers.

*[Page 63]*

Nevertheless, here and there were young people who rebelled and refused the yoke of religious law. One was, precisely, the rabbi's son, R. Hirsh, who became a Berliner, a follower of Moses Mendelsohn. Years later there was the well-known Dr. Israel Mikhal Rabinovits, one of the first members of the Lovers of Zion.

A thirst for enlightenment began to penetrate Jewish culture. The public began to demand that special teachers be assigned to Jewish elementary schools to teach Hebrew, Russian, and mathematics, "because," according to one report, "without these skills, a modern person cannot find his existence."

People began to study Hebrew, grammar, and also Russian, a fact substantiated by the abundant correspondence printed in the newspaper, ha-Melits in the 1880s. The newspaper was frequently found in Antopol homes. Prosperous families in Antopol also subscribed to the newspaper ha-Tsefirah. By 1905, Antopol even had a special agent for ha-Zeman. In addition to these Hebrew newspapers, Yiddish and Russian newspapers and other periodicals were delivered in Antopol.

The social movements of the Russian Revolution had a strong influence in Antopol. People of the town talked about Fradel Stavski, a woman who organized subversive activities in the town and was sent to Siberia.

The Bund was also active, as well as the Socialists.

Naturally, the Lovers of Zion movement and later the Zionist World Organization had a strong presence in Antopol. However, that is a chapter in itself.

Antopol boys and girls began to study Russian in the Russian school. They continued their studies in the gymnasiums of Brisk and other cities and went on to the universities, coming out as doctors and other educated professionals.

Mainly, the Jews of Antopol focused on Jewish studies. Boys studied in various rabbinical seminaries, the older more intelligent studying with the rabbi of the city or in the study hall by themselves. As a result, a number of these boys became renowned rabbis. At the beginning of the twentieth century, a small rabbinical seminary in Antopol was led by R. Benjamin (Shevelevits), Professor of Talmud. Boys from other towns as well as those from Antopol studied there.

Winds of educational reform reached Antopol, and the townsperson R. Aharon Lifshits established a reformed elementary school. The school existed for several years, succeeded by Israel's elementary school (Israel Volevelski-Wal), which had special class benches for the students and a teacher for Russian.

In those days, Antopol also had a private girls school led by Taibe Frume. Private teachers for Hebrew, Russian, German, and general sciences became the rule. Thus Antopol became a town known for its educational facilities, including a library containing books in Hebrew, Yiddish, and Russian.

The thirst for education increased after World War I. A Tarbut school was organized where boys and girls studied the Hebrew language. There was also a library known as the Y. L. Perets Library. Jewish elementary schools and rabbinical seminaries also opened in Antopol. The sound of Torah was heard in the streets, until it was silenced by Soviet orders to close the Jewish cultural institutions.

Then came the Nazis (may their memory be blotted out), who obliterated our brethren in Antopol. May God revenge their blood!

*[Page 64]*

# Colonies of Antopol Jewry

Jews from Antopol had a strong presence in the cities of Russia and Poland. As early as the 1880s, there were Jews from Antopol in Kishinev, Bessarabia. They had social relations in all fields and even had their own study hall.

Our brethren were present in Warsaw, especially in literary circles, where our townsperson, the Hebrew and Yiddish writer MoshehStavski (Satui), lived from 1905-1911. The Antopol geese merchants and pickle makers used to go to Warsaw.

An important center of immigration was the United States. It was a long haul to get there. One had to have a passport, to cross the border and be disinfected. Then one was aboard a ship for two to three weeks. In addition, America was not a kosher place for Jews. Judaism could not be observed there like in our native country. However, an American dollar was worth two rubles in Antopol!

People began to travel to New York and Chicago. These were the two big cities where one could earn a living and have a family. Brownsville in New York City was the former Jerusalem of the U.S. Jews from Antopol colonized it. Together with people from Kobrin and Horodets, they established their own synagogue. They named it the Society for Good Deeds of the Union of Brethren of Kobrin, Horodets, and Antopol.

One Jew from Antopol brought over a second. However, not all felt at home in the new country. Many returned to Antopol and rebuilt their new lives. Those who remained in the U.S. became citizens and contributed to the progress of the country. They established Associations and helped their brethren remaining in Antopol.

Many persons from Antopol, such as the Farber family (Farberware) and Shelomoh Margalit (oil and gasoline stations), were represented in US industry.

In the field of music, our brethren played an important part. Hazan David Futerman was one of the country's best cantors and was president of the Cantor's Union of the United States. Also, Roberta Peters, a member of the Futerman family, was a star of the Metropolitan Opera House in New York City.

The Jewish writer, Shmuel Dayksel, was the son of a Jew from Antopol who had a large tailoring firm in Kishinev.

In science, Jews from Antopol were well represented. Our beloved townsperson Dr. Feitel Berman, of blessed memory, was the administrator of the largest hospital in the world, located in Pasadena, California. Also, Dr. Meir Kletski was for many years the chief dentist of the Arbeyter Ring (Workmen's Circle) and wrote scientific articles about dentistry.

A Jew from Antopol, Professor L. Anderson (Aranovski), played an important part in the development of the atomic bomb, which brought an end to World War II.

The Antopol Jews in Chicago established a good niche for themselves, founding Associations and other institutions. The Antopol synagogue in Chicago was well known in town. Thanks to another Antopol Jew, Rabbi Jacob Grinberg of blessed memory, the rabbinical seminary Bet ha-Midrash la-Torah was established. He was a Professor of Talmud there until his death. In addition to teaching Torah in the seminary, Rabbi Grinberg wrote articles related to Jewish studies.

In addition to establishing themselves and Jewish institutions in other U.S. cities, Jews from Antopol were well known in Argentina, especially in Buenos Aires. They were among the first Jews who settled in that country.

A significant chapter of Antopol Jewry is written in the building and creation of the State of Israel. Israel had a special place in the hearts of the Jews from Antopol, who were not content with the prayer, "And to Zion comes a redeemer," and the like. They had already contributed to the building of the Land of Israel 200 years ago.

*[Page 65]*

In 1808 (the Hebrew year 5569), an immigration began of the pupils of R. Elijah, the Gaon of Vilna, to Israel. They settled in Tsefat, then ideal for the Gaon's pupils. There were not a lot of Hasidim in Tsefat. There were many more in Tiberias, for the Hasidim there had the upper hand over their opponents.

Travel to Israel took months; however, this did not keep them from going. Also, immigrants went to Israel from Pinsk and the area surrounding Drohitshin.

Jews from Antopol took part in that immigration. For example, R. Mosheh b. R. Akavia (?), escaped a pogrom in 1834 by fleeing to Tsefat. Changing his name to R. Mosheh Neeman, he settled in Jerusalem and participated in the public life of the city. R. Tsevi Montopoli was also active in the life of Jerusalem at that time. The immigration included entire families, evidenced by tombstones of small children whose parents were from Antopol.

In the 1880s, a Jew from Antopol with the family name Yahalom settled in Israel. One member of this family, R. Benjamin, was a founder of the town En Ganim, which was next to Petah Tikvah. R. Benjamin Yahalom was active in the community until the War for Independence.

Mosheh Yaakov Benjamin, or as he was called in Jerusalem, Alter of Antopol, holds a special place in the history of Israel. When he moved to Israel with his parents in 1863, he was quite young, just seven years old. Years later he was among the first builders of Meah Shearim, individuals who risked their lives to protect the community from Arab attackers. Alter of Antopol was also known as the first person to import herring from abroad to sell in Israel.

Renowned in the rabbinical world was R. Netanel Hayyim Pope, of blessed memory, who immigrated to Israel in 1891 with his wife and son, Yitshak Mosheh.

In 1902, the highly respected R. Yehezkel Saharov, of blessed memory, and his wife, Hayah Etel, and son, Yitshak Mordekhai, moved to Israel. Also, Yitshak Mordekha, of blessed memory, was prominent in the social life of Israel, and his children played an important part in the building of our land.

Thus numerous members of the Antopol Jewish community moved to Israel before the early Zionist leader Herzl. Later, other Antopol Jews responded to Herzl's appeal, and another immigration to Israel began, which is itself another chapter in history.

# The End
## By Israel Fernik

In 1960, our dear townsperson Dr. Feitel Berman, of blessed memory, wrote a letter to the elder in charge of Antopol. He wanted to hear news of his town of birth. He wanted to know how many Jews remain, what sort of life they lead, and so forth. Finally, two years later, he got an answer. It was not a private, direct reply. Instead, it was a public answer, printed in the White Russian journal Galas Radzimi that is published in Minsk, the capital city of White Russia to which Antopol belongs.

The case is this. The elder of Antopol, it seems, was afraid to take the responsibility to answer the letter. So he sent the letter to Minsk. From Minsk, a correspondent of Galas Radzimi went to Antopol. He wrote an article on the town and accompanied it with photographs. It is as if he said, "Have a look and judge for yourself how good it is to live in Soviet Russia."

And what did the correspondent see? A certain Isaac Berkovitsh Zaks, who seems to be a Jew, told him that the people in Antopol had suffered from the Nazis. They were White Russians, Jews, and Poles. Certainly, the reporter admits that only Jews were killed and no others. He continues writing that the people of Antopol fled into the forests. They were partisans. Even the elder in charge of the town became a partisan. Is this true?

The reporter is happy that the White Russians returned to Antopol and began to lead a progressive life, full of lectures and concerts. Things are really lively! The people of Antopol now study and read newspapers and journals.

*[Page 66]*

There are three schools in Antopol: a school where children study for 11 years (probably an elementary school with a gymnasium), a school with a dormitory (probably for the children of villagers not living in the city), and an evening school for workers.

The reporter also visited the town's library where he found 26,000 books and 30 different newspapers and journals in the reading room. There is also a bookstore that sells books in different languages, Russian language books, and translations into Russian from English, Polish, French, and German. However, what about books in Hebrew and Yiddish? You would not find such books, because there is no Jew living in Antopol.

In general, the cultural situation in Antopol is a happy one. There is a theater and distribution of two weekly journals that are published in Kobrin.

The reporter does not forget to mention that there is a church in Antopol. However, what about the Jewish study halls? What happened to them? The reporter is quiet about this.

He tells of the town's pride in its hospital. It has 14 doctors and 32 assistants. The hospital has three buildings, and treatment is free. When patients are in a dangerous condition, an airplane takes them to Brisk.

Antopol has a population of over 4,000, and 19 buses connect it with Minsk, Brisk, and Kobrin.

However, what about Dr. Berman's questions about the Jewish population? The elder in charge of Antopol and the reporter filled their mouths with water and were silent. The Jewish town of Antopol, which existed for 300 years is no more! And we Jews of Antopol, wherever we live, incline our heads to the ground and with a cry say the kaddish: May God's name be extolled and sanctified.

Who of us from Antopol does not remember the fence in the courtyard of the great Cold Synagogue? We remember when, after World War I, the synagogue, all five study halls, and more than half of the houses in Antopol burned down. After the fire, only the brick fence posts, around which grew grasses and nettles, remained in the synagogue courtyard. Of the study halls, only the walls of the two brick study halls remained.

In the 1920s when a new study hall was built, workers took down two of the six fence posts and used the bricks in the new construction. However, thanks to the protests of more thoughtful individuals, four of the posts were left as a memorial to the old synagogue courtyard. A new wooden fence was built, incorporating the old brick posts. Now pigs couldn't wander in, as they had done in the past.

Today, our town is only a happy memory for those of us who left at the right time for the big world, for Israel, America, Argentina, and other countries. But we who remain are the fence posts, the saving remnant of our hometown. We are left as reminders of our characteristic Jewish settlement, of our town, which bubbled and spurted with the goodness of home life and Judaism.

We are left to remember the Jews of Antopol over the years who truly had big hearts, who had hands open to give, and who had trust in one another. For example, we remember the Free Loan Association where every needy person could borrow without paying interest. My father, R. Motl Fernik, of blessed memory, served without pay as the Association's secretary during its whole existence. Some 450 families, 95 percent of all the Jewish families of the town, benefited from the benevolent Association. Prior to World War I, a similar institution had been founded with the money of R. Akiva Fishl Lifshits. My grandfather Hersh Leib, of blessed memory, was its trustee. Another benevolent institution was the orphanage. Under the devoted leadership of R. Hirsh Nitsberg, of blessed memory, numerous orphans were raised and taught trades. They came out true and fine youths and were a pride of the town.

*[Page 67]*

Because Antopol had no hospital, a medical supply society led by Nahum Volinets and his wife, Henia, of blessed memory, was active day and night. Even in the middle of the night, people could borrow medical supplies necessary for the care of the sick. Likewise, a burial society had members who went forth without compensation at any time to give rites to the dead. Also, a Passover supply fund provided every needy person enough to make Passover.

To my memory, no visiting preacher, poor man, or Rabbi failed to find at least two people to go out and collect money for him. And when misfortune – may it not happen to us! – fell upon someone, there were those who collected money to help. No one knew for whom the money was collected so as not to embarrass the needy person.

Larger settlements than Antopol could have been proud of the cultural institutions we had, both secular and purely Jewish. These included the study halls, a Hasidic prayer hall, a religious elementary school with 150 boys enrolled, a Tarbut school where 250 boys and girls studied, as well as two general Polish schools which were tuition free. Also, the Y.L. Perets

Library had thousands of books in Yiddish, Hebrew, and Polish, and the Shomer ha-tsair had a Hebrew library.

And what about our organizations? The great he-Haluts organization had over 110 members. The Shomer ha-tsair, Poyle Tsien, Freyheyt group, and General Zionists were almost always active. The Jewish National Funds, Keren Kayyemet and Keren ha-yesod, and the League for working Erets Yisroel also functioned.

We have our organizations to thank for the fact that we survived to remember our town. It was there in the clubs of he-Haluts and ha-Shomer ha-tsair that we youth were encouraged to make our way into the world. And now we are able to raise up a literary memorial to our destroyed but never-to-be forgotten town, which was called Antopol, so that all the perished martyrs – our dear parents, relatives, and friends – shall always have a memory in our hearts!

# My Town and My Family
## By Morris Asif

There were two streets in Antopol. One, Pinsk Street, stretched from the marketplace to the cultivated acres of land outside of town. The other, Kobrin Street, ran from the marketplace to the edge of town closest to Kobrin. The two streets were like chains with a ring, the marketplace, in the middle which held them together.

The marketplace was a large area with attractive stores in the middle and pretty houses all around. It was more times empty than full. Only on Sundays and on market days, and on fair days when gentiles came to sell and buy, was it crowded. At those time, it was a busy, happy place where Jews tried to earn money for the week and for Sabbath.

Like the main street in a small American town, together Pinsk and Kobrin formed the backbone of the town. Snaking out from the backbone were narrow, crooked streets with small houses, each with low windows and an earthen seat around the house. Altogether, the two main streets with their houses, orchards, and gardens and the narrow streets with their smaller houses formed the whole of Antopol.

Winter came early to Antopol, with snowstorms and winds and such a cold that mothers did not let the children out of the house until after Passover. Families spent long winter nights huddled around the stove. Snow stayed on the frozen ground until after Passover when it finally melted, leaving the town knee deep in mud.

Everything sprouted and bloomed in summer, and the birds returned.

In Antopol lived good people – the old and middle-aged and children, residing in the large and small houses. In the town were poor people who did not know how they would earn a living from day to day. There were workers, peddlers, brokers, and merchants. There was a small group of people who had a comfortable life.

*[Page 68]*

Everyone lived side by side with each other. On Pinsk Street was a house with a pretty orchard. On one side lived the wealthy Mordekhai Sheinboim. On the other side lived the carpenter Avraham Yitshak.

There, by the orchard, also lived my father, Aryeh Yozef 's of blessed memory, with his family. On the other side lived his brother, my uncle Israel of blessed memory, and his family. (They later moved to America with their children.) If the soot in a chimney caught fire, my father and uncle poured water on the flames to put them out. If there was a wedding, they served as waiters. If, God forbid, someone died, they were among the first to pay their respects. If someone had to teach manners to a gentile, they were the ones who stood up to him, with soft talk or with firmness.

My father was always prepared to help someone. If the person needed advice, material assistance, help in straightening out a misunderstanding, that person came to my father, Aryeh. God gave him another skill, that of a chiropractor. He could move a limb back in the right place. If a cripple could not turn his head, foot, or hand, Aryeh made the adjustment, and the person went away with a blessing on his or her lips. He considered such treatment a good deed and wouldn't accept money, even from gentiles who came to him from surrounding villages. Later, people use to bring him gifts such as sacks of groats, buckwheat, beans, and peas from their fields.

My father and my uncle worked hard. However, they were happy and waited like all Jews of Antopol for the Sabbath to rest and to thank His dear name.

On Friday, our dear true mother of blessed memory would get up when it was still dark to heat the oven and bake bread – white bread – for the Sabbath, as well as cake, piroshkes, and later cholent. When the oven was hot, she prepared a pot of grated potatoes for a baked pudding. (I can still taste its flavor!)

My father would arise early on Friday, as on all days, and go to the Study Hall to pray. He would come home from prayers, eat breakfast, and go to his workshop to work until noon. Then he closed up. After lunch, he went for a sweat in the bathhouse. This was his greatest pleasure. Coming home, father would have something to eat and then lie down on the sofa for a nap. When he got up, he put on his Sabbath clothes and went back to the

Study Hall to receive the dear guest, the Sabbath. He liked to pray at the cantor's desk. After prayers, he would come home, sanctify the Sabbath over wine, eat supper, and say grace. Then he was tired and would go to bed. On Saturday, he would arise early, drink tea with sugar, go to the Hasidic prayer hall to pray, come back around noon, wash up ritually, and eat. Mother would take out the cholent after the regular meal and then a good noodle pie. After he ate, father would sleep and then go to the prayer hall. When he came home, he separated the Sabbath and the weekday over fire, and then went to his shop to work. Thus things went until the next Sabbath.

This is how the people of Antopol spent their days, Sabbaths and Festivals, those who were better off and those who fared worse.

May the beloved souls of all our parents and of our sisters, brothers, and all members of the community not be forgotten.

# In the Old Home
## By Dobe Zisuk

My parents were not rich, but they had a good name and they earned it by giving help to unfortunate people who were poor or sick. Whatever they lacked for Passover – matzoh, wine, meat, and the like – my parents provided, not entirely with their own money. They persuaded others to give and saw to it that the needy were not ashamed.

*[Page 69]*

My mother, of blessed memory, was a woman of valor, and she guided her 10 children admirably. The youngsters studied with the best teachers, with even the girls learning to pray and to write.

I was the oldest of the children, and now I am the grandmother of grown-up American grandchildren. Still I cannot forget the pleasure of Passover eve in the old country. Two weeks before Passover my mother used to hire a gentile woman to whitewash the room and wash the bed sheets. Afterwards, as the room was already prepared for Passover, we had to eat from trays and watch out lest a piece of leavened bread should fall some place. To keep the sheets clean, we slept on hay or straw. The beds were not used until Passover. The table, benches, and everything had to be washed and scoured. Everything was washed piece by piece and put into the street. The room was left empty. After a hard day's work, it would have been nice to sleep on clean sheets, and certainly a good mattress would have been appreciated.

Several weeks before Passover, we would buy three pood (120 Russian pounds) of flour to bake matzoh in the first oven because my father and mother were very pious. When all the sheets of matzoh had been prepared, one sheet was left to grind up into matzoh meal for dumplings. We would bring out the mortar, sieve, and sifter from the attic. I, as the oldest girl, and my brother, two years younger, would go to work grinding, sifting, and pouring the meal into sacks. Often we lent the mortar and sieve to neighbors on our street. To this day, I can still smell the fresh aroma of matzoh.

To search for leaven, my mother used to take from a high shelf a wooden spoon that she had put there when there was a question with its being ritually clean. Then she would show father where pieces of bread were lying. He would carry his prayer book together with the wooden spoon and a feather and say with great concentration the blessing concerning the search for leaven. All of us children would say the amen after the blessing.

Concerning the seder, mother would place the cushions on the chairs for us to sit on, and father, in his white gown, would make a beautiful sanctification of the wine. After that my brothers sanctified the wine. Then the four questions were asked. All my brothers had to explain the haggadah, word for word. The seder lasted until midnight.

The old country doesn't exist any more, and one cannot expect these types of preparations to take place in the new country. However, I can tell you, dear people, that I carried on the traditions of Passover with my husband, of blessed memory, and my children no differently than my parents did, even though I was here in America. And even now I carry on just as we did in the old country. I wish that all Jews would carry out tradition here as in we did in the old country. The fear that Judaism is going under would not be so great if the younger generations were raised in pure Jewish spirit. Then they would remain, like us, Jewish in practice.

# My Town, Antopol
## By Y. A. Shulruf

Our town was not distinguished with richness and great commerce. As it was far from river ways and railways, the town's possibilities for commerce were quite small. However, the inhabitants were rich spiritually. The main thing was that they lived in contentment. The spirit of pious Judaism was in the air everywhere. Toiling and hard working, the Jews used to pray in public and listen to a lesson in a chapter of Mishnah, En Yaakov, or Hayye Adam. From the windows of the study halls, you could hear the reading of the Talmud. Work – everything – stopped on the Sabbath. On the Sabbath, one could even think that the grass and the trees ceased growing. The atmosphere was created by the rabbis of the time.

*[Page 70]*

In my childhood years, the big "cold" synagogue and the two study halls, the old and the new, were the centers of my life. Our town was wrapped in awe and holiness, concentrated around the aged Rabbi, the Nabozshni Rabbin, a genius and a righteous man. His divine image called forth respect, not only among the Jews but also among the gentiles. As I grew up, I heard many stories associated with him. His name was known far and wide. He was a righteous man who traced his genealogy way back and who sat on the rabbi's chair.

Who was the congregation and support of the rabbi? Craftsmen, storekeepers, and a merchants who could not allow themselves luxury without providing luxury to the rabbi. But he did not ask for such things. The townspeople asked the rabbi, as a righteous man, for advice and sought his blessings. The rabbi, a thin man, a man short in stature, led a great seminary with pupils for whom he arranged room and board and also taught them their lessons. In addition, he gave advice and cured their illnesses. Not only Jews came to him, but also Christians believed that the Nabozshni Rabbin could help and heal them.

One such case was as follows: A healthy smith had complained that "straw was in his stomach" and grimaced in pain. However, the rabbi told him to go home and he would be well. The smith said that he felt already like a newborn. And another Jew, someone called Joshua, said that he was on the point of divorcing his wife because she could not give him a child. However, the rabbi told him not to do that and blessed him. At the end of the year, as the rabbi said, Joshua's wife Lane bore him a girl.

The rabbi himself did not believe that he could help anyone. However, since people said that he could, he gave blessings so they could calm down. The rabbi's wife, however, was not happy that people bothered the rabbi.

"Pintshe, go eat. The groats will get cold," she called to him. To strangers she shouted, "Go home, what do you want from him?!"

When a woman giving birth was having a hard time and the midwife could not help, people went to the rabbi, and he said that God would help and they should place a shawl under the head of the woman giving birth. After such a birth, the rabbi held the baby at circumcision. If the circumcision took place on the Day of Atonement, it was a happy event. The scene is hard to put into words. The rabbi with his white patriarchal beard, his white robe, his white skullcap, and his white socks looked like an angel. Like a young man full of love, he covered the baby. However, when the ritual circumciser sang the scabrous tune "In your blood, live," a cloud drew over the face of the rabbi who sat on the chair of Elijah and a tear fell down his white beard.

Another story was told of Yavdokhe, the daughter of Tikhon, who had birth pains. The rabbi's wife was leaving her house with a sack in hand, heard the cries, and quickly ran to the rabbi in the study hall. It was just before Shavuous when the trees were in full bloom and the elder trees spread their aroma. Yavdokhe's cries were a dissonant note to the pleasant outdoors scene. The rabbi, who felt good, told his wife to take her shawl and put it under the head of Yavdokhe. In addition, he told her that he would be the person who would hold the child at the circumcision – absolutely. And she should, for the sake of God, not forget that.

The rabbi's wife smiled. "Aye, aye, Pintshe," she said. "Do you want to be the person who would hold the illegitimate child of the gentile Yavdokhe at the circumcision?"

The rabbi fell into deep thought. "Probably." He asked God that the messiah should come and that "Knowledge would cover the earth like the water covers the sea" and all the gentiles would believe in the true God.

Our town does not exist anymore. The Nazis and the White Russian bandits destroyed it. Near the Frishikhvos dam lie buried our dear and beloved (who did not even receive a Jewish burial or grave) in a mass grave. And together with them lie also buried our youthful dreams.

*[Page 71]*

# War and Occupations, 1914-1921
## By Shmuel Lifshitz

Upon the outbreak of World War I, the Russian government hung a conscription notice on the church in the market place. On a Sabbath afternoon in the month of Av (?), those conscripted from Antopol and its environs had to travel by train to Kobrin. With groans, tears in their eyes, and much anguish, the women, children, and elderly accompanied the young men to the train. I was then nine years old, and the memory of that scene is one I shall never forget. By chance, the day before there had been a solar eclipse. Everyone was shaken. The eclipse was a bad omen. (Later, the war broke out, and letters arrived from the front and from the wounded in hospitals.)

The young men went on the Sabbath to the loading area. Trains left without let up for the front with ammunition and soldiers and came back with the wounded. I must also point out that anti-Semitism increased. People spread rumors that all the Jews were for the Germans and sent their money to Germany.

At the fortress in Brisk, people prepared for a big battle. Many fled, which let to Antopol becoming overfilled with Jewish homeless. They were settled in study halls and, where possible, in private homes. The town devoted itself to helping the homeless. In our home (that is, Moshe Isaac's house), which was on the synagogue courtyard, there was a kitchen where food was prepared for the homeless.

On the last night before the Germans came, we didn't leave our home. At the time, a battle which lasted about 13 days was being fought at the Horodets River. We could hear the shooting in Antopol. The Russians had burnt the town eight days earlier. They burnt the stores around the four sides of the marketplace and Mazurski's mill, which was powered by a diesel motor. Eight days later, the last night before the Germans entered, the watchman told us to prepare to leave our homes because soon the entire town would be burnt. There would be no battle in town because everyone was leaving since tomorrow at noon the Germans would enter.

We prepared ourselves, hid the little money we had, and packed our things in the ice cellar. Our family consisted of grandfather, parents, and three children. We left our home at midnight. We went through David Kaplan's garden to the fields where we met more Jews and also other members of our family, one of the largest in town.

While lying in the fields, we could see the town burning on all sides. We heard the shouts of the escaping soldiers, so we also fled farther and farther away. We met up with Jews from the town and also homeless refugees. Of course, we were also homeless. The synagogue courtyard, the synagogue together with the study halls, our home, and the bath were all burnt. The German army had entered in the morning.

Gradually, the population returned to the ruined town. As Antopol became completely filled with Jews, the Jewish refugees and the local Jews took over vacant gentile houses and also settled in the nearby villages of Frishikhvost, Zshalive, Zenivie, and Tarakan. At the same time, our Jews began to supply themselves with food.

As it was before the holidays, the grain crops were already in the barns. The Antopol Jews began in a primitive fashion to beat with sticks the full ears of corn and to prepare bread. People from the big cities, it is a pity, had to come to our small town for us to instruct them how to get some grain and afterwards clean and grind it.

Thanks be to God, the winter came late, and we dug up the potatoes which were still in the fields. Later, there was frost and after it went away, we dug up potatoes which had already frozen. We used them to bake puddings. Understandably, the grain around the town was quickly used up. This happened before the German government, which took everything it could get, had a chance to seize our grain and before it could establish control.

*[Page 72]*

The Germans immediately began to take over. They created districts. The district of Antopol was from Horodets Bridge to the village of Brashevitsh. The Drohitshin district began from Brashevitsh. The villages in the Antopol district were Frishikhvost, Zshalive, Zenivie, Tarakan, Shukatsi, and Rusheve. The Germans set up a civil administration.

A mayor was selected for Antopol. He had to know the German language. The first mayor was a limping, homeless Jew from Brisk, who caused a lot of trouble until we got rid of him. We replaced him with a person from Antopol. Then a council of four people was picked to organize the gathering of grain from the villages for distribution to the people and also for complying with requisition orders from the Germans. The Germans had stopped all travel. There were no trains for a certain amount of time. To go from one district to another, a pass from the general staff was necessary, but it could not be obtained.

All the better horses had been requisitioned. From time to time, horses were taken to a veterinarian to be examined, then branded and recorded. The Germans completely controlled the distribution of the horses. I should comment here that a horse was worth a fortune. The person who had a horse would be able to get food, and those who did not would go hungry. It was forbidden to take food from the village to the city. There was a nightly curfew at 9 p.m. The entire male population from ages of 14 up served as forced labor. Their work was to repair roads, to bring different products to the train (which began to operate for military purposes), and to load supply wagons. The Jewish officials had to supply people, horses, and wagons for all this work which was compelled by the German military.

In 1918, the revolution in Russia broke out. Trotsky made a peace agreement with the Germans in Brisk-Litovsk. Then all the peasants who had left the entire region began returning to their homes. They found their houses burnt, in ruins. Many had no doors or windows. The fields were overgrown with wild grass. One can only imagine how bad the situation was. At that time, the Germans withdrew. Numerous gangs sprang up, robbing, stealing, and murdering. At the same time, many prisoners of war returned, among them lots of Jews. The Jews in Antopol organized a self-defense effort and began to govern. Elhanan Lifshitz, who had returned from Russia, headed the self-defense unit. Nehemiah, the quilter, kept the weapons at home. He lived on the marketplace in an apartment in Esther Shemuel Rusel's house. Travelers spread news from one city to another, thus it took some time to hear that the Belokhovtses were in Kobrin. They waited until the Polish Army entered. They then joined the Polish Army to fight against the Red Army, which had been able to overcome all the other armies in Russia. People used to meet in Nehemia's apartment to discuss the news and to make the best decisions they could.

One Wednesday evening, we sat with Nehemiah the quilter. Suddenly, his wife came into the room, frightened. She said that several cavalry had just come to the house of Avigdor, the village chief. She had heard them speaking Polish. We immediately panicked. Nehemiah and my father and a few other older people went out on the balcony to intercept the cavalry while others quickly removed the weapons from the room by the back door. There was great fear, because we had had an announcement a few days before that the people of Antopol should take their guns to Kobrin and surrender them to the Polish government. From the other side, the Red Army had sent money and instructions to buy weapons we were to hold for them until they arrived.

Several scouts arrived in town for two or three days. On the third day, the Red Army came to Drohitshin and to Antopol. The Red Army that came to Antopol was disorganized. It was a large group of soldiers of different ages, many were young and many were elderly. They came on foot and lacked weapons. Some did not even have a rifle.

*[Page 73]*

However, every one of them had hand grenades slung around them. Since they came at dusk, there was a great deal of confusion. Finding quarters for such a big mob was a critical problem. In our home, soldiers were quartered in each room, and we had to share our supper with them. Finally, the soldiers were all housed and went to sleep. We didn't even put up a watch. The Poles and Belakhovtses came in at dawn with machine guns, cavalry, and artillery. The Red Army did not have time to flee. The soldiers ran with their pants in their hands and fell like flies from the rifle bullets and the machine gun fire.

Separately, both armies came into town. The Polish Army came through Kobrin Street; the Belakhovetses, through Rushever Street. Both armies came to the market in an orderly fashion. Afterwards, they went to search the houses, supposedly for Bolsheviks. In reality, they did this to rob and murder.

They shot three Jews: a youth, Moshe, Fal Tsherniuk's son; Nehemiah's son from a nearby village; and Efrayim the wagoner, the father of four small children. They wanted to murder more people but were easily bought off. The first three Jews they shot they hadn't asked for money. Immediately, upon opening the door they seized the victims and shot them. No one left the houses. At nightfall, the soldiers left. Then people came out in masses from the houses for the funerals of the victims.

In Zakazele, they murdered all three Jewish families.

Mainly, in Antopol, the Poles cut off the beards of the Jewish inhabitants. After the soldiers left, things slowly normalized. The roads opened up. News began to come from America; a little later, also help.

Support came from the Joint Distribution Committee and from Americans who had families in Antopol. The Joint sent material help which was distributed to children, and a kitchen was opened to provide them with lunch. The kitchen was in the brick synagogue, the only one rebuilt at that time. Later, help from America increased. American relatives began to provide assistance.

In 1921, the Red Army led by Trotsky became stronger and attacked the Polish Army. Again misery returned to Antopol. Jews with their cattle, horses, and wagons were seized. It was still worse when the Russian Army came back through Antopol. It was great luck, even a miracle, that it happened during the summer. All the men in the town from 14 through 70 hid for a long time in the forests; young women and girls joined them. Polish soldiers remaining in Antopol looted the town as only the old and children remained to defend it.

The first two scouts of the Red Army came riding on horses with light machine guns on their shoulders by way of Zshaliver Street with the greeting: "Hello, Comrades! Aren't there Poles here?"

Immediately, several Polish soldiers who had hid came toward them, hands up. A little later, the Red Army came in from Pinsk, Zanivier, and

Zshaliver Streets into the market. The Russian Army set up a civilian administration named Revkom, which was composed of Jewish and Christian representatives of the population who had to carry out the Army's orders. It must be said that the entire army, despite the fact it had fought and suffered hunger, did not steal. They would ask for something to eat and if they could dig up some potatoes in the field. Conditions became worse for us when the Polish Army received help from Western governments and began to push back the Soviet Army. However, the war did not continue for long. When our world opened up again, we started over with aid from families in the United States. The American dollar had great value, because everything could be bought with it.

We Jews sat on our suitcases ready to immigrate. Unfortunately, it was not easy, because immigration was severely restricted. Those who were able to get out did so with great difficulty. Finally, they were safe.

*[Page 74]*

# Religious and Cultural Life
## By P. Berman

The synagogue courtyard was in the center of town. Clustered there were the religious and communal buildings of Antopol. It was probably the place where Jews settled first and then spread out to other parts of town.

When I was a young boy, the synagogue courtyard was the only paved place in town and, therefore, suffered little from the deep mud of winter and spring. Surrounding the four sides of the courtyard were the buildings of the cold (unheated) synagogue, two study halls, and the rabbi's house. Beneath the old study hall were the bathhouse and the almshouse. The old cemetery adjoined the courtyard.

The cold synagogue was the highest building in the city, other than the Provoslav church which stood in the marketplace. The architecture of the synagogue was the well-known type of Polish and Lithuanian synagogue architecture described in literature. I have seen pictures of such synagogues, which seem like copies of our own in Antopol. I don't know how old our synagogue was. It had been repaired many times and probably rebuilt a long time before I was a boy.

As a child, I remember the synagogue as a solid building, clean and without external ornamentation. In my child's eyes, it was the greatest and prettiest building in the world. Inside the synagogue, it was always dark because the large Gothic windows were high up, not far from the ceiling which was probably two stories higher than the ground floor. The walls were painted dark gray, and on one wall the matso hung in a special tin can which when lowered marked the distance one could travel on the Sabbath.

The white and gold ceiling was a round vault entirely covered with paintings including depictions of all kinds of animals -- deer and lions and also even, as I remember, a creature with one horn, probably the mythological unicorn. Below them were painted the 12 constellations. Under each was a Hebrew inscription such as "scales," "fish," scorpion," and the like. Under the animals were also descriptions such as "Run like a deer" under a picture of a deer.

The raised platform was in the middle of the synagogue near to the door. And on the east side, as usual, was the holy ark with engravings and paintings, which took up a lot of space. The height of the ark went up to the ceiling. It was painted gold, and at the very top were painted two hands giving the priestly blessing.

The women's synagogue was on the second floor, above the chapel, and was quite a large room. The eastern wall had a gallery with openings through which the women could look into the men's synagogue and follow their prayers.

Throughout the year on Sabbath and holidays, people prayed in the cold synagogue. There were very few people praying in the winter, mostly elderly craftsmen. People did not study there; they only prayed and said Psalms.

People say that at one time the sexton of the cold synagogue was a Jew with the name of Abraham'l. He was a small old Jew. However, he had the strength to come every Friday afternoon to the marketplace and call with a hoarse voice, "Come to synagogue!" Thus is derived the family name Shulruf ("call to come to synagogue"), and thus are his children and children's children called today.

When I was a boy, the sexton was Elye, a handsome Jew with a big red beard. He was also a teacher in the elementary school, which was in the chapel of the cold synagogue.

What we called "the new study synagogue" was, in truth, not the more recently built of the two study halls in the marketplace. The old synagogue was a lot newer. It was, however, built on the original site of the old study hall, which had burnt down years ago, and the name "old" remained. The new synagogue consisted of great rooms divided with a long brick furnace between the men's and the women's synagogues.

*[Page 75]*

A lot of the established important people of Antopol prayed there. R. Hersh, one of the three rabbi's who remained in town after the funeral of R. Pinchas Michael of blessed memory, was the religious leader of the new study synagogue. And when the disagreement between the Tsahnlies and the Gages died down, the established people, mostly, were on his side. Efrayim Lifshitz, the fabulously rich man in town, and his family prayed here, except his son David who prayed in the old synagogue with his father-in-law.

Samuel Sbarshtsik, the reader of the Torah on the High Holidays, belonged to the study hall. Here also prayed the hunchback, one of the important storekeepers in the marketplace and the owner of the only two-story brick building in town, the building in which the pharmacy was located. People often also saw R. Hetskel, known as the man living on Rushever Street. He was a handsome Jew and a great scholar who was mostly occupied with learning and was little interested in worldly matters. R. Hetskel used to study "En Yaakov" with people.

Yaakov Hayyim, the ritual slaughterer, was a clever Jew who was interested in many communal matters. He was one of the chief leaders in the societies that took care of charity and other general matters of the city.

As in other study halls, people studied a lot. There were young people who spent the entire day in study. One of them was Yaakov Shelomoh Henokhs. He had a stagecoach which brought merchandise every week to Antopol storekeepers.

Leizer, the sexton of the new study synagogue, was a tall powerful Jew with a long black beard and quick movements. I remember how on Friday afternoons he would go from bench to bench lighting the lamps which hung on chains. He earned the greatest part of his livelihood from bookbinding. Landowners of the surrounding estates always brought him books, in all kinds of languages, to bind.

## The Old Study Hall

When the study hall was quite old and ready to fall down, it was rebuilt with new walls. However, the name was never changed so people just called it the Old Study Hall. As a reminder of the past, they built into it here and there pieces of wood from the old building, as R. Pinchas Michael, of blessed memory, told them to do. Wooden boards were laid as paving to the rabbi's house so he wouldn't get his boots muddy when there was mud in Antopol or dusty when there was no mud.

The remodeled study hall was a large, modern building with many places for worshippers, self-taught students, and the numerous youths who used to sit and study with Rabbi Mikhael. A long tile oven took up almost all of the west wall. Under the reading platform, a long table and benches were placed around the walls. Several steps led down from the vestibule to a chapel where a class of elementary school pupils studied. The women's section was on the second floor with a separate entrance.

My father, of blessed memory, spent almost his entire time in the Old Study Hall. I, myself, as a young boy used the study hall like a part of our house. After elementary school and on Sabbath and festivals when we weren't in school, I was always in the study hall. When I was older, I studied there by myself under the supervision of my father.

Remaining in my memory are some interesting individuals who were among the many people who always prayed in the Old Study Hall.

For example:

Yekutiel, Beyla Hannah's husband, prayed in an eastern corner beside the Holy Ark. His wife was a woman of valor and carried on the business for the entire family. He himself spent all of his time in the study hall. He was of small stature, had a big black beard with side curls, and a quiet voice that was a little hoarse. He was always studying and was little interested in secular matters. His two sons, as I remember, were the only young men in the study hall with long black beards.

*[Page 76]*

Avigdor Sirota, the town's mayor, was one of the important, well-established people of Antopol with connections in all-political and philanthropical matters. He had a prominent place in the Old Study Hall.

Yankel the doctor was one of the finest individuals often found in the Old Study Hall. He was one of the great experts in the general practice of medicine of the time, and people used him more often than the Polish doctor. He was also interested in and took part in all the important institutions in Antopol. A highly honorable man, he did a lot of good for all.

The Old Study Hall had two sextons: Gedalyah, the chief sexton, and Yenkel Menkes, the under sexton.

Gedalyah was in charge of bookkeeping, entering income and expenditures. He kept accounts and collected debts from individuals and, in general, took care of the business of the study hall. He also called people to the reading of the Torah, led the prayers, and read from the Torah when necessary. In addition, he arranged for blessings-of each person called to the Torah, of newborn daughters on the occasion of their naming, of sick men or women. He was a jack-of-all-trades, knowing many crafts. For example, he could build a house or a brick oven and did all kinds of carpentry work. Gedalyah was killed in the war between the Bolsheviks and the Poles.

Menkes, the assistant sexton, did all the manual labor such as sweeping, cleaning, and heating the building and was one of the two gravediggers of the burial society. He called the congregation to penitential prayers and to the reading of the Psalms. Naturally, he was a very poor man, and his wife did day work in private homes.

In the study hall, people studied by themselves and in groups such as the Talmud Society, the Mishnah Society, and the En Society. Sometimes young people studied the whole day there. In the evening, all the tables had lamps, and the traditional Gemara scholars' chant was heard all around. Often, the study hall was lit all night, and young people held a watch and studied until early morning.

There was one small problem about the study hall. It's windows overlooked the old cemetery, creating a sense of dread among some individuals.

# The Rabbi's House

Near the Old Study Hall, the rabbinical residence was a large house probably built in R. Pinchas Michael's time. There were five big rooms with a kitchen and a built-in Sukkah which was used most of the year as a pantry. The big baking oven and a long stove which took up a great deal of space in the middle of the house heated the entire structure in the winter. A large dining room also served as a waiting room for people who came to see the rabbi. It was where every Thursday yeast was sold. Lining the walls from floor to ceiling were shelves filled with old books. Several years after Rabbi Mikhael's death, his oldest son, Abraham Mosheh, came and took the books to Brest-Litovsk, where they were all destroyed a short time later in a great fire.

One thing I particularly remember was that on the ceiling above the rabbi's seat at the dining table was a spot that had been deliberately left unpainted. The wood was blackened with age. The spot was left in this condition, a custom in the homes of pious people, in memory of the destruction of the Jewish Temple in Jerusalem.

The rabbi spent most of his time in the second large room where he conducted sessions of the rabbinical court. There he made decisions concerning the kosher code and other matters of the townspeople. I remember a small bookcase built into the wall about which my father told an interesting story from the time of Rabbi Mikhael.

*[Page 77]*

The old rabbi had once on a Purim after prayers invited the entire congregation to his house. He promised to give them "wine from the wall." No one doubted that Rabbi Mikhael had the power to draw wine from the wall. They were all a little disappointed, therefore, when the rabbi, smiling, took out a bottle of wine from the built-in bookcase and took a drink with the congregation.

## The City Bath

A short distance behind the study hall was the city bath. Men went to the bathhouse every Friday; on other days of the week, it was heated for women.

The pool for ritual bathing was used every day, not only for women, but for pious men who also immersed themselves.

On top of the steam boiler was a whistle which could be heard all over town. It was blown in the morning to call people to the bath. And on Friday afternoon, it also blew to tell the women to light the Sabbath candles. Often on Friday afternoons, the rabbi would go to the bath and drive out those who might be late going to synagogue.

The bath keeper lived in a house beside the bathhouse. Half of his house was used as an almshouse where traveling poor people stayed. A mentally handicapped person, David Ber, usually worked in the bathhouse. He was one of a number of such persons, men and women, who lived in Antopol, as in other towns in the region, and for whom nothing could be done. Fortunately, these individuals appeared only to be depressed, at least in Antopol, and I don't remember their causing any trouble.

David Ber came to our house often. He kept his phylacteries with us and came to pray almost every day. He never wore a prayer shawl. Perhaps he was never married. I remember him as a short middle-aged man with a black beard. He spoke little. However, he complained frequently about himself, saying, "The man is a living ruin." His comment was well known about town and often used when people made fun of someone who complained about his health.

# The Synagogue Courtyard
## By A. Varsha

The synagogue courtyard was the nerve center and the barometer of the town's inner life. Sometimes events began here which affected Antopol for a long time. Meetings of different associations were held here, and decisions were made and important general amendments passed that often had an influence on the life of the entire community.

The courtyard echoed with the sounds of happy events as well as sad ones. Here were set up the wedding canopies for most of the marriages. Each time a funeral was held, a deep sadness fell over the courtyard. If the deceased was an important person, the funeral procession usually stopped in the courtyard and a funeral oration was made.

On Sabbath and festival days, the courtyard was filled the entire day with people dressed up in their best Sabbath clothing praying and studying, and a festive mood filled all corners.

A large crowd often came to the synagogue courtyard in the middle of the week when a well-known preacher gave a sermon in one of the study halls. Some of the preachers could draw a big crowd, particularly on a winter night when the windows were closed and the air inside was oppressive. The lamps flickered and could not light to their usual height. The crowd was thirsty for a good word, mainly from a fiery Zionist speaker, and was content to suffer the cold and stand pressed together for a time like herrings in a barrel, listening.

The general happiness and tumult of Simhat Torah and Purim and the holy sadness of Yom Kippur and Tishab b'Av remain in my memory in connection with the Antopol courtyard of over 50 years ago.

*[Page 78]*

During the rainy season, a pool of water formed in the synagogue courtyard and spread as far as R. Hersh's house. The pool was quite useful. First, people used the water to put out fires, frequent guests of Antopol. Second, people used to go to the pool for the ceremony of casting out sins into the water on the New Year's.

Since the destruction of our dear town, the synagogue courtyard remains an orphan and cries together with us.

The entire structure of the cold (unheated) synagogue was supported by just one beam. The beam was carved and divided the synagogue under the dome from north to south.

Once I crawled along the beam – carefully keeping my balance while feeling as if I hung to life suspended by a hair – to examine the nails that had been hammered in long ago during construction. The antiquity of the synagogue, I believe, is confirmed by the fact that no factory-made nails had been used.

I clearly remember the artwork I observed as I made my way along the beam. First there was the frieze on the margin of the vault. The 12 constellations were painted on the frieze in burnt umber in dark and light hues. This painting was a masterpiece. Despite the passage of 300 years, the paint had lost none of its original color. In my imagination, I could see the master painter at work with his brush.

Over the holy ark, he had painted musical instruments illustrating Psalm 150. You remember the guitar and harp, the ram's horn and flute, the cymbals, and drum. The painted instruments were so real I felt I could take them each up in my hand. The old master was an artist of divine grace. He also painted animals on the dome, and I believe that his intention here was that even a beast is redeemed when it enters God's house.

Now behold the holy ark. In our region, in bigger cities, I have never seen such a large ark. Our ark was about three stories tall! Its carved doors spread themselves like wings over the eastern wall. Their white and gold light radiated over the entire congregation. The gold paint was doubtlessly about 300 years old yet it had not peeled nor split anywhere. No one could forget the carved doors on both sides of the curtain of the ark and how the cherubs would fly out when the ark was opened. The painting and the carving were probably completed soon after the erection of the building because the scaffolds became a part of the building.

A mystery remains. Who were the master craftsmen? They left no sign of themselves; some believed they were not from Antopol.

A few years before the synagogue burned down, taking with it both study halls, it was improved by Hayyim Zelig the carpenter who built a new platform for reading the Torah. Shelomoh the painter dedicated himself to decorating the platform, and masses of people from near and far came to view its glory.

No wonder our grandfathers, fathers, and I took such great pride in it. To think that such a poor small town possessed so special a spiritual treasure.

## Synagogues and Study Halls

The brick study hall, which stood between the market and Pinsk Street, was not an old building. It was called the brick study hall to distinguish between it and the other study halls made of wood.

The sexton was a small thin Jew named Mosheh Hershel. He was the cemetery caretaker of the town. Every Friday on Pinsk Street and in the marketplace, Mosheh Hershel used to call out, "Come to synagogue," and he would announce the important meetings that were to take place. When he was in his cups on Simhat Torah, Mosheh Hershel used to pretend he was reading from a plate the entire rain prayer. Afterward, he would sing, "I am a wall," which suggests a good quality. Then he would add another – "bright like the sun" – even though wandering in exile.

*[Page 79]*

Sarahke was a treasure. She devoted her life and fortune to decorating and making the study hall more beautiful.

Friday nights, Mosheh Zelig the storekeeper sat beside the stove and studied with the congregation the chapters of the Torah to be read on

Saturday together with Alshekh's commentary. Sabbath afternoon he used to teach En to the congregation.

In addition to the different books in the brick study hall, there was an old concordance. If a dispute arose about a Biblical quotation, people went to the study hall to consult the concordance.

# The Nobleman's Synagogue

Various explanations are given for the name "Nobleman's Synagogue." Some say that the nobleman Brever donated the building as a study hall. For that reason, it received the name. Others say the building was bought from the nobleman Shepelya, and the name is taken from that. In any case, no noblemen prayed in the study hall. The Jews from Kobrin Street and the surrounding streets prayed there, ones who were lazy or too infirm to go to the synagogue courtyard.

One of the prayer leaders at the nobleman's synagogue was R. Avraham Yitshak, "with the shoes." Why was he called "with the shoes"? The explanation is that he was a pious Jew. He didn't want to be "modern" and wear boots like the modern secular people. Therefore, he wore shoes with straps that he laced up his legs, like people did in earlier times.

Avraham Yitshak was an established Jew. He was among the first to own an acre of land on Pinsk Street. He was the husband of the well-known righteous woman Rachele who worked day and night to help poor people. They were the parents of R. Yaakov Leyb and Meir David Shterman, who each owned an acre of land. They inherited their father's voice and led prayers for the congregation. Let us hope that their prayers were accepted in the Heavenly Temple of Prayers.

# Meir Podot's Study Hall

The study on Kobrin Street was called MeirPodot's Study Hall. Different legends circulate about Meir Podotin. People said that Meir Podot had the voice of a lion. When he prayed in his study hall on Kobrin Street, he could be heard in other corners of the city on Pinsk Street.

How did Meir Podot become famous as a leader of the congregation in prayer? No other than R. Pinchas Michael made him famous. The story is as follows: Once during the additional service on Yom Kippur, the cantor became sick. R. Pinchas Michael asked, "Who can lead the prayers?" They told him, "There is here a young man who can lead the prayers."

The young man was Meir Podot. R. Pinchas Michael asked him, "Can you lead the prayers?"

Meir Podot answered, "I have never led the prayers."

R. Pinchas Michael answered, "Go and lead the prayers."

From then on, Meir Podot was known as a great leader of prayer.

People said that Meir Podot belonged to the Hasidim of the town of Kobrin. The Rebbe of Kobrin invited him to be the leader of the prayers in Kobrin. And the Rebbe spoke to him thus: "If you can take it upon yourself to act in the role of the sacrifice offered in forgiveness of Israel's sins, you may go lead the prayers." R. Meir Podot agreed to accept that condition to lead the prayers.

*[Page 80]*

That legend explains how R. Meir Podot became well known. He was a great lover of the people of Israel and risked his life for them in leading the prayers.

## The Hasidic Chapel

In Antopol, no special chapels existed for Hasidim as in other towns. Apparently, not a lot of Hasidim lived in Antopol. Therefore, there was only one Hasidic chapel where all the Hasidim in town prayed. The Hasidim of Stolin, Kobrin, Lubovitsh, Slonim, and Trisk prayed there, also. Although they belonged to different traditions, they lived in peace among themselves. Berish, the butcher's father, donated the building. The Hasidic chapel was famous for its collection of books on Jewish mysticism.

Individuals we should not forget include Leyzer Mikhal, a Hasid of Stolin, a learned Jew, not a noisy man, a quiet, agreeable Jew. Henokh, the elementary school teacher, was a Hasidic follower of the R. of Trisk. He was learned in Jewish mysticism. Then there was Berish, a Hasidic follower of the R. of Kobrin, a clever Jew who was one of the town fathers. And who doesn't remember Nathan Getsel? He was a true Hasidic follower of the R. of Slonim. He had a high fervor, but his fervor never caused him to harm anyone.

When a celebration for a Hasidic Rebbe took place or a Hasidic Rebbe came to Antopol, all the Hasidim sat at one table, drank a toast, took leftovers from the Rebbe's plate, and went to dance together. And they all went together to their deaths. May God revenge their blood!

## The Glory of Youth

Together with the five study halls, the cold synagogue, and the Hasidic Chapel, there was also until 1915 a prayer quorum of the Glory of Youth Society, which consisted of nearly 20 young men who worked in various crafts. The members of the Society were quite friendly among themselves.

The Society paid the salary of a rabbi, Mosheh Hersh the bookbinder, a tall Jew, a devoted scholar with a small, sparse, not full, beard. On Friday nights, he studied the Pentateuch with Society members; on Saturdays, Hayye Adam and Mishnah.

The prayer quorum met in Breyne Rive's apartment which was near the market between the brick buildings of Akiva Fishel Lifshitz and Hayyim Grinberg. People prayed there only on the Sabbath and at festivals. Following afternoon prayers on Sabbaths, they would eat the third Sabbath meal celebrating like the Hasidim, although they were far from being Hasidim. Each Sabbath, a member provided the food for the third meal, which consisted of challah, herring, beer, and the like. After the ceremony to separate the Sabbath from the weekday, they sang songs such as "He who separates" and "God said to Jacob." They also sang "Don't fear my servant Jacob."

The Rabbi Mosheh Hersh collected his salary by going around to Society members' apartments. They received him with the honor due a rabbi and paid as much as each had pledged. Once, about 1910, the prayer quorum met a number of times in the apartment of Meir the nose, who was also a member of the Society.

Then there took place a truly joyous event for which the Society had long awaited. A new Torah scroll was written. With great rejoicing Society members carried the new scroll under a bridal canopy to Breyne Rive's apartment. Some who accompanied the scroll held aloft poles with naphtha lamps decorated with colored paper and cutout inscriptions. Some played musical instruments as they walked along; others sang and danced. Not only members of the Glory of Youth participated in the festivities, but all the Jews of Antopol shared in the joy of fulfilling a commandment. People drank toasts, danced, and ate all along the way until they got to Breyne Rive's apartment. The celebration continued late into the night. We can't say that the Antopol Jews were unable to enjoy themselves when they had the occasion.

*[Page 81]*

After World War I, Shelomke Menahem put a lot of energy into reestablishing the Glory of Youth Society. Members met every Sabbath in the new study hall in the synagogue courtyard, and Shelomke Menahem taught them and led them in debates.

In addition to the synagogue, the five study halls, and the Hasidic Chapel, there were in Antopol three prayer quorums in private homes.

# Memories of the Elementary School, 1923-1926
## By Rabbi Shalom Podolevski

In the early twentieth century, few towns in Europe were so tightly bound and mutually dependent as were the villages of Antopol and Horodets. Antopol would not have been Antopol without Horodets, and Horodets would not have been Horodets without Antopol.

Antopol shared with Horodets its spiritual, professional, and cultural resources. The last rabbis of Horodets were born in Antopol: R. Hayyim Grinberg and R. Aryeh Grinman. When a person from Horodets needed a doctor or a midwife, he or she had to come to Antopol. Also, the pharmacy and the bank were in Antopol.

However, the most important thing that Antopol made available to Horodets was the elementary school. Horodets had at that time one elementary school teacher. Even if he had been the greatest of pedagogues, he could not have taught all the children in town. Therefore, when children became too old for the Horodets elementary school teacher, they went to Antopol where they boarded during the week. On the Jewish Sabbath, they walked the highway home to Horodets, returning to Antopol on Sunday. Sometimes, a Jewish or gentile wagon driver would give the children a ride.

I still remember a warm summer day after Passover around 1922 when my father, of blessed memory, walked with me to Antopol so that I could register for elementary school. At the time, the school building was under construction, and elementary classes were spread out over Antopol's five study halls. My father had to go through a complex procedure to register me.

First we had to see the bursars. The first bursar was Hershel the Black. He was a Jew with a handsome black beard with streaks of gray. He was of stately appearance and looked more like a preacher of ethics from Kelm than a resident of Antopol. He spoke with assurance, like a person secure in his authority. He talked for a long time with my father about Antopol's good elementary school, where nearly all the town's youth studied.

When we finished with the first bursar, he gave us a receipt for the second bursar, R. Yaakov Hayyim, the ritual slaughterer. R. Hayyim's house was exactly the opposite of Hershel the Black's. Hershel's house was in the middle of a quiet orchard filled with aromatic flowers and sweet smelling grasses. However, R. Hayyim's house was on a narrow, noisy street, and the slaughterhouse was on the balcony. Gathered around the house was a goodly number of people carrying chickens. The cackling of roosters and hens mingled with the voices of women and peasants in the marketplace.

My father went with me into the house and presented Hershel the Black's receipt. Hayyim looked like a merchant, not a ritual slaughterer. He was a clever Jew, a good person with a lot of experience. When we arrived, he was in the middle of eating and did not have much time to speak with father. After a few words of conversation, he finished eating, quickly said grace, and wrote a receipt stating that I should be admitted to elementary school.

*[Page 82]*

Then we had to walk to the women's study hall where we found Yudel, a small Jew with a severe appearance who sat at a great table. Around him sat about 20 youths from 10 to 12 years of age. Yudel, the teacher, showed me where to sit. I hardly made it through class before my father came to take me to where I would board, the home of Moshehle Matos, an elderly Jew who was a shoemaker and a fine and good person.

After Sukkot, R. Hayyim, the ritual slaughterer, gave me a note to go to a higher level elementary school teacher, R. Shelomoh. He appeared to me like an angel from heaven. I always had an excellent relationship with my teachers. But the closeness I had with R. Shelomoh'n would be hard to duplicate.

R. Shelomoh was in his 50s, a great scholar and a person of deep understanding, a big heart, and much love for children. I don't know how R. Shelomoh came to teach at the Antopol elementary school. He was from Sislovitsh, Poland. He had studied in rabbinical seminaries and knew how to be a true pedagogue. He took a personal interest in my education and instilled in me his devotion to study, his commitment to education, and compassion for my schoolmates. However, people used to murmur that R. Shelomoh's ideas were too modern. We, his pupils, cared only that he was good for us. For me, R. Shelomoh became identified with my home, my father, and my education. He had already directed, as was done in modern schools, a Hanukkah play presented by the two upper classes. Our class, the second highest, was the Maccabees; the most advanced class, the Greeks. We studied Talmud, the Tractate of Kiddushin being my favorite. In truth, R. Shelomoh put every word in our mouths.

I remember how he would take me to another study hall to tutor me alone, so that I would learn faster. I was a good pupil, as were the other youths. I will never forget R. Shelomoh and Antopol. Thanks to that town, I had such a wonderful teacher.

After having studied with R. Shelomoh a year, I was placed with my relatives and friends, Kalman Kuprianski and Greblovski originally of Horodets, in an upper class.

The teacher was the brilliant rabbi, R. Yozpa who came from Kobrin and was well known in the rabbinical seminaries of Novorodek. He was in his early 30s, quite handsome, tall with a black beard and a rabbinical appearance. His walk was quick, and he carried himself like that of a person of Mir or Radin, rather than of Novorodek. He lived on Pinsk Street, and when he walked through the marketplace, his stately appearance called forth much respect, not less than that given the rabbi of the town, Volfson.

R. Yozpa would ask the students, "Read from a page of Talmud." He himself gave lessons in the manner of a professor of Talmud. He was not as capable a teacher as R. Shelomoh. However, he encouraged students to study independently and to become rabbinical scholars. He spent a lot of time talking with us as we studied the Bible, piety, and virtue.

His manner of teaching was to develop the student intellectually and emotionally. We sat with R. Yozpa in the order of the letter xyz. The best student sat first, the second best second, and so forth. The youths from Horodets – Kalman, Barukh, and I – sat together facing R. Yozpa. Kalman and Barukh were my two best friends, and I sat between them. When the teacher wanted one of us, he used to say, "Horodets!" On each side of us sat 12 Antopol youths, making a total of 27 pupils.

The most capable and best of us was Yaakov Gordon who later moved to Argentina. Others were Yosef Levin, Ben Tsiyon Garber, Ezra Sanke, the future rabbi R. Yaakov Pester, Yisroel Fernik, Yisroel Volovelski, and Aharon Volinets. About 10 of R. Yozpa's students, the best and most talented of the Antopol elementary school, went on to study in rabbinical seminaries in Kobrin, Kamentis, and Mir. They became scholars, pious men, and the pride of the Antopol elementary school. It is a great tragedy that Hitler's merciless hordes murdered them. There remain few Jewish religious scholars from that happy time, scholars who perpetuate the ideals of R. Shelomoh and R. Yozpa.

Praised and sanctified be God's great name!

*[Page 83]*

# Bertshe and Education in Antopol
## By Yosef Veitsel

At one time, no organized educational institution existed in Antopol. Perhaps there was an elementary school for poor children. However, it must not have been very important because I don't remember it. In general, the condition of education was for "every man to do what was right in his own opinion." If a Jew, sadly, had no income, he became an elementary school teacher. Some elementary school teachers, I've heard, could not learn the children's lesson themselves. "Of what value is a teacher who can't study himself!" However, if someone did become an elementary school teacher and continued for some time, he became or was looked upon more or less as an authority in the occupation. (If he really was a good for nothing, he didn't last long as a teacher.)

When Hayyim, of blessed memory, my father's first born, was growing up, elementary school education improved in our town because of my father's influence. He selected the elementary school teachers himself and actively took part in what went on in the classroom. Sometimes he came to the classroom and listened to the children recite their lessons. When parents had a youth Hayyim's age, they always wanted to put the child in Hayyim's class. In the course of time, the class became filled with the selected children of established people. No children of strangers were accepted into the class.

Each elementary school class was like an individual institution within the school, with each class having its own specifications. The lowest class in elementary school was taught by Yankel Perkis, the Pentateuch class by Yitshak the Lame, another Pentateuch class by the rabbinical scholar Rashi, and the first Talmud class by Gedalyah the Sexton.

When Hayyim finished his course with Gedalyah the Sexton, no higher class was available in town. Father asked R. Aharon to start a class for Hayyim and selected other students for it. Thus Aharon began to lead the highest class in Antopol. When I was about four and it was nearing time for me to go to elementary school, my father taught me the Hebrew alphabet and language. Then I studied with Yankel Perkis one year, with Yitshak one year, with Gedalyah two years, and with Aharon one year. Then Aharon told father that he had nothing more to teach me and advised him to send me to a rabbinical seminary.

Thus developed the educational system in Antopol at the end of the nineteenth and beginning of the twentieth century. It was my father, Bertshe the storekeeper, who brought order into education in Antopol.

# R. Henokh, the Elementary School Teacher
## By M.L. Koshtshuk

At first sight, anyone could recognize R. Henokh as something of a holy man. This was because of his walk, the way he carried himself, and his dress. He was a small Jew with a pale loving face and a pensive air of eternity. He had two long curled sidelocks, a long wide black beard, and a black silk belt tied around his waist. From his belt hung two pretty black tassels. A black skull cap was under his hat. He wore a small wool prayer shawl with long fringes bouncing over his knees. He used in numerous ways a fine red handkerchief which hung from one pocket. He used it especially to drive away flies. Even the flies were created by God's hands, and he observed the Biblical injunction, "And His mercy is on all His creations."

R. Henokh had in the second pocket a snuff box, a small flat box which he had inherited from his grandparents who had gotten it from the righteous Rebbe himself, who had sniffed snuff from it. The red handkerchief was also useful for other things: to cover his mouth when he went into the street so that demons could not enter and so that he could not gossip. Also, to cover his eyes in case he met a married woman on the street.

*[Page 84]*

His walk was in moderate steps, slow while he was absorbed in thought about God, worship, and Jewish mysticism. However, you should have seen him when he hurried to prayer. It was hard to keep up with him! He almost ran when it came to fulfilling the religious commandment to give thanks for the Creator of the world. And, with a friendly smile, he would wish everyone a good morning and a good Sabbath.

R. Henokh's occupation was that of elementary school teacher. He did not do this to earn a living or as a spade to dig with to his advantage. The main reason that he was an elementary school teacher was to spread Judaism and Hasidism and to fulfill the commandment, "You shall teach your children." He did not seek out rich children to earn a huge fee for teaching them.

God had matched him with a woman, a real woman of valor, as was fit for such a righteous man, Hasid and mystic. His wife could charm away the evil eye, an evil spirit, and also toothaches. She could make acute pain go away. She could squeeze mumps. Understandably, she did not take compensation for doing these things. People went to her to be charmed, because all knew she was married to a holy man, R. Henokh, who had revealed to her the secret of charming according to Jewish mysticism. Therefore, ghosts and demons were afraid of her incantations. If someone insisted on paying her, she pointed to a charity box marked "Meir, the miracle worker," and she told the person to put the compensation in the box. She also applied cups to draw blood. She was an expert in the matter of the health of small children. She was able to recognize if a child did not feel well and would quickly call the doctor and would tell her husband to pray to God for the child. And God would bring the child back to health.

R. Henokh was also a good teacher, and his students were quite attached to him. He never hit them like the other teachers did. His method was not to strike a child but to enlighten him with talk of ethics and to make him fear hell, so that he would cry. As a teacher, R. Henokh was special. Even from a distance his students were recognizable. He so strongly influenced them that they too wore long earlocks and sometimes even Hasidic belts. It was because of their belts that his students got into fights with the non-Hasidic youths who would pull at the tassels, causing the belts to become untied and fall off. Then there would be blows.

During World War I, when the Russian Army left town, the soldiers set the houses on fire so the entering Germans would have nothing they could use. Usually, people knew when their homes were about to be burnt. Hastily, they removed various possessions: bedclothes, furniture, cooking pots.

They took them to the fields and to the Christian cemetery from where they could see their houses. R. Henokh's family saw that their house was already burning but R. Henokh was missing. They shouted to find out who had seen him last. A neighbor said that she had seen him go into the house with his prayer shawl and phylacteries under his arm. People ran to the house and saw him inside. Houses all around were burning, and his house was also on fire. He had his phylacteries on his head, which was covered by his prayer shawl, and he was praying the Prayer of the Eighteen Blessings. When the Germans entered Antopol, R. Henokh was dead. He deserved a burial, but we could not do him the honor.

It is painful to think about those who have left us, but they are not forgotten. May R. Henokh's soul be bound up in the bond of eternal life.

*[Page 85]*

# R. Meir Yosel, the Elementary School Teacher

## By M.L. Koshtshuk

Meir Yosel, the elementary school teacher, was a Jew, who God forbid, never pursued earthly rewards. His whole life was spent as a scholar of the Talmud. When he left school for the day, he went to the new study hall to study Talmud by himself. This was his schedule, winter or summer, Sabbath or festival. He only went home to eat and sleep. Despite the fact that he was one of the greatest teachers of Talmud in town, he lived like a poor man. He resided in a rented apartment of two rooms in someone's house. His wife, Zlote, kept a little store and had in addition a factory to make the old style bonnets that Jewish women used to wear. Zlote's bonnets, made with flowers and bunches of grapes, were famous.

In the study hall, Meir Yosel sat right at the edge of the west wall. This is where he kept all his books, which saved him time and trouble. Was it possible that no one looked at him or took note of him? It was possible because, so to speak, you had in him a Jew who always sat bent over his volume of Talmud, quiet, not praying aloud as other Jews did. For example, Ore the elementary school teacher and Binyamin the ritual slaughterer filled the entire synagogue courtyard with the tune with which they used to study. However, who did one search out from behind the stove to have the honor of standing with a Torah scroll on the platform to say the special hymns for the Feast of Tabernacles? Meir Yosel, the elementary school teacher.

If you were to look at Meir Yosel, you would think that outside of the study of Talmud he knew nothing of the happenings of the world. And you would be right. How could such a person know about worldly affairs? To know them, he would have had to give up time from his studies of Talmud.

When it came time to blow the ram's horn on New Year's, when the Rabbi R. Hersh, of blessed memory, went up to stand on the platform, the quiet Meir Yosel stood beneath the platform to guide him on the blowing of the horn. It is amazing how that duet of extreme tenor came forth in such wonderful harmony. R. Hersh would make the walls tremble when he blew the horn. However, it was Meir Yosel's sharp whining blast of the horn that penetrated the loving hearts of the pious congregation.

Nevertheless, Meir Yosel had a sense of what was going on in the world. It is possible that he used to listen to the speech of the "Foreign Minister" of the new study hall. That person was Shelomke Menahem, a martyr killed by the Nazis, may God revenge his blood. He used to carry on about the politics of the world.When he came to pray, whether early in the morning or in the afternoon, a crowd of people who listened enthralled by his explanations of worldly events always stood around him. The main sources for his lectures were the correspondent Itshele's "Political Letters" in the Friday edition for the Jewish Sabbath of the daily Yiddish newspaper, Moment, and Nahum Sokolov's "We Talk of Matters of State" in the Hebrew newspaper, ha-Tsefirah. Meir Yosel never went up to Shelomoh's seat in the study hall because he had not only heard the reading out of the newspapers that Shelomoh gave but also saw all the particulars and nuances of all the war fronts and the Emperor's Courts that Shelomoh gave in sign language to Mosheh, who could not speak (Kive the wooden).

If you were a stranger and came into the new study hall and took a look at Meir Yosel, you would think that Yosel was only sleeping over his book. But, suddenly, he would turn the page and take his beard into his mouth. His eyes would look confused, something not being clear to him. Neither his beard nor the rereading of the text could help him out of the hard spot. Finally, he would seek help from Binyamim, the ritual slaughterer, who after the rabbi was the greatest scholar of Talmud in the new study hall. And with Binyamin's help, everything became clear. The wrinkles on Meir Yosel's forehead became smooth. A satisfied smile lit his face, as if he wanted to say, "It is thanks to God that I was able to overcome the difficulty and understand the passage."

*[Page 86]*

He would take out a snuff box and with a sharp sniff fill both nostrils, just like the most wealthy man. Then he would go back to the study of Talmud.

# Rafael, the Elementary School Teacher
## By Mosheh Leizer Koshtshuk

Who among us does not remember Rafael, the elementary school teacher and Hasid of Kiobrin? R. Pinchas Michael, of blessed memory, used to ask him and his small elementary school pupils to say psalms for the sick. Rafael would say certain chapters of psalms and shake himself. The children would shake themselves, just as he did. He would call out the name of the sick person, and all the children would shout, "Amen." The children each received 13 kopecks for this service. Naturally, Rafael didn't lack for pupils. His house was next to the Hasidic chapel, and he would step outside to call the students to study or to ask them to be quiet, not to shout. He was tall, handsome, with a blond beard, and he dressed in a long wool prayer shawl with fringes hanging down to his knees, as is fit for a Hasidic Jew. He held a whip in one hand with five lashes, according to the number of the books in the Pentateuch. The other hand he held in his bosom. He had to carry the whip with him always because once a pupil stole it. He had a hard time finding it, and what use is a teacher without a whip? He inherited the whip from his father, who was also an elementary school teacher.

At times, he would remove his hand from his bosom and take his small beard into his mouth and sing. He was a good singer. People used to hear Rafael sing at various happy occasions: at a wedding, at a circumcision, or with musicians when a Torah scroll would be brought into a synagogue. On such occasions, he sang, "Who will find a woman of valor" and "Good are lights that He created."

When he was an elementary school teacher, he would take his pupils and go to the house of a woman in childbirth. Together they would say, "The Angel who redeems from all harm should bless the woman in childbirth and the child." Then all the children would shout with their squeaky voices, "Amen," as loudly as they could, and he would go on to read the "Hear, O, Israel." The mother of the woman in childbirth would then give the children a reward of a handful of peas, beans, and kernels and sometime 13 kopecks. Then they would run out with a shout, "Good night to the new born and to the woman in childbirth."

Rafael would also give the woman in childbirth a copy, handwritten or printed, of the "Songs of Ascent." He would place it at the child's head or hang it on a window or door as a watch, that demons should not harm him.

On Sabbath mornings in the summer, Rafael would take his pupils to pray in the big, cold synagogue. The tall Jew would walk, as was his fashion, with long strides, causing the hem of his belted Sabbath caftan to flap around him. The children ran after him like small chicks after the mother hen. Even when he was in deep thought, he might snap the fingers of his right hand and sing a tune. He would always make himself happy, because to be happy is a great commandment, as it says in the Bible, "Serve God with happiness." Sadness is the greatest sin. It belongs to the Devil, God forbid. It destroys your health. Then you cannot serve God. Such did this holy Rebbe of blessed memory teach. Also that it is as important to say psalms before prayers as it is to learn a chapter of the Mishnah. It is not without good reason that Rafael the elementary school teacher was called Rafael the angel.

# The Tarbut School
## By Beylah Kletski-Libenfroynd

I can't remember exactly how old I was when I went to school. I remember one thing surely. It is that when I went to school for the first time I could already read and write Hebrew. I also could translate into Yiddish the first chapters of the book of Genesis in the Pentateuch. Probably, I had learned by listening to the private classes that my older sisters and brothers took.

*[Page 87]*

I heard the word "school" a long time before I went to it. We heard our parents repeat, "A school will be opened for the children. The children will begin to attend school." I waited impatiently for that day although I did not understand what it meant. Finally, that happy day came. We washed up and dressed in our finest clothes. Our parents took us to school for the first time.

The new school was a big incomplete building of red brick, built in 1913 and meant to serve as the town's hospital. The Jewish study halls were burnt in World War I, and the new hospital building served for a long time as a study hall. After the war, when the Zionist movement in Poland had begun to grow roots in the Jewish cultural life of the big and small cities in Poland, the local Zionist leaders in Antopol got the idea to turn the former hospital and study hall into a modern Tarbut school. It was as if the building was created for that purpose.

It was separated from the gray, poor Jewish town on four sides by a wide meadow surrounded by fields. At first sight, the school became part of us.

In the beginning months of the first school year, the lectures frequently took place outside the school building and often consisted of games and songs on the green meadow.

In the winter months of the first school year, the lectures were given inside in the unfinished rooms which had no doors nor windows nor floor. We sat on simple unpainted benches.

Our first teacher, Zaretski, a young tall red-haired Jewish pupil of one of the newly established Tarbut teacher schools in Poland was a great authority for us. He was always happy and in a good mood. He taught us the first pioneering song, "We immigrate to Palestine with song," "The shepherds have gathered around the fire," "God rebuild Galilee." And many other songs. At the end of the first school year, Zaretski left us to continue his studies. His place was taken by the woman teacher Fayanes, a daughter of a Bialostok rabbi, who had finished a Hebrew gymnasium in one of the Polish cities. She stayed a year in the Tarbut school with us. She taught us to read and write, also Pentateuch and to declaim the poems of Bialik and Tshernihovski. However, she left after one year to continue her studies. Later, she lived in Rehovot in Israel and had a high post in the Ministry of Education and Culture.

Our third teacher, the founder of the Antopol school, was Yisrael Lifshits, a native of Antopol. Yisrael Lifsits (Lif) later lived in Montreal, Canada, and became a well-known pedagogue and author. While he was our teacher, the school was finally finished. The rooms were furnished with tables, school benches, and chalkboards, and the walls were decorated with pictures.

Teacher Lifsits also established the first parent-teachers association, and with its help worked out a program of school studies. He also became associated with the General Bureau of Education in Poland, which at that time was in its infancy. Lifsits directed the school according to the instructions from the Bureau of Education and from the parent-teachers association. He also began to teach me regularly four to five hours a day. The language of instruction in all subjects was Hebrew. We learned the following subjects: Hebrew, Bible, general and Jewish history, geography, natural sciences, Polish, music, and arts and crafts.

The teaching personnel began to increase with the arrival of Feldman and Serbin. Feldman was a great enthusiast of the modern Tarbut school and was devoted to Hebrew language instruction and pioneering Zionist thought. He threw himself into the work with great devotion, and so the teaching in school became more interesting daily.

*[Page 88]*

Serkin, a woman teacher of Polish, was a great devotee of Polish literature and taught us first the poems of Maria Kanopnitska, Mitkiewicz, and Slavatski. She also began to read with us the Yiddish stories of Eliza Arzeshkava and even Proust.

It was then that a library was established in Antopol, which in the beginning consisted of books on Enlightenment literature: Mapu and Smolenski and from our poets Bialik, Tshernihovski, and Kahan, as well as the works by Feierberg, Frishman, and others. Later, there were translations from world literature: Anderson, Jules Verne, and Dickens. There were also Polish language books. Although I was then 12 or 13 years old. I had already enthusiastically read "Ahavat Tsiyon" ("Love of Zion") and "Ashmat Shomron" ("Guilt of Samaria") by Mapu and "ha-Toeh be-darkhe ha-hayyim" ("The Wanderer in Life") by Smolenski and the interesting stories of Feierberg and as well as the fantastic translations of Jules Verne and even Sinkiewicz's novel, "Be-esh uve-herev" ("By Fire and Sword"), which I then understood in a childish fashion. I also became an accomplished student of Polish literature.

The Jewish holidays were a special enticement for us children. A celebration was held in school for each holiday. All of us, pupils and teachers, prepared carefully for such a celebration. The school building was decorated with our national blue and white flags, with real flowers and branches in the summer holiday months, and with artificial ones in the winter.

We pupils used to give speeches about the national and religious character of each holiday and also about the meaning of the holiday during the period of our ancestors in the land of Israel, who were farmers, and we tied each holiday to nature.

We also became actors in dramatic productions. On Hanukkah, we changed into small Maccabees, who courageously fought the cruel Greeks. On Purim, we took part in a Purim play, which showed the history of "The Scroll of Esther." On Passover, we showed the history of the Exodus from Egypt, fleeing slavery for freedom. On Pentecost, the happy spring holiday, we made outings to the nearby fields, plucked flowers, wove wreaths, and decorated school and home with grasses, greens, flowers, and branches. Acting out these holidays in our imagination returned us to the time when the Jews lived peacefully on their own land, celebrated their holidays, and bravely fought for their freedom.

The first core of the organization ha-Shomer ha-tsair was founded in our school. In our free time, we gathered to hear lectures about the development of the land of Israel. We would sing pioneering songs and dance the horah, and in the hearts of each of us there developed a deep desire to leave the Diaspora and immigrate to Israel where our ancestors had lived, as we learned in the splendid stories of the Bible.

In the beginning, we were an all girls' school. The boys in the town still spent day and night in the confines of the Jewish elementary school, studying from early morning until late at night with a rabbi who had a whip in his hand and lectured about the Talmudic scholars Abaye and Raba.

The first boy attended our school in 1923. He was my brother. My parents had decided to take him our of the Jewish elementary school and put him into a school with a broader perspective.

The second boy was the son of one of our woman teachers. Slowly the old-fashioned Jewish elementary school began to empty itself of students. The boys in town became pupils of the Tarbut school.

In 1924 came the end of my happy life in Antopol and my studies in the Tarbut school. My parents decided to leave town and move to Vilna. With a heavy heart, we said good-bye to my dear, loving teacher and my first classmates in school, to whom I was devoted. In the evening at the going away party, which was arranged for my brothers and me, we received as a gift a volume of selected poems of Saul Tsherniehovski, beautiful in blue binding with gold letters. This book of splendid poems was for many years a symbol of our first happy, carefree childhood years.

*[Page 89]*

# Aharon Lifshits, the Hebrew Teacher
## By Shemuel Lifshits

One of the first modern teachers in Antopol was Aharon Lifshits. Aharon was a capable young man who had been to Ruzshinai to study with R. Binyamin'en, in the Razshinayer rabbinical seminary. He also had a pleasant voice and studied with the cantor of Rozshin, Zisel Rosata.

When Aharon returned to Antopol, he brought back with him a good grasp of knowledge in Russian and Hebrew.

In the early twentieth century when the movement to improve elementary schools spread over Russia, Aharon opened in 1900 an "improved elementary school' in Antopol. He took as a partner Joseph Liberman from Pinsk. His improved school consisted of two rooms with special benches and tables for the pupils. Aharon taught Talmud in Russian, and Leberman taught Bible in Hebrew. Hebrew was studied from modern booklets, such as "Bet-Sefer Ivri" ("Hebrew Book") from Rozovskin and "Moreh ha-signon" ("Teacher of Style") from Tawiow. With Aharon, people also learned Jewish history, "Divre ha-yamim li-vene Yisrael" ("History of the Children of Israel") by Ben-Yehudah and Lerner's "Moreh ha-lashon" ("Teacher of Language").

Aharon also taught his pupils to sing. He organized a choir and prayed on New Year's in the brick study hall and on the Day of Atonement in the synagogue. He kept up his improved elementary school for several years until younger teachers came and also opened a similar elementary school. Then Aharon immigrated to America where he continued his profession. He also became a ritual slaughterer and a cantor in different synagogues.

Around 1912, two young men of Antopol went into business together. They were the bakers Yisrael Badanes and Shelomoh-ke Menahem. They opened an "improved elementary school" for beginners according to the system of learning Hebrew in Hebrew and taught in a modern way, boys and girls together. I studied with them for my first three semesters. The school existed until the German occupation.

Because it was a financial success, other teachers began to open "improved elementary schools" in Antopol. One of them was Nahum the teacher (Berl Leyb, the cutler's son). His class was in his father's house. In his class, people studied with the same method as with the teacher Yisrael Badanes. There was still another teacher, Leybush. His class was in a big room in the house of Binyamin, the Talmud professor.

In addition to the "improved elementary schools," private lectures were also given in homes and in the elementary schools. These were to teach the children to write Yiddish and Hebrew and to do mathematics. One of the teachers was Shelomoh-ke Menahem's, a good Hebraist and a Zionist and also an activist taking part in each of the town's public affairs.

And who does not remember Alter Sholem, the ritual slaughterer? He was a teacher in the elementary schools and gave lessons in private houses. He was a teacher in 1915 in the public school, which was in the village Torekan, and went to America after the war.

In addition to male teachers, female teachers and writers also lived in Antopol. One was Tybe Frume. In her house on Kobrin Street, she taught a class for girls and also gave private lessons. After World War I, she went to America to live with her husband, Rozenfeld, in Miami.

*[Page 90]*

# Political, Social, Economic, and Fashion of Life

## Political Movements in Antopol

### By Dr. Meir Kletski

The beginning of the 20th century brought great innovations that dramatically changed the life of the Jewish population in Antopol. Before then everything was relatively static, even monotonous. The establishment controlled individual and social life. For example, Avigdor the town elder, with the help of a few cronies used to decide how to have the population legally relate to the outside world, that is the Czarist government. The "Gages" and the "Tshaplies" decided the religious and spiritual life, the relationship of the population to the rabbis. The young generation learned only to obey and to submit to the elders, the establishment. Cultural education consisted primarily in learning Yiddish and Hebrew. The young boys used to get their cultural education in the elementary school, and the girls got theirs at home.

The beginning of the end to this order came at the turn of the 20th century. A revolutionary movement initiated in Russia greatly influenced developments in Antopol. It brought great changes in the private and social life of the entire population, especially the youth. The fresh winds that blew over all Russia, reached the smallest towns, including Antopol.

People began to wake up from their lethargic sleep. The Russian revolution had begun! Jewish youth and Christian youth began to protest not only against the Czar and the bureaucrats but also against the old leadership and its restrictions which lay like a stone on the life of the population. In Antopol, this led to the formation of two major parties, which were to play an important role in Antopol: the Bund, which had a membership of around 150, and the Socialist Zionists (S.S.), which had a membership of about 100.

Young people were swept away by the revolutionary socialist movement. There were also in Antopol some individual members or sympathizers of political parties other than these two. For example, Fradel Stavski belonged to the Socialist Revolutionaries, and the Novigrudskis belonged to the left wind of the Social Democratic Party. However, these individuals used to cooperate with the town's Socialist Zionists or with the members of the Bund because these two parties were better organized.

The initiators of the movement in Antopol, as was the case in all the other small towns, were those young men who, in order to work, took the opportunity to tear themselves away from the sleepy town and travel to the cities.

There they came into contact with other workers. They became real proletarians infected with revolutionary ideals. They worked in the big cities throughout the year; however, on holidays, they bought a new suit of clothes and came home to Antopol. In the home town, they would meet with their old friends and would advise them to follow their example and move to the cities where everything was alive, in motion, to get work there, train for an occupation, or even study a trade in Antopol and become self-employed. At the same time, they told their friends how interesting life was in the cities, that there were organizations like the Bund, the S.S., and other parties that were struggling for a better, more beautiful world, for freedom and justice for the Russian population in general and especially for the Jews. I remember among these agitators only the names of Noske, Yitshak Leyb's (), who were among the first pioneers of the Bund and Nathan David Velvel's (Glatser) and Leyzer Farber, who helped organize the S.S. They influenced me to become a member of the S.S. Among names of those I remember as important activists in the S.S. there were: Eliyahu Klarfeyn, Akiva Sirota (the son of Avigdor, the town elder), Shaul Volfson, Perets Hurvits, Feytel Berman (R. Moshe's son), Yisrael Volovolski, and a few others. We were the leaders of the S.S. movement in Antopol.

*[Page 91]*

As soon as the party was organized, we began a strong cultural movement among the youth in Antopol. We used to gather in different homes where we would give lectures to members. They would study the theory of the S.S. in Yiddish and in Russian. We would get different proclamations, brochures, and books from the big cities, like Pinsk, and the like. We would read the works of Kautsky, Bebel, Liebknecht, also literature composed about the S.S.

In the evenings or on Sabbath afternoons or during the holidays, we used to go the Birzshe, which was on Kobrin Street. Boys and girls, intellectuals and simple workers, proletarians and idle people used to go together. We wanted to show the older people that every person is equal, that there is no difference between poor and rich, educated and ignorant. But those who were not educated enough, we taught politics so that they would be aware.

We used to go altogether to the Birzshe. The members of the S.S. would be on one side of the street and the members of the Bund on the other side. Often our group confronted theirs, which led to hot debates about the two opposing parties. The Bundists claimed that we were not revolutionary enough, that we were not capable of leading a class struggle because we did not have enough proletarians among our members.

These discussions often became heated and led to fist fights between members of the two groups. However, the two parties would unite and cooperate when it was necessary to face the police or an enemy, as in the case of pogromists, and so forth. The following is an example.

An important fair was going to take place in Antopol. A short time before the fair we heard rumors that reactionary ignorant peasants would come to the fair to make a blood bath against the Jews. Therefore, we had to prepare for that day. Feeling that our own forces would not be sufficient against so many pogromists, we asked the help of the self-defense organizations from the surrounding cities. Horodets announced it would send several "boys." And Kobrin sent a large group, about 30 people.

The day before the fair, we called an assembly in the old study hall. To this assembly came also simple Jews, Jews with beards and side curls. Among them were healthy people, strong Jews who could strike back if need be. Among them was also the short physically weak Shemuel, the scribe, who was ready to defend his brethren. To defend ourselves we all joined together. The day of the fair all the young men, like welldisciplined soldiers, marched in the streets, mainly at the market, many with revolvers, with lances, and the like. The police also walked around and watched. They took good notice of us but didn't bother us. The day passed calmly and no one caused any trouble. Everyone was pleased.

Taking advantage of such a rare opportunity of having so many people from Kobrin and other cities come together, both political parties, the Bund and the S.S., decided to hold a general mass meeting at which we could discuss the various theories of the parties, sort of a symposium. We assigned the speakers who would represent the two parties. The writer of these lines was supposed to represent the S.S. and one of the Kobrin Bundists had to speak for the Bund. We all gathered in a room around eight o'clock at night. The room was at the end of town. We were about 200 people, boys and girls. We sent several young people into the main streets to watch for police. Everything went well, for a short time. The Kobrin Bundist began his speech, bringing out the importance of the Bund and the role which it plays in Jewish life. All paid attention. The mood was upbeat. Suddenly, however, the mood changed to confusion and fear. A young man, obviously upset, ran in and shouted, "Police!"

Instantly there was panic. Many of the gathered began to jump out windows to flee, but only a few succeeded. The rest were forced to return because the police had stationed themselves around the windows and doors and didn't let anyone leave. We all put away our weapons and waited quietly but with great trepidation to see what would happen. We heard a knock at the door. The young man guarding the door opened it. The first person to come in was the Chief of Police.

*[Page 92]*

After him came police officers of various rank, about 10 men altogether. Everyone turned to look at the Chief of Police to see if he looked mean and severe. We saw that he looked friendly. We even noticed a smile on his face. He went over to our representative and immediately calmed him, saying that the police had not come to arrest us, only to talk to us. He wanted to know the reason so many people had come from the surrounding cities to Antopol. Our representative from Kobrin told him the following:

"As is known, pogroms had happened against the Jews in various cities. We heard the rumors that some peasants had decided to attack Jewish storekeepers and rob them. We came here mainly for the purpose of calming the storekeepers and to show them how a pogrom can be avoided. If, for example, a drunken peasant wanted something from a storekeeper and did not pay, the storekeeper should not pay too much attention to that. A small fight could lead to the spilling of blood, which must be avoided at any price."

The young man ended his comments by expressing the hope that in Antopol nothing bad would happen as it did in other unfortunate cities. The Chief of Police accepted what he heard. He assured the speaker that as long as he was Chief of Police in Antopol no pogrom would happen here. He asked us all to go home and told the youth from Horodets and Kobrin to leave as soon as possible. We disbanded with quiet satisfaction.

We organized youth of Antopol considered our encounter with the police a great victory. We felt that we could breathe easier, that we could meet again with more assurance. However, we became overconfident, foolhardy, and needlessly provocative, and this led the mild-mannered Chief of Police to crack down on us. For example, the police arrested of some of our most important activists, including Fradel Stavskin.

My participation in the S.S. Party ended when I left Antopol in 1907. It is probable that the activity of other members ended about the same time.

# The Awakening Revolution: Zionism in Antopol
## By E. Tsaytelzon

The establishment of a homeland, the redemption of the Land of Israel, had always been a Jewish dream. Along with numerous other towns, Antopol participated in the movement toward this goal. For example when the Lovers of Zion association was founded, people began to set out plates in the study halls for donations on the day before the Day of Atonement.

In 1887, 10 rubles were collected in Antopol. That was a lot of money in those days. Among the activists were Shemuel Pisatski (the future Shemuel the scribe) and Yosef Grinberg. The money collected rose to 30 rubles in 1890. And it appears that the Jews of Antopol did not just give token donations. Some of them were also members of the Lovers of Zion organization.

Unfortunately, this reawakening did not last long for new winds began to blow, spring winds, which also came to Antopol. New movements arose to free Russia of Czarism. These movements took hold of our youth in Antopol, and the movement to free the Jewish people cooled. However, the chill did not last long. Deep in their hearts glowed sparks, which rose up again after the great disappointment which our brethren suffered in Russia. Zionists in Antopol again began their holy work such as buying shekels to give as donations, collecting money for the Jewish National Fund, and setting out plates for collections in study halls on the day before the Day of Atonement. Some not only helped collect money but immigrated to the Land of Israel to renew it and themselves.

*[Page 93]*

Not a large amount of money was collected in 1903, a total of 13 rubles and 60 kopeks. However, the collection proved that Zionism was still alive. In 1911, the sum rose substantially: 47 rubles and 90 kopeks were collected on the day before the Day of Atonement. It is noteworthy that in 1913, despite a year of bloody oppression in Kiev, the plates in Antopol on the day before the Day of Atonement collected 22 rubles and 19 kopeks!

The activists helping with that collection were Menahem Rubashevski, Berish the lease holder's son, Shelomeh-ke Menahem's, Hillel Kletski, and Yoel Leyb the mason. They sowed the seeds of the future immigration to the Land of Israel movement.

# Revolutionary Movement
## By Aryeh Shkolnik

In 1905, when the revolutionary movement spread throughout all Russia, our small town of Antopol was very much involved. The entire youth, as well as a number of workers, overnight as if by magic developed revolutionary awareness. They called out, "Czar Nikolai, down with him." From time to time, they brought in orators from Kobrin and Brisk and held secret meetings.

One of these meetings was held on a wintry Friday night in the old study hall way up in the women's section. Early on Sabbath morning, the women came to pray and saw the mess the socialists had made. They found cigarette butts, matches, extinguished lamps, and the like. The women were furious and with excited voices cried down to the men's section, "Come see what the heretics have done. God knows what troubles these rejects will bring down on us!"

And still later, during prayers, the commotion increased when Falk, Shemuel Tevye's son, acting under the influence of the previous night's speakers protested the blessing of the Czar. When the cantor started to give the blessing on behalf of the Czar, "who gives salvation," Falk banged a table, mounted the platform, and declared, "I don't want to have the blessing who blessed' said on behalf of Nikolai! Czar Nikolai. Down with him!" There was much tumult and shouting. Angry Jews pounded on the youth and struggled to throw him out of the study hall. However, Avigdor the town elder shouted, "Jews, stop! Let us not bring troubles on ourselves!"

# Women Revolutionaries
## By Mosheh Setavi

Fradel Stavski, the daughter of Efrayim and Bashke who were among the most respected people in Antopol, became a social revolutionary. She wanted immediately to overthrow the Czar and establish a socialist regime in Russia.

The authorities in Kobrin knew about her and sought her arrest. Fortunately, her uncle Misha Stavski was in Antopol. He put her in a sled, covered her up, and took her to Drohitshin. From there Fradel was sent to Krementshug where her grandfather R. Yaakow Shemuel lived. From Krementshug, she went with her father to Yekaternislav. However, she remained active as a young revolutionary. In 1910, she took part in an attack in Yekaternislaw Province. She was caught and sent to prison in Siberia.

Fradel was not freed until 1917, when the Russian Revolution broke out. She left for Moscow, married Mosheh Barotshenko from Bessarabia, and became employed by the town's main library.

Fradel's youngest brother, Gershon, who was in America, kept in contact with his sister until 1939. From then on, he heard nothing from her. Is she still alive? Is her son alive? Where is her husband?

Such was the fate of one female revolutionary in Russia.

*[Page 94]*

Another was Yehudit Feldshtein. For her revolutionary efforts on behalf of the Russian Social Democratic Party, she was sent to prison in Siberia in 1895. There she became sick with tuberculosis and was sent back home.

She resumed her revolutionary efforts and printed literature on a press which she kept hidden in the attic. In 1920, the Poles found some of her pamphlets and accused her brother of belonging to an enemy political party. He was arrested and served time in Kobrin. Finally, he was freed on parole.

## Medical Help and Medical Institutions
## By Prof. P. Czerniak

Before 1850, no doctor lived in Antopol, and medical help was in the hands of "grandmothers," sorcerers, good Jews, rabbis, those who charmed, and those who simply thought they knew how to doctor. At that time, diagnosis was simple: 1) sicknesses with fever, 2) stomach pain, 3) wounds, 4) broken joints and bones, and 5) craziness.

With a mentally ill person, a paralyzed person, the deaf and dumb, hysteria and the like, people would go to a good Jew, a rabbi, or a charmer who would say a good word or pray that the trouble would go away.

Fever, stomach pain, and other internal sicknesses people used to heal with the help of popular grasses like chamomile, linden, nettles, and the like. To warm a person, sacks of sand were used. To cool a person, pieces of ice. Wounds, blisters, and bleeding were treated with cobwebs, pellets of dough with honey, grated potatoes, roasted onions, rolls with milk, and other similar means.

Special customs were observed for pregnant women. At the end of the pregnancy, they put a salt-filled amulet into a pocket. After the birth of the baby, the child and mother had to be protected from demons and evil spirits until the circumcision took place. They placed the Songs of Ascent from Psalms on the bed. After the afternoon service, they would come to the child's room to read the Hear, O, Israel prayer. The children and their teacher who came were given cooked peas. The ritual circumciser used a powder which he made from rotting pine wood to cover the wound after doing the circumcision.

Among the White Russian population in the 19th Century, there was a well-known gentile from Tshernovits who fixed joint and bone breaks. Aryeh Yozefs (Osipovits) also used to practice as a doctor. He charmed away the "evil eye."

Organized in Antopol from the earliest times were societies for social relief such as Visiting the Sick and the Almshouse. Money was collected in specific boxes. The treasurers distributed the equipment such as bleeding cups, leeches, and the like. They also took care of night sessions and service to the sick, giving them drinks, massages, etc.

In the years 1850 or 1860, Moshe the "doctor" began practicing. His medical knowledge was developed in the Russian Army, where he worked as a practical nurse in a military hospital. When he returned from military service, he married, settled with his wife on Kotlior Street, and became the father of two daughters and a son.

Moshe the doctor wrote prescriptions but mainly distributed to his patients medicines that consisted of castor oil, quinine, and different herbs. When he examined a sick person, he first took the pulse, examined the throat with the help of a spoon, wrote the prescription, and was paid a fee of 10 or 15 kopecks. He also pulled rotten teeth.

Around 1875, Yenkel the doctor arrived and was in competition for patients with Moshe. He was an orphan and had studied in an Antopol rabbinical seminary. When he was called to military service, his teacher collected around town a sum of money, a bribe, to ensure that Yenkel would be placed in a military hospital where he would learn something about medicine. Bribing whomever could help paid off, and after several years' service in medical institutions of the Tsarist Army, Yenkel received his training as an assistant surgeon. After his return to Antopol he married the sister of Aryeh and Falk Tsherniak, began his medical career, and took his seat among the synagogue treasurers. He was a smart Jew, an earnest person, and strong willed as well. At his hand, wild boys suffered hefty blows.

*[Page 95]*

A cholera epidemic broke out in Antopol in 1895. Moshe and Yenkel the doctors mobilized practical nurses and the Almshouse and Visiting the Sick Societies. All worked hard to fight the severe epidemic, which cost many deaths. The medical treatment consisted of giving patients whiskey to drink and rubbing their feet.

Yenkel the doctor didn't talk much. He was either deep in thought or worn out. He smiled only at the naive questions asked by Jewish mothers. In serious cases, he didn't want to accept the responsibility himself and consulted a real doctor such as Dr. Saratshinski or Dr. Veynshteyn in Antopol, Dr. Prabulski in Kobrin, Dr. Pines (eye doctor) in Bialystok, and Dr. Yevsienko (surgery) in Pinsk. In 1915, Yenkel left Antopol with other war refugees and did not return until 1918.

I remember when I finished the gymnasium in 1930 and decided to go to France to continue my studies. R. Avigdor the town elder, of blessed memory, found out and went to my mother, of blessed memory, rebuking her that she would let me live among gentiles. She asked friends and her brother-in-law Yenkel for advice. He made a quick decision: "Let him go!" Later, in 1932-33, when I came home for summer vacation and went to visit Uncle Yenkel the doctor, he quizzed me at length about my studies, what up-to-date knowledge there was about internal organs and the head.

"Only listen," he would tell me. "I envy the knowledge you are studying and acquiring." He had such a love of science.

After 62 years of medical work in Antopol, Yenkel the doctor died in 1937 of a heart attack at the ripe old age of 80 and some years.

During the same period, from the end of the 19th Century until the beginning of the 20th Century, several women practiced medicine in town. Especially known was Ester-Hayah the grandmother. She was a short strongly built Jewish woman who lived in town from 1860 to 1914 and had a hundred "grandchildren" at whose birth she assisted. She made the necessary preparations and looked after the women giving birth. She would walk with the woman in labor and say in jest, "Come, I will go with you even to the attic." Everyone knew where she lived because almost all the women giving birth came to her for help. Early on she lived in an apartment as a neighbor of Mordekhai Sheynboym. Later she bought a house from Naftali Volinets. She died in 1914, at the beginning of World War I, at the age of 80.

Another "grandmother" at that time was Grandmother Bashe Yente who lived on Kobrin Street. She was almost everyone's beloved "grandmother," and in gratitude, people sent her gifts of food on Purim.

In 1905-06, a diploma-holding midwife, Manye Gershtein, lived in Antopol. She was born in Smorgan in Vilna Province. She married an Antopol youth, Berel Gershtein from the Lifshitses.

Another "grandmother" was Itke the midwife who lived as a neighbor of Bendet the kettle maker. She was a thin sympathetic girl who quickly made a name for herself. She became quite popular in 1908 after struggling with a difficult birth. Although the local Dr. Saratskinski and Dr. Gershuni from Kobrin were present at first, they both gave up and left. Itke remained alone and after great effort delivered the child. Both the baby and the mother survived. In 1923, Itke married Shelomoh Podolevski of Horodets, and in 1928 they immigrated to America.

At the same time, Avraham Volf 's daughter practiced as a midwife. She studied the profession in Brisk and began to practice in the village Derevnaye. However, in 1915-18, hungry peasants used to attack and rob. Then she went to Antopol and was very much loved there. In 1925, she went to Pinsk where she continued working in her profession.

*[Page 96]*

The list of women specialists would not be complete without Esther-Rahel Garfinel (the Getekhe), who had an office in the homes of Zaydl Bratsken and Zalman Kuilbe. Her patients also included gentiles. For that reason, she was called the gentile assistant surgeon. She applied cups for drawing blood, cups that were especially shaped for this purpose. Her office overflowed every Sunday. She died in 1914 after many years of practice.

The epoch of assistant surgeons and grandmothers ended in 1905 when the town got its first doctor with a diploma, the Pole Saratshinski. He had a wife and a daughter named Zosya. No one knew where he came from. People say that he came from Pruzshen and that his wife belonged to the Polish nobility in Warsaw. He had a reputation as a friend of the Jews, and even learned to speak Yiddish. He made calls at the homes of the Jewish sick, driving his carriage led by two red and white horses. He visited the poor free of charge and even gave them money to buy medicine. Saratsinski fled from Antopol in 1914.

In the years 1910-1912, when Saratsinski was still in Antopol, the established people in Antopol began to be more concerned with medical problems. The synagogue treasurers would halt the reading of the Torah on the Sabbath and agitate to build a city hospital. The work was then begun. First Dr. Shats was brought in 1910 and the walls of the hospital were built on a pretty site not far from the naphtha reserves. When World War I broke out, Dr. Shats left Antopol so the idea of operating a city hospital went unfulfilled. The building was then used as a study hall as the old study hall had burned down. Later, in 1919-1920, the building became the Tarbut school for Jewish children of Antopol.

During the harsh war years, 1914-1918, when Dr. Saratsinski, Dr. Shats, and Yenkel the doctor were away, a student of medicine Lipa Zagorodski from the Lifshits family, Itsel Burshteyn, Yudel the writer's son-in-law, also a student, the assistant surgeon Yenkel, who was not a student, and another assistant surgeon Yenkel, who used to say "no harm will come," were responsible for medical help in Antopol.

Yenkel, who said "no harm would come," examined the sick in this fashion. First he would take the pulse. Then he would put his wood and paper tube on the chest and listen. Third he would put a spoon down the throat and say, "God will help, it will be good, you will get through, no harm will come." Accordingly, he was called "Yenkel, who says no harm will come."

In the later period of the Russian Revolution and afterwards in the time when one regime followed another, many doctors passed through Antopol, mostly army doctors. These doctors distributed medical help to the population of Antopol and its surrounding region. People say that in 1918 a young Jewish doctor came to town with the Russian Army. He would visit every home to which he was called, not charge a fee, and distribute free medicine such as castor oil, aspirin, and quinine. He liked to receive white meal from which he used to bake pastille cakes in Turiansky's and distribute them to the soldiers.

A tall Russian doctor, who was a narcotic, also practiced for a short time. He didn't like the place and left in 1919. When the war was over, Dr. Weinstein with his wife the mid-wife and their son, a student in the gymnasium, arrived in 1925 from Lithuanian. He worked hard and helped the sick, especially those suffering from tuberculosis, who were quite numerous. But one morning, Dr. Weinstein committed suicide while shaving, cutting the arteries to his neck. His son, who had finished the gymnasium and had begun to study medicine in Vilna, was too young to take over his father's position. Therefore, Mrs. Weinstein brought Dr. Narkin from Pinsk.

Dr. Narkin settled in a house on Pinsk St. and with great energy began his job. In a short time, he became popular among both the Jewish and Christian population in the surrounding villages. He was devoted to his patients and always wanted to know if the medicines he prescribed worked. He made follow-up visits, and his patients liked that. He also used to take care that plums and almonds should be put away and not cause angina. His brother who was a medical specialist in Pinsk visited town from time to time. Dr. Narkin was responsible for the direction of the Insurance Fund for workers and office employees. When it came to small sicknesses, people used to visit Yenekl the "doctor," who had come back to Antopol in 1918.

*[Page 97]*

In those years, the Christian assistant surgeon Tshernik settled in H. Kulik's house at the end of Pinsk St. and treated patients. He made himself out to be quite important, saying that he read medical journals and healed his sick patients with progressive methods. When he did not succeed in healing the sick person, he would send to Pinsk or Warsaw for advice, arguing that doctors in the close-by cities did not know any more than he did.

Before World War I, people went to Naftali the doctor in Horodets to treat their teeth. He had studied dental medicine a few months in Warsaw. When Naftali settled in Kobrin and Vitkin came to Horodets, people went to Vitkin who had a diploma in dentistry. Such was the situation until World War I when Vitkin left Horodets.

Dr. Shagan, who settled in Antopol in 1927, practiced dentistry. In case he had to remove decayed teeth, which took manual strength, he tried to appear young and energetic so that the patients would trust him. For that reason, he dyed his gray moustache black and smiled at the young patients. Dr. Shagan paid close attention to cleanliness, and when a peasant did not wipe his boots immediately before sitting in the dentist's chair, he would get a lecture. Dr. Shagan was very strict when he treated decayed teeth and demanded his patient's attention. He knew his work well, and his fillings lasted many years.

As for medication, three sources existed. The first was from the assistant surgeons, who themselves prepared medicines from different grasses and who received prepared medicines from pharmaceutical companies for testing. and lastly from the Sick Insurance's pharmacy.

The second source was the pharmacy established by Lifshits in 1900 in Grinberg's house. The pharmacy was later run by the pharmacist Seletski. Later, in 1912, when a school to prepare students for entering the gymnasium opened in that house, the pharmacy moved to Mazurske's house. The pharmacist Neidits worked there.

The third source of medication was pharmaceutical stores operated under the Sick Insurance. The first was opened by Mosheh-Aharon Ozernitski in Sirota's house. After his death, the business was run by his wife, Henia. Later, Hershenhorn opened a second pharmacy store where he also made medicines.

Thus it happened that, in the 15 years after World War I, Antopol became a small medical center serving its own residents and the populations of the surrounding area. Working in Antopol were a doctor with a diploma, two good assistant surgeons, several nurses (among them the woman Visotski), a mid-wife with a diploma and several "grandmothers," a doctor of dental medicine, a pharmacy and several pharmaceutical stores, and later also a doctor of veterinary medicine who settled in Gurin's orchard.

In the 1930s, the chances to get medical help improved in Antopol because four Antopol youth studied medical science. As one of them, I had finished my studies in 1936 in France and returned to town. The French diploma did not give me the right to practice medicine. To do so, I had to pass certification in Vilna. Afterwards, after working a year in a hospital in Brisk, I opened an office in Antopol.

At the same time, Rafael, the son of Dr. Veinshtein, continued his medical studies. Also studying medicine were Dr. Shagan's son Joseph and Avraham, of the Pinsk landowners, who went to study in France. They all showed signs of being good doctors.

*[Page 98]*

However, war broke out on September 1, 1939, and events were to develop in another direction. Studies were temporarily broken off. I received an order from the Polish government to establish in Antopol four centers for first aid for wounded soldiers. On the fourth day of the war, a large battle took place in Kobrin at Lake Mukhovets. The first wounded were brought from there to us in ambulances. It did not take long, and the Russian Army marched in.

When the Russian government took over, medical help was given to the populace free of charge. A polyclinic was established in Lifshits' big house. Private medical offices were closed in the course of time. In Yankevitses' house, which was at the end of the Kobrin farmland, a hospital was opened.

However, two more wooden houses were moved and set up in one place for the purpose of giving Antopol its first hospital of 60 beds. The hospital had divisions for inner diseases, childbirth, and infectious diseases. Surgical centers were opened in the three nearby villages. The medical personnel in Antopol changed. Dr. Narkin returned to Pinsk. Yenkel the doctor died. Two other doctors came from Minsk as well as a sanitary inspector, several assistant surgeons, and a registered nurse. An administrative authority was created, and I took the post of director of the hospital and polyclinic.

A new war started in 1941, and to our great misfortune the German murderers entered. Everything was destroyed. They did not have to take care of the health of the population. On the contrary, their solution was to kill everyone. The Russian doctors fled. I, together with Dr. Zonshein of Brisk who was in Antopol as a refugee, were imprisoned in the ghetto. Rafa Veinshtein and Yosef Shagas did not have the chance to finish their medical studies in Vilna and were imprisoned in the ghetto.

In the last orgy of killing, all the medical workers in the ghetto were murdered. They were: the young, almost handsome Dr. Veinshtein, Dr. Shagas, the mid-wife Veinshtein, the pharmacists Neidits and Ozernitske, the registered nurse Visotski. The medical centers in the villages were closed. I together with my wife, Gitel (Feldshtein), fled and went underground with the partisans and until July 1944 were in the forests and marshes of the Antopol region.

The Russians took Antopol back on July 22. I again got the task of organizing medical help in the Antopol region. However, unfortunately, whom was I to help? Antopol remained without Jews. Here I go among the ruins, and I see no Jewish faces. I don't have any more Jewish patients to help. All those who were alive three years ago, struggled, created, and grew did not exist anymore. I was writing prescriptions for those who were happy when my brothers and sisters were murdered. However, as a doctor, I could not but help them. I only had to see them as sick people. I left Antopol, no longer a Jewish town, in 1945. Strangers took over. I learned in 1962 that only one Jewish family lived in Antopol. The marketplace was empty. Trees grew there. However, the hospital had grown and had a surgical division. The outpatient service functioned as before. Antopol became a typical White Russian Soviet town. And for the Jewish Antopol, let us say, May He (God) be extolled and sanctified.

# Photographs

**Yeshiva Students from Antopol**

**At the mass grave, Soviet government officials and delegates of the survivors honor the martyrs.**

**A Jew, wrapped in Talit and Tefilin,
says Kaddish after the first martyrs.**

**A Landmark in Antopol**

**Yudel der Schreiber, one of Antopol's earliest educators**

**At the Cemetery**

**Amongst silent friends**

**Sara Zunszajn**

**An ensemble during the German occupdation, 1916,
Is led by Eliah Gvirtsman and sons.**

**Private girls school is headed by the teacher Teibe Shagan (Frume).**

**Geese traders Hershil and Tzajtl Shterman**

**Ida Wolinetz**

**The Hehalutz in Antopol**
*Farewell to member Hayyim Osipovits who was making aliya*

**Haim Asif on a Sport's Day in Antopol**

**Women partisans during the war...**

**Women partisans after the war**

**Talmud Torah Administration**

**The teacher Israel Wollowelsky and his class**

*[Page 108]*

# Hebrew Messages

## History of the Community
### By Akiva Ben-Ezra

Polesia is known for its swamps. It is between the Bug and Dnieper rivers. This region belongs to Russia. After the Riga peace agreement in 1921, Poland received the province of Grodno and parts of the province of Pinsk that belong to Polesia.

The swamps cover half the region. It is thanks to the swamps that the Swedes were halted before Pinsk (1706) led by

. Napoleon also had a hard time with the swamps in Polesia (1012). The Germans were halted there in 1915.

Between the swamps and sand there were forests of pine and small streams. The fish in them of various kinds support a part of the population.

The forests of Polesia were once known for animals of prey, such as wolves, foxes, bears, and the like. Frequently, these animals attacked the surrounding settlements.

As the forests were cut back in the last hundreds of years, the number of animals of prey decreased which reduced the danger to the surrounding communities.

The population of Polesia is mainly composed of White Russians divided into two groups – those assimilated to Polish culture and those assimilated to Russian culture.

Likewise, Poles, Jews, Russians, Germans, Hungarians and gypsies dwell in Polesia. The Poles numbered 10 percent of the population and Polish princes once ruled the entire region.

The Jewish settlements until their destruction by the Nazis also made up 10 percent. They lived mainly in cities and towns and earned their living from commerce and crafts. A small number were farmers. Their cultural level was higher than that of the other inhabitants.

One of the branches of commerce in the region was forestry. The forests of Polesia were famous. Jews controlled this commerce. Jews owned the forests and hired gentiles to cut them and bring them on rafts to Germany.

Poland and Lithuania were united in 1569. The principality of Lithuania opened its doors to Polish culture and institutions, especially to the Catholic Church. The Church tried to make its influence decisive in all spheres of life and was very successful at that. The region slowly assimilated to Polish culture. Understandably, this angered the Cossacks and was expressed in the revolt in 1648. Farmers joined the Cossacks and together they plundered and killed for two years. Much Jewish blood was spilled before Poland defeated the Cossacks.

In the spring of 1706, the Swedes under their king Carl the 12th made war against Poland. The swamps of Polesia stopped them and Poland remained untouched until 1772, the year of the first partition of the country. Then, White Russia was taken over by Russia. After the war of 1793-1795, Russia got more provinces, among them Grodno. As mentioned above Napoleon invaded and also had a hard time with the swamps. The Poles attempted to revolt twice against the Russians, in 1830 and 1863.

These revolts caused the Jews great suffering at the hands of both sides.

The region was quiet about 100 years. However, during that time the Jews suffered at the hands of the Czars.

World War I had the Germans rule for a short time and exert a certain influence on the life and culture. After the passage of the Ukrainians and the Bolsheviks the Poles returned in March 1919. Peace came to the region in general. However, the Jews suffered persecution and bloodshed.

In July 1920, there broke out battles between the Poles and the Bolsheviks.

White Russians also took part in these battles under the leadership of the General Belakhovitsh on behalf of the Poles. However, the "Belakhovitses" also spilled much Jewish blood and wrote a sad chapter in the Jewish history of the region.

*[Page 109]*

The peace accord in Riga was signed in March 1921 between Poland and the Soviet Union. Poles ruled the region until 1939 – the start of World War II. Then, the Red Army came and conquered the region and ruled it until June 1941 – the outbreak of the German-Russian war. This is when the Germans conquered Poland and the Ukraine and even reached the gates of Leningrad and Moscow. What happened after the Nazi beasts of prey came and the bloody events is the topic of this memorial book.

# Antopol
## By Prof. P. Chernyak

## Physical Geography

It is one of 30 similar towns in Polesia, which has the greatest swamps in Europe. The region is 150 meters above sea level. The latitude is 52 degrees 11' north and the longitude is 24 degrees 42' from Greenwich. The town lies between Kobrin, Drohitsin, Radostov, Zaprod, not far from the big swamps spreading south, east and northeast. These swamps take up nearly 56 percent of the area of Polesia. Antopol, like other settlements takes up a small area. However, at its edge, especially at its east, there are many swamps.

## Hydrology

There is no river in Antopol. The Karolvski Canal, whose length is 79 kilometers and width 20-30 meters, and depth only 2-2 1/2 meters is about 10 kilometers distant from town. The Poles began to dig it before 1795. It was finished under the Russian Czars. In 1941/42, the Soviets deepened and widened it to make it more suitable for the many shipments by boat loaded with wheat to Nazi Germany in the direction of the Bug and Visla and to receive from it coal and metal ores in the direction of Zamokhvets, Pripets, and Dnieper. These were the times after the MolotovRibbentrop "dealt" under the sponsorship of Stalin-Hitler. In the winter of 1941/42 about 5000 prisoners from Asiatic Russia were brought to Antopol and under conditions dug to deepen the canal. They also built a military airfield nearby.

From the hydrological viewpoint the region in which Antopol is found belongs to the boundary of the area separating the Baltic Basin to which the Bug and Visla flow and also the Shatsrah-Nieman of the Black Sea Basin to which the Pripets Dnieper flow. There is a second canal called "Oginski", which joins the Shatsrah with the Yesioldah and the Pripets. This canal is smaller than the Karolvski. Its length is 50 km., width 12 meters. It was dug in the 18th century. According to this description, we see that the region of Antopol is an important hydrological area. Besides these two big canals, there were dug in the Polesia area canals for drying out that had an area of 2000 km. In 1935, Queen Bonah began building canals when she received Kobrin and its region from King Zigmont and began to bring to this region Mazorian colonists, who apparently reached only Grusheeva, about 3 km. from Antopol.

The Kralovski canal passes through Horodets – 8 km. from Antopol – and there is found the sluice and high bridge through which also passes the highway joining Pinsk to Brest through Antopol.

Ground water level is very high in Antopol. One only has to dig some meters in order to have a good well for drinking water. Many wells were dug in the courtyards of the town, especially in the years 1930-40, when cement pipes for wells began to be produced by Fodorovski of Antopol. Farmers in the entire region bought these pipes. Many people dug wells.

# Climate and Precipitation

The climate in Antopol and the region is influenced by the fact that the town lies in a closed area, low and swampy and wet, in a continent that stretches from the Ural to the Atlantic and between the Black Sea and the Baltic.

*[Page 110]*

We don't have in our possession climatic measurements from Antopol itself. Rather, we have data from Pinsk and Brest and there is no essential difference. Summer stretches from the end of May until the middle of September. The temperature is 17 degrees C. The highest temperature is in July and the first half of August. Winds blow in the summer from the west and northwest. It happens that there are strong storms with rain. However, most of the summer is without clouds. After hot days there is dense fog at night, which comes from the surrounding swamps and covers a thin layer on the dry ground.

The winter is severe and mostly cloud covered. It is accompanied by snow, which lasts for three months and water freezes, especially in the swamps, which serve as good roads. The lowest temperature is in the second half of January. Because the winter and summer are long, the spring is brief and lasts about two months. This is the time when the swamps spread and their area is the greatest around Passover. The winter sometimes has strong rains and the skies are mostly cloudy. The amount of rain is significant – coming to about 600 mm in a year.

# The Ground

From a geological point of view the ground is built of a layer of granite and above different layers of chalk and sand. In the diluvium period the region was all covered by immense glaciers, which came from the north. Because of the hills of granite above the banks of the Dnieper the glaciers could not advance and remained in place in the Polesian plate. After the glaciers melted, there remained swamps and rocks and soft ground. People think that there was a sea previously and that the glaciers partially filled it up. Much plant growth was in the swamps and wild regions were formed that take up about a third of the region. In other places there are layers of kaolin and there were even formed regions of "black earth".

People began drying the swamps in the 15-16th centuries. Then, there began the orderly working of the land for agriculture. In the 17-18th centuries the Cossacks and Haidameks destroyed huge regions and killed the inhabitants, and especially the Jews.

After the efforts of assimilation to Polish culture, there began under Elizabeth II and Nikolai I the assimilation to Russian culture, especially after the revolt of 1863, and the bringing in of agricultural workers to colonize.

However, most of the good land belonged to different princes. After World War II when the Soviets ruled in Antopol, there were set up two collective settlements: Pruvmayski (near to Frishikhvost) and Guberniah–south of Antopol.

# Plants

The plant world included wild plants, especially in the region of the swamps around Antopol. There was a lot of grass for grazing. Much land was forested, 25 to 32 percent (1926). The majority was pine, 65 percent of all the trees. There were berries to be harvested in the forests and the people of Antopol enjoyed them.

Agricultural plants included: oats, rye, wheat, barley, flax, potatoes, cabbage, garlic and sunflowers. In Antopol itself many regions were cultivated by gentile farmers and also by Jews owning plots of land. The Jews raised mainly vegetables (tomatoes, cucumbers, etc.). Farming methods were mainly primitive, especially in the villages. They used only natural manure. Agricultural cooperatives began to form in the years 1930/32, especially dairies. They began to bring in animal feed and better seeds.

# Animals

The animal world was very rich. The forests had bear, wolves, wild boar, antelope with big horns, beaver, hares, etc. These were widely hunted. The number of birds was not less rich. They were in the forests and swamps. There were 16 types of ducks, storks, pelicans, etc. The rivers and swamps had more than forty types of fish. There were also a lot of frogs (who at different times broke the quiet of the night with their croaking). There were snakes, ants, bees, mosquitoes, and small and bothersome flies, especially in the swamps.

*[Page 111]*

# Inhabitants

The number of inhabitants of Antopol was different at various times of development. In good times, the number went up to 3,000. However, epidemics, immigration, and murders took their toll and did not let the number of people grow. The majority of inhabitants were Jews. The rest included Polishoks (that is locals), White Russians, Russians and Poles.

The inhabitants lived in primitive houses (huts). They dressed in homespun cloth, until manufactures were imported from factories. They had a pale colored skin. They had long oval faces, a wide forehead, straight nose, and chestnut hair. They were quiet, spoke little and thoughtful. They were patient, conservative, not diligent, and despite the wealth of water were not clean. The adults sometimes would rest on the ovens. The children were serious and worked. The majority religion was the Pravoslav and represented in Antopol by the Orthodox Church. However, the farmers believed in all sorts of myths and there were many Baptist sects among them. They typically wore a straw hat. The Poles began to come in to the region in the 16th century. During various periods, they had a big or small amount of new immigrants. After World War I, there was a large amount of immigration to the area. Among those who came was the mailman Krominski, the hangman of Antopol Jewry.

# History of the First Jewish Settlement in Antopol
### By Mosheh Falk

The researcher and teacher R. Yeshayah Aharan Ozranitski, of blessed memory, devoted a great deal of his time to genealogical research about the history of our town. He would work day and night at his shelf of ancient books at home. He would glean many facts about early Antopol from them. I loved to read his writings and researches at that time. They would have been an important source in writing this book. Unfortunately, all the writings of R. Yeshayah Aharon, of blessed memory, were burnt in the big fire in our town of 1915. What I write now is from my memory of what he wrote.

In the year 5160, there was already a dense Jewish settlement in the region around which was built in the course of time the town of Antopol. In the year 5210 (1450), there broke out a serious plague suddenly in the Jewish settlement.

The nearest princely palace sent out an urgent command to destroy with fire the community and its inhabitants. The command was executed immediately and not one person escaped from the Jewish community.

There were only about twenty Jews outside the community on business, who survived. When they returned, they found only a pile of ashes and burnt bones. They immediately covered the ashes and bones in a layer of earth. At the end of the seven days of mourning, they erected for themselves a tent for communal living about a thousand cubits east of the cemetery. Afterwards, they raised the area of the cemetery by about two cubits of earth with the help of friendly Christians of the area, who helped them with their wagons to bring the earth as a cover and comforted them. Likewise, they planted a growth of trees to the number of those killed.

In the year 5280 (1520) the King Zigmund I passed and saw the pretty stand of trees that had grown up in the meantime. He halted to look at this pretty sight. Then, the local princes, who accompanied him, told him the story behind the trees. The king asked to see the brave Jews and their new settlement.

He was led to the Jewish houses. He was received with great honor in the study hall that was erected in the common dwelling tent. The king praised them for their bravery, their honest lives and friendly relations with their Christian neighbors and for their faith in God and man.

*[Page 112]*

Afterward, the king went with the heads of the community to the direction of the cemetery. He stood about 50 cubits in front of it and declared: all the plain you see in front of you belongs to you. Right up to the settlements around you the place belongs to you. I suggest calling your city Antopol, because I see Antipoli-tikah in your pleasant lives. As a sign of recognition of your goodness and faith, I donate a sum of money sufficient to build a great synagogue in this place.

The king left the settlement with wishes for its growth. Then, the settlement began to grow and develop. Professionals were brought and the building went on for ten years. The majority of professionals decided to remain. They built themselves nice houses and got work for themselves building palaces and monasteries in the lands and villages of the region. When the building of the synagogue was completed, a delegation from the city went to invite King Zigmund to the opening of the synagogue.

In the year 5290 (1530) the king and his companions arrived at the gate of honor that was set up in the cemetery facing the entrance of the synagogue. The king appeared at the gate and at his sides I see in my imagination those accompanying him, R. Avigdor Sirotah, the mayor, R. Hayyim Kotlar, the ritual slaughterer, and R. Hershel Nitsburg. Facing them stand in honor and glory, R. Tsevi-Harsh Ralimovits and Rabbi Mosheh Berman, with the Torah scrolls in their hands. Among them, R. Laizer the sexton holds a silver tray with bread and salt and a gold key to the entrance of the synagogue.

However, when I wipe out the thoughts of my fantasy, I remember what happened after that – the destruction of the Jewish community at the hand of evil people and hundreds of years of dear Jewry wiped out with cruelty. May the memory of all of it be blessed.

# Location of Antopol and its History
## By Akiva ben Ezra

Antopol, or as the Jews called it – Antopolye, lies at the side of the railway from Pinsk to Kovrin, a km. east of Horodets and 29 km west of Drohitshin, in the district of Kobryn, within the province of Grodno. The geographical location of Antopol is in Polesia, rich in swamps and forests. Antopol received its share of this "wealth". Not without reason was the place called with the accompanying name "swamps of Antopol".

Near to Antopol, on its west side, from the highway that goes to Kobrin, there extended some decades ago a thick forest until Horodets, on the south side. On the way to the village of Rusheve, there was also a thick forest. In this forest there were wolves, bears, and also a multitude of snakes.

It seems that ancient Antopol began on the highway to Kobrin, in the spot where the forest ends and continued until the old cemetery that was located by law outside the town.

When was Antopol founded? When did Jews begin to settle in it? There are few historical documents on which we can rely. We must make due with the guess that the Jewish community was founded in the year 1604.

According to Polish documents (from the period in which Antopol was under Polish rule), the town is mentioned in 1718 in connection with the building of a monastery. In that document it says that the generous Lady Antoninah Zamolskah built the monastery. It is for that reason that the town was called Antopol (that is, the city "Polis" in Greek of Antoninah).

## Changes of Rule in Antopol

The region of Polesia belonged to different governments at different times due to revolutions and historical change. The Lithuanian Archduke Gdimin conquered Polesia in the years 1315-1341.

*[Page 113]*

After the union of Poland and Lithuania in 1386, the Lithuanian Archduchy opened its doors to Polish culture, especially to the Roman Catholic Church. The Roman Catholic Church used all means at its disposal to increase its influence in all areas of life. Slowly and with success, the Church completed the assimilation to Polish culture of Polesia.

This situation roused the anger of the Cossacks and brought about the famous revolt of Chmielnitski in 1648. The Cossacks revolted and plundered over a period of two years. Much Jewish blood was spilled in 1648-1650 in Polesia, until the Polish army overcame the Cossacks. In the spring of 1706, the Swedes under the leadership of their King Carl the 12th declared war on Poland. However, the swamps of Polesia forced them to return home that year. History does not record the fate of the Jews of Antopol in those years. However, the Jewish community had a folk saying "This is reminiscent of the Swedes" to indicate something that happened a long time ago. Poland was saved and remained complete until 1772, the year of the First Partition. In 1793-1795, the provinces of Minsk, Vilna and Grodno passed to Russia.

The Province of Grodno had 8 districts: Grodno, Lida, Novogrodok, Slonim, Volkovisk, Pruzshani, Brisk, and Kobrin. Antopol was included in the district of Kobrin. Not a long time passed before Napoleon Bonaparte's war on Russia (1812). This did not pass by Antopol. Battles took place in the town, from which the inhabitants, including the Jews, suffered.

The Poles in the region were not happy with Russian rule and tried twice to revolt in 1830 and 1863. However, these two attempts to revolt were definite failures.

These rebellions had a bad effect on the Jews of Antopol and the surrounding region. They suffered from both combatants. Many residents of Antopol supported the Poles. They took care to give them food and asylum. They did all this even though the Pole in hiding shouted to his Jewish savior: "Leprous Jew, remove your hat!"

The Russians did not forgive the Jews and punished them severely for supporting the Poles. Punishing Jews was quite easy for the Czarist authorities and the Jews of Antopol had to suffer various Czarist decrees.

The land around Antopol belonged to squires and the Jews used to pay them a land tax. In 1904, the Jews paid taxes to the Lady Estate Holder, Sofia Dilitrivnah Voitash. She had 4,500 dessiatina of good land and 100 dessiatina of not good land (A dessiatina is a measure of land consisting of 2.7 acres). Thanks to her administrator Mordekhai Shainboim, she did many good things for the Jews of Antopol.

The region of Antopol was quiet of wars for about 100 years, until the Ninth of Av in the year 1914 when World War I broke out and lasted until November 1918. At the end of the summer of 1915, the Germans conquered Antopol and the surrounding region. Many Jewish homes burned down and the Jews settled in the abandoned homes of gentiles, who had fled to Russia. The remaining number of Jews in the town began to organize and arrange their daily lives. However, the Germans ruled harshly. Their rule was especially hard on the youth, who were caught and sent to work in different places or had to work hard in the town itself.

The German conquerors began to assimilate the town to German language and culture through the "Folks-Shule" and the Jews of Antopol young and old began to learn German and to accustom themselves to the Germanic way of doing things. This order lasted until November 1918 when the Germans began to return to Germany. The months until the end of 1918 were months of anarchy. Finally, Antopol was added to the jurisdiction of the new Polish State. Then, began the "legal" terror. The new Polish government took plunderers and murderers under its protection. The Poznantshiks continued to plunder, pull out Jewish beards and make pogroms. It did not take long and Antopol became an area in dispute between the Russians and Poles. In 1919, the Bolsheviks came to Antopol and began to arrange their "order". They dial not stay long and the Polish legionaries returned to Antopol. With their return begins a new period in the region. The Poles forced their authority on the region and much Jewish blood was spilled. Likewise, there was great damage to Jewish property.

*[Page 114]*

The region began to quiet down and the inhabitants began to rebuild their lives. Then, the war broke out between Poland and the Bolsheviks (July 1920). At first, the Russians were victorious and they already reached the gates of Warsaw. However, the wheel of fortune reversed and the Polish army began to push back the Russians. Meanwhile, the soldiers of General Belkhovits, a leader of the White Russians, began to help the Poles. The help of the soldiers of General Belkhovits to the Poles is a topic in itself, which is written in history with the blood and tears of the Jews. In 1921, the peace treaty of Riga was signed between Poland and Russia. Antopol was included in Poland. The Polish government began to enforce severe rules in hygiene, which were mainly aimed at Jews. A law of compulsory education was also instituted for children.

Poland also instituted a draft to the army, which Jews did not like. Nevertheless, many young Jews served in the Polish army, with distinguished service. Thus, the years passed until the outbreak of World War II (August 1939). Then, the Bolsheviks came and conquered among the rest Antopol. A Soviet regime began in town. Contradictory news began to arrive. Some said that the Red Army brought salvation, not only spiritually but also materially. Others informed in a masked fashion that the Red paradise was indeed a hell. The Russians ruled the region until June 1941 when the Nazis passed the border with Russia and conquered all of Poland and Ukraine and continued on the road until right up to Moscow and Leningrad.

Antopol fell into Nazi claws. The Jews of Antopol did backbreaking work, were tortured and locked up in the ghetto. However, they did not submit. They fought in the underground, did acts of sabotage, and ran to join the partisans in the forests.

However, Hitler, may his name be blotted out, was stronger than them. He destroyed them and wiped out all the rest, the old, women, and children. The years of the murders by the Nazis were from June 1941 until July 1944. They will not be forgotten forever! With a curse on our lips, we will remember the disgrace of these human beasts, who destroyed hundreds of Jewish communities, among them, our dear town of Antopol.

In July 1944, the Red Army conquered Antopol, which is included up to the present in the Province of Kobrin in White Russia. However, its dear and holy Jews are no more. Thus ended 300 hundred years of the Jewish community in the town of Antopol.

# The Economy of Antopol

We don't have much news about the economic life in Antopol in its first years. Likewise, we don't have details about the Jewish population during that period. However, from different sources, we concluded that the Jewish population continually grew.

In 1847, about 200 years after its founding, the Jewish population was 1,108. It didn't take long and in 1360 the Jewish population was 1,259 out of the general population of 1,563. If we take into account that during these 13 years, the town had fires, the net gain in Jewish population is very noticeable.

In 1897, the Jews were already the majority in town and numbered 3,137 out of 3,867. In 1904, the general population was 5,235 and the Jews clearly numbered over half. Antopol grew in this period. Pinsk St. grew in length, almost until Prushikhvost, and the surrounding side streets became full of Jewish families.

How did Jews earn a living in Antopol? What brought about their dispersion over the length and width of town? Most of the Jews in Antopol were farm workers. They grew potatoes, onions, beets, cucumbers, radishes, and more. The farm workers were called "Morgovniks" (from the word morag, about half a hectare of land). They farmed the land behind their houses, especially in Pinsk and Kobrin streets. There were those who worked the land themselves, and there were those who hired gentile help. When they grew vegetables, they loaded them on wagons to bring them to markets in surrounding towns. At the beginning of the twentieth century, the industry of pickled cucumbers developed. These were sold throughout the country and even reached . Barrels were filled with cucumbers and placed in cellars, so as not to spoil during the winter. Dealing in cucumbers gave many families in Antopol a good living. This branch of commerce flourished until World War I.

*[Page 115]*

The second great industry in Antopol was fattening geese for sale. During the 1890s, the Jews of Antopol began to sell fattened geese. They would bring geese from distant regions of Russia and raise them in special coops. They would fatten the geese with oats and millet. Then, they would sell them in Vilna or Germany. This commerce lasted from the Feast of Tabernacles until the end of the month of Shevat. From here came the expression, "It is forbidden for a goose to hear the reading of the Scroll of Esther on Purim". Purim falls in the Hebrew month of Adar, which follows the month of Shevat)." The Russian geese were big and weighed a lot. Their neck was long and they had a raised beak. These "characteristics" brought the geese to the attention of great rabbi's, which discussed them in books of rabbinical response. The great rabbi Ben- Tsiyon Shternfeld devoted 18 pages to the topic of the geese of Antopol (See "Shaare Tsiyon", vol. 1, p. 123-141, Piterkov, 1903).

Merchants and commercial agents from different cities used to come to Antopol, and geese merchants from Antopol would frequently travel to Vilna. As a result, they established their own prayer quorum, that of the geese merchants of Antopol in Vilna. Their prayer leader was Hershel (the blond) Shterman.

In Antopol, there were olive oil presses, mills powered by horses, windmills for flour, and brick factories for the needs of Antopol and the surrounding region. An important business in town was the factory to process flax. The first person to establish the branch in town was Efrayim Volyusher. Mr. Volyush got a name for himself in Antopol and the surrounding region, mainly because of his loud whistle heard in the surrounding region. There was a plaster factory in town supplying plaster for ovens. The marketplace with its concentration of stores was in the middle of town between Kobrin and Pinsk streets. In about 1890, there were 42 stores in town, in which the Jews sold different wares to the people in town and those living in the villages.

On Sunday, the gentile villagers of the region would come with their products to sell to the Jews and in exchange would buy cotton, salt, ornaments, clothes, and the like. The main income was from the gentiles, especially on the annual fairs, called by the names Desiatikha and Troltsa. The fair Desiatikha would take place on Friday, 10 weeks after Passover. Hence, its name–the tenth Desiat.

The reputation of the fairs had a wide audience. Merchants from different cities would come to Antopol to trade and Jews from the surrounding towns would come to place orders for their needs. During the fair days Antopol was like a noisy beehive. It was difficult to pass by all the people in the market place.

Development in the region did a lot to help the economic life in town. In 1840 when the royal canal from Pinsk to Horodets was built (known as the "Dnipro-Bogaski Canal") Antopol also supplied workers for the project, through a local Jew named Yaakov Shmalevits.

In the 1880s when the railway was built between Zshabinke and Pinsk, the Lifshits family, Antopol merchants in forest products, supplied the railway ties. The railway gave work to many people from Antopol, Jews and gentiles together. Another big project was building the highway in 1908-1910, which was between Antopol and Horodets. This road made it easy for wagon drivers to get to and from the railway station in Horodets.

*[Page 116]*

In Antopol at the beginning of the 20th century, there was a Bank for Loans and Savings, which made it possible for the merchants in town to receive interest-free loans. This bank was in the house of Avi-gdor Sirotah. Its accountant was Perets Gorvits (Hurvits), who afterwards became a dentist. The bank began to operate at the outbreak of World War I. It was reopened in 1921, when Antopol began to recover. In 1924, the bank had 194 members. In the period between the two world wars, a "Free Loan" Association was established, with the generous help of Mrs. Esther Kornblum, who came for a visit from the United States. The "Free Loan" Association did a lot to help the economic condition of the Jews of Antopol. Little by little the town recovered. A railway stop was built on the way to the village of Sveklits. There the train stopped for a short time. The mail was brought from there. Before that, it had been brought from the train station in Horodets.

In 1928, an autobus line was inaugurated between Kobrin and Antopol. It also aided the development of commerce. In 1935, a small electric power station was built, which supplied electricity for lighting and also powered a mill to grind flour. The United States was a big source of income for Antopol before World War I. Many men who had immigrated to the United States used to send financial support for their wives in the form of cash in dollars. In exchange, two rubles for each dollar were received. The parents of immigrants also used to get support. When World War I was over, there was increased support from the United States.

The government of Poland, and especially Minister Grabski, began to block Jews from earning a living. However, to where could one flee? The gate to the United States was closed, so there began two streams of immigration. One stream turned to the Land of Israel. The other turned to Latin America (Argentina, Brazil, Cuba, Mexico, and the like). Thanks to the two streams there has remained memory of the community of Antopol. Immigrants from Antopol helped to build their adopted countries and especially the Jewish State of Israel. Those Jews from Antopol, who do not live In Israel, also helped to build the Jewish State. Those who moved to the Jewish State took an active part in its life and development.

# Culture in Antopol

Antopol, like other Jewish towns in Polesia, had a developed religious identity, Religion provided the general framework, to Jewish life. The rabbis set tone in all spheres of life. All life was conducted according to the Code of Jewish Law. Even though it was a hardship to live according to Jewish law, the Jews of Antopol carried out all its paragraphs. It is told that more than one hundred years ago, the Jews of Antopol made a partnership with the Jews of Drohitshin to buy citron in order to carry out the commandment (of making a blessing over It during holiday of Tabernacles). Thus, it happened that an the intermediate days of the festival of Tabernacles that a team of horses was hitched to a wagon to bring it or return It to and from Drohhitshin a distance of 32 km., just one way. However, here and there were Jews, who did not want to walk in the ploughed furrow of Jewish law and rebelled. One of them was the son of the Rabbi R. Mosheh-Hirsh, who became a follower of the enlightenment school of thought of Moses Mendelssohn. He was known for years as Dr. Yierael Mjkhaj Rabinovits, one of the first of the Lovers of Zion and translator of the Talmud into French.

The thirst for knowledge began to penetrate more and more. The community began to request to bring to the Jewish elementary school teachers for Hebrew, Russian and Mathematics. Thus, began the study of Hebrew, grammar, and Russian. We find announcements about this in the Hebrew newspaper ha-Melits from the years 1884 to 1889.

The Hebrew newspaper ha-Tsefirah began to reach a few subscribers in Antopol. In 1905, the town had a special agent for the Hebrew newspaper ha-Zeman. Newspapers and periodicals in Yiddish and Russian came in. The reader's thirst could not be satisfied. The different movements during the Russian revolution had much influence in Antopol. People in Antopol were able to tell the story of Fradl Stavski, who carried out revolutionary activities and was exiled to Siberia. There were activists of the Jewish Bund, S.S. (Social Democrats) and Lovers of Zion. Afterwards, there came the Pioneer Jewish groups on behalf of Israel, which took hold in Antopol. The youths and young ladies of Antopol began to study Russian in the Russian government school. Afterwards, they continued their studies in the gymnasiums in Brisk and in other cities. From there, they went to universities. They went out as doctors and practitioners of other free professions.

*[Page 117]*

The Jews of Antopol put a strong emphasis on Jewish studies. The youth of Antopol would go to learn in different rabbinical seminaries. Adults would study with the local rabbi, or learn by themselves in the study hall. Not a small number of students graduated the rabbinical seminaries as rabbis. Many were invited to assume rabbinical positions in bigger cities.

At the beginning of the twentieth century Antopol also had a rabbinical seminary. Its head was R. Binyamin (Shavlevits). Pupils from nearby communities came to study at this rabbinical seminary. New winds began to blow in the traditional Jewish elementary school. Then the reformed Jewish elementary school was founded. It was administered by a person from Antopol, R. Aharon Lifshits (Lif). The reformed Jewish elementary school lasted a few years. Then came the Jewish elementary school of R.

Yisrael Volovelski- Vol, who had special chairs for students put in and also brought a Russian teacher.

Antopol had in those days a private school for girls directed by Mrs. Taybe Frumes (Shagan). Private teachers for Hebrew, Russian, German and sciences of different types were already accepted in town.

Antopol became famous for its thirst for knowledge. The library, which held books in Hebrew, Yiddish, and Russian, was a help in education. The thirst for education increased after World War I. Then, the Tarbut School was founded in which youths and young ladies studied Hebrew as the language of instruction. Likewise, there existed a library in the same of Y.L. Perets Library. Jewish elementary religious schools and rabbinical seminaries were also opened in Antopol. The voice of Torah was heard in the streets of town, until it was silenced by the Soviets, who closed down the Jewish cultural institutions and the Nazis, may their name be blotted out; who destroyed what their predecessors did not manage to destroy.

# Settlements of Immigrants from Antopol

The Jews of Antopol were to be found in the big cities of Russian and Poland. Already in the 1890's, Jews from Antopol lived in Kishinev and kept up there a unified group and study hall of their own. They were also to be found in Warsaw, mainly in literary circles. Of fame there was the Hebrew-Yiddish writer Mosheh Stavski-Satui (1905-1911). There also came to Warsaw the duck and cucumber merchants from Antopol. The United States became an important center to absorb immigrants from Antopol. It certainly was a long way. A passport was necessary. Then, one had to pass through medical quarantine. Afterwards, the boat trip took 2-3 weeks. Upon arriving in the United States, the immigrants could not be as religiously observant as they were at home. However, the desire to expand horizons and develop overcame everything. They traveled to New York and Chicago. These were big cities in which they could live with dignity and build a home. However, they also went to Brownsville, which was called the Jerusalem of the United States. It became a type of Antopol community. There, they established together with immigrants from Kobrin and Horodets a synagogue called "Mutual Benefit Society, United Brethoen of Kobrin, Horodets, and Antopol.

Each person brought a friend over to the United States. Each person helped another to make a new life for himself. However, some could not adjust and went back to Antopol to build a new life. Those, who stayed in the United States became citizens, and began to participate in its development. They founded associations and gave much help to those people who remained back home in Antopol.

*[Page 118]*

Many from Antopol integrated themselves into United States industries, such as the Farber family in the branch of metal cooking ware, and the family of Shelomoh Margalit, in the branch of gasoline stations. Many other people made a name for themselves in the United States. In the field of music: the cantor David Futerman was considered one of the greatest cantors in the United States. He was also president of the "Cantor' Association" In the United States. Roberta Peters, star of the Metropolitan Opera In New York was also a member of the Futerman family. These people made a name for themselves in the field of science: Dr. P. Berman, of blessed memory, who was the director of the hospital in Pasadena, the biggest in the world. Dr. M. Kletski, who was for many years the chief dentist of the Arbeyter Ring and author of many articles in his professional field. Professor Herbert L. Anderson (Aranovski) was a person who took an active part in the development of the atom bomb in its first years.

In Chicago, many people from Antopol had important positions. They founded associations there and different institutions. The Antopol synagogue in Chicago had a name for itself in all the city. Our townsperson, Yaakov Grinberg, of blessed memory, founded the Bet ha-Midrash la-Torah in Chicago. He was its main professor of Talmud until his death. Rabbi Yaakov Grinberg also did not just make due with teaching. He also maintained a correspondence and wrote on the Science of Judaism.

Jews from Antopol were also to be found in other cities. There they participated in public activities in general and in Jewish activities in particular. Jews from Antopol had an important place for themselves in Argentina, especially in Buenos Aires. It is possible to say that they were among the first Jewish immigrants to this country. The Jews from Antopol played a big part in the building of the State of Israel. The Land of Israel was of great concern to people from Antopol. They did not just make due with saying "And a redeemer will come to Zion".

There were already people from Antopol known to be living in Israel two hundred years ago. In 1808 (Hebrew year 569), there began the immigration of the pupils of the great Rabbi Elijah of Vilna. Seventy people went to the Holy Land and settled in Tsefat. Tsefat was then the ideal place for the pupils of the great Rabbi Elijah of Vilna. This is because there were not many Hasidic Jews in Tsefat, while in Tiberias the Hasidic Jews outnumbered the non-Hasidic Jews. The trip to the Holy Land took months. However, no difficulty stopped them or their brethren from Pinsk and Frohitshin. We again find Jews from Antopol in Tsefat in the name R. Mosheh Akiva of Antipoli, who was saved from a pogrom in 1834. R. Mosheh fled to Jerusalem and he was known as R. Mosheh the trustee, who was active in community life in Jerusalem. Among the activists in Jerusalem in this period was also R. Mosheh Tsevi of Antopli. In the way of the history of these years we also find the tombstones of children, whose parents were from Antopol. We learned from this that the immigration from Antopol comprised whole families.

In the 1880s, there settled in Israel a Jew from Antopol named Yahalom. One of the members of that family, R. Binyamin was among the founders of En Ganim near to Petah Tikvah. He was also active in matters concerning the entire Land of Israel until the founding of Israeli Statehood.

Mosheh Yaakov Benjamin, or as he was called in Jerusalem, "Alter of Antopol," was an important person. When Mosheh Yaakov immigrated together with his parents in 1863, he was still a child of seven years of age. After the passage of time, he was among the founders of the neighborhood in Jerusalem called, "Meah Shearim." He was the first to bring salted fish to the market.

R. Netanel Hayyim Paper, of blessed memory, who in 1891, immigrated together with his wife and son Yitshak, was well known in the rabbinical world. In 1902, some important families left Antopol for the Land of Israel. Among them was R. Yehezkel Saharov, of blessed memory, together with his wife Hayah Etel and his son Yitshak Mordekhai.

*[Page 119]*

Yitshak Mordekhai, of blessed memory, was very active in community life in the Land of Israel. His children had a big part in building the country. Thus, lived and worked Jews from Antopol in the Land of Israel still before Dr. Herzl's appeal.

After that appeal, the immigration increased more. And as we said above the Jews of Antopol had a big part in building the country.


# The End

In 1960, our townsperson the dear Dr. P. Berman, of blessed memory, wrote to the official in charge of Antopol. In his letter, he asked what remained of the town of his birth. The answer reached him finally two years later in the form of a report in the White Russian newspaper "Galas Radzimi", which is published in Minsk, the capital of White Russia. It had a description of the town after the war. It appears that the official in charge of Antopol was afraid to answer the letter himself and sent to Minsk for an answer. From Minsk a special correspondent was sent by the newspaper to write about his visit accompanied with photos.

## What did the correspondent see?

One person with the name Isak Berkovitsh Zaks told him that among the victims of the Nazis in Antopol were White Russians, Jews, and Poles. There was certainly a ghetto in the city. However, there is no mention that the people locked up were only the Jews. He says that the inhabitants fled to the woods. They were there with the partisans. He also stated that the mayor was a partisan.

The correspondent melts from the happiness of telling that the White Russians have again conquered Antopol. They have established a progressive regime. There is a lot of culture, lectures, and concerts. In general, really a paradise.

Antopol today has three schools. One with 11 grades of study, one with a dormitory (apparently for children of villagers) and an evening school for workers. The correspondent visited the municipal library. It has 26,000 books and about 30 newspapers and periodicals. There is a bookstore. It has books of different kinds in Russian and translations from English, Polish, French, and German. However, what is the situation with Yiddish or Hebrew? There is no book in either of these languages. This is because there is not a Jew remaining in Antopol.

The correspondent does not forget to mention that there is a church in town. However, what about the study halls? To where did they disappear?

There is a hospital with 14 doctors and 32 assistants. The hospital has three buildings. There is no charge for service. In the case of an emergency, the sick persons were evacuated by airplane to Brisk. Antopol has a total of 4,100 inhabitants. There are 19 buses giving the town transportation to Minsk, Pinsk, Bisk and Kobrin. This is all.

Thus has ended a Jewish community that lasted for about 300 years. And we the Jews of Antopol, wherever we are, bow our heads and with a voice full of tears say: May His great name be extolled and sanctified!

# Antopol, as I Saw it in My Childhood
## By Shemuel Turnianski

Antopol was about 90 km. east of Brisk on the Bug, on the Brisk-Moscow railway. When you came from Brisk to Antopol you would pass through these stations: Zabinkah about 30 km. from Brisk, Kobrin, about 60 km. and then the small station of Norodets, through which passed the Dnieper-Bug Canal. It was then about 7 km. to Antopol. The population of our town was about 3,000. Of this, three quarters was Jewish and the rest White Russians. It was characteristic of that region.

*[Page 120]*

The houses were mainly built of thick, big wood. The roofs were tiled. The houses were lit with kerosene lamps and had inside plumbing. Water was drawn from primitive wells with a bucket raised by a pole. It was brought home in pails. This was not an easy job in the winter with temperatures of minus 30 degrees below freezing. Whoever could afford it, got a gentile to bring home water. A stove served for heating and cooking. Wood had to be bought in advance, so that it would dry and easy to burn. Those who could not buy it, had to use wet wood, which did not burn well. The kitchen was the place to wash. Each morning during the cold, the layer of ice had to be broken in the barrel, in order to wash. Many houses had roofs of tin or straw. Most homes were simply furnished. Only in the rooms of the youth was the wooden floor stained red. Young girls also had a sofa covered in yellow fabric and springs inside. The walls were decorated with embroidered colored threads describing views from the Holy Land and the Biblical environment.

Main Street was the only paved street. The other streets were unpaved and had no sidewalks. Everything was under mud in the spring and fall. Therefore, all the inhabitants needed boots or rubbers on their shoes.

The main street from Kobrin on the way to Drohitshin was divided as follows: Kobrin St. had a length of about 1 km. The market square was on the south side of the street. It was about 400 meters in length. Pinsk St. went out from the square about 1.5 km until it reached the village of Kopelnevkah in which one Jew lived. From there the way led to Valkah and to some other villages in which only gentiles lived. This street was paved with big stones.

Parallel to Kobrin and Pinsk Sts. on the north side, there began Rushever and Zanivier streets, whose length equaled almost that of Kobrin and Pinsk streets. On the other side was the gentile street, Kutelirskah St. At an angle to it was Shlos St., which began from Kobrin St. and continued until Gorin's garden. After it was the street of Lefer Fridman and -Hayyim the ritual slaughterer, Shlos St. and then Yoel Alley, the narrow alley of Shimlikhah, the alley of Hayyim Lifshits, and the small alley of Aba the builder. These were the streets on the right side.

From Kobrin on the way to Drohitshin on the left side was the alley of the old cemetery and also of the synagogues and the Rabbi's house on the square called Synagogue Courtyard.

Onwards was the alley of Asmelinker and the Alley of Yosel the tailor, the alley of the study hall surrounded by a wall and the alley of the Mugilkes (the former Christian cemetery) and the alley of Mordekhai Tserniuk. The market square was built in the form of a square 400 by 400 meters. It was surrounded by houses, among them stone houses and also a building of two stories. Within the square was a smaller square, which included 48 stores – 12 stores on each side of the square. Northeast of the houses and stores was the cabin of the firefighters with its tin roof. In the middle of the market there was Fravoslav Church. Its bells rang on every Christian holiday. Near to it were planted different beautiful trees. Young people came there in the spring to pluck lilacs. This was a sign of love. There were also Pistachio trees, from whose flowers a tea was made. Between the trees rose a big stone pillar with a nest for storks. On the south side, one came to the garden of. It had pools of water with reeds, beautiful trees and fruit trees. It served as a place to boat and stroll for the people in town.

For a while there was a field for soccer. There was also a castle in the garden. It was burnt by the Germans when they retreated in 1917. Near to it were some stables for horses. The boulevard of trees on the east side led to the railway station. On the south side it led to the thicket of trees of Gorin. On the north side, the length of Courtyard Street was a hill of sand, which served for some time as a soccer field and later as a market for cattle.

To the east side of the end of Zanivir St., there were hills of sand that also spread south, to the Christian cemetery (Frishikhvost) and north to the Pohonyah, land belonging to Jews and used to pasture horses and cows. The length of Zanivir St. was an old Christian cemetery, the Mogilkes. The hill was a place for children to play and to pasture the sheep of the farmers. In the middle of the street was located the Study Hall of R. Meir Podot and after it the old Jewish cemetery, in which was buried R. Pinchas Michael, of blessed memory, the famous rabbi of Antopol.

*[Page 121]*

North and west was the alley in which were the study halls, the Synagogue Courtyard, in which until 1914 was the big synagogue, called the Cold Synagogue. Its roof was in the form of a round cupola. Its ceiling had the paintings of the 12 constellations. Near to the big synagogue were the old study hall, the new study hall, the bathhouse and the old graveyard.

More recently, there was there also an icehouse. Ice was brought there in the winter and kept there for medical needs and to make ice cream in the summer. As said above, the icehouse was brought to the Synagogue Courtyard during a later period. At that place, there was also a big tank to store kerosene that reached town in some wagons. The ground was watery almost all the days of the year. Passage was even hard with horses. Southeast to Pinsk St., the way continued about half a km. to the village of Frishikhvost, and finally Roshver St., on the southwest was the orphanage.

And today, all this does not exist in mapping our dear Jewry.

# Antopol and its Jewish Population up to World War I
## By Abraham Lifshits

Antopol is situated on the main highway between Pinsk and Brisk in Lithuania. The town of Drohitshin is to the east and the small town of Horodets to the west. The latter's railway station also served Antopol. As a typical Jewish town Antopol was able to raise up many generations of faithful and devoted Jews, scholars, known activist scholars and great rabbis learned in Torah, who left the town and whose fame went before them. The scope of Antopol Jewry's activities was very diverse. The inhabitants at the two ends of town were farmers and were called Morgovnikes. Most of them lived on Pinsk St, in the east part of town, and the rest lived in the west part of town on Kobrin St.

There were only a few industrial plants in town. Among them, we should list the two flourmills. Near to one, which was powered by steam, there was an accompanying serious enterprise to process the wool from the region's Christian farmers. This was on Roshvah St. A diesel motor powered the second mill of Mazurski. It was located on the market square. A number of Jewish families earned a good living also from the windmill. The majority of people in Antopol were merchants. All the stores in the city belonged to Jews. Among them were the stores for manufactures, building supplies, work tools, iron merchandise, stores for the sale of alcoholic drinks, stores for cigarettes, and more. Some of the Jews were butchers, a trade that passed in inheritance from father to son. Some entered into exchange with the gentiles. There were also merchants in forestry products, which traded with the nobles who had estates in the region. Every noble had his Jews in whom he trusted and did business. Some of them bought forests and some of them the grain and forest products. Some of them bought milk products, and others the industrial products of the noble.

Many of the people of Antopol were craftsmen, mainly copper engravers. Mainly estate owners, who had to set up copper pipes to purify alcohol, employed them. Making brandy was done on the estates. These craftsmen earned a good living up to World War I. This war brought a shock to many branches of industry in town. The government bought up all the copper for the war effort and even confiscated household items of copper. This brought an end to the copper industry in Antopol.

*[Page 122]*

There were three factories for non-alcoholic drinks in town. They sold the product to the surrounding villages. Even this industry came to a halt during the war. This was because of a lack of the materials to keep it going. Even the Mazurski mill, which was in the marketplace, was burned down completely by the Russians during their retreat. It was not rebuilt.

The chief industrialists in town were Binyamin Mazurski, Betsalel Mosheh and Mosheh Lifshits. There were a lot of craftsmen. They dealt in building, carpentry, and painting. There were also shoemakers, tailors, seamstresses, masons, wood carvers, glaziers, and other craftsmen. Some of them did not find work in Antopol. They earned their living by working for the farmers and estate holders. They would leave town on Sunday and return Friday afternoon. It frequently happened that they would not be home for the Jewish Sabbath. Some people from Antopol earned their living from fruit trees of the many estates around town. They would buy the fruit while it was still on the trees. They would take their families to the fruit trees, set up tents, guard the fruit, and when it was ripe pick it and market it in town. In Antopol, there were many families of wagon drivers, who earned their living from the traffic with the train station. This occupation passed in inheritance from father to son. The family had a right to earn a living this way.

Some like Itsye Nyunes and Mordekhai Mantiles, earned their livelihood poorly by transporting sand and building materials with their horses to Jewish houses. They dug up this material in land belonging to no one, located behind Kotelyarski St. This business was not enough to support their families. Itsye Nyunes would also transport the dead in his wagon to the cemetery distant from town about 2 km. It is noteworthy to remark that despite the poverty of these two Jews they did not spare any effort to educate their children. Itsye's son studied in the Jewish religious elementary school and got excellent grades.

To end the picture, I will mention Chaim, the chimney sweep. He was nicknamed Chaim Chimney. He was also called Chaim Diesiatnik. This was because of the additional task he had to complete his living. His main Job was to clean each month the house chimneys to prevent fire. His second job was to watch out at Jewish weddings that no uninvited guests came and to set up the tables for the banquet after the wedding. As was mentioned, villages surrounded Antopol. Therefore, this town had a big and beautiful market. At its center was a row of stores. Those who were able sat near to the market and its edges. There was a market every Sunday. In it the peasants from the region would bring their wares for exchange and to buy their needs. Besides the weekly market, there were two big yearly fairs. One was called Distikha (ten weeks after Easter) and the other was called Troytse. Merchants from other cities would come to these fairs.

We should say that Antopol was not on a river. People had to get their water from wells. However, not all the wells had good drinking water. Only one or two of the wells had sweet water. Therefore, there were water carriers, who drew water from Shagan's well or another well and supplied customers. There were Jewish and gentile water carriers. However, the woodcutters were only gentiles.

There were a few bakers in Antopol. Most of them baked only barley bread or white bread. A few baked pastry for weddings and the like. The simple bakers would bake pancakes from wheat. Many people wanted to buy these warm pancakes, especially Jewish schoolboys in elementary school or the study hall. Every family, even the wealthy, would bake every Friday white bread in honor of the Sabbath and special white bread for the town's poor. Some people would gather these charity breads and secretly distribute them to the poor, so as not to embarrass them.

Being a sexton was another occupation that really did not support its workers. And who did not know Leizer the sexton in the new study hall? He was a Jew who moved quickly. He was also a bookbinder. He acted only as a sexton without pay, in order to serve scholars. Besides these two, there were sextons in the old Synagogue, the study hall surrounded by a wall, the study halls on Kobrin and Pinsk Streets and in the Hasidic house of prayer. The income from all of this was small and the people engaged in it also did other kinds of work.

*[Page 123]*

There was a special ritual slaughterer among those in town. He was R. Yaakov Hayyim the ritual slaughterer. R. Hayyim was a distinguished person, to whom every one turned. He was the living force behind communal life in Antopol and he was decisive in it. Besides being a ritual slaughterer, he was also a ritual circumciser, the best in town and in the towns and villages near to Antopol. He also had a sweet voice and honored G-d and the people in town by leading prayers on every holiday. The ritual slaughterers in town had a hold on this profession and when a slaughterer married off his daughter, he gave his son-in-law a part of the business in town. Thus, R. Binyamin Skidleski, the first son-in-law of R. Yaakov was appointed to being a ritual slaughterer. R. Taakov Hayyim at the end of his life inherited his profession to his youngest son-in-law R. Eliezer

Bernshtein, who was the last ritual slaughterer in town, since he was killed by the Nazis.

May their memory be blessed forever.

# World War I
## By Mosheh Falk

With the end of the period of my childhood, I became more moderate and serious. I tried to work and also began to read a lot. Daily I read the two newspaper dailies Haynt and Moment. The Beilis trial interested me a lot. I read Bialik's City of Slaughter a lot. I already learned to sing ha-Tikvah by heart. There was a big picture of Herzl hanging on the wall. On another wall was a messianic theme: "At the end of days, the wolf and sheep shall live together..."

Suddenly, there appeared on the streets announcements calling for a general draft for war. The population was bitter and sad. There was not a house in which the crying of women and children was not heard. They were being separated from the men in the family. We grew up suddenly and began to sense a new situation. Twice a day I ran to the post office and impatiently expected mail. I would soon have my Bar Mitzvah. My sister sewed a bag for phylacteries for me and my sister Blumah brought me a beautiful pair of phylacteries. However, the celebration was modest. Our house was full of refugees from Brisk and we also slept in the attic. We shared all with the refugees. Chickens and ducks disappeared from the city. We offered everything we had to the unfortunate. I myself offered the pair of phylacteries to a refugee and lost them. I was sad to have also given away the bag for the phylacteries into which so much love had been put into its making.

Month followed month. The Germans conquered and also Brisk fell to them. My father buried in the ground all his work tools and also the property and equipment we had at home. The city was full of Cossacks and a Cossack was commandant in the city. We sat locked up at home. The fear was great and we already heard shots in town. We went to live in the fields behind the city. The soldiers plundered all they found. They even took the boots from the feet of the men. Towards evening the smoke went up from the town they set on fire. My father ran to save the Torah scrolls from the study halls. When he came home at evening, he was full of soot and dropped from exhaustion. We revived him and he went back. He found the entire town burnt. However, he put the Torah scrolls in a house that survived.

We went to our burnt house. My father found the hiding place of our valuables. My mother was in tears and clasped her hands in despair. Acquaintances came and advised us to enter for the time being one of the gentile houses. The inhabitants had fled. However, mother refused to live in the house of a gentile. Finally, our in-law Shelomoh the painter came and took us to live with him. We left my childhood house and went to live in our in-law's house. Itke, Shelomoh's daughter, went to live with her three children in her parent's house. We got two of her rooms. We immediately began to think of establishing a study hall in the temporary building meant to be a hospital. The building was completed by the time of the High Holidays.

*[Page 124]*

After the High Holidays, the youth was taken to perform forced labor. They took me and my friend Yisroel-Mendl, the son of Yaakov Hayyim, the ritual slaughterer. The next day the two of us were sick with typhus. My dear friend died of the disease. As to myself, my mother did not close her eyes or leave my bed for eight days and prayed to G-d to take her in my place. I got well and she got sick and died. Her good eyes accompany me always.

# In the Gates of Torah
## By A. Ben-Ezra, R. Pinchas Michael, of blessed memory

We assume that the Hasidic Rebbe and the regular orthodox Rabbi are two different types and they cannot be mixed up together in one person. This is because the Hasidic Rebbe is a miracle worker and leader to the ignorant masses. The regular orthodox rabbi is a professor of law, a scholar among scholars. One kingdom does not touch another in this regard. However, there is historical evidence for a mixture of these religious types in one person. There were some great people, who had mixed in them the qualities of the Hasidic Rebbe, a person of feeling, sharing in the troubles of the masses, and the qualities of the regular orthodox Rabbi, with great retentive and analytic powers, coming to a sharp point in the law. Some people could handle both of these in themselves.

Still before Baal Shem Tov (ca. 1700-1760), the founder of the modern Hasidic movement, we had personalities like Judah b. Samuel he-Hasid (d. 1217), of the medieval Haside Ashkenaz, Judah Loew ten Bezalel (ca. 1525-1609), of Prague and other religious personalities, who combined in themselves the qualities of the Hasidic Rebbe and the regular orthodox Rabbi. Even after the spread of modern Hassidism, there appeared some rabbis of mixed type, such as R. Seckel Wormser of Mikhelshtat (1768-1847), R. Elijah Guttmacher of Graidits (1796-1874), and people like them.

A rabbi of mixed type was R. Pinchas Michael, of blessed memory. He united in his person the vast and analytical knowledge of the Talmud and a caring personality, drawing to himself thousands of people, Jews and gentiles. They came just to see him and to receive his blessing.

R. Pinchas Michael was born to his father Yitshak Eizik and to his mother Breinah Heniah in 1808 in the city of Sharshev (Grodno province). R. Eizik was the grandson of the great Rabbi Yehoshua of Pinsk, a descendant of R. Eleazar ben Samuel Schmelke of Amsterdam (1665-1741), author of Maaseh Rokeah and on his mother's side of Meir ben Isaac Eisenstadt (1670-1744), author of Panim meirot .

R. Pinchas was an only child. However, he did not act like an only child. Only children are usually pampered and not scholarly. This was not the type of the youth Pinchas Michael. He was devoted from childhood to worship and study. His parent's ideal was not a secular one of accumulating wealth and possessions. Rather, it was a spiritual one, of attaining knowledge of Torah and wisdom. Pinchas Michael worshipped and studied all the time and eagerly acquired rabbinic knowledge. Of the rabbis who influenced him, we know the name of only one, R. Asher ha-Kohen (1797-1866), the author of Birkat Rosh. R. Pinchas Michael tried to be modest like his mentor. He learned from R. Asher to make due with little. Accordingly, he did not seek a rabbinical appointment until about the age of fifty, as did his mentor, R. Asher.

He even imitated his mentor in his own literary output. Just like his mentor composed a commentary on the Tractate Nazir, so did he. Certainly, Pinchas Michael's composition is not as full of casuistry as that of his mentor. As his mentor, he was extremely diligent and went without sleep. He did this to such an extent that his father asked to sleep one hour in the afternoon to fulfill the commandment "Honor thy father..." It was from his father R. Yitshak Eizik that he inherited the great love of the Jewish people and devotion to matters of charity. As was the custom in those days, his parents married him off at an early age. He took as a wife Moshkah daughter of the wealthy R. Yehiel Mikhl of Pasval, who was a great grandchild of R. Jehiel ban Solomon Hellprin (ca. 1660-1746), author of Seder ha-dorot. His wife kept a store and maintained the household so her husband was free to just study.

*[Page 125]*

Already in the days of his youth, R. Pinchas Michael was known to be familiar with the Talmud and its commentaries. Then, he began a correspondence with rabbinical luminaries about the Early and Later Commentaries to the Talmud. He established himself as a critical analyst of the text. He began to write down his commentaries to Talmud, Rashi, Tosafot, Isaac ban Jacob Alfasi, ben Jghiel, and Nissim ban Reuben Gerondi, until it became a thick book. However, he was humble and made no big deal of this. He would even listen to the youth studying in the study hall and accept their opinions. When he did not understand Rashi, Asher ben Jehiel, Me1r ban Jacob Sch1ff or Israel ban Gedaliah Lipschutz, author of the commentary to the Mishnah Tiferet Yisrael, he would not be assumed to say: "I do not have the merit to understand" or "They were so profound that I did not understand them", and the like. However, when he would understand a disagreement between Asher ban Jehiel and Meir ben a gloss and not his words at all".

In places where it is clear to R. Pinchas Michael that Samuel Eliezer ben Judah ha-Levi Edels was not correct, he does not even accept him and writes: "His explanation is confused" and "His answer is contrived". Mainly, he accepted Rashi's opinion but not always.

It was not only in Jewish law that R. Pinchas Michael held forth but also Sharshev, R. Pinchas Michael's birthplace, was known for its rabbis and great scholars. R. David, author of Homot Yerushalayim on Shulhan erukh, Orah hayyim, held the rabbinical post there. It is said about this rabbi that according to astronomical calculations he wanted to have the new moon each month be celebrated for three days instead of one or two and wanted to have the scroll of Esther read on Purim for an additional day on the day of the holiday known as Shushan Purim. R. Pinchasben Azriel, ha- Levi, of Amsterdam, the author of Nahalat Azriel also had a rabbinical post there. Likewise, R. Eizk hakohen, author of Shaare Yitshak also held a post there.

R. Asher ha-Kohen, 1797-1866, pupil of R. Hayyim ben Isaac Volozhiner, 1749-1821, also held a rabbinical post there. R. Asher was the author of Birkat Rosh on the tractate of Berakhot and commentary on the explanations of Rashi and Tosafot and Birkat Rosh on the tractate of Nazir and commentary on Maimonides' legal decisions.

In the beginning, R. Asher ha-Kohen did not want to earn his living as a rabbi. He was a merchant until the age of fifty in Sharshev. During leisure hours, he would sit and study. Torah. Finally, he accepted the request of the town's wealthy people to accept a rabbinical post there. However, he did not remain long. This is because in 1852 (the Hebrew year 613) he was appointed rabbi of Tiktin (Grodno province) at the request of the town's leaders.

When R. Asher ha-Kohen became rabbi of Tiktin, the leaders of the Sharshev community sought a rabbi capable of carrying on the intellectual position of the post in their community. Finally, they chose R. Pinchas Michael to replace R. Asher ha-Kohen. They saw in him the same scholarly type as his mentor, erudite in Talmud, modest and capable.

R. Pinchas Michael was just as modest in his rabbinical post as he had been as a private person. He was friendly to the masses. He listened to what they said, participated in their sorrow, and helped them. He especially treated children with respect and addressed them as "You" (second person plural). Despite his popular behavior, R. Pinchas Michael was known as a scholar, who was asked for answers by famous rabbis.

*[Page 126]*

On the other hand, the common people turned to him for advice in their daily lives. His house was open to every poor person. Thus, he was rabbi in Sharshev for eight years until 1864 (624). This year has a new designation in the life of R. Pinchas Michael, because in this year he left his birthplace, Sharshev, in which he grew up and took root and came to the town of Antopolyah (Antopol in Russian), in the Kobrin district, in the province of Grodno.

Antopol was famous not only among the Jews in the Antopol region. Rather, it was also famous outside of the boundaries of this province. It is a true fact that this town, which was almost forgotten to the Russian government was known to the Jews for its famous rabbis knowledgeable in Jewish law and mysticism. The saintly mystic R. Moshes Tsevi was rabbi here for forty-four years from 1818 to 1862 (578-622).

R. Mosheh Tsevi was known not only for his knowledge of law and his knowledge in Jewish mysticism. He was also known for his good disposition, his good feeling to the public and individuals. People would come to him with both spiritual and worldly matters; this person in material matters, this one about earning a living, and this one about physical or mental health.

After R. Mosheh Tsevi's death, R. Hayyim Zalman Bresloi, a descendent of the great rabbi Yosef David of Mir, was rabbi. Apparently, a quarrel broke out and he had to leave Antopol after two years and settle in Mir. The rabbinical position in Antopol was waiting for its true inheritor. A number of rabbis, learned and educators, were candidates for the rabbinical post in this small town. However, not a one of them satisfied the desire of its Jewish inhabitants. This was because the rabbi, who would inherit the rabbinical position would have to be a continuation of the rabbinical tradition in Antopol and satisfy all groups of people with his fatherly attitude towards all his congregants.

It wasn't easy to satisfy the Jews of Antopol, who numbered more than one thousand inhabitants. This is because all of them were learned in Judaism. Some were scholars who gave lessons in Gemara, like R. Yekutiel the blacksmith, and others like him.

The heads of the community found only one rabbi fit for the post. This was R. Pinchas Michael, full of Talmudic knowledge and love for his fellow beings. The town's leaders overlooked his speech deficiency, the fact that he stuttered. They knew that it was not a physical defect. Rather, it was the result of quick thought and rapid mental grasp. They looked at his simple nature, both in his way of teaching and his life style, his good nature, and his immense knowledge of Talmud and commentaries. These qualities made him the appropriate heir to the rabbinical post of Antopol.

Before he accepted the post, he told the town's leaders that he did not want a salary. Rather, he would have an income from his wife's sale of yeast. On the first day of the month of Heshvan, 1864 (624), R. Pinchas Michael came to town. The entire city was happy to receive its new rabbi. Finally, Antopol received a rabbinical authority that merited the two crowns – learning and good reputation. Everyone wanted to hear his first sermon. It would certainly be studious with references to earlier and later commentators on the Talmud, as was the manner of contemporary scholars.

However, R. Pinchas did not deliver a sermon like this. The people did not hear law from him. Rather, they heard lore and ethics. In order to fulfill his responsibility, he discussed a matter of law at the end. This is also God's manner. He did not address the children of Israel when they came the first day to Mt. Sinai. They were tired from the journey. So, it is with the commandments that God gave to them.

*[Page 127]*

First, he gave them easy commandments, like the priest's share of the dough, new meal offering, and afterwards, leave offering, tithes, sabbatical year, and jubilee year, which were harder. "When God gave his commandments, He took a gradual approach, instructing us to act justly and kindly." Pinchas Michael passed from statements of Jewish lore to Jewish ethics. He repeatedly warned about the observance of easy commandments, such as praying on time and value of study.

He expanded on the value of study. Almost all of his first sermon was devoted to this topic. These are his words: Everyone, even if he worked for a living in crafts or trade, has to diligently set aside time for study of Judaism, whether a little or a lot, each according to his ability, or to listen to others in this study, each according to his ability. God will not request a person to study hard things, only what he is able. The point is to do something. And to guard oneself from idle talk, especially in the study or synagogue, learning Judaism is important. The woman should help her husband by also working to earn a living, like Zebulun the merchant provided for his brother Issachar, enabling him to study.

The first sermon that R. Pinchas Michael preached in Antopol was the program according to which he acted all his stay in this town. He explained in it the principals of his method in law and manners. This is primarily because he was a teacher of Jewish law. He would repeat these ideas in almost every sermon. Teaching of Jewish law should be done simply, without trying to show off. There was a need to guide the heart in study and not to study externally. Every person should learn according to his nature. "Some people are able to study better before going to sleep. Some are able to study better when they awake, because then their thoughts are quiet and rested."

In addition to the study of Jewish law, there are two more fundamentals: prayer and charity. These are the three principles on which he based his sermons and private conversations. R. Pinchas Michael deviated from the established custom that a Rabbi would only give a sermon twice a year: on the Sabbath before Passover and the Sabbath between the Jewish New Year and Day of Atonement. He gave a sermon on every holiday. He would stand before the congregation on the Sabbath between the New Year and Day of Atonement, wrap himself up in his prayer shawl and weep. The congregation would weep after him. This was his "sermon" by which he stirred the people to repent and do good deeds.

Most of his sermons were not sharp. Rather, they had work of ethics and admonishments for daily living, like keeping the Sabbath, doing deeds of charity, feeding the poor, and keeping accurate measures for weighing goods. He stood up for these matters and called out for their observance on every occasion. He was firm on studying simply. He studied and taught others by this method. His method was to simply explain the obtuse without being far-fetched and wordy. Rather, he used a logical explanation and set up the text correctly and with brevity. R. Pinchas Michael used this method in his short explanations that were precise to the Tractates of Nazir, Temurah, Meilah and Tamid.

His explanations could be described as a little that contains a lot. He knew the secret of reduction in writing. He knew what to put down and. what to omit. He acts this way in his explanation to the Talmudic Tractates of Ternurah, Meilah, and part of Tamid. Like in his introduction to the explanation of Nazir, so he does in his explanation to the other tractates of the Talmud, apologizing and saying: "Behold, I understand how little is my value and my intelligence. It is certain that there are things that I do not understand".

R. Pinchas Michael kept this manuscript with him for many years, certainly because he did not have the money to publish it. He kept it until he got instruction from heaven that he must publish it. Then, he gave it to the publisher. His explanation immediately found a wide audience, because it was so precise.

*[Page 128]*

Directly or indirectly, R. Pinchas Michael influenced thousands of Jews, whether they heard him speak morality or wisdom or whether they only heard of his name. During his lifetime he was already a legend, passed from father to son and grandfather to grandchild. Every one talked of the righteous man, who listened to every, one turning and who did not differentiate between Jew and gentile. This is because "a gentile also has to live". He was a father and patron to every suffering and bitter person that came to him from a distance. Among those coming were Jewish scholars, merchants, craftsmen, women and children. If a tragedy happened at home, they immediately ran to the righteous man. If a Polish squire did not want to renew a lease, they turned to R. Pinchas Michael to seek advice. If someone was dangerously ill, they called for the aid of the righteous man. The righteous man would say: "I don't know, God will bless you".

R. Pinchas Michael became the emissary of those turning to him. He would add these people to his prayers in saying the Shemonah Esrah. He did not act as a typical Hasidic Rebbe. He would not receive gifts. At the most, he would take some pennies for poor students. The purse was tied one's neck and he would put into it and take out counted pennies for the needs of charity. Charity is one of the pillars of the Jewish would. Therefore, he would repeatedly warn about keeping this commandment at every opportunity.

R. Pinchas Michael would actively participate in the troubles of poor Jews. He would say: "It is very hard for a Jew to earn a ruble". He meant that a Jew had to work really hard to earn a living. Therefore, he would be lenient in ruling on kosher slaughter or mixing meat and dairy. This is in spite of the fact that he would oppose the Hasidic method and customs. Nevertheless, when it came to decide if a cow was kosher according to ritual law, he accepted the opinion of the book Daat kedoshim, a Hasidic Rebbe in Caliela.

Once a poor woman came to tell him that she had mixed dairy in a meat dish. The rabbi asked about her children and what they ate. When he heard that that were actually hungry and would benefit from the meat dish, he ruled that she should feed her children.

He was not only bothered by daily matters. He was also asked about things that could not be postponed, such as we have mentioned above. His sharp eye penetrated into Jewish life in distant America that was just taking shape. This was at a time when the Jewish community in the United States was still small and the practice of Judaism there was weak. He would advise his questioning people to immigrate to the United States. He used to say: "Go to America. You will earn a living there. And he would add: "Keep the Jewish Sabbath."

Like Rabbi Salanter, who was his contemporary, he advised people to immigrate to the United States. This is because he saw the wave or pogroms taking place against the Russian Jews. What about himself? He wanted to live in the land of Israel. However, his people would not let him go. He would accompany everyone immigrating to Israel, whether a tailor, shoemaker, merchant or property owner, some distance outside the city. To live in Israel was very important to him. Just desiring to live there made Jewish redemption a possibility. He would explain the statement: "Because of four reasons our ancestors were redeemed from Egypt ... because they did not change their language and their name." A person desiring to settle in another country changes his language, his name and clothes and accustoms himself to the ways of the country. However, the person who desires to return to his ancestral home acts the opposite way. This is why the Jews were redeemed. Despite all the difficulty of slavery, they did not cease to believe that they would return home and therefore they went from slavery to redemption.

Rabbi Pinchas Michael had advice on how to be redeemed and get out of difficulty. This was accomplished through observance of the Jewish Sabbath. Therefore, he would encourage those fearing his sermons to hurry up to receive in the Sabbath. For example, he asked artisans and their workers to leave their shops early, in order to exit the bathhouse in time.

*[Page 129]*

R. Pinchas Michael would take it upon himself to enter the bathhouse a long time before sunset with a rod in his hand and "whip" those delaying to leave. He would whip them out of love. R. Pinchas Michael objected to bodily punishment. Once he slapped on the cheek a youth of 14 years of age for hitting his playmate. R. Pinchas Michael regretted doing this and he could not concentrate on his prayers until he approached the boy and asked for his forgiveness. When the boy forgave him, he held his hand and was very happy.

According to his nature, R. Pinchas Michael was forgiving and easy going. Many people took advantage of this weakness and used it for their personal good. One wicked man forged his signature and traveled from city to city to collect money on behalf of the Jewish religious elementary school in Antopol. R. Pinchas Michael put an announcement in newspapers and asked the rabbis of the cities to which this man should come to take the notebook containing the forged letter and burn it. He asked only this and nothing more.

A wicked person also took advantage after the fire that broke out to Antopol in the summer of 1885. This was when 80 houses were burnt. And on the twentieth of June of that year another fire burnt one hundred and twenty houses. The Jews of Antopol became extremely poor and sent messengers to collect funds on behalf of the victims.

The elders of the town used to talk about the first fire that happened about 1869 as a historic event in the life of the town. This is because almost all the town went up in flames. In that year R. Pinchas Michael went out with R. Netanel Hayyim Pappah, one of the wealthy people in town, far away on behalf of the victims. They came up to St. Petersburg. Everywhere they were received in a friendly fashion. Thanks to these two distinguished townspeople the city was rebuilt. Jewish life again took its course and forms.

R. Pinchas Michael returned to the town and its Jews. He cared not only for his flock but also for the entire Jewish community. Once he said to R. Yekutiel husband of Belah Hartakes: "It is better for you than for me, because the world does not depend on you." People came from everywhere to see him and did not give him rest in spirit or body. Moshkah, his wife, used to drive out those coming to their house saying: "He is not able to help and he does not know how to help. Leave him alone! " As many as she would drive away, more would come.

And what about his study of Torah? Behold, a person is required to study "day and night". Therefore, he fulfilled the Talmudic statement: "The nights were only created to study (Tractate Eruvin 65). He would sleep a little and almost all the rest of the night he would study Torah. As a result, he had an amazing knowledge of Talmud and Codes. This was "up to the point that all the luminaries of his time treated him with respect."

Lack of sleep, many cares and strong devotion to studies caused R. Pinchas Michael to develop a severe internal illness. Following the advice of doctors, he went to Berlin for an operation. When he set out for Berlin, he also prepared for his death. This is because who knows what tomorrow will bring in such a situation. A person must leave an ethical will for his household. R. Pinchas Michael wrote such a will. Although the will was written to his sons, a person who reads it carefully with open eyes will see that this will represented his fundamental beliefs. We see his democratic attitude and opinion about the state of the poor and artisans. In his time, the artisan had an inferior status. The most important person was the Jewish religious scholar. Therefore, he tells his children to marry their sons to the daughters of scholars. "Do not seek out the rich, give your daughters to a good and scholarly person, even if he comes from a family of artisans. To do so is not contemptuous, as fools say. It is more contemptible to be one of the rich, who lose other people's money than an artisans who lives from the work of his own hands and is dear to G-d."

*[Page 130]*

R. Pinchas Michael also had an aesthetic sense and a desire to treat others gently. He asks that books be bound well, "because this is a glory to those who do so in this world and the world to come." R. Pinchas Michael warns: "Do not curse, even a gentile and even a living animal, and raise your children pleasantly and not with blows, only with good words...and be advised not to sadden any person, and especially a servant, because they are daughters of fathers like your own. Therefore, take care to honor them and you merit much good.

Likewise, he warns about household peace. A man must be easy going to his wife, even when she makes his life miserable. He advises not to bother quarreling, because it is hard for a husband to win in a quarrel with his wife. The husband should give his wife the benefit of the doubt. He also warns his daughters and daughter-in-laws to watch out for the honor of their husbands and not to make them sad "even with small talk".

He warns against sadness and anger several times, "Because sadness and anger are of no help in correcting anything. Remove sadness and anger and trust in G-d in all your affairs."

He also advises to give a tithe on behalf of the poor and poor relatives and for other holy matters. The money for this is to be kept as if it does not belong to the giver. If earning a living should not be so easy, do not go to ask the help of a saintly person i n another town. This is "because in every city there are people, who fear G-d and are able to beseech Him for the sake of the needy." This is also the case in physical needs. First, a person should ask mercy for himself from G-d. At the same time, he should ask others to seek mercy for him. Just as he was in his lifetime a representative for all the needy, so he promises to help those asking in the next world.

The admonishments of R. Pinchas Michael are similar to the admonishments of R. Asher of Stolin, of blessed memory, who was the son of R. Aharon, of Karlin, of blessed memory, the founder of Karlin Hasidism. He also warns some times about observing the Sabbath and adding a little extra time to it over the legal time of its entrance and exit. He warns about the need to set times to study Torah, to give a tithe and the likes of this.

Was R. Pinchas Michael influenced by the Baal Shem Tov's Hasidism? Did R. Pinchas Michael incline to Hasidism? We can answer the last question certainly in the negative. On the contrary, from anecdotes brought in his name, we learn that he was opposed greatly to the Hasidic way and Hasidic Rebbes. How are we able to reconcile his two different tendencies? Certainly, the two opinions are correct. In his youth, R. Pinchas Michael was a great opponent of the Hasidic way of life. However, he came closer to Hasidism in his last years. Sometimes, he would pray in the prayerhouse of the Hasidim of Stolin.

R. Pinchas Michael was rabbi of Antopol for twenty-six years. Not all the years were good and peaceful. It happened more than once or twice that a person attacked his spiritual leadership. R. Pinchas Michael forgave the insult quietly in his heart. We should say the truth. Not all of the inhabitants of Antopol saw the high value of this rabbi. An anecdote told in the name of R. Pinchas Michael will shed light on the attitude of the Jews of Antopol to him.

Once he was asked, "Why are you not as important inside the town of Antopol as outside of it?" R. Pinchas Michael answered, "The Biblical section when read in its place and time of reading is not very important. This is because we read it in the three weeks between the breach of the city walls of Jerusalem and the destruction of the Temple. However, when we read it outside of its place, as the last section of the Torah reading on a holiday, then a lot of money is paid to be called to the Torah for its reading. Pinchas in its own place does not have such recognition but Pinchas out of its place is more important."

*[Page 131]*

Thus, after his death people used to stretch out on his grave and ask him to intercede for them. It was not only the masses, which came to his grave. Rather, intellectuals and enlightened people used to come yearly, each as the rich Jew, Luria, of Pinsk. Everyone began to recognize the great importance of their pious man and rabbi, who lived as one of the holy and left the world holy after his death.

Thus, they say that on the new moon of Adar 1890 (650), R. Pinchas Michael took sick with typhus. He lay some weeks in a bed from which he did not get up. However, his mind was clear. When the time for prayer came, he awoke and prayed. On the last Sabbath of his life, he made + tie blessing over the reading of the Torah, and said to his family: "I am a guest. A guest must get the chance to say the blessing over the reading of the Torah". At the end of the Sabbath when he separated the passing of the holy day from the coming secular weekday, he wrote a card to be rushed to the Rabbi of Pinsk. He told in it of his coming death. He invited him to the funeral and asked forgiveness from him. Likewise, he informed him that in the case of the dispute in the place in Maimonides that the law is in accordance as he, the writer of the postcard, said. The day before the 17th of Adar, his soul exited in purity.

The town immediately wrapped itself in mourning. Runners went to Horodets and Kobrin to give the bad news of the righteous man's death.

Many from these towns, both Jews and gentiles, went to the funeral. The following rabbis gave the eulogy: R. Yehoshua Yaakov Rabinovits, rabbi of Horodets, Rabbi Tsevi Hirsh Rabinovits and R. Mosheh Berman, son-in-law of R. Pinchas Michael, R. David Rushkin, and R. Pinchasb. R. Eliyahu of Lida, the spiritual leader of Kobrin. They eulogized him near to the synagogue and near to the study hall on Pinsk St. Afterward, they came to the old study hall in which the deceased prayed. The luminary, R. Yosef Shaul Epshtein, rabbi of Kobrin, led the mourning. Thus, ended the episode of the life of R. Pinchas Michael, of blessed memory. And with his death ended a shining historical chapter in the history of the town of Antopol, whose Jews participated in its writing.

# Section from the Ethical Will of R. Pinchas Michael

My dear children and son-in-laws, since I am going to a distant city, I shall write you some ethical statements, even though you do not need my thoughts, since you are able to read books on ethics. Nevertheless, a father is responsible to energetically teach his sons ethics and we do learn from elders.

Our scholars, of blessed memory already spoke at length and warned about this in Midrash on the beginning chapters of Exodus. First of all, trust in the Holy One, Blessed be He, with a strong and firm trust. I know that all Israel trusts In G-d. Nevertheless, there is a difference between people's trust. Generally, when you have success in all your affairs through the grace of G-d's help, G-d forbade you think at all that because of your wisdom and understanding you have done well. Only give thanks to G-d's grace that he did well with you. Don't let your inclination entice you to make a lot of business deals. As our scholars of blessed memory have said: If he has a measure of money called a maneh, he wants 200 maneh of money. Really, it is very hard for a man to make due with what he has and not to make a lot of business deals and bother himself with doing a lot of grand things. It is worthwhile to think always that I should be careful, lest if I am not honest, G-d will remove me from success, and the door will be closed. For that reason, be happy with what you hate, which G-d has gracefully given you. And if your portion in life is restricted and you have need, trust in G-d and don't be sad. Sadness will not help you correct your ability to make a deal. Only ask mercy from the Holy Blessed be He and ask pious people to pray for you. For this purpose, you do not have to travel to other towns for help. In every town, there are pious people. And be very careful of lies and deceit, and even take care to keep your verbal agreement, because this is a very great measure of truth. And be very careful when another person's money is involved, because people who trust in G-d, do not desire the money of others. This is because G-d can give you sustenance with permission and honesty. Then, you will experience a physical and spiritual relaxation. You will have time to pray and to study. Our scholars of blessed memory have already said: "The first generations, who set aside fixed time for study, and who had strong faith, and only worked part-time, the Holy One, blessed be He, sent them a blessings in everything they did." It is certainly hard for us to be compared to the first generations. What is possible to do is to learn from them properly and to take ethics from them and learn good qualities. An enlightened person will pay attention to study his actions.

*[Page 132]*

When it comes to the study of the Torah, I should have spoken first about this. Certainly, our rabbis of blessed memory have already said, "Earning a living has priority over the study of Torah." Therefore, I started out first to warn you about how to conduct business and about the quality of self-assurance. These two things are interrelated. When you completely rely on G-d, you will have more time to study. Therefore, take care, my beloved sons and son-in-laws to study every day a leaf of Talmud and to review it well.

Don't think that your ability to make deals and do commerce will be spoiled, because of your study. It is not true, because it is impossible. The

Holy One, blessed be He, watches over in detail what happens to a person. And the study of Torah is considered as valuable as all of the commandments. Therefore, how is it possible for a person to suffer a loss from studying? If a person studies Torah, the Holy One, bussed be He, will sooner or later compensate him or he will be saved by means of his study from a bigger physical or financial loss. This is because the Holy One, blessed be He, thinks in depth of what shall be done to a person.

When it comes to household expenses, beware of spending too much for luxury, especially in a time when it is very hard for you to earn a living. Don't envy people, who spend excessively for wood and stones to make their houses pretty, and other unnecessary items. They will eventually lose their honorable place in life. They will also cause others to lose their money, sometimes a little, and sometimes a lot. Our scholars, of blessed memory, have already said to judge carefully before making expenses. They said that a person should spend less for food than that for which he has the money. Someone who deviates from the statements of our scholars, of blessed memory, is a person who acts as if he has separated himself from life.

Let us return a little to the matter of study. A person should learn every day the code of law book Hayye adam, so that he may learn how to carry out the day-to-day commandments. He should also study the prayer book Derekh ha-hayyim. This involves no great effort to study a little after prayer from the prayer book one uses to pray. However, the Holy One, blessed be He, adds all our actions into a big account. When the Holy One, blessed be He, helps you to marry your children, may they live to the age of marriage, for G-d's sake, don't think about money. And don't put a burden on yourself. Our scholars, of blessed memory, have already said, "You should give money to your daughter as you should do to your son:" They qualified this by saying that you should give to your daughter a tenth of your property. We know that it is hard to make due with a tenth of your wealth in buying the clothes for your daughter and the other extra expenses that everyone talks about.

Many people, may it not happen to us, have become impoverished, because they gave a large dowry to their children and spent more for wedding expenses than necessary. This is done, because of lack of trust that they will get a good match for their children. It is not, like the fools say, to spend beyond one's means and to trust in G-d not to be impoverished. This is not true. If they would have had strong trust in G-d, they would take a youth, who studies well in the rabbinical seminary but is badly clothed and barefoot. They should trust in G-d that he will help the new couple earn a living. However, they don't do that. They only trust in their coarse intellect. Therefore, my beloved, match up your sons, as the scholars of blessed memory said, with the daughter of a scholar, and don't look for a girl with rich parents. When it comes to wealth, the most that one can hope for is that the money will last over three generations, as is stated by our scholars, of blessed memory. You see this happen always to the very rich, even those of them who are truly pious. This is because even if they are truly pious, who knows what their children or grandchildren will be. Who is greater for us than Nakdimon ben Guryon, for whom the sun broke through the clouds, just as it did for Joshua. This is according to the statement of our scholars, of blessed memory, "There are three people for whom the sun broke through the clouds." Nevertheless, his daughter rebelled against him, may the Holy One, blessed be He, have mercy. You should see to give your daughters to a good and scholarly man, even if he comes from a family of craftsmen. This is not contemptuous, as the fools say. More contempt belongs to the families of the rich, who lose other people's money. However, craftsmen live from their work and they are dear in G-d's sight.

*[Page 133]*

In case, you are able to make a match among cousins in our own family, according to the statement of our scholars, of blessed memory, "A person, who marries in his own family and tribe does something very good." It talks at length about this in the Midrash Rabbah to the section Hayye Sarah in Genesis. "Plant seed from the wheat of your city, because it is likely to bring a successful crop. And so did Abraham, our father, say to his servant to get a bride for his son Isaac from his native land, Ur Kasdim, because the people from there are likely to succeed in bringing forth a holy seed." When your sons grow, it is worthwhile to send them to a rabbinical seminary for study, because they will learn in an orderly fashion. I am very sorry that I did not study in a rabbinical seminary and am not able to explain to you from personal experience its great value. However, whether you send or do not send your son depends on his nature. Send him only if you understand it will benefit him to travel to study and it is according to his desire.

Take care to study Midrash Rabbah every week for the portion of the Torah read in synagogue. Take care that in the course of the year you finish the Midrash together with the Scrolls, because it is a great and important thing to do. Study simply. This is especially the case, since there are explanations that can be understood well. And if there are places, which apparently are not understood and do not have a sufficient explanation, understand truly that this spot has a sublime secret. I also received from the luminaries of our time, may their memory be for the next world, that in places in the Midrash, the scholars hid secrets like the treasures of secrets hidden in the folklore in the Talmud. For this reason, don't stop studying Midrash, because of some places that you cannot understand.

My dear children, when you have to earn a living and not every person is free from doing this, at least be sparing in your talk as much as possible. Think that the time you save from not talking, you can spend with a book, even books on ethics, Pentateuch or Prophets; so that you may merit the world to come. Someone, who blessed memory said, "Everyone, who talks a lot, comes to sin." Don't think that for the sake of business that you should talk a lot. This is a lie! People who talk a lot for business, do so because they lack trust that the Holy One gives success.

When it is time to pray, forget about business matters. Think of the sublimity of the Holy One, blessed be He, and simply on the words of prayer. Try to do this every day. Don't despair if G-d forbid you are not able to do this sometimes. This is one of four things at which you need to try a lot.

When it comes to books, don't buy the Biblical Apocrypha that tell foolish and fine stories. Our scholars have already said, "...he who brings Biblical Apocrypha into his house, brings in confusion."

*[Page 134]*

This is even true about the Book of Ben Sira. His book deals with ethics and earning a living and has fine words. Take care not to read it. Truly, one should not learn from the great people of the generation, who sometimes read it in some places. As our scholars of blessed memory have said, "They allowed the Family of Raban Gasliel to study Greek Wisdom, because they had to deal with the authorities. In the case of Mamonides, of blessed memory, he was able to learn things that caused bitterness and a r e comparable to serpents. He digested all this and turned it into honey in his stomach. Who can be compared to him? Nevertheless, he was criticized truly in many statements. The educated person will find the sources in their places.

See that you purchase a set of the Talmud and Codes and other Holy Books. This is because sometimes a person is prevented from studying for lack of owning the necessary books. When others rush to beautify their houses with silver vessels, wood and stone colored in red, see that you beautify your houses with Holy Books, which are bound well. Their binding shall be a glory to the people having this done in this world and in the world to come.

In all matters, whether physical, suffering some sickness, G-d forbid, or monetary, seek first G-d to ask mercy from Him, and inform the public of your sorrow, so that they shall ask mercy for you. Likewise, in all matters concerning arrangements of marriages of your descendents, and all matters from small to big, make your request to the Holy One, blessed be He. This is because in His greatness and his humility, he will not despise the suffering of the poor.

When you go to sleep, I don't have to remind you to say the Shema prayer before going to bed. This is because even the ignorant are careful to do this. I warn you strongly to think about some holy matter before you sleep. This may be a section in the Mishnah or Talmud or Pentateuch, or anything else that you are able to read. And with this thought in mind, you shall go to sleep. When you wake up in the middle of the night from your sleep, also do not think about the world's follies.

And be very careful to wash your hands upon waking, even in the middle of the night. Nevertheless, if it is impossible to wash your hands for some reason, you may think about matters of Torah. This is because you may not recite words of Torah if your hands are not clean.

My beloved, be very careful with domestic tranquility. Treat leniently your wives and household members and servants. Just as a person wishes to earn a living well, so he should be careful in this matter. Don't talk a lot with your wife. And if sometimes, she causes you bitterness, don't argue with her. It is best to leave your wives and go to the study hall or to the synagogue and not to argue with them. This is because it is hard to prevail over their foolishness. And our rabbis of blessed memory have said, "They were created from Adam's rib. Therefore, it is hard to appease them." And judge them on the side of merit.

Likewise, in city matters, you should see to act only in peace and flee from dispute as you flee from fire. Don't accept an appointment, even to be the treasurer of the study hall, whose job is to call the people. The exception is that you should accept to be the treasurer of an elementary school, because the study of Torah is considered as valuable as all the other commandments.

In this way, be very careful to advise them to study Torah and to give them food and clothes. Likewise, in visiting the sick you should take care as much as possible. As far as the rest of the associations, it is better not to be a member, especially those involving mediation and accepting money. I advise you strongly on this.

In the matter of commerce, you should be very careful not to trespass, even in a situation permitted by law, such as to put a store next to a store. This is because success in this is unexpected for many reasons. We have already seen this. And if sometimes it is hard for us to follow this advice, I have already said that things go easier for a trusting person, and that G-d will help him. In the matter of loans, if you are able to take care not to loan or take a loan on interest, this is very good. This is because it is true that merchants, who do big deals borrowing money on interest almost always see in the end that such action is not successful. At least try and do as little with matters involving interest as possible. Take care that a bill of obligation is properly written according to religious law, as is explained in the book "Hokhmat adam" (Wisdom of mankind).

*[Page 135]*

Take care about swearing an oath and accepting a ban, because on the matter of swearing truly, a person can be really punished. Try to compromise, so that you do not need an oath. In the matter of welcoming in the Sabbath, be very careful to welcome it in early. Warn strictly your wives and servants, because the commandment of the Sabbath is great and has a value equal to all the Torah and the commandments. We have not seen such a case in the other commandments, as occurs in the case of the Sabbath, where someone who does not keep the Sabbath, G-d forbid, does not keep the entire Torah.

My beloved, be very careful about the matter of charity from the viewpoint of being miserly. The Torah has already warned against this and called a miserly person wicked. This also applies to carrying out household expenses, one should not be miserly but should find a middle ground. My children, be very careful when you give a tithe. Keep the money for the tithe secure with you as if it were not your own money. Give it to the poor and your relatives, and as the need arises, to other matters that are holy.

In our times, we must be more diligent, because the Sabbaths and Festivals were only given to study Torah, as our scholars, of blessed memory, have stated. And the author has already spoken at length about this in the holy work called Brit Avraham. It is worth reading this. Be very careful regarding the commandment to put on phylacteries. And for the sake of G-d, do not make the boxes holding the parchments from the Torah big. It is very good that they be small. The passageway for the strap on the phylactery for the head should be two fingers wide. This is so, G-d forbid, they are not put on the forehead and separated from the proper position on the head. Be very careful about observing the commandment of wearing fringes on the corner of your garments. Have a fringed garment with you even when you are traveling.

Generally, in the matter of all the commandments, do not be miserly. And the Holy One, blessed be He, will make up for your need. Make honoring Heaven the main thing. Following this principle, you should not talk in the study hall or synagogue. This is a sanctuary. You do this for the sake of G-d, may His name be blessed.

My beloved and dear ones! You should have love and unity among you and always seek the welfare of your fellow man and woman. I have tried to publish my novellas, which the Holy One, blessed be He, has caused me to express on the Talmud and also the Response of my predecessors. These are arranged, and everything that is out of place can be put back n order. Nay sermons are also arranged. And if you wish, publish these works.

My daughters and daughter-in-laws, be very careful about the honor of your husbands. Don't cause them anguish even in a small matter, G-d forbid. Never utter a curse, even against a gentile, and even against animals. Accept the Sabbath early and quickly. Raise your children by guiding them with words and not with physical blows. Use only good words. Our teacher and rabbinical authority the pious luminary, Elijah of Vilna, has already advised us about this in his ethical will. Read it always, because it is a cure for the soul.

Remove from yourselves the quality of sadness and anger. Trust in G-d in all your matters. And the rest of the statements and laws, which a woman should follow, has already been published in Yiddish. Read these always. Be careful so as not to cause a shy person sadness, and especially your servants. This is because they are also, understandably, the children of the Biblical Patriarchs. Therefore, take care to respect them and you will have a lot of merit.

*[Page 136]*

To the people of my city of Antopol, which is dear to me, may the Holy One, blessed be He, have mercy on you end keep you from all harm. There should be goodness and grace in your borders. Be advised to pursue peace and avoid disputes.

And I have asked you to forgive me with a full heart, whether in matters involving money or in things prohibited or allowed. Announce this in the study hall and in the synagogue. And I also forgive you in every detail.

I will ask you to keep the amendment to our communal law not to have a wedding on any Friday in the winter, and in the summer, it should not occur after 4 pm in the afternoon.

And I have asked that you study in the first year of my death a chapter and a half of Mishnah every day, so that you may finish at the end of the year all of the Mishnah. And that you say after the study of the Mishnah the prayer "Ana", which is published in the book of Mishnah. And I will also pray for your behalf as much as I am able. And I will do as much as I am able for you. And I have asked Yaakov ha-Kohen, may the light of his knowledge shine, and Mr. Tuviyah and his son to study every day a chapter of Mishnah and afterwards that they should pray and say Kadish di-Rabanan. And with the help of G-d, I will intercede on behalf of R. Yaakov ha-Kohen as much as I am able. Generally, I will intercede on behalf of everyone who studies Mishnah for me.

And I admonish all my townsfolk to live in peace with one another. Certainly, I will not forget to do what I am able to, on your behalf. And for everyone who shall express to me a specific request, I will try to do all I can. This is because I shall work upon my death, as I did when I was among you, to try and help others as much as I am able.

My dear daughter, I ask you not to be too sad, because you are weak and your health may suffer. Generally, what the Holy One, blessed be He, does is for the good. It is forbidden to cry a lot. One should receive what the Holy One, blessed be He, does with true joy. And I am not crying when I write this, because I expect the mercy of the Holy One, blessed be He, and that I will have a joyous report to tell. This letter, which my son Avraham Mosheh, may the light of his learning increase, will be copied by my son Meir Elazar and his son-in-law, may the light of his learning increase. You will safeguard this copy. Whoever wants to copy it shall be allowed to do so. You should try to print the composition on the Talmud, the Mishnah, and whatever is written on codes. The Holy One, blessed be He, will help you.

I am your father and father-in-law, who seeks your welfare with love. I write this today, Sunday, 20th day of the month of June (Sivan), 1897 (657), in Berlin.

*Note: The sons of R. Pinchas Michael were: 1) Avraham Mosheh Groisleit in Lithuanian Brisk; 2) Meir Elazar in Pinsk. His daughters were: 1) Toibay Beilah; 2) Roikhl; 3) Mikhlah, who married Rabbi Aba Sirkin, rabbi of Sharshev.*

*Their sons are: Duber, Yosel, Elazar, Eizik. Their daughters are: Toibah, PInah, and Breinah. Breinah married R. Mosheh Berman of Antopol, who inherited the rabbinical post of R. Pinchas Michael in 1892 (652). In 1921 R. Mosheh Berman came to the United States and was accepted as the rabbi of the orthodox synagogues in Los Angeles, California. He died on September 22, 1931 (Heshvan 691). His sons are: Professor Feitel Berman, expert in cardiology, In Los Angeles, and chief director of the Los Angeles Regional Hospital, which is one of the biggest in the United States, and Pinchas(Pintsheh), a poet in Yiddish. His daughters are: Leah Silberman and Feigel Duber, the son of Mikhlah, had a son and daughter. The name of the daughter is Feigah and the name of the son is R. Avraham Wants. After the Holocaust, only the son survived and he came to New York. The Rabbi R. Aba (called now Tsiyens) taught in the R. Yitshak Elhanan Seminary. He is now rabbi of one of the synagogues in the Bronx, N.Y. and the head of a rabbinical seminary located there.*

# R. Mordekhai, of Blessed Memory
## By Ben-Ezra

"Everything depends on luck, even a Torah scroll In a synagogue" (Zohar, section of Numbers called Naso). This simply means: sometimes people forget to read a large size Morah scroll, and take out of the ark a small size Torah scroll and read from it. Thus is the luck of books people and cities. Sometimes but very rarely a small and far away town has a greater reputation than a big city and makes a place for itself in history.

*[Page 137]*

This was the fortune of Antopol, a town placed in a swamp, in the district of Kobrin, Grodno province. This small town, in which a hundred years ago, there lived only 1,108 Jews was famous for its saintly rabbis. In addition to the rabbis learned in Torah, who held a rabbinical post in this town, there were Jewish craftsmen, who would go early morning to the study hall to study a page of Talmud. Among them was a blacksmith called R. Yekutiel, who would teach a lesson in Talmud to people rich in means and learned in Torah.

It was due to the good fortune of Antopol, that among the great rabbis, who held the rabbinical post there, was the luminary R. Shemuel, who was later appointed to be the chief rabbi of Karlin.

In 1921, Mosheh Berman came to the United States and was accepted as the chief rabbi of the orthodox synagogues in Los Angeles, California. He died on September 22nd of 1931.

Note: His sons are: Professor Feitel Berman, expert in cardiology and chief director of the Los Angeles Regional Hospital, which is one of the biggest in the United States, and Pinchas(Pintsheh), a poet in Yiddish. His daughters are: Leah Silberman and Feigel. Duber, the son of Mikhlah, had a son and daughter. The name of the daughter is Feigah and the name of the son is R. Avraham Zaiants. After the Holocaust, only the son survived and he came to New York. The Rabbi R. Aba (called now Tsiyens) taught in the R. Yitshak Elhanan Seminary. He is now rabbi of one of the synagogues in the Bronx, N.Y. and the head of a rabbinical seminary located there.

"Everything depends on luck, even a Torah scroll in a synagogues (Zohar, section of Numbers called Naso). This simply means: sometimes people forget to read a large size Torah scroll, and take out of the ark a small size Torah scroll and read from it Thus, is the luck of books, people, and cities. The righteous and mystic rabbi, R. Mosheh Tsevi, the father of Rabbi Joshua Jacob and Dr. Israel Michal Rabinowitz, served 42 years (1818-1862), 578-622, in this town. R. Mosheh Tsevi was known not only for his learning and great knowledge in the written and oral law and Jewish mysticism. He also had a developed character and the ability to feel for the individual and public. People used to come to him both for spiritual and practical affairs. One group of people came to him for their professional affairs and another group of people for their medical and psychiatric care.

The luminary R. Hayyim Zalman Bresloi, who was afterwards president of the rabbinical court in Mir and a professor of Talmud there, officiated as rabbi in town. Antopol was not only famous for its rabbis.

It was also fertile soil to train rabbis, who afterwards served other communities. Among the most famous were these two rabbis: the righteous rabbi, Yitshak Mrsh, who afterwards was rabbi in Simiats, Grodno province, and R. Mordekhai-Li.

In an environment saturated with Jewish law and mysticism, R. Mordekhai was born in 1837 on May 3rd (Iyar 597). His parents were: his father, R. Mendel and his mother Sarah. R. Mendel was a miller. This was the origin of their family name Weitsel (wheat seed). R. Mendel was not known as an analytical scholar. He was rather a Jew familiar with basic religious books as well as Jewish liturgy. B;:") Mendel was known in Antopol and outside of it for his ability to lead Jewish prayer services.

Mordechai, the son of R. Mendel the miller, was seen already in his childhood as an exceptionally brilliant person. He did not make due with his usual studies in Jewish elementary school. He would stay after school and study Jewish law after formal classes were over. At that time, he got the nickname, Mordekhai- Li. It was felt in his youth that he was born to greatness.

*[Page 138]*

People tell this story of Mordechai, when he was eight. He came home to eat his meal and asked his mother, "Please give me my meal!" His mother replied, "Immediately, my son." The small child went to the oven and saw rolls being baked. He said: "The way the rolls are being baked makes them unfit for consumption by Jews according to ritual law!" His mother rebuked him for comments on the ritual fitness of her kitchen. He held his ground and added, "If you doubt me, go to the rabbi, and ask him how to bake rolls In accordance with ritual law."

The mother of R. Mordechai-Li. went to the rabbi and asked him how to bake rolls in accordance with ritual law. The rabbi asked her, "How did you know to ask this question? Who told you?" The mother said, "My son, Mordechai-Li, told me to ask this question."

The rabbi studied the matter and said that the rolls were not fit for ritual consumption. From that time on, Mordechai-Li became famous not only as a studious child, but also as a person who knew Jewish law. Before the year was over, he became the pupil of R. Yitshak Hirsh, the rabbi of Antopol. R. Yitshak Hirsh observed that his young pupil did not just concern himself with straight forward rabbinical works that discuss the legal questions of what is permitted and what is forbidden and what is fit for ritual consumption and what is unfit for ritual consumption. He also studied mystical works, which are outside the legal tradition. These books attracted the attention of Mordechai-Li.

R. Yitshak Hirsh, who was an authority on both the Jewish legal tradition and Jewish mysticism, did not permit his pupil to study books other than on the topics of Jewish law. This was because he thought that first a student should fully study Talmud and Codes. It was only after the study of these topics that a person could study Jewish mysticism.

The pupil Mordechai-Li studied diligently with R. Yitshak Hirsh for six years. He was ordained at the age of fourteen with rabbinical ordination.

The reputation of R. Mordechai-Li went beyond the boundaries of Antopol. Many of the important people in town wanted him for a son-in-law. Finally, R. Shimon Volvol, a rich, important Jew, was able to marry him to his daughter, Chayah. He agreed to pay the couple's living expenses all their lives. In addition to the bride and living expenses, he gave an invaluable study tool, especially for R. Mordechai-Li., a diligent student and lover of books. It was a case of books, whose value was 500 rubles.

Free the concerns of earning a living, R. Mordechai-Li studied Talmud and related books day and night. He was always repeating aloud his lessons. To keep from sleeping, he put his feet into buckets of cold water. While studying, he forgot about basic human needs, such as eating, drinking, etc. He studied for the sake of studying, not to make profane use of his studies. However, when the matter of charity was involved, to come to the aid of the poor or to fulfill the commandment of redeeming captives, then he carried out the following Biblical sentence himself, "It is time to act on G-d's behalf. People have abrogated your law (Ps. 119 and 126)." He would leave the study hall, step deeply into the swamps or snow, and go from house to house to collect money. He didn't pay attention to his fingers becoming chapped from the cold.

And if it happened that some tough person would not give as much as he was able, R. Mordechai would enter the kitchen, take a club and threaten him. Understandably, the person submitted to R. Mordechai, and gave as much as he was assessed to give. This was because he knew that Mordechai was not collecting for his own sake.

R. Mordechai-Li did not only occupy himself with legal matters. He had this principle: "Everyone who saves one Jewish soul, is comparable to one who has saved the whole world." The individual represents the community and the entire community is each of its individual members. Each individual member is to be considered as making up the entire community himself. This was the point of view according to which Mordechai.-Li. lived his entire life.

*[Page 139]*

There was established a rabbinical for youths fit for ordination in Pinsk. Among were the founders of the seminary the mystic R. Mordekhai Zakheim, president of the court of Pinsk, and R. Avigdor Tosfah, rabbi of Karlin. R. Mordechai-Li. wanted to study with the mystic, to be influenced by him in the study of Jewish mysticism, and to further his legal studies from the immense knowledge of R. Shemuel Tosfah.

R. Mordechai-Li traveled to Pinsk, and studied three years with these two spiritual giants. He especially was drawn to Jewish mysticism. However, his rabbi, R. Mordechai Zakheim, forbid him to study openly this type of knowledge. He used to study it secretly when people were asleep. The reason of R. Mordekhai Zakheim was that if it would be known that R. Mordechai-Li was a mystic, then he would be considered to be a miracle worker and crowds of people would visit him as they did the Bal-shems. The people's visits would interfere with his studies. After receiving ordination from R. Mordekhai Zakheim and R. Shemuel Tosfah, R. Mordechai-Li returned to Antopol. He was accepted to be a rabbinical judge in town. This appointment requires an interpretation. This is because R. Mordechai-Li was not the son of a rabbi and not the son-in-law of the rabbi, who inherited a rabbinical position. He was the son of a miller and the son-in-law of one of the simple Jews In town. Thus, If R. Mordechai-Li was appointed judge in town, this shows that he was worthy of the great appointment and got it only because of his knowledge and contributing qualities.

In 1864 (624) the pious rabbi, R. Pinchas Michael was appointed to be rabbi of Antopol. These two great personalities got along fabulously. The two of them stuck together. They studied together and took care of the individual Jew and the Jewish community. They paid special care to the spiritual and physical wounds of the individual Jew. From the moment R. Mordechai-Li became friendly with the pious R. Pinchas Michael, of blessed memory, the reputation of R. Mordechai-M increased, both because of his genius and his righteousness. Many communities offered him a rabbinical post.

However, the community of Antopol did not let him leave. This fact may serve as how popular R. Mordechai-M was with the Jews of Antopol.

A big fire broke out in town in the year 1870 (630). Almost all of the town was destroyed by the fire. Most of the Jews were without income or housing. In that year, the Jews of Bitan (Grodno province) asked R. Mordechai-Li to accept the rabbinical post there. R. Mordechai-Li accepted. However, all the Jews of Antopol could not make peace with this. How was it possible that their delightful townsman R. Mordechai-Li could leave? Was it not enough that they had become impoverished and they would also have to give up their glory?

A dispute broke out between the communities of Antopol and Bitan. The Antopol community said that R. Mordechai-Li belonged to them. The community of Bitan said that R. Mordechai-Li would be their rabbi. The end was that one night R. Mordechai-Li left town. People said that the important people of Bitan stole him away. It is worthwhile to say that R. Mordechai-M came to inherit the post left empty by the righteous rabbi, R. Shelomoh-Li, of blessed memory. There are some legends about that man. The community of Bitan was small then. It had only about one hundred families. They could pay him only fifteen rubles a month. However, R. Mordechai-Li was glad to accept. When his wife complained about what was going to happen to her, R. Mordechai-Li tried to entice her with these words, "Was the wife of Jacob the shoemaker better than yours?"

It was typical of R. Mordechai-Li to make do with little. This was also his attitude to the poor. He would say, "I and my family have more than enough. Why should I not help a rich man, who has become poor, or any poor person? Why should I not make it easier to a poor woman, who has given birth?"

*[Page 140]*

He did everything secretly. He hated publicity and was afraid of it very much. His fear of publicity prevented him many times from taking part in public works, which had to be done through assemblies and with great publicity. This quality of modesty and avoiding honor was the most typical of R. Mordechai-Li. This quality was basic and rooted in the enticing personality called R Mordechai-Li.

Even though R. Mordechai avoided publicity, nevertheless, his reputation was praised by thousands of Jews. They came from near and far to Bitan. This one came to get the blessing of the righteous rabbi. And this one came to ask him a question in a time of trouble. And one of the luminaries and righteous men of that period, R. Pinchas Michael, of blessed memory, would ask those who asked him for some cure, "Why do you come to me and not a wise and righteous man like R. Mordechai-Li? Travel to him!"

And thus, people did. When the name of the righteous man of Bitan or R. Mordechai-Li of Bitan (R. Mordechai-Li Bitener) became known, they traveled to him. Thanks to the crowds that mobbed his home, the Bitan Jewish community began to flourish. Wagon drivers, inns, stores, and all the inhabitants of town got good business. Not only did the material condition of the town improve, its spiritual position became significantly better under the influence of R. Mordechai-Li. In Bitan he founded a seminary for grown youths. Many youths came to study with him. R. Mordechai- Li taught according to healthy logic. He avoided hair-splitting as much as possible. Incidentally, he used to mix in jokes and daily events in his words. This is because R. Mordechai-Li was a wise person and had knowledge of what was going on in the world.

The needs of the Yeshiva and community took most of his time in the day. He founded an Association to provide free clothes to the poor pupils of the Jewish religious elementary school. He obtained more support to provide lodging for poor travelers, and similar charitable associations.

He regarded the poor and lonely as a part of himself and he devoted his strength to help them. This is because "the natural duty towards one's fellow human being and Jewish law demand us to answer the requests of every man and woman." The function of the rabbi is not only to decide what is the law about milk and meat products fit for ritual consumption. It is to lead the people and give them moral aid. For this reason, R. Mordechai-Li complained about rabbis who don't make it their habit to answer all those seeking help.

During the day, he would help people with their private concerns and also deal with public concerns. At night, he would study Jewish law until dawn. During his study, he would write down novellas and answer response.

R. Mordechai-Li stayed eighteen years in the town of Bitan. He lived a private life of suffering and poverty in this town. He suffered because the young wife he had married died on March 8th, 1881 (the eighth day of Adar 641) after years of sickness and suffering. He remained a widow and had to raise his small children. R. Mordechai-Li suppressed the pain of his private life. However, he had to deal directly with the pain of those who came to his doors for help. The Jewish people coming to him had a lot of needs and he felt it was his duty to find help for those suffering. He gave good advice and words of comfort.

He made Bitan an important place during his stay. It became a major center since everyone came there to see him. He encouraged the thousands of people who came to him by speaking lovingly and truthfully. He did his duty to the point of self-sacrifice.

Many communities wanted to appoint R. Mordechai-Li as rabbi. He declined until he received an offer from the community of Korlits (Minsk province). The brilliant luminary, R. Eliyahu Barukh Kamai, was rabbi there for several years. R. Kamai was Professor of Talmud in Mir and profoundly influenced his rabbinical seminary. R. Eliyahu Barukh Kamai left Korlits in 1886 (646) to become rabbi of the city of Vaksna (Vilna province). The Jews of Korlits began to seek a rabbi fit to fill the place of R. Eliyahu Barukh Kamai, who was both knowledgeable and analytical. He also knew what was going on in the world.

*[Page 141]*

The Jews of Korlits decided to appoint R. Mordechai-Li. They sent some important people to Bitan, bringing an offer of rabbinical appointment with them. R. Mordechai-Li hesitated but finally they convinced him and he agreed. However, the Jews of Bitan did not agree. They protested his leaving. Some hotheads said, "We will break their bones! We will shed their blood if they take our rabbi from here!" Mordechai-Li called the hotheads to him and quieted them. Although they stopped being angry, they were very bitter against the people of Korlits.

In 1857 (647), R. Mordechai-Li was forced to flee to Kolits. He left at night, just as he had previously left Antopol for Bitan. The Jews of Bitan wondered what they could do to get back at the people of Korlits.

The day R. Mordechai-Li came to Korlits was a holiday for the Jews. The stores were closed and the craftsmen stopped working. Youth and old came to receive R. Mordechai-Li, who came to inherit the rabbinical chair of R. Eleyahu Barukh Kamai. It did not take much time for R. Mordechai-Li to become beloved to the Jews of Korlits. Everyone honored him, old and young. He immediately became famous as the miracle worker of Korlits. Jews and gentiles flocked to him from near and far. Some came to receive a blessing. Others came for medical or help or just for good advice. In addition, youths and adult students came to study in the rabbinical seminary founded by R. Mordechai-Li and to listen to his lessons.

R. Mordechai-Li gave lessons like an artist. The relation of R. Mordechai-Li. to his students may be seen in this event. The rabbi and author Ben-Tsiyon Eizenshtat was thirteen years old when he came to study in the rabbinical seminary of R. Mordechai-Li in Korlits. One time at the end of the Sabbath and after midnight, this youth was found lying down on one of the benches in the study hall. He used his winter coat as a pillow. It was dark in the study hall except in one corner there was a small candle burning. Then, R. Mordechai-Li entered the study hall. He put the books of Talmud together, which had been spread out, and left the study hall. Within ten minutes, R. Mordechai-Li's son entered the study hall, woke up the sleeping youth and asked him to go to the rabbi's house, where a bed was prepared for him. The youth refused this invitation, thinking that he was not worthy of this invitation, which would bring him so much honor.

After a little while, R, Mordechai-Li himself came to him and rebuked him for not coming over, "We know that the study of Torah and having a profession to earn go well together. If Jewish law takes concern that a person should be able to earn a living, i t certainly cares that he take care of his immediate physical needs! A person, who causes himself pain is a sinner in the sight of the Holy One, blessed be.

R. Mordechai-Li drew himself to all types of people with words of love. Everyone honored and respected him. R. Mordechai-Li did not stay long in Korlits. He was rabbi for only four years. He was called to serve in Ashmina (Vilna province). Ashmina was a bigger town than Korlits. It was famous as a city of people devoted to self-study and enlightenment.

The luminary and righteous rabbi, R. Hayyim Avraham Shapira was rabbi in Ashmina. He was the son of the famous luminary, R. Libli Shapira of Kovno. R. Libli Shapira of Kovno was the brother of the luminary, our master and teacher, Refael Shapira, Professor of Talmud at the Volozhin rabbinical seminary.

R. Mordechai-Li came to inherit the position of the luminary R. Eliyahu Perski. Mordechai-Li wanted to sit peacefully and devote himself only to Torah and community matters. However, he was not able to devote himself just to these things since he had to deal with people seeking healing for their pains. He was unable to send them away without trying to help. He had to listen to the painful lives of the thousands coming to visit him.

*[Page 141]*

For example, it was impossible for him not to pay attention to a woman about to give birth, who had no money and still needed a doctor. To whom could she turn in a decisive hour like this? Understandably, she came to R. Mordechai-Li, even if it were late at night. R. Mordechai-Li got dressed and ran to the cow, so that the woman giving birth would have milk to nurse her infant.

R. Mordechai-Li acted like a merciful and patient father. He would pay attention to everyone. This is because not everyone could elevate himself to study Talmud and novellas. Therefore, R, Mordechai-Li paid attention to the individuals bringing their problems to him. Besides individual matters, he had to pay attention to public affairs. There were groups to study Talmud and Midrash. There were youth sitting and studying Torah in the study hall in need of meals and clothes. There was no one to care for them except R. Mordechai-Li. He took care of their needs without publicity or making noise. He did it quietly and in secret. This is because "least my actions be known to people thinking that I did it only for attention and approval."

Rabbis complained that he did not participate in rabbinical assemblies. One of the greatest rabbis asked him why he devoted himself only to the needs of individuals coming to him. R. Mosheh answered, "My paying attention to the needs of Individuals is something that was assigned to me from Heaven to do. Perhaps, I will be able to help the individual who came to me, even a little. I know that my ability to do is weak. However, each individual that I help is added to that total number, which we call the community. Therefore, I am involved in public affairs. The public is composed of individuals, who make it up. I am trying to act as Jewish law instructs me."

He himself lived on as little as possible. He only ate meat on Sabbaths and holidays. He gave most of his salary to the poor. Likewise, he would give gifts to his visitors. There was a great change in the private life of R, Mordechai-Li in Ashmina. He married a second time. His wife was Malka, daughter of R. Avraham Grinberg, of Slonim, a rich and learned Jew. The new father-In-law took it upon himself to support R. Mordechai-M. However, he, himself, did not take all of the benefits offered him by his father- In-law. He lived a simple and modest life. Nevertheless, when it came to the purchase of books, his spiritual food, nothing stood in his way. R. Mordechai-Li paid attention to the purchase of books. He devoted himself to the purchase of rare books. The day that he added an important book to his library was really a holiday for him.

Just as he acted gently with people, so he was as hard as steel when it came to be zealous for G-d. He didn't back away from a powerful person. He rebuked the rich for oppressing the poor. If a person broke Jewish law, he left his private duties and went to fight G-d's war. The truth was always a candle lighting his way.

The life of a person is like a road and has different stops. Each stop has its signs. Each stop leaves an impression on the person delaying in it and staying there. R. Mordechai-Li had five stops in his life: Antopol, Bitan, Korlits, Ashmina, and the last stop of Slonim.

Slonim was well known as a Jewish city. Jewish luminaries had previously occupied the rabbinical position. They included R. MoshehR. Yehudah Edelman, R. Dov Berish Ashkenazi, and R. Eyzil Harif.

The rabbinate at the time of R. Mordechai.-Li was held in Slonim by R. Joseph Shlufer. He was called "the youthful genius of Dinaburg". He was the son-in-law of R. Eizil Harif. He had inherited the position of R. Joseph Rafin. Behold, R. Joseph Shlufer died in 1900 (665). The community of Slonim began to look for a worthy rabbi. It paid attention to R. Mordechai-Li. And what happened in the first towns, also happened in Ashmina. A conflict broke out between Ashmina and Slonim. Each town wanted R. Mordechai-Li. Finally, Slonim won the struggle and R. Mordechai-Li left Ashmina in the dark of night.

*[Page 142]*

R. Mordechai occupied the rabbinical post in Slonim for eleven years, from 1905-1916. He also acted like a Hasidic Rebbe. His being both the Rabbi and Rebbe was a strange fact. Here, you have the rabbi of a well known city, a great scholar in Jewish law and wisdom, to whom all the great scholars of Israel turn in response concerning law, who was an opponent of Hasidism and the son of an opponent of Hasidism. At the same time, he acted like the Bal-Shem Tov. Hundreds of legends grew up around him. However, R. Mordechai-Li did not see a contradiction in being both the Rabbi and Rebbe. Yet, he would complain to visitors coming for a blessing, "Why travel to me if you have Hayyim the blacksmith?"

Hayyim the blacksmith from the village of Holozin close to Pinsk was famous for his love of truth and pursuit of justice. He was known to be a person who would not benefit at all from others. On the contrary, this poor person would seek out other poor people to give them the cereals and vegetables, which he received from gentiles in payment for his work. He had the ability to dress the wounds of the oppressed and the broken of heart.

R. Mordechai-Li would sometimes send his visitors to a cripple known as a miracle worker. The youth lived in a village near to Beiki (Grodno province). Hundreds of people would come to him to ask for advice and for cures from him. This is because he also knew secular sciences. Nevertheless, R. Mordechai sometimes advised against other miracles workers, "Don't believe in the efficacy of this! On the other hand, don't have slight regard for even the blessing of a lay person."

Still, people did not give him peace. They would diligently seek him out day and night. The immigration to the United States increased at that time. People came to ask his advice on whether to go to the United States. This was because the United States had the reputation that even to land on its soil was an act not allowed by Jewish ritual law. R. Mordechai's answer was that if you wish to be a Jew living according to rabbinical Jewish law, you are able to do this anywhere. When his sister asked his opinion he answered, "The United States is not a country that makes a Jew impure. There will come a time when people will envy those who immigrated to the United States and the soil where we remained will be impure." This was a farsighted view, a look at a distant time and a different country.

Likewise, his view about settling Israel was that of a Jew devoted heart and soul to the vision of future generations. He would say, "If I knew that the Turks would give up Israel to us, then I would give the coat off my back to achieve this." According to Heikl Lunski, who wrote the biography of R. Mordechai-Li, he was a lover of Zion in theory and action.

His statements made a big impression on the community of those seeking him out and listening to his advice. When he looked at a person, his gaze penetrated the very soul of the person. Everyone trembled at the majestic sight of him in his old age. His long eyebrows cast fear on people facing him. His glance could be hypnotic. However, some refused to accept his authority, including a Jewish barber in Slonim and a Jewish photographer. The photographer was a tough fellow, who used to work on Saturday. When R. Mordechai found this out, he protested from the pulpit against violating the Sabbath. He warned the photographer not to work on Saturday. This happened a few times without result. Then, R. Mordechai-Li excommunicated him. The next day the photographer forced his way into R.

Mordechai-Li's house. He took out a gun and aimed it at him. People in the household shouted for help. Others rushed into the house, seized the photographer and gave him over to the police. However, R. Mordechai–Li, a forgiving father, came to court when the case came up and forcefully and successfully asked to have the charges dismissed.

*[Page 144]*

R. Mordechai-Li acted to save Jewish lives. He forgave insults to his honor. He didn't care about his health. He would go great distances and see the necessary officials. This was so that no harm should happen to a Jewish person. Heikl Lunski tells-about one instance when some youths were condemned to hanging because of rebellion against the State. R. Mordechai-Li took it upon himself despite his advanced age to go with great suffering to Vilna, so that he could ask mercy from the General Governor. Thank G-d his request was granted. Because of his intervention, the youths did not get the death sentence.

Suddenly, World War I broke out. The borders were closed. Many communities were uprooted. The Russians also poured out their wrath on Slonim before they left. The troubles of the Jewish people increased. R. Mordechai-Li could not bear to see the anguish of the Jewish people. Hiss strength left him. The evening before March 28, 1916 (Adar I 676), the saintly R. Mordechai-Li died. His light was extinguished, the light which illuminated days of darkness and trouble for the public and the individual!

## Spiritual Property

The spiritual property of R. Mordechai-Li was not very great. Only one of his books was printed. Most of his writings on Jewish law and response, which number in the hundreds, remained in manuscript. Among these is a very intelligent and valuable commentary on Shulhan arukh, Hoshen mishpat, and a big composition on the order Kodashim of the Talmud. There is a reason for this. R. Mordechai-Li did not want to publish what he wrote. When his friends pressed him to make available his hairsplitting commentaries spoken publicly, so that they might print them, they were surprised to learn that he never wrote them down. He had a phenomenal memory and he knew by heart both the Babylonian and Palestinian Talmuds, as well as the broad rabbinical literature around them. Once at the feast of Purim, he read before the assembled all the legal decisions of the Tosafot in the Talmud by heart.

Generally, R. Mordechai-Li did not have hairsplitting arguments for their own sake. He spoke simply and logically and his teaching was brief but good. Still in his youth he wrote a book according to this method and called it Aleh havatselet (Rose leaf), since his family name was also Rozenblat. He kept the manuscript among his unpublished writings. R. Mordechai-M. compared the hair-splitting lectures given at the finishing of a Talmudic tractate to the wedding dress made from fine fiber. However, no one minds the type of material, because the dress is not meant to be worn on the weekday. People look "only at its beauty and the splendor of its value. Therefore, they intend to make it glorious with embroideries of buds and flowers."

We hear with these statements a hint that hairsplitting arguments are not things that can exist a long time. They are only an external, lightning and temporary. R. Mordechai-Li lessened the value of hairsplitting arguments with statements like this.

Even though R. Mordechai-Li refused to publish his novellas, he finally answered those requesting him and gave to his friend, the scholar and enlightened person, Yehuda Idl Tsizling of Ashmina to publish some of his statements. These are included in the book Hadrat Mordekhai.

The book Hadrat Mordekhai is divided into four parts: 1. Tsitsim u-ferahim (speeches given upon finishing talmudic tractates in the manner of hairsplitting arguments); 2. Meshiv be-devar halakhah (response); 3. Novellas on Talmud, Codes, and Tosafot; 4. Kuntres Ben-Menahem (sermons).

In the speeches given upon finishing Talmudic tractates in the manner of hairsplitting arguments, R. Mordechai is the example of a person with familiarity and analytical ability. He goes down valleys and goes up mountains. He grinds up the valleys and mountains. He gives these in the way of rabbis, who give sermons when a Talmudic tractate is finished.

*[Page 145]*

However, this is not his way in response. Here he makes his conclusion according to the actual law. He negotiated with the great people of his generation on what is forbidden and permitted. He swims in the sea of the Talmud and casts his net on the first commentators and the later commentators. He makes an effort to permit what is permitted.

Here I have to point out something strange in the book Hadrat Mordekhai, the volume on response, section 9, p. 43-45. There is an old responsum, whose content is taken from the response of R. Akiva Eger, section 62. There is no hint given as to the source of this responsum.

Truly, this is a difficult matter. Certainly, R. Mordechai-Li did not want to publish this book to glorify himself. How is it that this responsum entered his books?

I am of the opinion that the responsum was not put in with his knowledge. I guess that R. Mordechai.-Li copied this responsum from memory and put it in his writings. When R. Yehudah Tsizling arranged R.

Mordechai-Li's writings, he thought that this responsum also belonged to R. Mordechai-Li and included it with the rest of his response. This has happened in many other rabbinical works.

The novellas on Talmud, Codes, and Tosafot are based on logic and acceptable. There is not found here mental gymnastics, which are confused and crooked. What we find here is straight and pure intellect, which makes a crooked path straight.

We also find this in his sermons. They are simple and a work of genius. We do not find here him jumping from matter to matter and putting together different types. We find in these sermons the lightning of genius, a rainbow of different colors. Such a sermon is of the type of a "hammer splitting a rock". This means, just as a rock is divided into different parts – big, medium, and small – so the lightning and sparks of his sermon come to unite into an important piece.

*[Page 145]*

# Rabbi R. Shemuel
## By A. Ben-Ezra

One of the first rabbis in Antopol was R. Shemuel of Pinsk. He was a descendent of Samuel Eliezer ben Judah ha-Levi Edels), a rabbinical dynasty going back to Maharsha. His father was Rabbi Aryeh Leib, the son of R. Klonimus, the rabbi of Pinsk.

R. Shemuel was one of the best pupils of R. Refael ha-Kohen (R. Refael, the elder), president of the rabbinical court of Pinsk. When he was nineteen, R. Shemuel received rabbinical ordination from R. Refael ha-Kohen. He became rabbi of Antopol at the age of twenty. We don't know how long he was a rabbi in the city. People say that he was involved in a difficult conflict and, as a result of this, had to leave Antopol.

R. Shemuel went to serve as rabbi in Karlin, near Pinsk. He was the first rabbi in Karlin and died there about 1821 (581). He was well versed in Jewish law. His name was mentioned as the "rabbi, luminary, great, familiar and analytical, light of the Exile, famous in his generation."

Among the writings of R. Shemuel are novellas on Talmud, response, and legends about the weekly readings of the Pentateuch in synagogue. It seems that he had an inclination to mysticism and Hasidism. He gave his agreement to print the Zohar by the Hasidic brothers Shapira, in Slavuta.

One of the descendants of R. Shemuel was also famous. He was the writer in the Enlightenment generation, Mosheh Aharon Shtaskes.

*[Page 146]*

# Rabbi Mosheh Tsevi
## By A. Ben-Ezra

Rabbi Mosheh Tsevi was the son of Rabbi Yisrael Rabinowitz, a descendent of a long line of famous rabbis. He was one of the great rabbis in our time, great in revealed law and Jewish mysticism. He was distinguished as a great mystic. R. Mosheh Tsevi was also a place to which the ordinary Jew turned. People would go to him to receive a blessing, amulet, or cure. He was also called, for example, together with R. Yaakov Lifshits of Minsk to confirm the signature in the complicated will of R. Shaul Karliner.

He himself did not write books. However, after his death, his son, R. Yehoshua Yaakov, published a pamphlet, "Hidushe halakhot ve-agadot," in the name of his father. We are able to examine his knowledge through this small pamphlet. R. Mosheh Tsevi did not make use of hairsplitting arguments to show his knowledge of Talmud. He preferred to study Talmud, Maimonides, or Tosafot for their simple meaning.

He raised a new and scholarly idea to explain ke-felah ha-rimon rakatekh (Song of Songs 4.3: "Thy temples are like a pomegranate split open"). This is explained by our rabbis of blessed memory: "The empty of learning among you are full of commandments like a pomegranate" (Sanhedrin 37). This statement is really difficult and not easily understood. However, R. Mosheh Tsevi explained it differently. The numeric value of rimon, resh (200), mem (40), vav (F), and nun (50) is 296. Felah (half) of the numerical value of rimon is 148, the same as the numeral value of kemah, kof (100), mem (40), and xyz (8) This means that Jews who are not expert in Jewish law but despite their lack of knowledge give money for the living expenses (kemah meaning flour) to support Jewish religious scholars will receive half of the merit that the Jewish scholars earn in the world to come.

R. Mosheh Tsevi was rabbi both in Antopol and Horodets. When his son was twenty, he gave him the rabbinical post in Horodets and remained rabbi in Antopol until his death in 1862.

The quotation at the bottom of the page is from Deuteronomy 32:7: "Ask thy father, and he will disclose unto thee, Thine elders, and they will tell thee."

# R. Hirsh (Rabinovits)

R. Hirsh was born in 1850 to his father R. Akiva Rabinovits of Grodno. He was a great scholar. He devoted his whole life to the study of the Torah. His wife supported the family from a store she owned. R. Hirsh married at an early age, as was the custom in those days. He married the daughter of R. David Yosl, who taught Jewish elementary school in Antopol.

He was already appointed to be a rabbinical judge at the age of twenty by R. Pinchas Michael, who held him in great esteem. He was a person of wide horizons and also got for himself knowledge in secular subjects, including high mathematics.

People say that once R. Hirsh was pondering a difficult problem in geometry. He asked the known mathematician, R. Hayyim Zelig Slonimski in Warsaw to seek a solution to the problem. He got this answer from Warsaw: "Slonimski of Warsaw does not know the answer to the problem of the person asking me, who I may address as the provincial Slonimski."

From that time on, R. Hirsh became known for his mathematical knowledge. If a student had a difficult problem with math, he would ask R. Hirsh.

R. Hirsh was extremely knowledgeable in Hebrew and Russian. He read newspapers in both languages.

Despite his great knowledge of rabbinical literature and general sciences, R. Hirsh did not boast. It was just the opposite. The tall rabbi, straight in posture, with a black beard and burning eyes acted as a friend to everyone. He knew how to comfort a person in a time of trouble and give spiritual help to members of his community.

Once when he visited his son, R. Mordechai, a professor of Talmud in Kobrin, a fire broke out. R. Hirsh did not hesitate. He climbed together with his son on a neighboring roof and helped to extinguish the fire.

R. Hirsh died in World War I. May his memory be blessed!

*[Page 147]*

# Rabbi Mosheh Berman
## By P. Likht

Rabbi Mosheh Berman was born in 1864 in Razinai, Grodno province. His father, R. Feitel was a professor of Talmud there many years. R. Feitel and his wife died when their son Mosheh was a young child. He grew up in the house of a well-known woman, Hodeske, who was their relative. This pious woman greatly influenced the child in forming his character and personality. Moshe studied in the rabbinical seminary of Razinai and afterwards went to Volozhin and Minsk. Finally, he came to Antopol to study with R. Pinchas Michael, of blessed memory.

He married Breine-Henie, the granddaughter of R. Pinchas Mikhal of Shershev. He lived a little while in Kobrin. After the death of Pinchas Michael and following a famous dispute, he was rabbi together with R. Hersh as rabbis of the town. After the death of R. Hersh, he was the only rabbi.

R. Mosheh was a quiet person. He was deeply immersed in his studies and in taking care of the welfare of the community. He was a warm Zionist and a worldly person. He also tried his hand at business in partnership with R. Avraham-Mosheh, son of R. Pinchas Michael. However, his honest character did not allow him to make a profit. Frequently, he would return his profits to the customers. As a result, his business partnership was dissolved.

After World War I, his two sons, Dr. Feitel Berman and Mr. Pintshe Berman, who were already in the United States brought him there. In 1921, R. Mosheh was appointed rabbi of the synagogue Agudat Achim in Los Angeles. He was beloved within a short time by the orthodox Jews. He was appointed president of the orthodox rabbinical court in the city. He also proved himself here as a disciple of Hillel, the elder, in his understanding of the circumstances of the existence of Jews in the United States. He himself remained all day in his prayer shawl and phylacteries in the synagogue and studied until late at night. When he returned home, he would continue studying until late at night.

R. Mosheh exchanged letters with many rabbis in the United States and was respected by all who knew him. He served as rabbi ten years in Los Angeles until his death on 22 Heshvan, 691 (October 1930). A memorial was held for many years on the day of his death, even after the synagogue moved to a new location. A structure to serve as a meeting place was raised up over his grave, as was the custom in the former place of his birth. May his memory be blessed!

The sentence at the bottom is from Exodus 17:14, but it substitutes the word "sons" for "Joshua": "Write this for a memorial in the book, and rehearse it in the ears of your sons."

# R. Mosheh Soloveichik
## By A. Ben-Ezra

R. Mosheh was born in Volozhin in 1879 (639). He was still able to celebrate his bar mitsvah in the great rabbinical seminary of Volozhin before it was closed by the Czar in 1892. In 1902, he married Peshe, daughter of the famous rabbi of Pruzshene, the luminary R. Eliyah Feinshtein.

He was invited in 1910 to be rabbi of Rasin. In World War I, he was rabbi in Kaslovits. In 1921, he arrived in Brisk. From there he went to Vilna. In Vilna, he was invited to be rabbi of Antopol after R. Berman left for the United States. He went from Antopol to be professor of Talmud at the rabbinical seminary "Tahkhemoni" in Warsaw.

*[Page 148]*

In 1929, he was invited to the Rabbi Isaac Elchanan Rabbinical Seminary in New York. When he went there, pupils came to him from all over the world. He taught for twelve years there. Among his pupils, there were later famous rabbis and heads of rabbinical seminaries.

R. Mosheh was known for his simple explanations and true research. He would search deeply for explanations in the Talmud. He was a good teacher, who knew how to give easy explanations and also how to enliven the study of the texts.

R. Mosheh Soloveichik died in 701 (1941). His many pupils, who studied the Torah from him became orphans at his death. May his soul be bound in the bond of life!

This sentence comes from Numbers 24:5: "How goodly are thy tents, O Jacob, thy dwellings, O Israel!"

# Rabbi Mosheh Wulfson
## By A. Ben-Ezra

Rabbi Wulfson had an early tie to Antopol. He was the grandson of R. Hayyim Zalman, who was rabbi in town after the death of R. Pinchas Michael. R. Mosheh Wulfson's father was R. Mikhal Yanushker, the author of Sefat ha-yam in three volumes, and the son-in-law of R. Hayyim Zalman. Besides the family line, R. Mosheh was known as a great scholar. He served many years as rabbi and professor of Talmud in Shtutsin, near Lida.

When the rabbinical post became open in Antopol after R. Mosheh Soloveichik left and a search for his successor begun, R. Mosheh Wulfson immediately became a candidate and was invited for the Sabbath. That Sabbath, he gave a sermon that was both hairsplitting and folkloric and that took hold of the attention of both the scholarly and simple at the same time. When the Sabbath was over, there was a meeting in the house of Akiva Fishl Lifshits, who was one of the thirty-three Jews having the right to vote in town. They unanimously voted for R. Mosheh Wulfson.

R. Mosheh knew how to get along both with the civil authorities and gentiles in town, using his fluency in Russian and Polish. He was devoted to community and institutional matters. He also took it upon himself to supervise the Jewish elementary school that met in the old study hall. They taught there Bible, grammar, and Hebrew.

Sadly, however, R. Mosheh did not have a long tenure. R. Mosheh gave the eulogy for the martyrs in 1929, after the riots and the destruction of the rabbinical seminary and massacre of its students in Hebron. Immediately after the evening prayers when he returned home, he had a heart attack and died.

He left a wife, five daughters, and an only son. His eldest daughter, Shifrah, married Rabbi Walkin. He was the last rabbi in Antopol until the destruction of the town. The second eldest daughter, Mikhlah, married a ritual slaughterer in Kobrin and died there in the Holocaust. The third eldest daughter, Leah-tseh, married in Zabinkah and died there in the Holocaust. The daughter Hayyeleh married Rabbi Hayyim, son of R. Avigdor Sirota. The youngest daughter, Malkeleh, died in Antopol together with her mother and brother.

# Rabbi Yosef David
## By Zalman Zeev Shahor

My father, the luminary, R. Yosef David, may the memory of the righteous be blessed, was rabbi and president of the rabbinical court in Antopol and afterwards in Semitits. He was born in Roznoi in Lithuania. His father was learned in the Torah and pious. His name was Rabbi Aleksander Ziskind Shahor, may the memory of the righteous be blessed. His mother was the righteous woman Reizl, daughter of the luminary, R. Zalman. He was rabbi and president of the rabbinical court in Roznov. He held the rabbinical position in place of his father, the great luminary of that generation, Rabbi Elhanan of Borisov, may the memory of the righteous be blessed. The grandfather, R. Aleksander Ziskind, was the son of Rabbi Hayyim Leib Shahor of Mir. They used to call him R. Hayyim Leib, the wealthy man.

*[Page 149]*

This is because he used-to carry out big business deals and would lend his money without interest to all needy. R. Hayyim Leib was the son-in-law of the known luminary R. David-L of Mir. He was one of the great rabbis of the city and one of the founders of the great rabbinical seminary of Mir.

My father, may the memory of the righteous be blessed, received his education in the rabbinical seminary of Volozhin and was devoted to Naphtali Zevi Judah Berlin, may the memory of the righteous be blessed, who loved him very much. When his father, may the memory of the righteous be blessed, held the rabbinical post in Antopol, Naphtali Zevi Judah Berlin used to visit him. The day of Berlin's visit was a holiday not only for Antopol but for all the surrounding towns. The luminaries of Torah from far and near would come to receive the visit of the rabbi of Israel.

After his marriage, my father, may the memory of the righteous be blessed, did not want to accept for himself the yoke of rabbinical office and chose to live from the work of his hands, from his warehouse. Many hours of the day, including the nights, he would study the Torah and his wife would lead the business. However, fate desired that my father would enlighten the skies of Lithuanian Jewry. So it happened that a fire broke out in town and my father's house and business burnt up. Thus, my father lost his property. At that time, the luminary and righteous man, Rabbi Pinchas Michael, may the memory of the righteous be blessed, died. He had been for years the president of the rabbinical court in Antopol. My father's friends brought him a letter of rabbinical appointment to the post in Antopol and urged him to take the post left vacant by Rabbi Pinchas Michael, may the memory of the righteous be blessed. He had no choice except to accept the offer and was accepted to be president of the rabbinical court in Antopol.

Rabbi Pinchas Michael had been famous not only as being great in Torah but also as a Tsadik and miracle worker. Many people used to rise early to his door to ask for his advice and to get a blessing from his mouth. When my father sat as rabbi in Antopol, people also came to him from all the surrounding area to ask his advice and to receive a blessing. My father tried to chase away those that came to him, saying that he was not a Tsadik or a miracle worker. However, it did not work. The bitter people did not stop coming to pour out their bitterness. Without choice, he was forced to answer their requests and give them advice until he got a reputation in all the area as a luminary, scholar, and doer of good deeds.

My father was both familiar and analytical in Jewish learning. About his familiarity, I heard from R. Yeshayah Grinberg, of blessed memory. (He was one of the veteran teachers of the elementary school Shaare Torah in Tel-Aviv-Yafo). He used to study Torah with my father, may the memory of the righteous be blessed. Once my father sat at home and studied. R Yeshayah Grinberg entered the library in which my father sat so that he could get a book to study. My father asked him: "R. Yeshayah, which tractate do you need?" He said to him: "Such and such a tractate." "And what tractate are you learning?" "Such and such a tractate." "If so", said my father to him, "you are on page so and so and you must look at page so and so in the second tractate." It was to such a degree that my father's familiarity with Jewish sources had reached, may the memory of the righteous be blessed.

My mother, may the memory of the righteous be blessed, told me that when he was still young, people would put a pin on the first page of any tractate and my father would recite by heart everything printed on that page. The luminary R. Meir Berlin used to say that my father was able to write by heart the talmudic references called Mesoret ha-Shas without looking at any book. This is because my father was familiar with the Talmud and Codes, just like a Jew, with the Psalm beginning with Ashre (Happy are they).

*[Page 150]*

My father, may the memory of the righteous be blessed, was gifted with an ability to explain that was exceptional. When he used to give the lesson to his students, they would be happy with his statements and feel as enlightened as if they were standing at Mt. Sinai. He loved every person of Israel as his own soul. Everyone in the city saw Father as their father and patron, a person who felt their pain and was prepared to help them in their time of need. His hand was open to all who sought it, and he would give to charity more than a fifth of his income. When a collection was arranged for an important matter, my father would be among the first to give. And, he would give the biggest contribution so that the rich people in town would not be able to get by with a small donation.

Thinking in a straightforward way was a firm foundation in my father's teaching. In his straightforward way, he would solve difficult problems when Torah judgments were brought to him. He would always try to study the problems in all their depth. The people who came for judgment were always amazed at their rabbi, who was comfortable in judging matters of commerce and economy just like one of the distinguished merchants. Those who came to him for judgment always left pleased, even if they lost their case because they saw the wisdom of the person judging. From the very judgment and the way it was formulated, they understood that they had made a mistake in their request and that the second person, who was judged innocent, was really right.

His nature as an exceptional judge went out in all the community. People came from near and far to his door for religious and civil judgments in complicated matters. Among the litigants appearing before him was R. Ozer Weizmann, the father of the first President of Israel, of blessed memory. He was a merchant in timber and from time to time had litigation with his partners and customers. Once there appeared before father, of blessed memory, three partners in a big deal. All of them were pious and honest. In addition to their business expertise, they were also familiar with bookkeeping. They asked my father to mediate their conflict. Father, after he had heard their arguments, requested that they bring to him their accounting books. The accountant brought the books and asked to give my father, of blessed memory, the explanations for the accounts. However, father said that that was not necessary. "I will find what I want myself." After examining the books, he found the mistake in accounting. After fixing the accounting mistake, there was no more dispute. Everything was settled amicably. This decision was heard in the merchant circles. And all of them saw in this a Solomonic judgment.

My mother, of blessed memory, could not restrain herself this time and asked father how he could arrive at the conclusion that the reason for the dispute was just an accounting problem? My father said t o her: "The matter is very simple. I saw before me all honest men. Not one of them wanted to benefit from any amount not belonging to him. If that is so, how could honest people like these arrive at such a sharp dispute? I came to the conclusion that an accounting mistake happened. After I carefully looked at the books, I found the mistake. Thus, I took the sting out of all the dispute."

The gentile population also heard of his reputation as a judge full of God's wisdom. A gentile who had a dispute with a Jew or with a fellow gentile would bring his case before my father, of blessed memory. This was done to such an extent that the civil judge, Sudvani Pristav, felt that the burden of judgment was greatly lightened on him. He began investigating why there was a drop in contending sides. As a result, he found out that the rabbi's reputation extended to the gentiles and that they brought before him their conflicts. He wrote a letter to my father and asked for an interview. Father agreed and the judge visited him, of blessed memory, and left enthusiastically. Father, of blessed memory, used his friendship with the judge for the sake of the oppressed. This judge became in the course of time a friend of the Jews. There were many stories circulating among the inhabitants of the region of father's, of blessed memory, advice. These stories bordered on the miraculous.

*[Page 151]*

Father served eleven years as rabbi of Antopol. Then, he was asked to become president of the rabbinical court in the town of Semitits, which was a big city and known in the rabbinical world. With the death of the elderly rabbi of Semitits, who was a Jewish luminary, the city was without a rabbi for many years. This was because of a disagreement among the sides in the city. When the communal heads of Semitits heard of the reputation of the rabbi of Antopol, they all agreed to make him, the luminary Yosef David, their rabbi and spiritual leader. A delegation of the leading people of the city traveled to Antopol to give father his rabbinical appointment. It was not easy for my father to leave Antopol and all the many friends that he had acquired there. However, the great people of the generation of that time insisted that he receive the position of rabbi in Semitits. When the communal leaders of Antopol heard that the community of Semitits gave their rabbi rabbinical appointment, the city became stirred. The communal leaders brought their arguments to the great rabbi, the luminary Hayyim Soloveichik of Brisk. The community of Semitits won the case. My father, of blessed memory, prepared to go to his new post. The people of Semitits were happy to welcome their rabbi, but the people of Antopol were in pain and worry.

When my father, of blessed memory, was going to leave Antopol, all the citizens-men, women, and children-gathered to take leave of their beloved rabbi. The gentiles also came to take leave of the great rabbi. A convoy of vehicles accompanied Father, and many people went on foot. All of them cried bitterly. It was difficult for them to leave him. When the news reached Semitits that the rabbi was close to town, all the people went out to welcome him with drums and musical instruments. The city of Semitits was happy.

My father, of blessed memory, came to Semitits the day before the Jewish New Year 660 (1900). The city was cloaked in double festivities for the High Holidays, the following holidays, and the honor of the new rabbi, who came to serve after many requests. The holiday of Tabernacles was very joyous in Semitits that year. Those still alive from that time tell a lot about the happiness of the festival. The happiness of the second night of the festival was greater than in previous years because of the entrance into office of the new rabbi. My father, of blessed memory, was a wonderful preacher, who always kept getting better. He would spill out pearls of the Torah and wisdom at all times. On the Sabbaths and the holidays the community would accompany the rabbi to his house. There would follow a well-prepared sanctification of the festival over wine. My father, of blessed memory, would talk about matters of the day. Since there were hasidim in Semitits, my father would also intertwine hasidic statements into his sermons. For the third meal ending the Sabbath, Jewish scholars would come. Then my father, of blessed memory, would mention statements about Jewish law and hairsplitting Torah studies. At the end of the Sabbath, the town's prominent and communal activists would come to take advice about how to handle communal matters. My father took care to fix all the communal buildings that had run down during the strong disagreements that preceded his appointment.

Semitits had my father for only six years. My father died in August 1906 (eighth of Elul in 666). Deep mourning came to all the near and far communities. People came from all over to his funeral. The great rabbis of the generation participated in the funeral and eulogized him. Among them were the luminary, Rabbi Naftali Tsevi Yehudah Berlin of Volozhin, who was his uncle, and Rabbi Yehiel Mikhal Epshtein of Novohorodek, who was the author of a commentary on the Shulhan arukh, and also his uncle. Two of his former pupils were there. One was Rabbi Meir Berlin, the son of his brother, who in his final years lived in Tel Aviv. The other was Rabbi Yitshak Kosovski, who was the son of the uncle of the rabbi, Rabbi Shaul Kosovski-Shahor, and brother of his wife, our mother, Lifshah, may the memory of a righteous woman be blessed.

*[Page 152]*

# Rabbi Yitshak Elhanan Walkin
## By A. Ben-Ezra

R. Yitshak Elhanan Walkin was born in 1900 to his father, the luminary R. Aharon Walkin, and his mother, the daughter of R. Ben-Tsiyon Sorotskin.

His unusual abilities were recognized already in his youth. When he was thirteen, he was accepted to the famous rabbinical seminary in Mir (under the leadership of the luminary R. Eliyahu Barukh Kamai and R. Yeruham Libowits). He studied there from 1913 until 1915 and afterwards studied in the rabbinical seminary of Radin. However, he continued to long for the rabbinical seminary of Mir. He endangered his life by crossing the border and reaching Poltavah, the place where it was newly established.

In addition to his devotion to his studies, he was devoted to his friends and helped them in difficult situations, especially at the time of the typhus epidemic. He finally got that also. When he was well, he returned to Lithuania. There he taught for a certain time in the elementary school of Kelm. When the rabbinical seminary of Mir returned to its usual place, he also returned to it.

When R. Mosheh Wulfson died, R. Yitshak Elhanan married his daughter Shifrah and also inherited the rabbinical post in Antopol. He was busy in communal service and was beloved by young and old. When the Second World War broke out and the Bolsheviks entered town, he did part of his work secretly. However, when the Nazis entered, R. Yitshak Elhanan died together with his community.

May God avenge their blood!

# R. Binyamin Rosh Yeshivah
## By Mosheh Falk

R. Binyamin, Professor of Talmud. He was a Jew good of appearance and excellent in character. He always walked with straight posture. When I knew him, he had a long white beard and a moustache, which was white from age and brown from smelling snuff. He was very humble and didn't interfere in any matters at home or outside of home. His only desire was to teach Torah to his students. Every three years he would complete the study of the whole series of talmudic tractates, studied daily. At the same time many of his day pupils continued to hear his nightly lessons on talmudic tractates.

R. Binyamin raised many generations of people studying Talmud and talmudic scholars in all the period of his happy life. Even his brother Aharon, who was older than him by 18 years, studied with him. Afterwards, he went to the rabbinical seminary in Volozhin. The known scholar R. Yenkel, husband of Beilah Hanah-kes, studied with him, as well as R. Aharon Asher Volinets, R. Yenkel Papah, R. Itshe, husband of Sarah Menyes, R. Leizer Yenkel, and others. They inherited from him their familiarity in the Torah and their devotion to its study. R. Binyamin was a Jew, who could hairsplit and who was familiar with all the treasures of Torah and its secrets.

I knew R. Binyamin and his family very well. They were our good neighbors. Our house was next to their house. When I first walked, my first visit was to their house. His wife, aunt Hayah, as she was called, acted to me like an aunt. And not only did she treat me as family but also all the family did. I knew the eldest son, R. Motel, only from his visits at home and in our house. He lived after marriage in Kobrin.

*[Page 153]*

However, the daughters, Malkah, Sarah Vitah and Mikhlah, were like sisters to me all the days of my childhood. Generally, all the family was friendly with our family, and especially with my brothers and sisters as the best of friends. They were like members of our household.

When I finished Jewish elementary school's first grade with R. Alter, in which I learned the Hebrew vowels, such as "Komets Ah", and left it already knowing all the blessings by heart, I went to study in the revised Jewish elementary school of R. Leibush, who taught us in the house of R. Binyamin and Hayah, our neighbors. I felt myself at home with them as if I were their child. Hayah and the daughters treated me with love. They would honor me with all types of sweets and with all that I just wanted. I would visit their house during my free hours all of my childhood years. Until I studied with him in the rabbinical seminary, I knew R. Binyamin only from the Sabbaths and holidays when I visited their house frequently with my father. He would come to R. Binyamin to solve a talmudic section or question that he encountered in his many studies in many books, old and new, that were in our house.

It did not happen just one time in the late evening hours or during the intermediate days of the festival when R. Binyamin was a little free from his studies that he would stand near the numerous bookshelves in our house and browse and search and collect a bundle of books. Each time he would exchange them for others.

For R. Binyamin, the professor of Talmud, my rabbi, teacher, and best neighbor and all his family, I devote with appreciation and respect these lines to their memory.

# R. Yaakov Hayyim, the Ritual Slaughterer
## By Rabbi Aharon Asher Volinets

I came to mention a special man among the inhabitants of Antopol. This man was excellent and distinguished in his qualities, generous and faithful with public matters and with the needs of everyone to fulfill their requests more than he was physically or financially capable of doing. He met everyone with a friendly greeting.

R. Yaakov Hayyim was a ritual slaughterer and circumciser. He was the son of Yisrael Zelig Kotlir, of blessed memory. He was the prayer leader and Torah reader, who had the best voice in the new study hall and afterwards in the walled study hall. On Sabbaths and holidays, and especially during the High Holidays during the additional prayers, he would always bring great joy in his prayers to all the assembled. About such an exalted man like this, it was said in the prayers of the prayer leader that he prayed with the prayers of an old man used to praying, and he had good looks and a big beard, and his voice was pleasant, and he found favor with people.

He was one of the thirty-three people who were elected with the signatures of all the people in town to decide in all communal decisions without complaint or any claim against them by the other people. He always went to the sessions to elect the rabbi in town and was the treasurer of the Jewish elementary school, in which he was active daily, and was the treasurer of the Society on Behalf of Visiting the Sick, which would pay for sick and poor people to visit doctors and get prescriptions. He worked hard to collect money for the poor to celebrate Passover. It could be said of him like it says in Ethics of the Fathers: "All who find favor with people, God finds favor with them."

He died in May 1933 (17 of Sivan 693), may his soul be bound in the bond of eternal life.

[Page 154]

# R. Mosheh Leizer, the Ritual Slaughterer, and His Friends
## By Tsivyah Shneider

The house of my father, R. Mosheh Leizer, the ritual slaughterer, was in the winter evenings a meeting place for himself and his friends, who would meet two or three times a week to study the Torah.

The most senior among them was Mosheh Avraham-kes, a scholarly Jew, who in the past was a bookkeeper for a lumber merchant. He lived off of support from his children in the United States and had stopped working a long time ago. Therefore, he would come in first. He was like a member of our household, and while he was waiting for the other guests, he would look at the public library in the study hall of Meir Podot, where my father was treasurer. He would also help set up the talmudic volumes and prepare tea.

The second was R. Shelomoh MikhalWulfson. He was a small Jew, who was prematurely gray. However, his soft eyes were like those of a child. My father used to say about him that he was the greatest scholar among them. R. Shelomoh Mikhal was a flour merchant by profession, which is his wife ran the business and he helped her. Actually, he was only interested in his studies of the Torah. Therefore, he came early to our house in order be released from his daily routine.

Then, my father would come. His friends were used to his being late since they knew that he was very busy. I remember his appearance. He was tall and thin and had a hard look. However, he had a golden heart. We all knew that the reason for his hard appearance was that he was in weak health and worked hard both as a ritual slaughterer and as a merchant each day, and in the evenings he would study until late by himself and together with his friends.

Two additional friends would arrive. They were Mosheh Eliyahu, a teacher of the Talmud, and Meir Yosef, a teacher in the Jewish elementary school.

Both of them were scholars. However, they had a hard time earning a living. When they sat at the same table with my father, they would forget all the problems of earning a living and their eyes would shine and their hearts would be full of love deep in the study of the Torah. Sometimes one of them would break out in a tune while discussing a talmudic section. All of them would listen as if they were one person to the one speaking with respect and mutual admiration.

I remember one winter evening in the dining room. My father and his friends sat at the table near the oven warming the room. My friends and I sat near another table and prepared lessons in Russian and Hebrew. My mother, of blessed memory, was sewing ritually fit fringes for prayer shawls for poor children. My mother always had a good nature. However, when she looked at my father and heard his teaching, she certainly dreamed about the world to come awaiting her through her own merit and the merit of my father.

# R. Avraham Yehudah Margiliyot
## By Aryeh Shkolnik

R. Avraham Yehudah certainly was not born in Antopol. However, it is hard to describe Antopol without R. Avraham Yehudah. He was born in Grodno in the year 1857 and grew up in Brest- Litovsk. He came to our city of Antopol to study with R. Pinchas Michael, of blessed memory. The young fellow was known at once for his sharp brain in studying and also playing chess.

Many wanted him for a son-in-law. Finally, one of the good people in town, R. Hetskl, the brother-inlaw of Efrayim Lifshits, got him. R. Avraham Yehudah did not want to be maintained by the support of his father-in-law, as was the custom in those days. Therefore, he became an elementary school teacher. He taught ten years. However, the occupation dial not suit him. He had creative force. He liked to do a lot. Among the rest, he built a factory for lubricant for wagon wheels. He earned a living from this. At the same time, he continued his religious studies and played chess.

*[Page 155]*

One day the income tax people came and arrested him. He escaped and spent the night in one house until he was able to hide with Efrayim Stavski for some weeks. He was dressed up like a woman and fled to Brest-Litovsk and from there traveled to the United States. He dealt in lubricants in the United States and was also known as a Jewish religious person and a prize-winning chess player.

After World War I, he went to live in Tel Aviv, near his son, and died in December 1939 (Israel on 4 Kislev 699). May, his memory be blessed!

# A Society to Study Mishnah and Societies for Other Studies

## By Rabbi Aharon Asher Volinets

I have brought in my book Shemirat Shabat (Observing the Sabbath) that the Rabbi of Brisk, of blessed memory, once saw in the study hall that two people were carrying paper and writing people's names on it. To the question by the rabbi as to what this was for, they answered to him that they were making a list of people to study Mishnah. The rabbi rebuked them and said: "What else shall you do? In a little while you will make a list for the Society of Sabbath Observers! Everyone is liable to study Mishnah or to hear the study of Mishnah, just as everyone is liable to observe the Sabbath. So why make a special society for this purpose?" This is what the above-mentioned luminary said about the people of the town of Antopol.

Antopol did not have a Society of Sabbath Observers. This is because all the people from youth until aged kept the Sabbath. It did not have a Society of Students of Mishnah because everyone present in the study all heard lessons in Mishnah. It did not have a Society to Study En Yaakov. This is because everyone paid attention to the study of En Yaakov. It did not have a Society to Study Psalms. This is because everyone said Psalms daily and on Sabbath nights in the fourth hour in the winter and in the summer on the Sabbath in the third hour all gathered in the study halls to say Psalms publicly. After saying Psalms, they sat at the tables to study Mishnah, En Yaakov, and Talmud.

There was also not a Society of People Praying in our town. Everyone came daily to pray in the study halls, as it is written (Psalms 55): "In the House of God, we go with feeling" (Regesh in Hebrew, taken as an acronym B. (barad, hail), R. (Ruah, wind), G. (Geshem, rain), and Sh. (sheleg, snow). There was no difference between the Sabbath and festivals and the High Holidays. So, it went with other commandments, like the Festival of Sukkot in which the booths built were equal to the number of houses. And about them, the Biblical sentence says (Exodus 19) Israel encamped them facing the mountain. Encamped is written in the third person past singular, meaning that all of them encamped as one person facing the mountain on which the Torah was given.

# For the History of Rabbi Binyamin Sakirlski
## By A. Ben-Ezra

He was born in Slonim to his father R. Yitshak in 1889. R. Mordekhai-Li of Slonim and also R. Hayyim of Brisk gave him rabbinical ordination.

R. Mosheh Binnburg of Smorgon was one of his rabbis. When he married Henyeh, daughter of R. Yaakov Hayyim the ritual slaughterer, he gave him as a marriage present a part of the ritual slaughtering in Antopol, and he was a ritual slaughterer in Antopol until he came to the United States in 1920. He functioned here as an examiner for kashrut in the Kraft Company. He died in 1945.

He became friendly with all the great rabbis in the United States. He exchanged letters, which included novella with R. Mosheh Soloveichik, R. Mosheh Razin (the author of some books) and other great people of the Jewish people. Among the rabbis, those people from Antopol who immigrated to the United States recognized him as a lover of Torah and people.

May his memory be blessed.

*[Page 156]*

# Rabbi Yitshak Lifshits
## By Shemual Varshah

Antopol was a town in the heart of Polesia on the railway line of Brisk in Lithuania to Pinsk. Some years after World War I when life returned to normal and new ideas were in town, the prominent residents and people learned in Torah, who were numerous in town, decided to fix up Jewish religious education. They wanted to give it the fitting image and form. They wanted to give it a basis and continue its existence. They also wanted to make it better. There was a question. Teachers were needed for Talmud, Rashi's commentary, and the Bible. The communal leaders appreciated what they had to do. They worked diligently with understanding and care.

They brought then to our town as chief rabbi, R. Shelomoh, of blessed memory. He was a former student of the rabbinical seminary of Volozhin. Some time afterwards they brought the luminary R. Yuzpa Davidovski (the author of Imre Yoself and president of the rabbinical court of Tchernowitz later). The educational institution established was a type of lower level rabbinical seminary. This was a lively institution, which promised a lot.

I knew in those days Yitshak from a distance. I frequently saw the pretty and tall boy among the youths who gave him great respect. However, I still did not have close contact with him. After some years in our young world, he already got a reputation for being the lion in the group in his class. When I was accepted to the classroom of R. Shelomoh, mentioned above, my father and acquaintances asked me with great interest: "To which class have you been accepted? Perhaps to the class of Yitshak Lifshits?" The class in which he learned was called by his name. He was its representative. When I was able to answer yes to this question, I felt happy. It was as if I had gone up in status that I was able to study together with him.

It was here that I met the acquaintance of the youth whose fame went from one end of town to the other. It is possible that the wonderful character of our rabbi was responsible for this. He was a gifted natural educator. If he found that someone had special talent, he always praised him. He would always bring this pupil's comments on the Talmud to the town rabbi. It was in Yitshak that the rabbi found someone to love. He became the crown of our class. The rabbi told us to learn from Yitshak: "Look and respect someone like this." He became a symbol to us. Our eyes always had to observe him.

Afterwards, we already found in the class of R. Yuzpa the sense of being in a rabbinical seminary. There were some elderly people studying there. However, the class in which Yitshak Lifshits studied was well enough recognizable. The chief role fell to Yitshak. He was at the head in learning and leadership. The rabbi esteemed his value and related to him seriously and with respect above that given to the rest of us. When I summarize my impressions from that time, I don't wonder at all. On the contrary, why should an educator not single out for praise an exceptional student if he deserves it. He was really outstanding in his learning and action. It is clear. The incisive look of the educator saw in him one meant for greatness.

I am only astonished at one thing. Why did all of us at that time give him such admiration? It is natural among youths to compete and be jealous and the like. However, see this wonder. In relation to him, none of us had such feelings. We saw that he was distinguished from us in a real sense that had nothing to do with intellect. He was physically taller than us. Even if we ran after him, we could not catch up. We accepted his status as a law, which could not be changed. Yitshak was always the leader and first person. He was the best. Yitshak was always the only one that each of us wanted to befriend and were able to do so. He was really the most exalted among us! It seemed to me that this characteristic view of him lasted all his brief life. On one hand, he was raised above all others. On the other hand, all others among his friends and acquaintances admired him.

*[Page 157]*

In general, the way he grew up was exemplary. His development was defined and studied, in an orderly and measured pace. Every phase of his physical development was accompanied by his spiritual development. One completed the other. The developments matched one another. He steadily went up. Goodness and nobility were recognizable on his face. These reflected his inner life, his inner strength, decency, contributive qualities, and straight way of thinking. It did not happen just once that we were blinded by the manner of his excellent development. We really could not look after him.

This young plant was transplanted from Antopol to a good spot, the big rabbinical seminary in Kobrin. He was fourteen then. I remember that we still had not left for a rabbinical seminary. Then, suddenly we were surprised by the visit of a real rabbinical student from Kobrin. He had managed to ascend in a short time up the scale of Torah study and piety. Even our new teachers were amazed at him.

He daily grew by continuous study at the rabbinical seminary of Kobrin. The professors of Talmud immediately recognized his value and his excellent abilities for Torah and knowledge and related to him accordingly. He used to create novella with clear thought. He was already recognized as a type of clear thinker. In short, he stood out in every way. He belonged among rabbinical students. He won esteem, honor, and favor. Despite it all, he remained modest. He was somewhat quiet as before. He continued to be this way and we were bound to him by bonds of pure love.

The days passed into years. Yitshak already went to another rabbinical seminary, that of Kletsk. When we all met at intersession in our town, he again stood out. One could see a thread of grace and kindness about him. I would say that a natural grace was spread over him and came forth from him. In connection with this, I remember one fact from our distant childhood days. The game we played most often was war. We played this game as a response to the World War that had happened close to our growing up. We would choose an army and generals. We would anoint Yitshak to be king!

The years 693-695 were his last period in Kletsk. His childish softness had already left him. His character had fully formed. He was already grown up in character. His spiritual powers grew up and came forth. He was aware of what was happening inside and around him. We talked frequently about different problems.We were always happy to hear his clear thoughts about this and that.

He was very zealous for God. However, he felt his zeal more than he verbalized it. It was internal zealousness; it was spiritual, lit up by a truthful light at its base. It was true zealousness. He would not cover up for anyone, no matter who that person was, even if it were his friend. He would give a sharp rebuke when necessary. His noble soul could not stand any deviations.

He was somewhat quiet by nature. He didn't like to make noise. When the day came for him to go to Israel, he deliberately avoided party celebrations. However, against his will, a big crowd accompanied him to the train station. Among them were the members of our Society to Study Talmud. This is because in the brief time that he spent in his hometown before going to Israel, he studied and taught in this Society. The members of the Society accompanied their young rabbi to the train station out of gratitude. After greetings and saying goodbye, he went on the train. He looked at the gathered crowd with eyes that were aware, compassionate, and full of longing. Did we think that this was the last time we would see this noble soul? Did we think that we were leaving him forever? Oh! Who would think, who would guess?! May his soul be bound in the bond of life.

*[Page 158]*

# R. Aharon Asher Volinets
## By M. Falk

R. Aharon-Asher was born in 1879 (640) in the town of Antopol, the province of Grodno in White Russia to his father R. Avraham Volinets, of blessed memory, and to his mother Ms. Esther Libe, of blessed memory. He was an important branch on an important and splendid genealogical tree of people great in Torah and Hasidism from many generations. According to the breadth of his heart in Torah and piety, he was worthy of the rabbinate. However, he acted like his ancestors and chose to be a working person and an innocent man, who earned his livelihood from his own work even if it did not pay well and to have a rich table set with Torah and wisdom.

R. Aharon was devoted from his early childhood to studies in Jewish elementary school and rabbinical seminaries. At the age of 14, he finished all his studies in Talmud with R. Binyamin, the known professor of Talmud in town. From here on, he made the study of Torah his trade, and dealt especially in Codes and Response until he was worthy of ordination. However, as was said, he refused to make his knowledge of Torah a tool by which to earn a living. He also completed at that time his general studies and became a person of learning and one familiar with worldly matters.

R. Aharon was the elder son of nine children in the family. He had the burden of helping to support the family. Thus, he began to teach children in the village of Rusheve, near town. He also gave lessons to the rich people in town from the Lifshits family. When R. Aharon was of marriageable age, important families with people learned in Torah sought him for a groom. In 1899 (660), he married Tamar, daughter of the rabbinical luminary R. Eliezer of Turkan, the author of the books Divre Hakhamim Ve-Hidatam, Leket Kotsrim, and others. The young couple opened a store in town for household goods and writing instruments with their dowry. God let them have success and their business grew with factories and agents from Warsaw, Brisk, Pinsk, etc. This is because they all trusted R. Aharon-Asher and his wife, thanks to their personal honesty and their fair dealing. R. Aharon-Asher did also not stop from keeping the commandment of honoring his father and mother and participated in earning a living for his parents' children even though he already had seven children at that time.

It should be mentioned in praise of R. Aharon that when he was at the height of his success, he actually carried out the principle of half his time belonging to himself and half his time serving God and the community. Each evening when he was free from his commerce, he taught Mishnah to the public of people praying in the walled study hall. Especially on the Sabbaths, he devoted his time and day of rest to giving classes in En Yaakov in front of a community eager for his words of the Torah. He was equally devoted to matters of the community and its needs. He was the living spirit in the Jewish elementary school and in the Free Loan Society. He also acted as chairman of the cooperative bank. He did not spare any effort to make it easier for borrowers who could not pay back their loans.

In the years of 1928-1929, when the Polish government put pressure on the Jews to pay taxes and many storekeepers and craftsmen lost all they had, R. Aharon Asher began to think about the future and especially the future of his children. After much examination and thought, he decided to agree to the suggestion of his eldest son, Yaakov, who lived from 1922 in the United States, and R. Aharon traveled to the United States in 1930. He did not find his proper place in the new land in the beginning. However, after a short period of time, he arranged himself somehow and brought over his daughter, son-in-law, and remaining grandchildren.

*[Page 159]*

After all his children arranged themselves at work and in businesses, the aging father did not have to worry about earning a living and he was able to sit peacefully in the study of Torah and worship. He poured out his broad knowledge and familiarity with the Torah into a series of books full of Torah content. He was able to put out these twelve books in the years in which he was free from earning a living in his old age: Porat Yosef (On Keeping the Sabbath); Osher avot (On Ethics of the Fathers); Tomer Aharon on the Tannaim (Scholars of the Mishnah); Imre Aharon on Prayers; Eshel Avraham on Akdamot (of the Liturgy of Shavuot); Imre Asher on the Synagogue; Likute Aharon on the Scroll of Ruth; Minhat Asher on the Giving of the Torah; Maamar Ester in Honor of the Sabbath; Osher Aharon on the Pentateuch; Likute Asher on the Book of Psalms; and Know What To Say Giving Answers To Questions Of Heretics and other articles.

I, the writer of these lines, received the manuscript of his last book and the money to publish it. The author, who was my friend and relative, asked me to arrange its publication in Israel. He devoted the income to the Free Loan Association for people originating from Antopol in Israel. However, when the book was being printed, the news came that R. Asher had died on the Sabbath, the 15th of Marheshvan 728 (October, 1967) in New York.

A noble figure of Torah and piety and an analytical and deeply knowledgeable, charitable and merciful man, he left in his death at a good old age his family, relatives, friends, and people from our town Antopol.

# The Walled Study Hall
## By Rabbi Aharon Asher Volinets

The walled study hall was built in 1886 (646). It was finished in the month of Elul 1888 (648). This was the date written above on the wall of the women's section. The chief treasurers, who faithfully built it day and night, were R. Yaakov Shemuel Stavski, of blessed memory, and R. Avraham, ritual slaughterer, of blessed memory. It was fit to write about them what it says in Psalms 132: "I will not give sleep to mine eyes, nor slumber to mine eyelids, until I find out a place for the Lord." The righteous R. Pinchas Michael, of blessed memory, sent a letter requesting funds to messengers, who brought it to all the surrounding towns so that money be collected to build the study hall and this cost a lot.

The form of the study hall, its character and height of its windows were like the synagogue in Kobrin. The walled study hall was built by the best craftsmen R. Barukh and R. Yosef, of blessed memory. They went to Kobrin with the treasurers to see the form of the synagogue and to fix and perfect the walled study hall according to this. Upon the successful completion, they celebrated the dedication of the study hall with the first penitential prayers of the year 1888 (648).

For the Sabbath prayers at the time of penitential prayers, they brought the cantor from the city of Horodets. At the end of the holy Sabbath, all the people of the city gathered to celebrate the dedication of the building. From donations collected then, they prepared the floor before the holiday. However, the study hall existed for a period of two years without the walls being whitewashed. Once there came to the city a famous rabbi and great speaker. All the people of the city gathered to hear him. When the speaker mounted the platform, he stood a few moments without saying anything.

However, he looked at the bare walls from every side and every way possible. Then, he looked at the bare ceiling. Afterwards, he opened his mouth and said: "Our scholars, of blessed memory, said in Baba Batra, leaf 60: When a person whitewashes his house, he should leave a little bare space [in remembrance of when the temple was destroyed]. And how much?'"

R. Yosef said: "The space of a square cubit."

*[Page 160]*

R. Hisda said: "And facing the entrance (as a memory to the destruction)."

"And what did the people of Antopol do?" the speaker asked with a loud voice. "They got together, decided, and said:Why should we make for ourselves a memory of the destruction in each walled house. Let us build a walled study hall and leave the whole structure without whitewash. This shall serve as a memory for the destruction for all the houses in the city."

His words made a big impression on all the listening assembly. They were all embarrassed, especially the wealthy, who lowered their heads. As is said: "I have been ashamed and cannot raise my head for shame." Immediately after the sermon, a good sum was collected. The next day the craftsmen began to fix the walls and ceilings.

This study hall was always a place of Torah, prayer, and a Society to Study Talmud continually, at whose head was the luminary R. Yosef David Rushkin, of blessed memory. Afterwards, the head was R. Mosheh Zelig Olishentski, of blessed memory. The town had a Society for En Yaakov and a Society for Mishnah. The ones who gave the lessons were R. Shimon, son of Sarah, of blessed memory; R. Yosef Shemuel Rasils; and R. Bertshe Meir Feivils, of blessed memory. I, who write these lines, taught the Society for some years. There was also a Society for Night Study. At the beginning of the night, two men taught one chapter of Mishnah. At the end of the night, two other men taught the second chapter.

So it was that youths and old people studied there until World War I when the walled study hall was burnt together with the synagogue and all the study halls by the Russian Cossacks fleeing the city from the German army pursuing them. The only thing remaining of the walled study hall for two years was the walls. Then it was that some people went to the officer in charge of town and got from him a permit to fix the study hall. They took a permit to get timber from the forest to rebuild the walls.

# Memories of the Walled Study Hall

# Written in my book "Shemirat Shabat"

Once when I was a youth studying in the study hall, a guest came and took a book and sat at a table near me. He was good looking and elderly. I said hello to him and asked him from where he had come. He muttered a few words. I asked him if he wanted something to eat. He was silent. I thought that this was a poor and hungry person. I saw to it that he got something to eat and he ate. Afterwards, I got from prominent people a place for him to eat daily. Once, when I asked him about his former position in life, he told me his story as if it had happened to anot her person. I understood that he was talking about himself.

This man had been a rich merchant in a big city. Once when he fell asleep on a Friday night, he woke up. He thought about his life in general and especially that he desecrated the Sabbath. He took account of himself and decided from that day on that he would keep the Sabbath holy in all his personal doings and with all his wealth. When it was morning, he hurried to go to the study hall. Behold, Satan approached him in the form of a man who was one of his friends from the merchants in town. That man said to him, "Let us travel quickly to a place where merchants are gathering and we will do business there." He went with him without telling him about his pure and holy thoughts, lest he be mocked by him. He went with him. They desecrated the Sabbath.

The man tried to keep the Sabbath several times. Each time, he stumbled with one of the people who were his acquaintances. What did the man do? He left his city and went to another, distant from his home. There he was able to keep the Sabbath day holy and to keep the Torah and its commandments all the days of his life without any disturbance.

We can explain by this a statement of our scholars, of blessed memory, in Kiddushin, leaf 40: "Rabbi Elai, the elder, said if a person sees that his evil inclination has overpowered him, let him go to a place where no one knows him and let him dress in black clothes and cover himself with black clothes, and he will do what he wants to do in his heart." And Tosofot explains: "Walking distances and dressing in black break down the evil inclination and keep him from sinning." And, in the story above, we see a person whose evil inclination overcomes him. He wants to be a kosher and good Jew. However, he stumbles because of his acquaintances in his good path. "Let him go to another city, where he is not known, and he will do what he wants to do in his heart to worship God by keeping the Sabbath and other commandments."

*[Page 161]*

After some time, it was known to his rich sons in Moscow that the man was studying in the walled study house. They sent him good clothes and much money and rented a good apartment for him. There, they baked and cooked for him, and he lived some years in peace and honor. When he died, his sons came from Moscow, and they brought a pretty monument of marble with a good iron fence. They gave two hundred rubles to R. Perets Sofer to say kaddish all year round. And I thought of Psalms 37:

"Mark the man of integrity, and behold the upright; for there is a future for the man of peace..."

# Education, Culture, Institutions, and Movements
## By Sh. Turninski

If we want to define culture according to what this term means then we certainly cannot compare the level of our contemporary culture to that of former time. This is especially true of the town of Antopol. There were broad cultural activities in these detailed fields:

1. **Library.** The library as I knew it in its beginnings was my neighbor. It was in the other half of our house. The librarian at that time was Heshkah Kolodner. The reading books were in Yiddish, Hebrew, and Russian. It is interesting to especially bring out that work in the library was done by volunteers in every place it was. It is for this reason that the expenses to keep the library were small. A person could borrow books for a few pennies. The fee collected was enough to keep the library in good order. However, there was not enough for making more acquisitions of library materials. There came to the help here a group called Seekers of Progress. These were contributors who took the last pennies from their pockets to maintain the library. These people did not come from rich families. It was just the opposite. Most, like everyone, came from poor families. Later the library was transferred to the house of Hayyim Zelig Postol. He had a building in his courtyard in which the family Vladovski lived. His daughter volunteered to maintain the library. One of the first members of the group, Seekers of Progress, was Abramtsik Feldshtein, who devoted himself for many years to this matter. The third station for the library was a corridor in the Tarbut school.

3. **Torah studies.** Most of the Jewish community in Antopol was religious and the group Glory of Youth did not only leave a deep impression on its members but also on others. The members of the group, whose meeting place was in the house of Breine-Ribah, were busy with the study of Bible, En Yaakov, and Aggada. The members of

the group, to which my father also belonged, were especially enthusiastic on the Sabbaths at the time of the third meal (the last of the Sabbath meals). I especially remember when a Torah scroll was brought in. The celebration took place at the courtyard of Meir London. There was a tent covering eight meters long, colorful candelabra made out of paper, and decorations put up around the square of the courtyard. This was such an enthusiasm, which was not known until then in Antopol.

*[Page 162]*

4. **Zionism.** A group of youths founded in 1923 a Revival Group to pass on Zionist news and the study of Jewish history. They used to gather twice a week and read the writings of Frishman and Mendele, Sholem Aleichem, and others. At the time of the meetings, they would sing Zionist songs. They also prepared a play on the lives of the cantonists (youths taken into the Tsarist army). The members of the group also tried making new melodies and made a new tune for the Sabbath hymn "Yom zeh mekhubad mi-kol ha-yamim." They began to take up agriculture and preparatory work to prepare for immigration to Israel. Eliezer Ozarnitski, the son of Yehoshua Aharon, was the head of the group. They rented a field and planted it with buckwheat. They did not only deal in agriculture but even in simple labors like cleaning the market. They gave their wages to the Jewish National Fund. The place of mentor was taken by Avraham Turninski, son of Shemuel Eliezer, at the death of Ozarnitski. He, together with the instructor Yisrael Lifshits, began to teach lessons in Hebrew. Likewise, a Hebrew language library was set up in the house of Sarah Yahalom. Then, speakers from different parties began to visit Antopol to draw in youth. A group of the Y.S.A.Y. (Jewish Socialist Workers' Youth) was formed. It was a type of rightwing Poale Tsiyon youth group. Its central committee was in Pinsk. Members were busy with reading books and analyzing them. Likewise, they put on plays. For example in 1925, they successfully put on the Dorfs-yung by Leon Kobrin. They also played sports. Soccer instruction was given by Yashah Lifshits, son of Binyamin Lifshits, who came from Odessa. The first playing field was in a poppy field. Afterwards, we rented a field in the garden of Goren. They prepared it for competition between groups from different cities, like Kobrin, Drohitsin, and others.

5. **Education.** Basic education was as follows. Boys and girls began to study together. However, at the end of the first year, the sexes were divided. The boys went to the Jewish elementary school to study Pentateuch and to begin studying other parts of the Bible. The girls went to the Tarbut school. Afterwards, some of the children studied with private teachers. However, the rich kids were transferred to the elementary school with gentile youths.

6. **The German elementary school.** At the end of 1915, the time in which the Germans conquered the town, they opened a compulsory public elementary school in which Jewish teachers and also a German teacher taught. The teachers were Eliyah Klorfein, Mikhlah Shavelevitsh, the brothers Shimon and Yisrael London, the teacher Vlodovski (geography), the teacher Leibush (Hebrew) and the teacher Rivkah Shub (song). There was also the German captain Herman. As we said, attendance at the school was compulsory. Hence, the children of the Jewish

elementary school had to study there in the morning. This school was on Pinsk Street behind the house of Shelomoh Goldberg, the carpenter, opposite the house of R. Mordechai Sheinboim. When the Germans left and the Poles entered, the school was transferred to the house of Mordechai Goldberg. Secular and religious studies went on at the same time. It is worthwhile to mention some of the teachers in this school: the son of Rabbi Hirsh Rabinovits, rabbi of the town, the teacher Leibush for the Bible, and the teacher known as the son-inlaw of the tile maker.

# My Teachers
## By M. Polak

**R. Alter**. My first teacher, who kept a Jewish elementary school in a small house bordering the old graveyard, was R. Alter. Every day R. Binyaminkah would come and take me on his shoulders and take me to the school of R. Alter, a distance of five houses from us. In the first lesson when R. Alter taught us orally the vowel "o", this kind man threw us each a copeck. In doing this, he made us like studying.When R. Binyaminkah took me back home, I would run by myself to the store of Sheinah Rivkah or to the kiosk of Sarah Vitah or to the house of R. Mosheh Eiziks to buy sweets or soda or ice cream.

*[Page 163]*

R. Alter treated us as if we were infants and did not raise his strap except to frighten us. However, he taught us lovingly. When I finished two semesters with R. Alter, I already knew the entire alphabet and I even knew all the blessings by heart.

**R. Leibush.** After I finished studying in the elementary school of R. Alter, I transferred to the elementary school of R. Leibush, who had his school together with R. Binyamin, the Professor of Talmud, in the second house from us. I used to run to the school of R. Leibush and came always first so that I could receive my daily candy from his wife Hayah or her daughters. R. Leibush was a good teacher and taught us Hebrew and prayer. He also did not like to strike us with physical blows. He would only mutter some times in anger from beneath his moustache. We were really more afraid of his wife, who sometimes came to help him. Her hoarse voice would frighten us. The class was quiet when she was present.

R. Leibush would go out with us to walk during the summer in the garden owned by Goren near the ponds. There, we children would feel like fish in the water. He would take us on the thirty-third day of counting the

Omer (between Passover and Pentecost) to the forest and tell us stories and get our attention by his loving attitude to us.

**R. Avraham Hersh.** We studied four semesters with R. Leibush and afterwards went to study with R. Avraham Hersh. His house was near Esther the baker. This was also near our house. I was also one of the first there every morning. We started to study Pentateuch with R. Avraham Hersh. He was also one of the best teachers. To be sure, striking us physical blows was sometimes part of his conduct towards us. However, he really had no strength. We children would take advantage of his weakness. There were some children who were more disorderly than usual. When one of them would go wild, then also the rest would join him. The rabbi would take revenge on us only one day in the week. It was on Friday when we began studying the weekly section of the Pentateuch. The rabbi's tremolo voice would hurt our hearing. We would feel the pain for many days. Right up to this day, if you see someone with long red ears, you will know that he studied with Avraham Hersh in Antopol.

We also began to study the other parts of the Bible with him. I was very interested in the Books of the Prophets and was considered among the best of his pupils. I also received help and encouragement from my brother Aharon. My father, who also took care in matters concerning my studies, was partially satisfied with my knowledge. My mother was in seventh heaven when she saw the minimal satisfaction of my father.

**R. Yaakov Hayyim and Sarah Menyes.** His house was between that of R. Menahem the baker and that of Yaakov Meir the cart driver. However, for me what was important was that it was very near to my poor beloved aunt.

R. Yaakov Hayyim was thought to be an excellent and good teacher. His wife Sarah Menyes was a beloved and good wife and used to receive us in a friendly manner and treat us to sweets and fruit out of her good heart. There was an entirely different spirit in this school. We heard and listened to what the teacher said willingly and respectfully. He began to teach us Talmud, Tractate Bava Kamma. Certainly, I was not interested in the beginning. However, after the teacher's lively explanation, and also in order to please my mother, I began to listen attentively and especially to grasp the unique explanations.

However, I was especially drawn to the Bible studies. I even knew the first chapters of Isaiah by heart. Generally, we did not act out wildly and make the teacher angry. We would get rid of our wild nature outside on breaks. I would run with some of my best friends to my poor aunt, and every one of us would get a piece of candy. Sometimes we would run to Mosheh Mikhael's to see the calves and cows in their shed or to the stable of R. Yaakov Meir to see the horses and or to still some other interesting places for children our age.

*[Page 164]*

With R. Yaakov Hayyim we were free from fear in class and had freedom of action outside. We studied four semesters with R. Yaakov Hayyim and finished two Tractates, Bava Kamma and Bava Metsia.

**R. Avraham Zelig.** His house was almost at the end of Zaniviyah Street close to the Christian graveyard. R. Avraham Zelig was considered to be among the best teachers. However, the children thought otherwise. He was always in an angry mood. Woe to him who got his angry look. Even though I was among the best students, I had a personally bitter experience that happened to me one morning when for some reason I was struck by the teacher. I took out my anger and reactions on the two baskets with eggs that the rabbi's wife had brought for Passover. Likewise, I took revenge on the glass utensils and windows. Afterwards, I ran home and went to the attic to be alone with my pain. Meanwhile, people came to tell my mother how I was slapped in the face. When she went to the class and saw the damage I caused, her eyes went dark. The teacher himself spoke to my mother and asked for her forgiveness for having struck me for no reason.

The whole family was stirred up. However, the most practical person was my poor aunt, who also told my sister Blumah in Kobrin. Blumah came the next day to take the teacher to justice with the authorities. However, people had already begun to intervene on behalf of my teacher. R. Yaakov Hayyim the ritual slaughterer, to whom the teacher was related, especially intervened on his behalf. There likewise intervened Rabbi Hersh and Rabbi Mosheh. Finally, it was decided that the teacher would not be taken to justice before the authorities. However, he would sign an agreement that he would no longer strike a child.

It is clear that I did not learn much more in the whole half a year I still went to the class of R. Avraham Zelig. However, from our point of view, we children had a good time. When I ended my studies with R. Avraham Zelig, I began to prepare for the examinations to enter the rabbinical seminary. After I succeeded In these examinations, I came to study in R. Binyamin's rabbinical seminary.

**R. Binyamin, the Professor of Talmud.** The rabbinical seminary was in a corner room of the big synagogue. The total number of students studying was 13. We became more serious in the rabbinical seminary. The teacher would recite to us the Talmud lesson, and afterwards we would study it by ourselves. In the course of our study, he would ask us questions and give explanations. We studied all day in the rabbinical seminary. The day included the evening hours. The most difficult day was Thursday in the afternoon when people came to examine us. The course of studies in the rabbinical seminary lasted three years. I finished completely the Tractates, Kidushin, Gitin, Shabat, Berakhot, and others.

In addition to the studies in the rabbinical seminary, I also had private lessons in Hebrew and the Bible with the teacher Yisrael Yitshak, the son-inlaw of R. Mosheh the doctor, mathematics with the teacher Mosheh Hersh, and even Russian with Mikhlah, the young daughter of our neighbor R. Binyamin.

Write this for a memorial in the book and rehearse it in the ears of your children (Exodus 17:14, substituting "children" for "Joshua").

[Page 165]

# The Founding of the Tarbut School

## By Belah Liberfroind

I remember the frequent conversations of my parents about the Hebrew school, which was to open soon in town. Children would be able to get an orderly and improved education in it. We young people looked forward with expectation to the important event without being able to understand its meaning and with an innocent curiosity until finally the special day arrived. We were washed very well, had our hair combed, and were brought in holiday clothes by our parents for the first time to the school.

This was a red brick building, which was still not completed in 1913. It had been intended to be used as a hospital. When all the synagogues were burned in World War I, it served for a long time as a synagogue. After the war, Zionism, in all its streams began to take root in the public and cultural life of the Jews. The Zionist leaders in Antopol reached the conclusion that the public building, which was left by the people praying in it when they built a new synagogue, would serve no better use than as the modern Tarbut school. It seemed as if the building by its very nature had been meant for this purpose from the beginning.

A wide and grassy space separated the school from the sad-looking houses of the town. The building had lots of free space around it, which so-to-speak brought into relief the gray daily life of the Jewish district and the festive life, full of happiness, the shouts of the schoolchildren and youth free of care. There is no wonder, then, that the school quickly conquered the hearts of youth of all ages.

In the first months of the school year, our studies took place outside the building under the open sky. The school program included only games and singing. In the winter we were forced to go inside the classrooms, which were still incomplete. The furnishings were very poor. However, all of this did not disturb how the little kids felt, who benefited from the freedom for a few hours from the discipline of their parents.

Our first teacher, Zaretski, was a youth, who was straight in posture, light haired and always happy. He was one of the pupils of one of the first teaching institutions founded by "Tarbut" in Poland. He was accepted by us as an authority. He taught us pioneering songs such as: "We Go Up to the

Land with Song", "The Shepherds Gathered around the Fire", "God Will Rebuild the Galilee", and others. Zaretski left our school at the end of the year and traveled to complete his education.

Deborah, the daughter of Rabbi Paians of Bialystok, took his place. She graduated from a Hebrew gymnasium in one of the cities of central Poland and devoted one year to teach in our school. She taught us to read and write and recited for us poems of Bialik and Tschernikovski. She also left the school at the end of the year in order to complete her studies.

The third teacher, Yisrael Lifshits, who was a founder of the school, continued and completed what was missing in fixing the building, getting appropriate furniture for the classes, acquiring textbooks, etc. He organized a committee of parents, and in cooperation with it, he worked out a proper program of studies and got in contact with the educational office of Tarbut, which began to function at that time in Eastern Poland. The studies slowly entered their proper path. Meanwhile, the group of teachers increased. The teachers were joined by the gifted and enthusiastic pioneering educator, Feldman, and Sirkin, the teacher for Polish.

The library was founded at this period. In the beginning, it included the works of Mapu, Smolenskin, Bialik, Tchernikovski, Kahan, Feierberg, Frishman, and others. The library was expanded in the course of time and also included the works of Jules Vern and of the best Polish writers, Slovtski, Mickiewicz, Sinkiewicz, Prus, and others. The holiday celebrations, which were arranged in the school for every holiday and festival, took a special place in our awareness. The preparations for these events were carefully planned. The classes were ornamented with decorations and flowers. The programs were rich in songs, recitations, lectures of the teachers and educators about the essence of the holiday, about its place in the life of the nation dwelling in the Land of the Patriarchs, etc. Plays were presented on national topics taken from Jewish history. Education in the national spirit created and developed the nuclei of youth movements, which were seen as the natural continuation of the school classes.

*[Page 166]*

Only girls attended the "Tarbut" school during the first years of its founding. The boys continued to receive their education in the dark classrooms of the Jewish elementary schools and their teachers filled their soft brains with difficult talmudic sections from early morning hours until evening. However, it did not take long for the quick and outstanding development of the "Tarbut" school to cause the boys to leave the Jewish elementary schools. They were unable to withstand the enticement of the new institution. And even the parents were forced to submit and not to discriminate between their sons and daughters.

As the years went on, the Hebrew language was heard spoken by children in town. The graduates and pupils of the school established the youth movements, he-Haluts ha-Tsair, ha-Shomer ha-Tsair, etc. The founders of the school took pride in these movements.

# Notes About the Tarbut School

They maintained the school with some difficulties. The Polish government did not support Hebrew language schools. Only the parents did by saving their pennies even when they lacked money for their own expenses.

Their reward was that their children studied Hebrew and got an education in the spirit of Judaism and Zionism. This was everything that they desired.

These people were on the Committee for the School, who did their work whole-heartedly: The head of the committee, Mosheh Rabinski Tanyes, who devoted the great part of his life on behalf of the project and worked day and night without rest, Perets Gurvits, a dentist, Hayyim Vaytsel and Berel London. They kept the school going with their devotion and successfully overcame the difficulties piled on their way.

The teacher Shelomoh Menahems Gershtein taught private lessons even before World War I in Hebrew, Bible, and especially mathematics. I will also mention the teacher Nahum Kotler, who established in 1920 a Hebrew school for beginners. He taught reading and writing in Hebrew, with special emphasis on calligraphy and math. The teacher Shimon Goldberg accepted private pupils for lessons and helped students with the entrance exam to Tarbut school. He also gave lessons to pupils in the Jewish religious elementary schools.

The following are the names of the teachers from the Tarbut school: The teacher Serkin; the teacher Pines (now in Israel); the teacher Epstein; the teacher Yisrael Lifshits (now in Canada); Mosheh Feldman; Varshilski; Tsiporah and Aryeh Tserulnik; Walk; Zaritsky, and Ash. The principal, Mrs. Serkin, was the teacher for Polish, who came to Antopol from Warsaw. Her only son, Jacob Serkin, remained alive and came to Israel. He lives on the Kibbuts Dafnah.

We the pupils bow our heads in admiration for their memory.

The orphanage was founded in 1921. Its guiding spirit was R. Hershel Nitsberg, of blessed memory. Twenty-one children, who were able to take care of themselves later, passed through it until 1930. There were still 12 orphan boys and girls in it in 1930. The home was kept by contributions from friends in Antopol (40 percent) and organized help from immigrants to

Antopol in the United States (60 percent). The participation of the Polish government was limited to only 300 zlotas a year.

The composition of the administration in 1930 was chairman, Hershel Nitsberg; director, Sarah Rudatski; secretary, David Varshavski; and supporters, Mosheh Novik, Zlatah Mazurski, Heniah Volinets, Zisl Lifshits, and Avraham Feldshtein.

*[Page 167]*

# Free Loan Association
## By M. Polak

There was even before World War I in Antopol a Free Loan Association, which was maintained by 80 wealthy people, who made monthly contributions to it, each according to his ability. The chairman was R. Avigdor Sirotah, the treasurer was Zekharyah Gerber, and managing members were R. Hershel Nitsberg, R. Yaakov Hayyim Shoib, R. Yitshak Berkovits, R. Meir Shub, and R. Barukh Yiglom.

The amount of loans distributed to 70 families on the eve of the outbreak of World War I was nearly 2,000 rubles. During World War I the association was closed down. The new Free Loan Association was reopened in 1921 by a first gift from Mrs. Esther Kornblum from the United States. She visited Antopol in 1921 and gave 600 dollars to renew the activities of the association.

The amount gathered up in the association was nearly 3,000 dollars by 1930. The increased amount was due to 1,000 dollars sent by the sons of R. Wulf Leib Glutser from the United States. The organization of Jewish immigrants from Antopol in Chicago sent 500 dollars. The Joint Distribution Committee gave 600 dollars. Together with additional donations from people living in Antopol itself, the association was able to make 1,825 loans up to 1930 in the amount of 212,000 zlotas.

We should point out that the association was led by R. Motel Fernik, who was both its manager and treasurer in this period and who did a lot for the association. He especially gave help to storekeepers and craftsmen to pay taxes to the government. This is because they had very little income due to the great crisis prevailing then in Poland in all the Jewish towns and in Antopol, especially.

# First Aid Development in Antopol
## By Belah Liberfroind

Antopol did not have a doctor who graduated from medical school, just as was the case in any outof- the-way town. The White Russian population made use of all kinds of superstitious medical practitioners, such as knowledgeable people and sorcerers. The Jews used surgeon doctors and midwives (grandmothers), and the like. These were people who had served as doctors' aides in the Czarist armies and by observation had acquired elementary knowledge. They were able to grant first aid in an emergency. However, they could not examine the type of disease.

Mashah acted as a surgeon doctor from 1860 to 1905. He was an angry Jew by nature, without any education and, understandably, with no knowledge of medicine. He had only one treatment for all types of illnesses-castor oil. He also pulled teeth. It happened more than once that he pulled a healthy tooth instead of the decayed one. He appeased the complaining person in a case like this by not charging for pulling out the second tooth.

Yenkel the doctor also practiced medicine in Antopol from 1875 to 1915. He had more knowledge than Mashah. He was well liked by the Jewish population. He kept all his medical tools in his pockets.

The grandmother Esther Hayah acted as midwife in Antopol in this period. Her help to women giving birth was very primitive. There was also another midwife, whom people called Di Smutsikhe. She also used to apply cups to draw blood.

The White Russians in Antopol at the end of the last century knew of a gentile from Czernowitz and the Jew Aryeh Osipovits. They both knew how to deal with a limb that came out of its socket and how to set broken bones. Both also knew magic against the evil eye as a most tested medicine. Esther Gorfinkl, who was called Di Gotekhe, served as a midwife among the White Russian population in Antopol. She was accepted by them.

*[Page 168]*

The first doctor to graduate from a medical school came to Antopol in 1905. He was Dr. , who was of Polish origin. He made a place for himself among the Jewish inhabitants and was considered a friend. He even learned to speak Yiddish. He used to visit his patients in a carriage attached to two white-red horses, and he was liked by people. An additional doctor, Dr. Shats, practiced medicine in town during the years 1910 through 1914. This doctor was especially invited in connection with establishing a hospital in the period of World War I. He was considered to be the town doctor.

The hospital building became a synagogue. This was after all five study halls in town burned in World War I. The Tarbut school was placed in this building in 1920.

An especially good midwife was Itkah. She was liked by all the classes of the population. There were cases when she saved women giving birth and their children when the doctors had given up.

Difficult cases were turned to doctors in neighboring towns: in Kobrin, Dr. Gershuni; in Pinsk, Dr. Prebulski and Dr. Yevseinko; and in Bialystok to the dentist, Dr. Pines. Sick people needing hospital care were sent to Pinsk or Warsaw.

During 1914-1918, there also practiced Dr. Lipa Zagorodski, who had just finished his studies, and Yenkel, called "kayn beyz". This is because of his custom of calming his patients with the words "no harm". "No harm shall befall you!" The first doctor of veterinary medicine came to town at this time.

After World War I, two public institutions were founded in Antopol to take care of health: 1. "Visiting the Sick"; 2. "Free shelter". The founding members included Mr. Alter Slonimski. The job of these institutions was to get medicine and supplies for the sick, among other things. The first pharmacy in Antopol was that of Mosheh Ozernik. It was founded in 1911 and called "Small Pharmacy." Afterwards, a second pharmacy was founded, which took care of doctor's prescriptions.

There was a local dentist in 1918, Perets Hurvits, who was excellent in his profession. However, he left Antopol for some reason and settled in Drohotsin. His wife, from the family of Sirotah, lives in Israel and works as a doctor. A Russian doctor, whose name I shall not mention, practiced from 1921 to 1924 in Antopol. He was addicted to narcotics and not liked by the people. Dr. Weinstein, a good and beloved doctor, was in town from 1925 to 1929.

Dr. P. Czerniak was in town in 1938 beginning to practice medicine. He was born in town and attended the elementary school and afterwards high school. He had a reputation as a good student. He successfully completed his medical education in France and did postdoctoral work in the universities in Vilna and Warsaw. After two years of practice in hospitals, he settled in his home town. He began working as a doctor in May 1939.

During the last months of that year when Poland was attacked by the Nazis, the country was partitioned, as is known, between Hitler's Germany and Russia. The eastern part of the country, and in it our town of Antopol, was conquered by the Red Army. The new regime did not stay still. It acted in all aspects of public life and also made progress in medical organization. A hospital with 40 beds was founded and a clinic in which two doctors, who came from Russia, worked, a midwife, and people giving first aid. Dr. Czerniak established these institutions and directed them. He also established clinics in the area surrounding town, whose task was to serve the rural population.

At the end of 1941, the Nazis conquered the region from the Russians. As they advanced east, medical service in town was stopped and destroyed. Dr. Czerniak was brought with all the Jews to the ghetto. The Nazi enemies did not give up taking medical help from the Jewish doctor. Every day Dr Czerniak was brought under a guard of thugs outside the ghetto to take care of their sick. This continued until the ghetto was destroyed and he was saved together with his family from the claws of death.

*[Page 169]*

Someone with an imagination, and even the weakest one, will not find it hard to describe the importance of a doctor under the conditions prevailing in the ghetto and the danger tied to giving medical help and obtaining medicines, disinfectants, and the like. Dr. Czerniak's life was constantly in danger. Despite all of this, he didn't stop giving medical care. It is possible to tell many stories about his bravery and sacrifice during those mad days.

In 1945, when the region was liberated by the Red Army, Dr. Czerniak was appointed director of the hospital, the clinic, and local health department, which were set up again in Antopol. Dr. Czerniak received a decoration of distinction from the Russian authorities for the medical work he did during the war.

Dr. Czerniak and his family left Russia in 1946 when Polish citizens were given permission to return to their homeland. He continued to work in hospitals in different cities in Poland until 1950 when he finally decided to immigrate to Israel.

# The Pioneering Youth in Antopol Between the Two Wars
## By Mikhael Kosht

Burnt ruins, ruined remnants of walls, and sooty chimneys stood up like silent monuments of the Jewish neighborhoods in Antopol. This was the dark picture of the town after the Russians fled with the outbreak of World War I. Many of the Jews of burnt Antopol settled in the villages of Zaniviyah and Turkan.

There stood a big, isolated building of red brick on the street leading to the villages of Zaniviyah and Turkan between the Jewish side of town that was burnt down and the gentile side that remained intact. The house was empty. It was not burnt. However, it was not completed and mysterious. We children, who frequently went the way from Turkan to town, passed it. This house drew our attention always. "What was this building?" we asked. The house was meant to be a hospital.

Destiny gave the house of red bricks a much nobler function. When World War I was over, it housed the Tarbut school. We children of the period of 1920- 1930 got an excellent education in this school, a national Jewish education, and we studied the Hebrew language and literature in a basic way and tied our soul to the Land of Israel and to the first desires and dreams of immigration there. However, this house became a spiritual center not only for those directly educated there but for all the youth in town. From there came guides and educators to the pioneering Jewish youth movements.

The Hebrew library was founded in the building. The drama club presented plays in its auditorium. Meetings and assemblies were held in it at night. Even after the authorities took displeasure and forbade the activities to take place in it, the Tarbut school served as a base from which branched out the social activities of the youth for still a long time.

The first organization of youth in Antopol after the war, which lasted, was called Revival. Before this, there was a youth group called Hertseliyah, which did not last a long time. The initiators and guides for Revival were members of Young Zion, led by Eliezer Ozarnitski, of blessed memory, who died at an early age. The founding assembly was in the orphanage that was at the end of the street going to Roshbah. As we said, the activity of the group Revival immediately went on taking place in the Tarbut school.

The principles of the association were revival of the Hebrew language and revival of the Jewish people in the Land of Israel. We took responsibility for learning and using the language in daily life, first of all in all our meetings and closed assemblies. It is hard to say that we kept up with this principle of speaking Hebrew. However, this activity gave a push to founding a Hebrew library. There was already a Yiddish library existing in town for a long time. Members of Revival gave and collected tens of books like Ahavat Tsiyon by Mapu, Zikhronot le vet, Kalman Shulman's Mistere Pariz, Smolenskin's ha-Toeh be-darkhe ha-hayyim, and the like. By this we laid the foundation for the library, which grew, developed, and bought many new books. Our biggest success was in subscribing to Shtibel publications in Warsaw. Most of its books were translations from foreign literature. Many of the youth, born during the war, were unable to acquire knowledge of foreign languages. These books expanded their horizon and knowledge. The books most read were War and Peace by Tolstoy, By Fire and Sword of Sinkiewicz, Victoria and Slaves of Love by Knut Hamsun, books of Oscar Wilde, Jack London, and the like.

*[Page 170]*

The second real action of Revival was on behalf of national funds, especially the Jewish National Fund. Collections were made mainly by visiting houses. For example, in Purim, couples in costume would scatter, pass from house to house and ask for a donation for the Jewish National Fund. The happy couple would be the one that was able to collect the biggest sum. There were also disappointments in these collections. There were cases in which people not only would not give but would also insult and hold in contempt everything we held sacred. One such disappointing collection is fixed in my memory. This was in 1923. There was then a crisis in Israel. The Yiddish Language newspaper Moment printed a series of articles on great unemployment, immigration from the country, and despair. This was all accompanied by pictures. A sensitive person finished this collection by crying in secret.

We set up ties recognizing the youth groups in the region. We added a new topic to our set theoretical and practical ones: work. We began contemplating fixing the world by a new regime of work with no one exploiting and no one being exploited. We studied the problem of property and work, etc. We called our group "Development and Work." Then, one project that we began raised our esteem in the group, especially in Pinsk.We rented a field in the vicinity of the Tarbut school and made a vegetable garden. We planted firt potatoes. The goal was not only to prepare us for agricultural work but also for cooperative work and cooperative management and organization. We succeeded in producing a good crop of potatoes, whose profit in selling we devoted to the benefit of the library and funds for which we collected.

This first test of self-realization succeeded in proving to us the correctness of the idea that surely a person could demonstrate devotion, loyalty, and ability even in the condition of a collective group and public property. This idea was realized by many of our generation and stood the test of reality in the collective movement in Israel. With the unification of the parties Tseire Tsiyon and Poale Tsiyon in Poland, our group "Development and Work" was defined as the youth party of Poale Tsiyon ha-meuhadim (United Zionists). Afterwards, it went by the name of Freyheit (Dror In Hebrew). Ties already existed not only with the regional center in Pinsk but also with the center in Warsaw, which supplied us with newspapers and literature in Yiddish and Hebrew from Israel and made us responsible also for different local activities, such as elections to the Polish Parliament and the like.

The Polish government forbade the Tarbut school to be open for our daily activities. The activities were mainly done secretly in the private homes of members. We received permission from the authorities to hold events in the Tarbut school only in the case of public assemblies in which there appeared delegates, speakers from the central office or from Pinsk. The he-Haluts was founded at that time by us. It included wide groups of youth. The he-Haluts movement was at the height of its development in cooperation with members of Poale Tsiyon with the beginning of the fourth Aliyah to Israel in 1925. Masses of youth joined with the goal of immigrating to Israel. Those people who had completed school and were between the ages of 18 and 19 organized younger groups of he-Haluts ha-tsair. Comprehensive cultural work was then done in groups to study Jewish history, the history of Zionism and Socialism, and analyses and clarifications on topics, which were then most of interest. The meetings of the groups were always accompanied with song and dancing the horah. We used to walk in the streets of Antopol, young boys and girls, singing and desiring in our hearts to have a new life in the desired land. Individuals went on to kibutsim for training and some small training in the form of the employment office of he-Haluts, which accepted and carried out all types of work available in town: doing agricultural work, bringing out manure from the sheds, loading blocks of wood at the railroad station, and cleaning trash out the market after market days and fairs, These first pioneers, many of whom were rich people, did not shirk from doing any type of work. They didn't need to do this work to earn their keep and support.

*[Page 171]*

This was an Antopol in which studying for enlightenment and working mixed together. There was farming area bordering on it. Fields were planted and vegetables grown (thousands of barrels of pickled cucumbers were sent from it). Even the storekeepers and merchants in it had a piece of sown land near their house or a fruit tree growing near their house. Many of its inhabitants had a cow and chicken in their courtyard. The Jews living in Antopol were strongly built: blacksmiths, tool makers, wagon drivers, builders in wood and brick-experts known in all the region, shoemakers, tailors, and carpenters. There were even tree cutters, who would stand on scaffolds, one above and two below and quickly cut big trees into boards.

The young pioneers of Antopol were used to physical work and didn't need special training to get used to a life of physical work. They went out as pioneers to do all types of work, work usually done by gentiles. These were women, who were rich and were graduates of school and who went out to clean the market place from rubbish. These were youths who had higher education and went who bare-footed to take out trash from every courtyard. They were porters on the railroad and cut down trees in the forest. Certainly, this was a big revolution in the Jewish street, a quiet revolution, which the pioneering movement caused among the Jewish youth so that they could remove the shame and the low status in which generations had looked at physical work. They wanted to tear down the barriers and prevent discrimination, which was the portion of working people, so that they could raise up the status of the working man. This is what is called in our time equal human value. This was the corridor through which the pioneers passed to do actual work in Israel and the Jewish to take over the work and agriculture to the establishment of the State of Israel.

The gates of Israel were closed. Only lucky individuals managed to get certificates to immigrate. The crisis of the Fourth Aliyah began to show. Masses of pioneers were left with no way out and were swept in the stream of migration to the United States. As the number of activists in the movement emptied out, it began to decline and sink. At the beginning of the 1930's, the Shomer ha-tsair movement showed only brief signs of life. Individuals still succeeded before World War II in breaching the gates to Israel and going secretly to Israel in the illegal Aliyah 2, the famous underground Aliyah.

There ended with this a chapter in history full of glory of the pioneering youth in Antopol. It will not happen again. The terrible Holocaust uprooted a many-branched tree, a clear spring for a generation of proud Jews, closed up by the enemy. There are no more youth in Antopol, healthy in body and soul, carrying the vision of redemption of the nation and the individual. When the great time came for the rise of the Jewish nation in Israel, not many merited seeing it and we didn't merit seeing again those who didn't live to see it.

*[Page 172]*

I was able to see the town one more time. This was when the whole thing was about to collapse, at the beginning of 1939. The town was struggling for its economic existence. All public activity was silenced. There was no memory of the youth movement and even the Hebrew library was closed and sealed by government order.

The town was surrounded by a rising anti-Semitic movement, and behind the border, the great enemy was already waiting. The Tarbut school stood out like a lone beacon of light above the ruin of this gray life. I visited paths known to me after many years. I was invited by the teacher Feldman to a Tu bi-shevat (Jewish Arbor Day) celebration. I stood and told the children of Antopol about Tu bi-shevat in Israel and how we celebrated it in the collective settlement by planting gardens and bushes. The children sang songs of Israel and recited "I Don't Sing to You, My Country" by the poet Rachel. I taught them to sing this song and their faces lit up and their eyes burned with desire and love for the land they longed for.

How you have perished in your youth, dear and pure children of Israel. We lost you, the coming generation. As to our generation, this one that saw the loss and destruction still is at the beginning of its redemption.

# Fradl the Revolutionary
## By Mosheh Stavi (from his memoirs)

In the years 1908-1910 when he lived in Warsaw, in order to participate in the Hebrew literature there, the author Mosheh Stavi used to visit his hometown Antopol and also his relatives, especially, his sister Tsviyah Feldstein. He came in 1908 at the end of the summer to spend the holidays and remained there until after Sukkot. The youth used to gather around him, as it longed for Zion. At that time, Fradl appeared, a teenage girl, the daughter of his brother Efrayim and Bashke, the daughter of the rabbi Netanel Hayyim Pape. She was inclined to socialism and freeing the Russian homeland from the Czarist yoke. At that time, it was a custom that at the end of the Sabbath and holidays, the youth of Antopol would go to stroll in the garden of the landowner Goren. Then, the group would split into leftist and rightist factions. The rightists would sing Zionist songs and long for the Land of Israel. The leftists would sing songs of liberation and the rise of a Russian homeland influenced by socialism.

When revolutionary activity expanded, Fradl was among its leaders. We got news that the district police in Kobrin were about to arrest her. Mosheh Stavi was the only grown up man in the family then in Antopol. Her father Efrayim was in Kremantsiuk in the south. Mosheh took upon himself the task of smuggling Fradl out of town. They put her in a wagon and covered her up with different things. Thus, they brought her to Drohitsin. From there, they took her by various ways to Kremantsiuk. The young Social Democrat was then about 17. She remained some time with her grandfather Yaakov Shemuel Stavski, who lived in Kremantsiuk. Afterwards, she went to Yekaterinoslav together with her father, a grain merchant.

She joined in Yekaterinoslav a local revolutionary group. In 1910, she participated in an assassination attempt on the governor of Yekaterinoslav. Fradl was arrested and jailed. She was sentenced to hard labor in Siberia.

Her Social Democratic friends in the United States collected money with the purpose of freeing her or helping her in Siberia.

In 1917, when the revolution broke out in Russia, Fradl left Siberia and came to Moscow. There has been no trace of her since 1919.

This was the fate of a revolutionary in Russia.

# The First Zionists in Antopol
## By Mosheh Polak

We talked in our house about what was going on in Zion. This was also the case in other houses in Antopol where enlightened society gathered together to read everything in connection to Israel and Zionism. I especially remember one meeting on the second anniversary of Herzl's death. Yehoshua Aharon Orznitski stood and spoke at the president's table. Yoel Leib Muler and Aharon Asher Volinets sat at his side. Opposite them, on long benches, which had been especially brought from the study hall, a big audience of members of their movement sat listening attentively. I knew them all the period of m y childhood: Yisrael-Yitshak and Hayah Gorfinkl, Ore and Minah London, Heni (wife of Yehoshua-Aharon) and Tamar (wife of Aharon Asher) and Raizl (wife of Yoel-Leib), my brother-inlaw Yenkl Varshah, my sister Blumah, and my brother Aharon, and I myself among them, Etyah and Berl (Yakhnah's children), Leizer and Dinkah, Motl and Malkah Shvilvits, Feitl and Fini (Rabbi Mosheh's sons), Yenkl and Meir (Perets, the scribe's sons), Leizer and Leah Fridman, Akiva Serotah, Yisrael Bedane, Shelomkah Bershtein Yosl Vaisman, Alter and Dubah Zisuk, Alter and Toibah-Hanah Brushavski, Efrayim and Bashah Stavski, Motl and Bailah Frenik, Binyamin and Heniah Skidlaski the teacher Leibush and Blumkah, Yosef-Leib and Malkah Farber, Yitshak and Sarah Berkovits and still many others of their age and also people older. Even my father used to listen to their lectures in our house.

*[Page 173]*

I remember still other meetings, lectures and debates on the action of the Jewish National Fund, the founding of the Mizrahi in Vilnah, the Delegation for Settlement in El Arish, the pogrom in Kishinev, the proclamation of Yosef Vitkin, the founding of Poale Tsiyon in Poltavah, and on many different Jewish Zionist topics.

The above-mentioned friends, who were the first Zionists in our town, used to come to our house almost every week to exchange books in the city library, which was in our house. It had books that reached us from other cities according to our request. I especially remember the noble image of Yehoshua-Aharon, who used to come to us to buy books. He would frequently come to us at night. I would light up the shelves for him by candlelight. He would search, exchange, or buy the books of interest to him, that he researched in many fields of knowledge. Like that were Yehoshua-Aharon and his friends. We children studied, got sustenance, inherited, and also realized the desire and hope of the older enlightened generation, which desired so much the rise of a Jewish State and the Zion for which it longed. May their memory be blessed!

# Ha-Shomer Ha-Tsair
## By Hayyim Asif

We founded in August 1926, (626) a branch of ha-Shomer ha-tsair in our city with the help of Hayyim Goldberg and Goldshtein, who were leaders of the movement in Kobrin.

The Tarbut school then graduated its second cycle of students. We did not have a school to continue studying in town. Only some people, who traveled to Brisk or Pruzshani, had the means to continue their education. Therefore, with the founding of our branch, the vibrant and dynamic youth was able to have a wide program of activities, to work and advance itself. Youth, who learned in the Jewish religious elementary schools, and young people, who still had not found a framework in which to act, also joined us.

The branch conducted cultural activities in the beginning. Courses were opened to study the language and likewise to study the history and knowledge of Israel. After a short time, all meetings were conducted only in Hebrew. The Hebrew language was heard in every place, at home, in the street, and in lectures and debates. We created an Israeli atmosphere.

The activities were led by youth without outside help. Nevertheless, we should mention the devoted work of our hometown person, Shelomoh Yahalom, of blessed memory, who accompanied the movement from its beginning steps, guided, explained, and did a lot to set up the image of the movement and its activities. He traveled to Vilnah to study in a seminar, also finished his course of studies, and afterwards continued to study until he was also cut down and perished with the other victims of the Holocaust, which struck Antopol.

*[Page 174]*

There also already existed the Freyheyt and he-Haluts ha-Tsair movements at the time our branch was set up. There were quarrels between the different movements in the beginning. However, in the course of time, when we met at cooperative functions to raise money, it became clear to us that we had a shared goal and identical aspirations.

The branch founded a library solely for Hebrew books. The foundation for the library was in the books, which the members brought, each one from his parent's house. We bought new books with money, which we earned in working in the fields, gardens, and the like, as day laborers. I would like to point out that even though the people in town earned a living by labor, it was not accepted to see a boy or girl from a wealthy family do simple work like day labor. This activity raised the standing of work to everybody. The library grew from month to month. New books were added. Children from the Jewish religious elementary school would also come to take out books. It happened more than once that parents came shouting with claims to leaders of the movement that they were causing their children to leave the straight path of Torah Judaism for a secular way of life.

At the time of World War I, when the Russians entered town, the library had 1,000 books. The activists, who feared for the future of the books, buried them under the earth until the time of anger would pass. To our sadness and pain, they did not live to take them out of the depths of the earth because they themselves fell victim to the killing.

The slogan was a healthy soul in a healthy body. We would practice sports, exercise, and take nature walks. We would talk about Israel and our desire to realize immigration to Israel, to till it and make it bloom. Only a few of us succeeded in receiving certificates to immigrate to Israel. Some went on a temporary visit, as tourists to the Maccabiyah and stayed in Israel. Others wandered in boats for weeks and months under hard conditions. And if they were lucky and not stopped by British soldiers, they reached a safe shore.

# The First Pioneer Group
## By Mosheh Polak

Our house had a pleasant mixture of religion, Zionism and socialism. This education made it possible for me to absorb yet in the days of my childhood the longings of my family for Zion. I was happy when even my father, of blessed memory, was able to immigrate to Israel and to live in Jerusalem. He died in it in good old age in 1938 (698).

Since my brother Aharon, of blessed memory, was active in Zionist youth movements and the Mizrahi, which frequently met in our house, I also absorbed Zionism from this source. In addition to this, I absorbed it from the groups in which my sisters were active and from all those who came to our house in the course of time.

After the events of World War I, I passed a difficult period in sickness from typhus and malaria. My mother, of blessed memory, died in that time, and a close, rich relative of ours came to Antopol from the United States, wanting to take back with him relatives from all his family. I was also among those to travel. Not wishing to do so, I departed from my father and from my dear family and traveled to Warsaw in two railway cars full of youth. In the hotel in which we were staying, when I sat down to eat, I suddenly heard youths speaking Hebrew at another table. I asked who they were. They answered that they were pioneers traveling to Israel. At that moment, I decided to ravel with them and informed my uncle of my decision and desire. He still attempted to persuade me to travel with him. However, when he saw that I was firm in my decision, he blessed me to have success. The next day, after prayers and morning meal, my uncle took me to the Israeli Office to arrange my travel to Israel. I appeared as requested for a medical exam. However, to my sadness, the doctor didn't give me at permission to travel because of signs of malaria, which were still in me. Meanwhile, I made due with the promise of the doctor that I would get well soon entirely and I would receive permission to go to Israel.

*[Page 175]*

I left my uncle, who promised me to finance my trip to Israel the next time. I also took leave of my brother-in-law Yaakov, who went in my place to the United States with the rest of the young men and women. I also took leave of the group of pioneers going to Israel with the hope of seeing them soon. I returned to Antopol. My father was also happy for my change in travel plans.

When I returned home, my father and sisters tried to help me to get well quickly and prepare myself to travel. I began to prepare myself with agricultural work and began to work in different fields. Likewise, I prepared other friends to travel.

In the month of August 1921, we received an announcement from the Israel Office in Warsaw that we should prepare to travel. All of our seven members, aged 19, organized as a well-prepared group for immigration to Israel to build our lives for ourselves and all Israel in our homeland. The grownup Zionists and the youth in Antopol arranged a magnificent departing party in the month of December 1921 on the evening of the last day we were in Antopol. They accompanied us early in the morning with a choir and trumpets to the railway station.

After we passed in our travel the stations of Kobrin and Brisk, we again came to Warsaw and to the same hotel in which we lodged the previous time. After some days we left Warsaw and came to Vienna to the pioneer's lodging. We met a big group of happy pioneers streaming to Israel from the towns of Poland and Lithuania. We were all very happy.

We stayed some months in Vienna and continued by train on the scenic route from Vienna to Trieste, where we toured for one day and continued to Israel on a freighter, Bukovinah. We were one month at sea in the Mediterranean. We had very little to eat. We didn't change our clothes the whole time and slept on freight bundles deep in the ship. However, we didn't complain and didn't despair. We even danced on the deck.

We tread the soil of the homeland on March 6, 1922. The next day I was sent to Jaffa as a representative of the group to get work. I had some addresses of veteran inhabitants from Antopol. The first address, which I received from my father, was that of old acquaintances, the family of Avigdor Muler, which lived on Ohel Mosheh, a street named after their father, of blessed memory. I was warmly and well received by all the family. The oldest daughter Gutyah and her husband, Hayyim Karis, a building contractor, especially took interest in me. I stayed the night in their house. Hayyim took me to work the next day on pouring the roof of the building, which he was building for Mr. Grodetski on Shabezi St. Certainly, this work was not so hard. However, I received many cuts from dragging cans with liquid cement on my shoulders and back. However, the day passed quickly. I was happy from my first day of work in Israel. I went to the home of Hayyim and Gutyah. I washed and changed my clothes and shoes, which were wet from sweat and cement. However, I felt very good as if I had built that day a house for myself. I also went to work the next day on another building for Hayyim. Meanwhile, Gutyah found for me a rented room in the cellar of Mr. Zalivenski's house on Shabezi St.

I immediately informed by letter the group in Haifa of my success in finding work and a room. All of them came after some days. We stacked all our suitcases high up by the wall. We had a little space for ourselves on the stone floor.

*[Page 176]*

Hayyim Karis also gave Nathan Sirotah temporary work. It happened that once a day one of the three members of our group worked. Nahum Muler and the brother-in-laws Mosheh Skiletski and the Glazers sons, who were small contractors, helped us to get work. However, we didn't lack for anything. The reason is that we lived as a communal group. After a few months, we got in the Naveh Shalom neighborhood a normal room. We also received from the Sokhnut Agency in Jaffa a bed and mattress for everyone. We bought a naphta lam and a used table. We also bought a bottle of wine in honor of the big event, gave toasts, and danced until late in the evening. From there we passed to a big room in Brent St. There was a place for all seven beds along the walls.

Meanwhile, we continued to look for work. The author, Mosheh Stavi, of blessed memory, then moved from Beer Tuviyah to Naveh Tsedek with six cows giving milk. After some of my friends didn't succeed in getting used to working with him, I exchanged my place of work with the contractor Karis and let my friends have it. I began to work with Mosheh Stavi and was very successful.

Likewise, got some work with the Boneh (Building) Company, whose administrator was born in our town. He was Mr. Yehezkel Grinberg, an engineer and contractor, known from the railroads in Central Russia. Likewise, the Mazurski, Katinski, and Saharov families tried to help us. The latter even suggested to us to buy their factory, which made floors, in Jaffa. However, we didn't want to ask for money from home.

The conditions in Israel didn't get better. Except for me and Sirotah there was no work for the other youths. Before the year finished, four members decided to go to the United States. Only, Sirotah, Zeev Volinets, and I remained. We received from the Sokhnut Agency a small tent and erected it on the sand dunes of desolate Tel Aviv. We also succeeded in receiving work from the building company Solel Boneh on the Zaiger building. This was the first building past Allenby Street.

After many attempts, I succeeded in 1923 in bringing to Israel my sister Reitsah, and in 1924 I brought my father and my sister Raizl. In 1924, there also came from Antopol Shagan and Simhah Vinik, who joined our group. I received a cabin as a gift from Hayyim Karis, as a reward for my work. The five of us went to live in the cabin. In 1925, I accepted directing the work on the building of the Davar newspaper on the corner of Ahad ha-Am and Yavneh streets. I put up a cabin there and went to live in it. Here, I became independent and our collective disbanded.

I and Nathan Sirotah worked as a group. Zeev Volinets also worked with us without a field of expertise. However, Aharon Shagan and Simhah Vinik didn't get used to building work. After a year, they returned to Antopol.

Afterwards, Zeev Volinets also returned. Nathan Sirotah and myself, the two who remained, continued to advance ourselves in Israel. We were also company to Naftali and Sarah Volinets. Even though their situation was tough, they made us feel at home. This was very important to us, the first pioneering group.

# Economic and Social Life: Employment in Antopol
## By M. Polak and Sh. Turninski

## Artisans and Farmers

Most of the Jewish population of the town was artisans, who lived from their labor. The product of their work was not just for Antopol itself. Rather, and especially, it was for the surrounding area. Antopol was surrounded by more than seventy villages and estates. The big part, which was employed i n building, worked throughout the whole week, from Sunday until Friday afternoon on the estates and villages. It is worthwhile to state that the Christian population in town and in the villages worked in agriculture, in cutting trees, and in raising animals, cattle, sheep, lambs and goats, horses and pigs. The free professions, and especially building, were in Jewish hands. These are the number of families according to occupation.

*[Page 177]*

## Coppersmiths and Engravers (*Kotliares*)

These artisans formed the rich class in town in 1914. Seventeen families earned their living from this. These coppersmiths and engravers worked mainly for the landlords in various works: beginning in setting up the vessels for alcohol factories of the landlord Zavedski and ending in making different utensils of copper such as pots (fendlekh), special pots for cooking tea with a narrow top (bunke) so that the tea would keep hot during the morning hours and during the Sabbath afternoons, utensils for hand washing (kendel), and similar stuff. They made the vessels in their shop in town itself. Every coppersmith had a very primitive shop, whose characteristic tools were an animal skin bellows to blow fire, an iron anvil, iron and wooden hampers, and tongs.

This occupation ended after World War I at a time when factory products began to arrive in great quantity and cheap prices.

The faces of those doing this work come before me one after another: Hayyim Zalman Futerman, Tsadok Futerman, and the other members of their family; and the Kotler brothers, Berel, Leib, and Aharon Shemuel-simple good-hearted people, pious, and making sacrifices on behalf of their fellow Jews.

I remember the day that the Polish army entered our town and made a slaughter. Among the killed were Efrayim Pomerants (called Knipl), the son of Yakhneh and Mosheh Tserniuk (Falk's son). He was one of the self-defense members in town. He stood guard together with his friends and inhabitants of town in the time in between regimes. Berel Leib brought the dead to burial, both Jews and gentiles, paying out of his own pocket for the wagon and horse belonging to the gentile Mikitah Sviderski.

## Blacksmiths

They lived at the edge of town. Their smithy was next to their house. They mainly put on horseshoes for the gentiles' horses and fixed the wheels for their wagons. Together with this, they did other small work in iron, which they created primitively. They had on their anvil the same tools as the coppersmiths with the addition of various tongs and presses. About twelve families made their living this way. Among those doing this work, I remember: Avraham Yitshak Goldberg from Mogilkes Kotlerski Street; Aba Kantsiper whose smithy was opposite the abandoned gentile cemetery; Berel and Yisrael Koval; Shemuel Bekher (called Shemuel Meir the smith); Mosheh and David Goldberg; and Alter Brashvitski and his sons.

## Tinsmiths

They earned a living doing work generally out of town, in covering the roofs of landlords' houses or churches (kloysters), making their roofs. They also made milk-cans, funnels, lanterns, and similar stuff.

## Woodcutters (*Filshtshikes*)

Most of the cut wood was bought prepared from sawmills in the forests or from lumber stores in town. However, all the additional work and fitting was done on the spot by the building. This work was done by four families. The woodcutters had a greater physical strength than average. They cut trees for different building purposes, like preparing boards for walls of houses and for roofs.

How was this work done? When the trees cut in the forest were brought to town, they were sorted according to two classes. Thick trees, which could not be lifted, were cut by digging a pit about two meters deep and 1.5 meters wide and 30 meters long. Thin blocks of wood were put along the length of the pit. The tree, which was to be sawed, was placed on top. One of the sawers would go into the pit and his associate would stand on top of the tree. Thus, they would saw the tree's whole length. Small trees would be sawed in a different way, although according to this principle. The tree would be placed on wooden supports and sawed just like the heavier trees. I remember among those doing this work Avrahmil the Dorbla and Ezra called Klenik

*[Page 178]*

# Builders in Wood

These built the houses in town, which were all made of wood. The order of planning and building the houses was this way. The houses were mainly one story, built on a foundation of bricks, about half a meter above ground. Cut boards of oak were put on top of the brick foundation. Each board was several meters in length, as long as the house, about 20 centimeters in width, and about 30-40 centimeters in height.

# Stonemasons (*mulier*)

There were houses of stone in Antopol built by Jewish builders. However most of their work was building ovens for baking a n d cooking and ovens for heating and warmth in winter. Every house had ovens like this. A big part of the builders worked in building factories for producing alcohol on the estates of Zkezele and Rusheve. They were also employed in the factories for bricks and tiles in Rusheve. Likewise, they built ovens in villages and nearby estates. Generally there were great craftsmen in Antopol for building houses, ovens, and chimneys. The occupation employed 18 families.

# Gardeners

Most of the gardens were covered by wooden shingles (*shindlen*). Three families were busy with this work.

# Carpenters

There were carpenters in many specializations. They built doors and windows in buildings. They built furniture. All the home furniture was of wood. There were beds, clothes closets, bookcases, tables, chairs, and cases for wall clocks. There were carpenters who were artists, especially in the furnishings of the study halls. The Holy Ark in the big synagogue was exemplary. There were 18 families working in carpentry. Especially known were Yehoshua Varshah and Yaakov Shemuel Volinets.

# Wood Engravers

These made various items such as the legs of tables and chairs, wooden spoons for eating, the ornamental framework of cabinets, handles for work tools, cart wheels, ladders, the big pestle for grinding matsoh that every house had. Thirteen families were employed in this occupation.

# Painters

The painters in Antopol were excellent. They were craftsmen, whose reputation circulated abroad. They didn't only paint locally. They were called from distant places to paint houses. Among the most outstanding were Shelomoh Varshe (Shelomoh der maler) and his son-in-law Zisuk, husband of Dobe.

# Glaziers

Most of them were not at home for weeks in town. They traveled to local villages, to the gentiles. They fixed window panes for placement in new and old houses. We don't have to say that these glaziers did all the work themselves in Antopol. I remember the glaziers Mosheh London and his sons, Hayyim Zelig, Akiva, Bertsik (Dov), Naftalkah, and Yosil (called Yozef). Another family of glaziers was that of Zaidel Garfinkel. I remember a third glazier AsherSlonimski (der glezer).

# Locksmiths

They worked mainly on estates together with carpenters making railings and fences. Three families earned their living in this occupation.

# Covering Walls and Ceiling with Paper

A part of the houses in town had their walls and ceilings covered with paper. This was the same on estates. This occupation employed one family.

*[Page 179]*

# Chimney Sweeps

Every house had ovens and chimneys. They had to be cleaned twice a year. Two families earned their living in this occupation.

# Bathhouse Attendants

The main activity for this was Friday afternoon for men and weekday evenings for women. Two families earned their living in this occupation.

# Tailors

Men worked sewing clothes by order. I remember among them Yosel Fridman Yosel David Dubovski, and Raivel Gololtsenah. They earned a good living because people in town ordered new clothes for the holidays. Twenty-seven families earned their living in this occupation.

# Seamstresses

These specialized in sewing clothes according to fashion. They especially made wedding clothes for brides and women's clothes. This is because there were no stores selling prepared clothes. Five families earned their living in this occupation.

# Hat Makers (*Kirzner*)

They prepared winter hats from animal skins and also fur collars for winter coats. Sometimes, they made furs from valuable skins. Among them were Hayyim and Gedalyah Kaplan, who were called Sender Moshehs grandchildren. Hayyim Kupitski (Nushtskhes) also did this work. He came from Kobrin and married the daughter of Nathan, a shoemaker. He opened a workshop in the store of Shemuel Visotski. Four families were employed in this occupation.

# Wigs

Most of the women in town wore wigs. One family earned its living from this work.

# Barbers

Barbers also played instruments n weddings and other affairs. Two families earned their living in this occupation. Shoemakers. They sewed shoes and boots by order. I remember among them Nahum Volinets, who was one of the better shoemakers; Hershel (Stishes); and Avigdor (Klion), whose father was the night watchman called Yosel Klion. He used to try to lessen his fear by knocking with his stick and shouting during his watch time. The children of the town would surround him and walk by his side. About thirty families earned their living from shoemaking.

# Stitchers (*Shtefers*)

In contrast to their colleagues, the shoemakers, stitchers used to sew only the top skin of the shoes and boots. My deceased father, Hershber (Tsevi) Turninski, earned his living from this. Mosheh Tsertok, Nehemiah Melamed, Hayyim Podlovski, and others were also employed in this work.

# Tanners

Three families earned their living in a primitive operation of tanning hides.

### Strap Makers (Rimares)

They belonged to the rich class in town. Apparently, they made a good living. They made from hides bridles, harnesses, and whips for horses. I remember among them Zalman Altvaig, called Zalman Kolbe, the blond strap maker and Yaakov Vlianski.

There were also different occupations like making tiles, barrels for wells, and tiles for floors. One of the factory owners was Avraham Podrovski, who came from Homsk and married Faniah Shub.

There was also a workshop for making winter boots from felt and a bakery of matsoh. Understandably, there were also ritual slaughterers, a watchmaker (Zunshtein), and a photographer called Yashah Lifshits, who came from Odessa.

*[Page 180]*

# Butchers

The butchers went on foot or traveled to villages to buy a cow or calf for the Sabbath. Some of the butchers also kept cows from which they sold milk. Generally, a big part of the people in town had cows or goats to get milk from them. This occupation employed twenty six-families.

# Flourmills

People worked this in four ways: with the help of horses, wind, steam, and diesel mills. The eyes of the horses were covered. While they turned in a circle, they moved the millstones. They also turned a grinding stone that extracted oil from flaxseed. How was this done? They took flaxseeds. They put them in a wooden container. They heated them with the help of a hand oven, with burning coals and a small flame. The walking of the horses caused wooden boards to beat against one another. The flaxseed was smashed and the oil separated from the seeds. The pulp was used as cow feed. I remember these people who did this work: Mordekhai Kaminetski (Dvoshes), Yitshak Zidel called Yitshak Rihels, and his brother Pesah, whose wife was Hayah Gitl. The horse mills were on the other side of town. They were owned by Yoel Bendet and Binyamin Velovalski. There was an additional one owned by Maniah Kaminetski.The windmills were outside of town.

After World War I, the mills were burned by the Russians (who left the place according to the scorched earth policy). They began to build more efficient mills in their place. Even these were primitive because they were built of wood. As we said, they were built outside of town. They were three stories tall and could be seen from a distance. The wings of the mill were turned to the wind and this supplied the power. These were the owners of the mills. At the side of the cemetery was the mill of Yoel Bendet and the Velovalski brothers. At the end of Haroshover St. was the mill of Yudel Goldberg. At the other side of town was the mill of Velveleh (who was called crazy Velveleh).

There was also a steam-powered mill. Different work was done there. It not only ground flour but also groats. It also beat down woolen fabric for gentiles (This is called valush). This mill belonged to Gadiah Rubinshtein. It seemed also that his brother Efrayim was a partner or had a say in running this mill. And if he didn't actually work in it, he was called Efrayim fun valush.

The diesel mill, This was the best of all the mills. It was a small mill since the machines didn't need a big space. David Velvil Glader (der murgovnik) owned it. This mill was on Pinsk St. near the steps.

# Bakers

The bakers were divided into two groups, one being craftsmen whose profession was their craft and others who were forced into baking by circumstances. There belonged to the second group, for example, widows and divorced women who had to earn a living in the absence of their husbands. One of these, Freyde Shadrovits, the wife of Yenkele the shoemaker, who left her to her sighs and crossed the border to the Soviet Union, took up baking black bread in the house of Aharon, the son of the black (bearded) teacher (shvartser melamed). Afterwards, she began to also bake all kinds of bread that the other bakers baked. The rolls of Shimelikhe, the wife of Shimon Altverg, were well known. And people even came from Kobrin St. to buy the bread made from sifted flour (gebaytelte broyt) she made.

Most housewives baked for themselves bread from bran and white bread (dolots) for the Sabbath. They didn't need bakeries. Small bakeries also baked bagels, rolls, and the like. Most famous was the bakery of Yaakov Frakes, the parents of Yisrael Lifshits, the teacher. They baked rolls (madelbroit), poppies in honey, and a baked good of rice in honey. Everyone who passed his bakery was unable if he only had a penny in his pocket, to resist entering and buying one of this good type, tasting like a muffin in honey. A person salivated just from the sweet smell. He didn't just bake this but also a baked good of buckwheat flour in square pans. It tasted heavenly. And he was not the only one to bake this. There were also others who did so.

*[Page 181]*

Groniyah would bake half black bread, flat bread (pletsl), rolls, and especially baked bagels, which before baking were put in boiling water. They had a special taste. The bagels of our time cannot be compared to them.

I don't remember the year in which bakers were given permission to set up wooden booths, so they could sell their products in fairs and in the local market. They had their place between the line of stores on the east side and between the houses of Shemuel Visotski and Itkah Mairims, who married Leibkah Eliezer, the cantor's son. Among those who received permission to set up a booth like were for selling baked goods were Moshkeh Aizerkes Lifshits, Fridah Shedravitski, Groniah's daughter, and others. The flat bread bakery of Sheine Rivkah was known In its day in the alley of Kobrin St. Among the other bakers were Barukh Valdman (the noznik), and in Kobrin St., there was also the bakery of Barukh's brother, David Yosef Valdman.

# Bookbinders

Most of the books came from Vilna, Warsaw, and Bialystok, unbound. The books of the Talmud were especially bound in leather. There were also orders from abroad, and especially from the United States, for special binding. Two families were employed in this work.

# Watchmakers

There were craftsmen making watches. They would make wall clocks by themselves. Two families were employed in this work.

# Vegetable Growers (*morgovnikes*)

They lived near their plots at the edge of town (on Kobrin and Pinsk Streets). They were called *morgovnikes* /after the name of their plots of land. The plot of land was called morag, a measure of almost 3000 square meters. Their main work was sowing cucumbers, which they pickled and afterwards sent abroad. This was the main export of the town. The pickled cucumbers of town were widely sought after. They were called Antopol cucumbers. These vegetable growers grew several types of vegetables. I especially remember their onions.

At the beginning of the summer, we went in crowds to the plots to buy green onions meant for planting. It had a bitter taste outside and a sweet taste inside (after peeling the outer layer). I feel a special taste in my mouth when I remember these onions. A part of the plot owners also fattened geese and even oxen.

I remember among these: Hayyim Zanivier, the father-in-law of Mosheh Zelig, the fisherman; Leib Kaploshnik; Mosheh Shterman; Naftalkah Volinets; Tsimerinski; Hershel Shterman, called the blond; the brothers Volovalski; the woman Birakhtshikhe; and the Grinman family and its children, Leizer and Getsel.

# Wagon Drivers

There was no local station. However, there was transportation between cities. This was done by wagon drivers whose line of work was from town to the railway station in Horodets, seven kilometers distant. The wagon was simple and harnessed to one horse with seats made of small wooden ladders. A sack filled with straw was put on them. This transportation worked at all times, even in times of unrest. Once, when the Poles still didn't rule over the entire region and groups of robbers and murderers acted without interference in the region, Mordekhai Gershtein, the father of Gavriel Gershtein, and Yosef Volinets, the son of Tuviyah Volinets, were killed on one of the trips. After much trying on the part of the town's inhabitants and much opposition b y the wagon drivers, the train began to stop opposite Antopol.

Transportation was by omnibus (a wagon harnessed to two horses and closed like a freight car). Afterward, the first autobus was brought. It couldn't be used and sat like an unturned rock. However, in the course of time, the Jews learned how to work its motor and started using it. Then, there began the golden age of transportation in Antopol. Yosef Alters (London) was the conductor of the omnibus.

*[Page 182]*

# Gravediggers

There were three graveyards. One was ancient in the center of town and completely filled. It could not be used for burial anymore. There were two new graveyards. Besides the Burial Society, two families earned their living from grave digging.

Monument engravers. Two families engraved monuments on stones, which they brought in from outside.

One fine day the craftsmen in town began to organize. They founded the Craftworkers Association (Handverker Farayn). They claimed that t h e organization could be run democratically. Certainly, the first thing taken up was to fight against the only financial institution in town, the cooperative bank, whose funds came from its members' shares, a lot of credit from the Joint, and the deposits of the customers. I was an assistant to this bank's accountant. The craftsmen suggested that I be the secretary of their organization.

I accepted their suggestion. I organized the organization in the best way. The craftsmen took control of almost all of the institutions in town: the above-mentioned bank in which I work as a director and accountant, and after some time they also took control of the town committee. Our organization was an important factor. We took part in everything. Lectures were given and even plays of the Freyheyt were presented. The authorities didn't like it. However, the request was given by the Craft Association and this helped in getting permission from the Prefect in Kobrin and our police in town.

# Antopol and the Villages in 1939 Families: Workers

| | |
|---|---|
| 3 | Construction in wood |
| 1 | Covering wooden roofs |
| 10 | Carpenters |
| 1 | Engravers of wood |
| 3 | Locksmiths |
| 2 | Tinsmiths |
| 5 | Glaziers |
| 1 | Painters |
| 1 | Book binders |
| 8 | Copper engravers |
| 31 | Blacksmiths |
| 2 | Harness-makers |
| 2 | Tanners |
| 41 | Farmers |
| 40 | Shoemakers |
| 8 | Stitchers |
| 17 | Tailors |
| 5 | Seamstresses |
| 1 | Watchmakers |
| 32 | Butchers |
| 9 | Bakers |
| 2 | Chimney sweeps |
| 1 | Bath attendants |
| 19 | Carters |
| 2 | Upholsters |
| 7 | Factory workers |
| 1 | Photographers |
| 2 | Mediators |
| 5 | Guards |
| 5 | Peddlers |

*[Page 183]*

# Families Different Occupations

| | |
|---|---|
| 1 | Rabbis |
| 1 | Mayor |
| 4 | Ritual slaughterers |
| 13 | Teachers (especially in a heder) |
| 22 | Teachers |
| 6 | Accountants |
| 2 | Officials |
| 2 | Agents |
| 2 | Managers |
| 3 | Doctors |
| 1 | Midwife |
| 3 | Pharmacists |

## Factory and Business Owners

6   Manufacture of building materials
1   Manufacture of porcelain
1   Manufacture of oil
6   Flour mills
1   Ice house
1   Hotel
3   Saloons in the villages
3   Restaurants
7   Coffee houses and kiosks
56  Stores of all types
90  Merchants of all types
17  5 Mainly in the villages

*From a general population of 2,225 people, there were 505 workers, who were killed.*

# Occupations and Commerce
## Families: Different Occupations

2   Rabbis
2   Ritual slaughterers and examiners
55  Teachers (especially in a heder),
8   Teachers of languages and accounting
2   Scribes for the Scrolls of the Law, phylacteries and mezuzah
2   Scribes to write letters
4   Watchmen (mainly for fruit gardens)
6   Accountants and bookkeepers
4   Directors of monthly work
5   Doctors
1   Midwives
2   Pharmacists
2   Hotel owners, especially for merchants coming from the big cities
2   Saloon owners, especially for the gentile population in town and for farmers, who came from the villages every Sunday
6   Coffee houses, restaurants, and kiosks
1   Caretakers of horses for government use, called Potst
3   Manufacturers of oil and food products for animals
2   Manufacturers of wine, in a primitive fashion by hand from raisins
2   Manufacturers of soft drinks
2   Manufacturers of pitch and kerosene
2   Manufacturers of candles
2   Manufacturers of sweets

1    Manufacturers of porcelain

1    Ice house owner, especially, ice for soft drinks in the summer and ice to lower temperature

6    Traders in forests, who leased forests from the government and from Christian estate owners.
     They sawed the trees in the forests and sent the wood to different cities or abroad

5    Traders in the city of wood for building, families;

5    Traders in the city with wood for fuel

3    Pitch suppliers (Gentiles made it from the roots of the trees)

6    Traders in fruit gardens (There were those who leased big fruit gardens from gentiles.
     When the fruit ripened they would send it to cities or abroad)

*[Page 183]*

6    Land leasers (There were Jews who leased land from Christian estate owners.
     They would work it with gentiles and send the produce to different cities or abroad)

3    Traders in cattle and horses (They would buy cattle and horses in the villages and sell it to
     merchants dealing in hides from other cities)

3    Traders in pig bristles (They would buy it in the villages and send it on to Mezerits, Poland for finishing)

16   Traders in fowl (They would buy geese from distant places, fatten them and afterwards send
     them slaughtered or alive to the big cities, like Warsaw or Vilnah)

4    Traders in eggs (They would send big shipments abroad)

3    Traders in vegetables, especially cucumbers, which they would buy from the city or village farmers
     (Pickling cucumbers was an independent branch)

2    Traders in cheeses and butter (They would buy from Jews leasing in the villages and also from gentiles.
     Mainly, they would send it abroad)

2    Traders in mushrooms

3    Traders in cloth (The villagers would make cloth in a primitive fashion. The cloth would be sent
     to the United States)

3    Traders in fish and salted fish


# Families: Stores

4    Produce stores

32   Grocery stores

4    Stores for hides

2    Hardware stores

1    Store for pitch and kerosene

3    Stores for kitchen utensils

5    Stores for fancy goods

4    Fabric stores

2    Shoe stores

1    A store for writing instruments

1    A store for medicines

# Jewish Occupations in the Villages

1     Saloons
2     Inns
3     Keeping cows especially for making Swiss cheese and butter
4     Stores
5     Leasing land and working it
6     Blacksmiths
7     Trade with the villages
8     Shoemakers
9     Supervisors in factories for alcohol and bricks
10     Forest supervisors

*The total number was 178 Jewish families with 832 members living in 51 villages and estates*

# My Dear Town
## By Vardah Kusht

How can I write about you, my dear town Antopol? All of you lives in me and surrounds my being.

I am tied to you by my past. I spent twenty-four years in you. I used to look at the sunrise and dream. Everything was shining and rejoicing. I dreamed about my future. In the evening when the sun set and the flock went home, I summed up my actions of the day in the hope of realizing my dreams.

I loved to listen to the ringing of the church bells, to look at the storks building their nests in the spring. I felt the pain of the Jews working to feed their children. I saw the children of the Jewish religious elementary school returning home in the evening with lanterns.

On the New Year, I visited the synagogue and took in the sanctity of the house. I loved everything in you because I was born and educated here. There were my parents' and sisters' home. There I lost all my dear ones. You stand before me always and I remember every corner with love. Everything is clear in my memory. I go down your streets frequently and try to make a past impossible to make return come alive forever in my imagination. Is there a need to perpetuate your memory? You seem to be the embodiment of beauty, splendid with wide spaces, and populated. However, in reality you were only my small hometown. Around you were the swamps of Polesia through which a train didn't come for years to your boundary. Perhaps, this is under the influence of the lilac, which grew splendidly by my window. Every time it would bloom, I could not satisfy my eye in looking at it. Certainly, a lilac like this bloomed behind our house in the garden of the priest. We lived on the "Gentile Street" near the church, around which lilac bushes grew in abundance. We children couldn't resist the magic of its bloom and fine smell. We passed the fence and plucked flowers mainly for the Sabbath.

*[Page 185]*

Our house which was not big in room would expand when we sat in it, thanks to the big love that flowed from my parents. They gave us more than they could, an abundance of devotion, education, and love without boundary and condition.

I remember the Saturday nights when all our family gathered together. All of us were dressed up, the table shone from the light of the candles and the light of the eyes looking at us, which covered us with a feeling of the safety of being in a warm nest. We were well defended from any wind breaking in.

I will memorialize your image, my mother and father, in my heart with love all the days of my life: You reminded me, Mother, always of the poem: "Who knows your life, Hebrew woman?"

We attended the Tarbut school. We were devoted to studies, thirsty for knowledge. It seemed as if we had nothing but the Bible. We wanted our parents to be proud of us because we appreciated their efforts.

Our town only had two streets. However, it had in it a developed Jewish youth devoted to the Zionist idea. We were organized in the Shomer ha-tsair organization and as one who devoted herself to work I also have pleasant memories from that period.

The Shomer ha-tsair building looked poor from the outside. However, it was full of warmth inside. Singing and dancing didn't stop until midnight. What was not told and sung about our destined country in the heat of youth and hope to be among those realizing immigration. To our sadness only a few were able to reach the shores of Israel.

It is hard for me to write about you my city Antopol and I don't know what to put first. Shall I remember the garden to which we streamed every Saturday from the beginning of the spring or until the late fall? Or should I describe walking on the sidewalks back and forth with no goal but with the jumping and joy of youth? So passed the days of my childhood.

Shall I remember the market days in which we small children liked to wander and look at everything and to get a big impression of everything. Only in the evening of market day, we were afraid of drunks because we Jews were always the scapegoats.

Antopol! Thus, passed my youth free from worries in a house of devoted and loving parents. There, we were still all one family together. After that we began to disperse. I still remember more and everything. I will always remember.

I left my parents and sisters. I immigrated to Israel. I didn't believe that this would be a final separation from you, and I didn't think, my dear ones, that this would be your end. I didn't accompany you on your last way and I am sad because of this. I will always carry your image with love in my heart, and when I hear your name, Antopol, a trembling will pass in all my bones.

[Page 186]

# Memories of My Youth
## By Miriam Valodovski

My parents, Meir and Yehudit Shub, were from an old family in Antopol. In the course of many generations, they were rabbis and ritual slaughters (as the family name indicates, Shub, shohet u-bodek, ritual slaughterer and examiner).

My father was active in the community and quite a few of the inhabitants of Antopol immigrated to Israel, thanks to him. However, fate was cruel to him and precisely his daughter, the widow Niyotah with her two children, Avraham, aged 12, and Yehudit, aged 5, could not be brought by him to Israel. They died together with all the people of our big family, together with all the martyrs of Antopol.

Life in the small town with its low houses went on slowly and with great moderation. I remember the garden with the pretty pond, which we called after the name of its gentile owner Goren. The streets were sometimes full of mud. The inhabitants, who lived in them, were dear people, each one of them.

I remember one Hanukah night. They treated all of us at home with potato pancakes, as was the custom. And, afterwards, we the youth went out to walk in town. The Hanukah candles flickered in the houses and the smell of potato pancakes wrapped the town and enticed our appetite.

And behold the market place stands in front of my eyes. One day when I approached the market place, I paid attention that something had changed and the people had gathered to talk about what they saw. I also looked and saw that in the course of the night the youths inducted into the army had managed to pass the store signs from one store to another. This was done in the typical spirit of venting one's feelings in those days, as if they wanted to encourage themselves as they were about to be drafted.

These and other memories come to my face from the period of our youth. However, they cannot cure our pain at the loss of our family members killed in the Holocaust.

# My Grandfather's Farm
## By Belah Liberfroind-Kletski

I was born in the village of Frishkhvost. There passed here the first years of my childhood. The village was found at a distance of two kilometers from Antopol. The meaning of its name comes from the combination of two Russian words, Frishiti-khvost, that is, sewn tall, since the village was as if a continuation of the town.

In Antopol itself there was a long main street and at its center a square, which was embellished by stone houses and stores. The square served as the market place, and twice a month there were held fairs to which the White Russian villagers would come bringing for sale their agricultural products and manufactures. With the money they received in exchange, they would buy their different needs such as clothing, shoe products, haberdashery, etc., in the Jewish stores. From the two sides of the main street there continued unpaved streets. The inhabitants of the small wooden houses that stood on their length were poor people. The continuations from the two corners of the main street were called morges, the plots of land that belonged to Jews, who worked them and earned a living from their work. Around the town a wide meadow continued and fields of grain spread out, which could hide, among the tall stalks of grain, a person at his full height.

The village Frishkhvovst was one of those White Russian villages surrounded by gardens and courtyards. The farm buildings included a shed for cattle and a silo for grain and the rest of the agricultural products. Among the inhabitants of this village, there numbered two Jewish families. One of these was the family of my grandfather.

My grandfather had a patriarchal appearance. His face was decorated by a white beard. He always wore a long coat (kapotah). And like every religious Jew, he took care to pray the morning, afternoon, and evening. When he had time, he also looked at his Talmud.

*[Page 187]*

My grandfather's house stood at the entrance to the village. It was a pretty wooden house surrounded by a garden of fruit trees, which numbered more than two hundred trees. Not far from the house were the outhouse, the stable, and the building in which the sheaves of rye, barley, and other summer grains were threshed. In the winter, it served as storage for seeds and fodder. At the gate of the courtyard, there was the doghouse for a big dog, who frightened the peasants dressed in gray robes and sandals twisted from reeds growing in the area of the meadows. The well was found in the garden. There was a wild pear tree by it. Its ripe fruit fell into the water giving it a special fragrance.

Thus, life went on quietly and tranquilly generation after generation until the end came and the hand of the executioner also reached them.

Rabbi Mordekhai-Li, of blessed memory: Letter of the dream, which was sent to the luminary, Rabbi Michael, of blessed memory.

With the help of God, on Friday the 28th of Shevat (January 28, 1881), in the year 641, here in the holy community of Biten, peace and great salvation to honorable dear friend and friend of my soul, the great rabbi, the luminary, analytical and knowledgeable, knowing the revealed law and able to analyze it, the saintly and humble rabbi, famous is the honor of the holiness of his glorious name, Rabbi Pinchas Michael, the rabbi of the community of Antopol.

After greeting him, the honorable one of sublime Torah, I come to tell you an awesome tale. Undoubtedly, people will not reveal this to any person but will only hide the letter In a place where no one can reach, or tear it to pieces in a fashion that it shall not come to anyone's attention.

On the night of the past Day of Atonement when I learned my set lesson, I fell asleep, and a splendid-looking person with a beautiful face and big beard came to me. When I looked at him, I was startled. He took my hand and said, "Why do you sleep? Get up and call to God." And I was very startled and awoke and behold it was a dream. I said to myself dreams tell false things. Nevertheless, my heart beat and I was greatly afraid.

I fell asleep again on my bed. And behold in my dream, there came to me again the splendid man mentioned above and two men were with him. The two men said to me: "Know that this is a true dream and don't despair." And I was very astonished. Then, the splendid man mentioned above said to me: "Examine your deeds because I come on a mission from the world above to you."

Then, I recovered and I said to him: "On what mission do you come?" And because, I spoke aloud, I awoke from my sleep. And I saw and behold it was a dream, and I said again: "Dreams are not significant." Nevertheless, because my heart beat, I was frightened and I didn't sleep again that night. And on the Day of Atonement, I cried a lot in a fashion which I never did. And I didn't know why I cried so much. And I said to myself perhaps it is because of the above mentioned dream that I cry, because my heart beat, etc.

I didn't dream again until Shemini Atseret. Then, I slept in the Sukkah, as was my custom, and in the midst of my sleep the splendid man mentioned above came to me dressed in white. I was startled when I saw how beautiful he was and that he looked frightening. Then, the man came up to me and said, "Your crying helped a lot so that they sent me to make you understand and to tell you how to take care and to abrogate the decree."

And the man was silent and stood silent about a quarter of an hour. Then, I began to weep a lot in my dream and said: "I don't know what is the big sin, which I sinned, that sent me emissaries from the world above." And I cried a lot in my dream and because of the great crying I awoke from my sleep. And when I awoke, I didn't say that this is only a dream mid of no importance because I had seen him speaking.

And I was very happy on Simhat Torah when I was asleep, and in the midst of my sleep, behold the splendid man mentioned above came. The glory of his appearance was awesome and he was wrapped in white and he came close and said to me: "For how long do I have to bother myself on your behalf to come to you from my honorable place."

*[Page 188]*

Then, I recovered and said to him: "By the merit of the Torah and the Tannaim and which I have learned and studied, I ask you to tell me the matter of your mission and to explain clearly to me so that I can understand."

Then, he went with me to a beautiful and pleasant room ornamentally decorated. I could satisfy myself with looking at this. And he said to me: "Sit, my son, sit and I will reveal to you a secret matter. And this is my mission."

I sat on one chair and he sat next to me. And he said to me: "I am revealing to you secrets. You know that I am the rabbinical teacher Rabbi Y. ben Lev, and when I was alive in this world, I sat on the chair of judgment to judge between two men. Two men came to me to decide a case and one was guilty. And he didn't want to accept the sentence because he was a violent person. Then, I warned him with the known warning and left. The above-mentioned man, whom I declared guilty, came to me and struck me on my cheeks, What he did is inscribed on his bones until this day and he has no recovery from this."

I was startled and astonished and remained like a silent stone for about a quarter of an hour. And after this, the rabbinical teacher, Rabbi Y. ben Lev, of blessed memory, touched my mouth and said to me: "Why are you silent?"

Then, I began to cry a lot and said: "I don't know how to fix this because I have no knowledge about private matters and intentions." Then, the rabbinical teacher, Rabbi Y. ben Lev, of blessed memory, said to me: "You should know that it has been decreed for you that you are to buy a book of the response of the rabbinical teacher, Rabbi Y. ben Lev, and you are to learn it constantly until you know it fluently from beginning to end. Then, this person will have a big recovery and you will be able to go up from step to step". And he said this with a soft voice: "Why do you want to know the secrets of the Torah?

" I said to him: "How much time should I study the above mentioned response until I know it fluently?"

He said to me: "Not less than four years because in addition to this, you have to study your regular lessons, what is forbidden and permitted and the laws of torts. Therefore, you have to study at least four years."

And then, I said to him: "I don't have a copy of the response of the rabbinical teacher, Rabbi Y. ben Lev."

And he said to me: "You may seek and find them for sale, only I am going to reveal to you one thing, which is that you must buy this only from the rabbi of Antopol, who has the above mentioned response." And I said to him, "Why only from the above-mentioned rabbi?" And in saying this, I awoke from my sleep and was very startled. Then, I said to myself: "Perhaps, it is an idle thing to buy it from the above-mentioned rabbi because it is possible to buy it in another place."

And in any case, I had a lot to take care of in the city and I began to ask some people to get the book mentioned above for me. And about two weeks later, the splendid man mentioned above in my dream came to me again and said harsh words to me: "Why are you waiting to carry out my mission?"

And I said to him: "Am I not trying to buy it?"

And he said to me: "Didn't I warn you to buy it only from the rabbi in Antopol."

And I said to him: "What is the reason for this?"

And he said to me: "It is because you have studied with the rabbi in Antopol that you have the merit to be a messenger to him, and I shall reveal to you this matter."

"You should know that the above-mentioned rabbi also has some things noted in the world above about him because he began to prepare for print an explanation on the Talmud for the Tractates Temurah/Meilah [and this is because I don't remember if he said to me Temurah and Meilah or only Meilah], and he didn't carry out what he had prepared to do. Therefore, he also has to take care to do this. And from the money that he will receive from you for the response of the rabbinical teacher Rabbi Y. ben Lev, he will begin to prepare himself to print the above mentioned."

*[Page 189]*

And I said to him: "How is this matter connected one to another?"

And he said to me: "Do you want to know about the secrets of the Torah?"

And I said to him: "Why don't you go yourself to tell the rabbi of Antopol?"

And he said to me: "Do you want to know the secrets of the Torah?" He repeated and shouted: "Take care for the sake of Heaven to carry out my warning, a moral rebuke, and don't change from anything an iota. Then, it will be good for you and also others."

And because of the voice, I awoke from sleep. The next day I wanted to send a special messenger to tell you all the matter, only I was delayed a little because of public service in which I was a little busy.

And in the past week when I began to sleep at night in a lot of sadness on account of my wife, who became very sick, the rabbinical teacher, Rabbi Y. ben Lev, of blessed memory, again came to me and said aloud: "You should know that this is the last warning, which I am warning you, and the sickness of your wife is a sign because you have been lazy at my warning. Therefore, take care for the sake of Heaven to immediately send a messenger only to the above mentioned rabbi and buy from him my response and learn it until you know it fluently almost by heart."

Then, I awoke from my sleep in great fear and began to hire a special messenger to your honor, only I learned that the person delivering this letter was traveling to your honor on some matter. Therefore, my teacher and rabbi, have mercy please, have mercy to spread the wings of mercy over me and send me the response of the rabbinical authority, Rabbi Y. ben Lev. I will pay you what you want for it. Only hurry to send it to me and I will begin to do what I have to do. My wife is in great danger, may God have mercy over her. I ask you as an honorable Torah authority to pray for her.

Your strong friend in word and soul, writing from the depth of his heart with lots of tears. The abovementioned Mordechai, who lives here in this holy community.

About the letter of the dream, the comments of the researcher Akiva ben Ezra.

R. Mordechai-Li in the letter under examination was born in Antopol, still before R. Pinchas Michael came to Antopol. R. Mordechai-Li. was already teaching rabbinic law there. When R. Pinchas Michael became appointed the town's rabbi, he developed a friendship with R. Mordechai-Li. The two of them sat and studied and together they made legal decisions and cared for the Jewish public. When R. Mordechai-Li left Antopol, they didn't end their faithful friendship and exchanged letters between themselves on private and public matters. The letter printed here is one of the letters that R. Mordechai- Li sent to R. Pinchas Michael and was published. The letter was first printed under the name "Letter of the Dream in Kevutsat Kuntresim in Jerusalem." It is according to this edition that I am publishing the letter.

The first editor of the letter, R. Yitshak Hirshezon, wrote the following: The above-mentioned letter reached me by one of my acquaintances and students of the rabbinical seminary Shenot Eliyahu, who traveled on business through the city of Antopol and visited the above-mentioned president of the rabbinical court there. He stayed in his house and when he opened a book to study, he found the above-mentioned letter from the rabbi of Buten. He immediately copied it and sent it to us, and he put back the original letter in its place.

And in one of the letters to me, Rabbi Hayyim Hirshenzon, of blessed memory, wrote that R. Yitshak Horovits was the person who copied the letter and afterwards was a principal in Zikhron Yaakov and the father-in-law of the scholar Dr. Binyamin Menashe Levin.

*[Page 190]*

R. Meir Otenof told me these details in connection with the letter under discussion: Every week before the Jewish Sabbath entered, R. Pinchas Michael used to empty his pockets and give the items he took out to his grandson Alter, the son of Elazar, his son from Pinsk, so that he would bury them or burn them. Once Alter felt among the letters that R. Pinchas gave him the letter of R. Mordechai-Li. Alter didn't burn the letter spoken of but gave it to the scribe R. Mosheh Rozenburg (R. Mosheh der Shrayber) to copy it. R. Mosheh copied it. Thus, this secret letter became known to the Jews of Antopol. When R. Pinchas Michael was informed of this, he became angry with his grandson. Alter became sick and died a week later. R. Pinchas Michael wept a lot at his death. People say that the rabbi said, "You will have no more chances to be a fool again."

This letter was also published by David Vaisman under the name "The Great Terror in 1903 (663) in Mosdot ha-emunah of R. Mordechai Aryeh Nisenboim." The second edition (and another edition) was in N.Y. 1924 (684): The Amazing Dream, Tel Aviv 1939 (699). The letter mentioned above was also discussed by Mark Toleran (B. Rivkin), who researched dreams in the issue of the Yiddish newspaper Tog for March 4, 11, and 25, 1944.

The rabbinical teacher Rabbi Y. ben Lev mentioned in the letter is R. Yosef ben Lev, one of the great rabbis who lived in 16th-century Turkey. His response in four volumes was first published in Constantinople in 1573 (333) with the help of Hanah Donah Gratsiah and Don Yosef ha-Nasi. This book was also published in Venice in 1606 (366) and in Fiorda in 452

(1692) and in Amsterdam In 1722 (482). The book had such a large distribution that by 1722 it was hard to find.

The fact that he struck the rabbinical teacher R. Y. ben Lev mentioned in the letter on the cheeks is a historical fact. The name of the man who hit him was Barukh, a Marrano from Portugal, who lived in Saloniki. He was a rich and tyrannical man. The contemptible deed took place in one of the market places of this city in front of witnesses. In the year 1545 (305) (see R. David Konforti, Kore ha-dorot, edition by Kessel, p. 37; Shelomoh Rozanes, Divre yeme Yisrael be-Turgemah, v. 2, p. 58).

# Jewish Holidays
## By M. Polak

Purim was an especially happy day for us children. We began to feel the holiday at home with the good smells of the fish cooked with vinegar and the laurel leaves for the meal and with the pleasant smell of all the cakes Mother baked to send as gifts. In addition there were also the smells of the apples and pears kept in the attic and especially the smell of the oranges, which my brother Aharon would send us early as spirits. Understandably, I would take upon myself to be the messenger to deliver the gifts of food. The activity began mainly in the afternoon. However, I would start out early in the morning so that I would also be a messenger on the way back.

The gifts of food would be put on a big plate with flowers, which my sisters warned me not to break. The plate had two big pieces of cake, one white and one brown, and three pieces of cake filled with all types of filling. Likewise, we also added one orange, one red apple, one pretty pear, a piece of chocolate, and some pieces of candy wrapped in different wrappings. Around the plate was a round carton, higher than the cake, covered by a white ironed handkerchief, whose ends were gathered on the bottom of the plate. As a messenger, I got paid and could also taste the food. Thus, my pockets and stomach were full at the end of the day.

*[Page 191]*

Standing out in importance after the sending of the gifts of food were the Purim plays (Purim shpil). I and my friend Shimon would dress up as an elderly couple. Shimon would bring us the old silk coat of his father, and my sisters would fold it and arrange it so that it would fit me. They also put a rag into the old hat of R. Mosheh. Still, it fell down over my ears. They made the white beard from flax and stuck it with glue. Even the broken cane in my hand added to the splendor of my beard. They outfitted Shimon my friend in a black silk dress and the first wig of my mother. When we walked past the houses like an elderly couple, they didn't recognize us. It should be known that in a place where they didn't recognize us, they gave us a bigger gift. Our friend Yisrael-Mendl would accompany us and hold a big purse. When we entered each house, he would declare that the gift was for a widow and orphans. We didn't miss any house. Even the widow for whom we were collecting gave us a donation!

Generally, all the Jews of Antopol gave generously. When my mother gave the money to the rabbi's wife, she decided how to divide it among the widows. We had the satisfaction that we did our part to help the needy.

I would also run to the study hall so that I could fulfill the commandment of making noise at the mention of the name of Haman during the reading of the Scroll of Esther. I would build the noisemakers myself. Sometimes, I would have the help of my friend Zaidel, who was an expert in this work. Before Purim, I would go to Meir the carpenter and take from him broken pieces of wood and I would engrave at the home of my friend Gedaliah's father, a carpenter, teeth from the spindles my sisters saved for me around which was wrapped their thread for sewing. I would make with these raw materials big noisemakers. Understandably, I would save the biggest for myself and I would sell the rest or exchange them with my friends for other toys.

Passover and the hall. And afterwards, I would with great concentration, thinking over all my possible sins during the year that past. Likewise, I would help my father prepare the study hall. I would sweep out all the study hall, dust and set up all the tables and chairs in their place, put kerosene in the lamps and clean them and their glass, and fill up the vessel for the washing of the hands with water. I would reveal all these good deeds to God to weigh them against my sins.

*[Page 193]*

And behold it was already the day before the New Year's. I completed all the tasks given to me and I stood on the platform where the Torah was read with my father. I paid attention was in awe. I didn't miss a word of the prayer.When the prayer was over, we greeted on another to be written and inscribed immediately for life in a good year. We went home spiritually uplifted and entered the Ten Days of Repentance in awe of the Day of Judgment.

I had the extra work on the day before the Day of Atonement of putting shelves around the walls in order to place on them boxes full of sand in order to hold up in them the great white candles in memory of departed souls. Likewise, I would bring plates from home and put them at the entrance door written with the names of the institution receiving the gifts.

The afternoon prayer was very early. Everyone, who lay down to say confession, would be lashed 39 times with a strap by my father. After that, each person would put charity in every plate he found necessary. I would stand by the table to see that the labels did not fall out of the plates and be exchanged. When the afternoon prayer was over, I would put all the plates with the money inside a chest that stood on the platform where the Torah was read and close it. After that, I would sweep out all the study hall, put all the long candles into the boxes of sand, run home to eat before the fast and to dress in honor of the Day of Atonement, then and return to light the candles and the lamps. My father would come to the study hall with a white gown and with a white belt and skull cap with silver embroidery. He would stand on the platform where the Torah is read and say the prayer of expiation. And when the cantor R. David would begin "With the knowledge of God", there would be silence and all the congregation would tremble with fear until he would finish "And God said that I forgive according to your words".

My father would remain all the night in the study hall in prayers and beseechings, and I and my mother would go home. My mother would arise early to go to the study hall. Afterwards, she would return to wake me and to take me with some food. After the memorial prayers, we would go behind the study hall and finish all the meal. After the blowing of the shofar and finishing the prayer we would return home. After that, we would again return to the study hall to clean it and to air it out and to write down from memory all the donations from those being called to the reading of the Torah. And returning home, we would make the first preparations for preparing the Sukkah.

For the Holiday of Tabernacles, the building of the sukkah began on the day following the Day of Atonement. A layer of dust filled the sukkah, which had to be cleaned again, after opening the wings of the roof. The wheels, which opened the wings, were greased and branches were brought for a roof for the sukkah. Some apples and pears were hung under the roof. The walls were decorated with pictures of luminaries and a picture of the Temple. Colored chalk was used as a decoration. Behold, the sukkah was prepared and pretty. Father would also sleep in the sukkah in addition to eating in it. Guests would also come to us, family members and friends. We would be happy. My brother Aharon would supply us with a citron and palm branch. I would run with the palm branch and citron so that our relatives would be able to participate in the commandment of blessing the citron and also to have others participate, whom my father wished to honor.

When I came to the palace of R. Mordechai Sheinboim, the dogs inside the gate would frighten me. However, the gatekeeper would take me by the hands and have me enter inside. They would give me a ruble of money for my effort. My savings bank would still increase more afterwards because on the day before Hoshana rabba, I would hasten with father to Goren's orchards. We would cut big piles of willows near the pools for hoshannot. I and my sisters would clean them at home and wrap them in bundles of seven pieces and tie them with straps from the palm branches of the preceding year. Afterwards, I would sit by the entrance of our study hall and would accept any price given. I would give the money to mother and take a part of it for my savings.

*[Page 194]*

I would participate together with the grown ups in their happiness on Simhat Torah. My father would give me a small Torah scroll and I was able to participate with him in going around as one of the adults. I was also able to enter with the Torah into the women's section and especially to have my mother and aunt benefit from kissing the Torah. The children would follow me with envy. When prayers were over, my father would invite a part of the substantial people to his house for the sanctification of the wine. People would go on to dance at home and in the street. Everyone was happy.

There were no classes all the eight days of Hanukah. However, I was immersed in what my sisters read about the bravery of the Maccabees, about Matityahu, Judah the Maccabee, Yonatan, Hanah and her seven sons, the bravery of Judith, and the miracle of the can of oil. Even father would take time to play with us children with the dreidel, chess or checkers, and even cards. The night before Hanukah, I would hasten to the forest to bring soft branches and, with the help of my father or also my friend Zeidl, who was an expert in making and engraving molds, we would pour liquid tin to make dreidels. We would receive the tin from the spoiled type my father got at work as a bookbinder. Zeidl would also bring the tin seals from the sacks of flour, which his father, R. Refael, the baker would give him. We would use mother's pot to melt the tin and a copper spoon to stir it and would pour it into the molds. We would make dreidels of all sizes and market them in class. So that merchandising would be permitted in class, we would first of all give the rabbi dreidels for his children. Certainly, I was not a great merchant. Sometimes, I would give on credit and not care to collect. Most of my earnings would come from money received as Hanukah presents. I would give it to my mother to keep and only stash a part away for myself.

The Fifteenth of Shevat was famous for the great number of weddings made on it. My sister Blumah's wedding was also on the Fifteenth of Shevat. We would study half a day and half a day we would hasten to the orchard of Goren to the frozen ponds to slide on the ice with ice skates we made ourselves or in small sleighs. Mother would give us fruit at home for the holiday: Saint John's bread, figs, and dates from Israel.

# Water for Tashlikh

## By A. Varshah, From the book by A Varshah, Yorn Fun Fayer Un Blut

Each town was graced by special qualities that distinguished it from the other towns: its legends, heroes, and similar stuff. Each settlement had woven around it magical stories from the past and from current events.

We, the children of Antopol, listened with a thirst for the words of our elders on the glory of our town, about which they talked with feelings of honor and respect. Certainly, it was not a small matter that we had in our cemetery the structures built over the graves of R. Moshesh-Tsevi, of blessed memory, and R. Pinchas Michael, may his merit protect us. Which city in all the region had such merit as this? And we had the "cold" synagogue, whose name went forth in all the region as an ancient and beautiful building. And there was a long list of well-known rabbis that the ancient rabbinical seminary had given to the world. And generally, the great number of learned people, who were found in the city until now. All of this filled each heart with feelings of pride and happiness.

*[Page 195]*

However, it sometimes happened that a person from a nearby town would visit our town and with a wave of his hand make as if it were nothing all our glory. This caused us, mainly the children, disappointment and dejection. Their crushing argument was: "Do you have a river or a bridge? Do you have a railway? Behold, it is not even possible to get a divorce in your city..." People from Horodets had arguments like these and similar arguments, which filled their mouths with praise for the great pleasure caused by bathing in the river, swimming, diving from the pier, or rowing boats in the evenings beneath a canopy of stars, and the like. While the people from Kobrin got a lot of mileage out of mocking the town, which was entirely muddy with no paved roads or sidewalks and didn't even have wagons for transport.

However, when a person from Kobrin like this was taken for a walk in the courtyard garden, his genealogical tree collapsed. He was moved and enchanted by looking at the wonders of nature so that he was prepared to give up ten bridges and to give all the military barracks in exchange for such a wonderful place like this to spend time. Truthfully, the garden didn't belong at all to the city. The city belonged to the courtyard. This is because the inhabitants of the town paid their taxes to the owner of the courtyard. The entrance to the garden was not gained easily. Nevertheless, the inhabitants of town didn't restrain themselves from boasting and saying: "The garden is ours'. The courtyard is ours'." They felt superiority toward other towns that is to say guests and friends coming from there when they put together all the riches and valuable antiques in the courtyard, its gardens, and forests.

Around the courtyard itself there was spread a row of legends tied to loves, quarrels, and murders. However, that didn't touch the town itself. These matters that concerned the owners of the courtyard, the list of women led astray, barons, who were shot, etc., were not added to the genealogical matters of our town. The exception was one spot in the pleasant courtyard about which it was possible to say that it belonged to the Jewish town. And this is the glorious pool of water to which the Jews went on Rosh ha-Shanah to say Tashlikh.

The pool was found to the left of the entrance gate and was decorated with trees and bushes. It was like there was a wondrously carved framework around the picture of this pleasant pool, which lay spread out facing the blue sky and felt the eternal prayer that came from the broken hearts of the local Jews on the first day of the Jewish New Year. And it seemed that if someone happened to pass near this pool on the other days of the year, he would really hear the small voice of holy words that rang out in a wonderful harmony somewhere: "Sing righteous, sing to Him..." And whoever had a good sense of hearing was able to listen to the singing of the Heavenly Hosts.

However, it was not easy for the Jewish congregation to reach these peaceful waters on the most holy day of the year. The gate was always shut. Every year, it was necessary to send a delegation to the baroness to ask her for special kindness and to let the Jews come to pray at the pool in her garden. There were two intermediaries in the city who had permission to enter the palace. The one was Hayyim , that is Hayyim Grinberg, and the other was Shelomoh the painter. Since Hayyim took his time to go to the court, he would rely in everything on Shelomoh. However, it is worthwhile to note that there was never any certainty that the gentile baroness would open that year the gate. This is because every New Year there spread rumors of her anger at the Jews, who came over the bridge and ruined her garden, trampling the flowers. And for the sake of the truth, this was not at all a false charge.

And therefore, when the day before the New Year's arrived, the Jews thought of the pool and their heart was full of fear, lest the baroness not open the gate and God forbid the sanctity of the holiday be disturbed. They were full of anger x great intention while their swaying bodies were reflected in the image of the pool, which received and hid their secrets in the recesses of its water.

*[Page 196]*

While the sun slowly set, the prayers spread out on the water. They were the great song to God from His people Israel, which exists forever. The people left the shore of the holy water and went back to the study hall with sure steps and a relieved heart. Everyone felt and hoped that they were written up for a good and happy year.

The gate was shut again with its lock and bolt. The pool and the trees at its side continue to sing their eternal song, "From the depths I called you."

# The Murder of Yonah the Miller
## By A. Slonimski

This was in the year 1908. On the Sabbath after Sukkot, there was a meeting in the garden of the priest against the Russian authorities. Two groups of youths went on this Sabbath before the evening and sang revolutionary songs: the group of Fraydl sang international, proletarian songs and the opposing group sang national Jewish songs. Mosheh Stavski and the pharmacist were in the latter group.

The police came when they heard the singing and arrested three youths who demonstrated: the tailor from Odessa, Stavski, and the pharmacist. The girls went with the boys to the police commissioner.

*[Page 197]*

When they all entered his office, he shook hands, like a gentleman, with the girls. He ordered the girls to leave and arrested the boys. When the Sabbath was over that evening, Yonah the miller was murdered. Upon hearing shouts from the miller's house, people began to run and the police commissioner also left his office. Running was hard for him and he shouted in the direction of the house to arrest the murderer. The arrested youths took advantage of the confusion and left peacefully the place and even went to the house of the miller. When people got there, they found the miller lying on the floor with his head bashed.

The murderer, a Russian gentile who had fled Siberia, hid in the forest near Antopol. Before evening, he entered the house of Yonah. When the latter returned from evening prayers, he attacked him, took some rubles from his pocket, and afraid lest he inform the police commissioner, killed him. Yonah's wife, who tried to protect her husband, was severely wounded and died some days later. The murderer fled.

This murder caused a big storm in town. From that day, it was decided to keep a good watch on the town every night from 10 p.m. until dawn. The gentiles were very afraid at this decision of the Jews. They hid in their houses and didn't dare to go out during these hours.

The Jewish inhabitants didn't rest. They diligently began to search for the murderer of Yonah the miller. They found him after a few days in the nearby town of Horodets when he was asleep at the bank of the river. They put him in chains and took him to Antopol. The murderer was put in jail in one of the available stores. However, he refused to talk and admit doing the murder.

At that time an unknown person came to town. He entered the hotel of Eizik Rubinshtein, ate a meal, and refused to pay. Eizik ran to the police. The visitor was arrested and put in jail in the same store that held the imprisoned murderer. The two jailed people didn't have anything to do with one another at first. However, the new prisoner took out a bottle of brandy after a short while and offered his fellow prisoner a drink. While the new prisoner took a drink, he cursed the Jews whose fault it was that he was now in jail. Then, the first prisoner opened his mouth and the two began to find fault with the Jews. Slowly, the first prisoner felt that the other prisoner shared his views and was his faithful friend. And as it says in the Talmud, "when wine enters, the secret is out." The murderer began to reveal his guarded secrets, how he came to Antopol and how he killed Yonah the miller and his wife.

The next day the prisoner who had refused to pay for his meal was taken out of prison. It was revealed that he was a detective, who had been sent by the police to get a confession from the murderer about the murder and some details on how he carried it out. The fact of not paying for a meal in the hotel of Eizik Rubinshtein was only an excuse for his arrest so that he could be imprisoned together with the murderer.

The Jews thanked the detective, who succeeded in his task. It was a holiday for the Jews of Antopol when the murderer was brought in the streets of the town to the police commissioner. Two people held him on each side. A crowd gathered to look at the caught murderer. One Jew tried even to approach and hit him. The murderer was tried and sentenced again to twenty years of exile at hard labor in Siberia.

# From the Memories of a Teacher in Antopol
## By Dr. M. Zagor (Zagorodaski)

Antopol was the last one of the towns in the region of Polesia in which I stayed.

I taught mathematics at this time in Pinsk and my small wage was not enough to live on. Therefore, people advised me to go for a period of time to a small town. They directed me to Antopol, with recommendations to the young Ms. Yahalom, whom they knew to be enlightened and good-hearted. She really helped me to get lessons in good homes. She herself invited me to be her German teacher.

*[Page 198]*

The family Yahalom was one of the best families in Antopol. When the Sabbath was over, the best people in town would come to drink tea and discuss various topics, especially commerce and forests and timber. I would also visit them sometimes on these occasions. However, I didn't make the acquaintance of the guests and I knew few of them. Since I continued my studies and prepared to take tests, I didn't think much of the town because it certainly was not different from other towns in the Pale of Settlement. However, I was proven that I made a mistake.

There was a rabbinical judge there, who was interested in engineering. He was Rabbi Tsevi Hirsh Rabinowitz, who had read the book of H. Z. Slonimski, Guide to Engineering. He used to solve questions on engineering during twilight. When he found out that there was a scholar from Pinsk in town, he addressed me in writing with a request to meet him when the Sabbath was over. I answered him and visited him. We talked about engineering, and I solved some questions that had bothered him. Once he asked me a question that even I had difficulty to solve. I sent the question to my brother Y. H. Zagor in Warsaw so that he would ask an answer from H. Z. Slonimski. I received from my brother this answer: "The Slonimski of Warsaw does not reach up to the ankles of the Slonimski' outside of Warsaw." This meant that he could not answer the asked by the rabbinical judge from Antopol.

The person spreading enlightenment in Antopol at this time was really a gentile, the local Christian doctor, Dr. Bik. He had a good library and he lent his books to whoever asked him. Ms. Yahalom also used to borrow books from him. It seems that many of the Jews in Antopol used this gentile's books. I also used to borrow books from him and helped to spread enlightenment. During the Sabbaths, I would carry on discussions with children and youths about different topics and sometimes on our Torah and its numerous commandments about the soul, God, the Garden of Eden, and more topics. Generally, I tried to enlighten the children and expand their opinions.

I have a good memory of the town of Antopol, especially since I found in it a desire for enlightenment and diligent men and women, who helped to spread it.

Dr. M. Zagor is the author of Milon kol-bo le-haklaut and more important books, on the topic of agriculture. He did a lot for Israel.

A selection of folktales from the period of R. Pinchas Michael, of blessed memory, selected by A. Ben-Ezra "

A Jewish Burial." The story told by Avraham, the butcher, and he begins: "Do you remember the butcher Tuviah?" Everyone nods. This Tuviah had a father named Hirshl. You certainly don't remember him. This Hirshl was also a butcher. He used to go to the villages and negotiate with the gentiles. He would leave after the havdalah ceremony at the end of the Sabbath and return in time for the candle lighting ceremony for the next Sabbath. In those days the gentiles and the merchants were different. It was important for them. No one would sell until Hirshl had expressed his opinion.

Once on a Sunday at dawn, Hirshl left his house. After he prayed, he ate, put a piece of bread and his prayer shawl and phylactery bag into his sack. He hid some money in a pocket hanging from beneath his shirt, took his walking stick in his hand and put his coat on his shoulder. It was the end of the summer. Hirshl thought that he would return home on Wednesday or at the latest Thursday morning. This is because all the town was waiting to have meat for the Sabbath.

On Tuesday evening Hirshl appeared to his son Tuviah in a dream. Tuviah saw in his sleep that his father appeared to him. Tuviah was astonished that his fatter came home so soon, and he asked, "Father, where is the cow?" And he answered that it remained in the village. "Why then were you in such a hurry to return?" Then, he answered that he didn't come willingly. How he shall not have any peace for himself until his bones should have a Jewish burial.

*[Page 199]*

Early in the morning Tuviah hurried to the rabbi and told him the whole story. In those days, the saintly R. Pinchas Michael was still alive, may his memory be blessed. He asked Tuviah how his father appeared to him and how he entered the house, whether as people usually enter or don't usually enter. Thus, they were speaking and behold Tuviah's two brothers came looking ill. They were working in a forest about ten miles away and their father appeared even to them in a dream. They got up early and at dawn went to town to find out what this was.

Everyone understood that this was not a simple matter. The rabbi asked: "Where did your father go?"

Tuviah answered him: "To Homitsits."

"How much money did he have with him?"

They answered him: "He had sixty rubles in his pocket."

The rabbi gave them his blessing and ordered them to go the same way that their father went. The three brothers came to the first village. They stood and asked: "Was Hirshka here?"

They answered: "He was." They showed him where he slept and told him what cows he saw.

They came to the second village. The townspeople said to them again: "He was here, prayed, ate breakfast, and went on his way."

They came to the village of Homitsits and went directly to Prokop, from whom Hirshl was supposed to take a cow. They found Prokop standing in the courtyard and fixing his wagon and the women working in the garden. The brothers opened the gate and entered the courtyard. Prokop pretended that he didn't see them come in and continued his work. They said to him: "Hello, Prokop!"

He replied: "Greetings and blessings." He didn't stop working.

They asked him again: "Was Hirshka here?"

The gentile said to them: "No, he wasn't here. I didn't see him at all." He didn't raise his head from the block of wood on the wagon that he was shaving at that time. Suddenly, the brothers looked at the handle of the axe in Prokop's hand. They saw that he had just now shaved a new one. And at this moment the three brothers felt that this was the axe with which their father was killed.

They stood and made an excuse that they wanted to buy hay. Was it possible for Prokop to show them the hay in his threshing floor? The gentile put down his axe, opened the threshing floor for them, and stood and watched how they put their hands deep into the hay and checked it, lest it be rotten underneath. And when they returned from the threshing floor, the gentile turned and said to them: "And I was already amazed that Hirshka is not here and I also need money."

The brothers went to the side and discussed what to do. They had a heavy heart. Their father was no longer alive. They had no doubt of this. However, who knew if they could find his body. Behold, "a thief goes one way and his pursuers have to go a thousand ways to get him." This is what people say. The brothers decided that they have to pass the garden and the meadow behind it. Each one went his own way and made different excuses. This one went to the field to look at cattle, and this one went to the garden to take vegetables for dinner.

Thus, the brothers went looking at what was around them. Perhaps, a mound would be found and signs of fresh digging in the earth. While they were looking for this, Tuviah found a groove in the ground and saw that a sack was sticking out and a pair of shoes was sticking out from the sack. Tuviah began to call and shout. The brothers hurried to his call and came and took out the body of their father.

When Avraham was finished speaking, R. Ber the sexton asked: "Do you remember the words of the saintly man, of blessed memory, when they brought the corpse to town?" And what did he say? Avraham didn't remember the statement. The saintly man, of blessed memory, said that Hirshl wouldn't have been given permission to appear to his children in a dream except for the merit due him for the "days" on which he fed the children of the Jewish religious elementary school and for the merit due him for inviting guests to his table for the Sabbath. This is because that the evil man, who killed him, was going to take the dead man's body out of the groove the next night and hide it in the shed under the manure.

*[Page 200]*

"Good Advice." Once a Jewish man came to him and told him his problem: "Rabbi, I am a clerk in a forest. My employer is a hard person and he certainly wants to fire me and to take away my income. And if he fires me, I have no choice but to become a vagrant and to go begging with my family. Please, rabbi, give me good advice as to what I should do."

Rabbi Pinchas Michael asked him, "Do you live together with your family in the forest?"

The clerk answered, "No, I live alone. How can I bring my family when I am in suspense and don't know what will happen tomorrow?"

Rabbi Pinchas Michael said, "If so, listen to my advice and have your wife and children brought to you."

The clerk was startled: "Rabbi, you don't know my employer. He is angry and excitable. When he sees that I have brought my family, he will be angry and immediately evict me."

Rabbi Pinchas Michael calmed him: "Don't be afraid. Listen to my advice and God will help you."

The clerk went and followed the advice of Rabbi Pinchas Michael. He brought to him his wife and children and settled them with him in the forest. He trembled, awaiting the day his employer would come.

The owner of the forest came and saw the clerk living with his family. He was angry and strongly rebuked him. However, after a short time, he made peace and was satisfied. And not only that, he raised the clerk's salary and married his daughter, who had come of age. When the forest was cut down and no workers came, he transferred his clerk to another of his forests.

Sometime later, the clerk came to Rabbi Pinchas Michael and thanked him for his good advice, which came out of his scholarship.

Rabbi Pinchas Michael said, "In my opinion, this was a simple matter. A Jewish person, even if he is one of the most difficult, will not harm his fellow man, supporting his wife and children. Jews are merciful people, descendents of merciful people."

"The Saintly Man on the Roof." Once, a fire broke out in Antopol. As usual, they began to save the houses of the rich people in town. No one paid attention to the houses of the poor people. R. Pinchas Michael, of blessed memory, went on top of the roof of the house of a poor man, which no one had hurried to save.

When the people saw the rabbi sitting on the roof and not coming down by himself, they hurried to save the rabbi. However, Rabbi Pinchas Michael, of blessed memory, called from on the roof: "I will not go down from the roof before you also save this house."

When they began to save also the house under discussion, the saintly man went down from the roof.

"Punishments." The building of the study house En Yaakov, or as it was called the study house of the butchers, in the city of Pruzinah went on for some years. And this is the reason for the delay in building it. A new Provoslav priest came to the city of Pruzinah. He was the head of the priests in the district of Pruzinah. His name was Gomlitski. Once on a Friday when the priest about whom we are speaking went to a bathhouse, he passed the study house under construction. He turned and asked the people with whom he was walking what sort of a building this was. When he heard that this building was going to be a Jewish study house, he asked to measure the distance between the building for the study house and the courtyard of their church. He saw that the new building was too close to the church. What did he do? He reported this in a letter to the district city Horadna. An order came from there to stop building the study hall.

*[Page 201]*

Some years passed and the building was not completed. What did our brethren, the children of Israel do? They sent a messenger to the saintly man, R. Pinchas Michael, of blessed memory, to ask of him advice. And R. Pinchas Michael promised them that everything would turn out well. And behold the Day of Atonement came. And when the cantor started to say "Let our supplication go up in the evening and let our salvation come in the morning", a cry was heard from outside: "Fire!" And behold the threshing floor of the priest Gomlitski was on fire. From there the fire spread to the church, a wooden building that stood next to the threshing floor. And after a little while, there was no trace of the threshing floor or of the church.

And again the above named priest wrote a report to Horodna, as follows: The Jews are responsible for this fire, having made it, so that it will be possible for them to finish building their study hall.

Two important officials came from the city of Horadna, the provincial prosecutor and one of the head priests. They asked the priest Gomlitski who was in his threshing floor that evening. It became clear that on that day two gentiles were threshing his produce. He gave them after their work glasses of brandy. After drinking they returned to the threshing floor. They lighted their pipes and slept. Meanwhile, one of the gentile's pipes fell on the hay in the threshing floor. This was the cause of the fire in the threshing floor and the church.

The priest Gomlitski got his punishment. Once he came to the post office to pick up the mail sent to the church. There was money included in the letters. Gomlitski took the money for himself and left. However, a person can't get away with things forever. So it happened that he received an order for demotion to serve as a regular priest in a far away region. This decree caused him mental instability. And after some time, he became crazy.

In the city of Kosovah in the province of Grodno, there was a brandy distillery. There was a Jew named Shelomoh in it that city. The gentile estate owner liked Shelomoh and appointed him in charge of his distillery. And behold, there arose a certain gentile, who envied Shelomoh. He made up some stories about Shelomoh to the owner of the distillery, who fired Shelomoh and put the gentile in his place.

Shelomoh came to R. Pinchas Michael, of blessed memory, and told him what happened. R. Pinchas Michael called together ten Jews and blessed Shelomoh in their presence. Just a few days past and the gentile we mentioned got drunk and caused a big, monetary loss to the gentile estate owner. The gentile estate owner got angry at the gentile and returned Shelomoh to his place.

Kadish Otanof was an elementary school teacher in the village of Volitski near Horlovits. His wife Gronah used to sell brandy to the gentiles. And behold one of the gentiles of the village used to bother her and not let her sell brandy. He would send the police every time to check her permit. And that wicked man would also kill the geese, which she fattened.

Once, Gronah came to the rabbi to tell her troubles. The rabbi told her to find out the name of the gentile and the name of his mother. However, she shouldn't tell anyone about this. Gronah told the names to the rabbi.

This took place in the month of Heshvan (November). And in the month of Kislev (December), the gentile about whom we are speaking traveled to the forest. A fight broke out between him and another gentile. The latter went and killed the wicked gentile.

There was an investigation as to who the gentile murderer was but he was not found. Gronah told the story to the rabbi. And the saintly man said, "This will remain a hidden secret."

There was a story about Yudil Tornoyar, the son-in-law of Mendel Palavski, who lived some years in the village of Toronoyah. This Yudil had built his house on the land of one gentile of that village. The gentiles of the village enticed the owner of the land to force Yudil to leave his house, and then they would be able to buy Yudil's house for half its price.

*[Page 202]*

Yudil came with his brother R. Lazar from Hutiva to R. Pinchas Michael to ask advice. The saintly man answered: "Keep calm, he will not drive you out. You will continue living in your house."

And Yudil Tornoyar returned to his village. When he got to Toronoyah, people told him that the owner of the land had died. And our Yudil lived in his house until his death.

In the village of Darvanoyah near Antopol, there lived a Jew named R. Yosef Rubinshtein, or as he was known in the village, R. Yosef Darvanoyer. There was one gentile in that village who had five sons. All of them were completely wicked. They would enter R. Yosef 's tavern, get themselves drunk, and not pay. They would break the furnishings, and sometimes they would also hit the owner.

This above-mentioned R. Yosef came to Rabbi Pinchas Michael, of blessed memory, to ask his advice. The saintly man first said, "Prepare to receive the Sabbath." Afterwards, he said, "Give them to drink as much as they want, and they will not bother you any more." And so it was. The father and one son got alcohol poisoning from drinking too much. One son was ground up in a windmill. Another son died from a flesh wound. One went crazy, and one disappeared. These tragedies happened in one year.

People say that the child who went crazy got up one night, opened the stables of the village, and took out the cows. He himself was strong like a cedar tree. He stood outside, dressed only in a shirt, his eyes raised to heaven and kept on looking without harming any one.

Once, there was a quarrel between R. Shemuel the tailor and his partner. They went to R. Pinchas Michael for judgment to settle the dispute. The rabbi said that R. Shemuel was innocent. Then, his ignorant partner jumped up and said to R. Pinchas, "I will not accept your judgment. I will listen to you, like I listen to a cat." This happened Friday before the Sabbath.

He went home and told his wife the story. In the afternoon when his wife gave him fish, the household cat jumped on him and bit him on the lips with his teeth. He began to shout and chase way the cat.

However, the cat didn't pay attention. His lips bled and he couldn't get rid of the cat. His wife ran to R. Pinchas Michael and asked his forgiveness. The rabbi gave his walking stick to the sexton and said to him, "Go chase away the cat." The sexton went and chased away the cat.

Once Hetskel the wagoner got angry at the rabbi. R. Pinchas Michael threw him out of his house. People say that all the members of the household of Hetskel died of tuberculosis. He was left without any descendents.

This story happened around 1905 during the days of revolution in Russia. The young people of Antopol would gather in the cemetery outside of town.

At one of the meetings Shabtai Kolodner, the son of a candle maker and a youth of fifteen, went to the structure around the saintly man's grave and said: "Old man, old man, don't you say that you are able to bring the messiah. Where is your messiah?" He was paralyzed on the spot.

In one village near to Antopol, there lived a Jewish tenant farmer. He had a Jewish woman as a servant. She had loose morals. Finally, the gentile estate owner took her to his home. One night the threshing floor of the gentile estate owner went up in flames. The Jewish girl about whom we spoke came and said to the estate owner that the Jewish tenant farmer burnt up the threshing floor. Meanwhile, the tenant farmer was put in jail until the end of the trial.

Then, the tenant farmer's wife went to R. Pinchas Michael to ask for help. The rabbi said that God would help and that her husband would go free. A few days before the trial, the rabbi sent his sexton to the Jewish woman to warn her not to give false witness. However, she told the sexton that she would say what she wanted. Then, the rabbi sent his sexton still another time and again she gave the same answer. Thus, she answered the third time. The rabbi heard the sexton and said: "God will help and she will not testify."

*[Page 203]*

The day of the trial came and it was held in the district city of Kobrin. At the time of the testimony being taken in the trial, the judge asked the gentile estate owner, "Where is the witness?"

"She is in the hotel. However, she is sick," answered the estate owner. "She is lying in bed and unable to come to court."

The judge ordered the estate owner to bring the witness in her bed to court. When they brought her in bed before the judge, he asked, "What do you know about the matter of the Jew?" However, the Jewish woman was unable to speak, as she had become dumb of speech. The Jew went free.

"Draft to the Army." Once in the time of the draft to the army, many Jews were taken and gentiles exempted. Belah Hanakes came to the saintly man to complain before him about this unjustness. When he heard of this unjust deed, he struck the table three times and said, "Master of the universe! Enough wicked people have been freed from the draft!" Immediately after this story, they began to exempt the Jews.

People say that once there was a complaint about the wickedness of an official in Brisk di-Lita, who was cruel to Jewish youth and drafted them to the army. In the beginning, he gave the excuse that it was not easy to kill a gentile. Finally, he was silent, as if he agreed that the complaint was a just one. After a few weeks, the gentile got a stroke and died.

"And the Brandy Became Vinegar." Some Jews had a brandy refinery. As is known, there was a tax on every barrel of brandy. However, the Jews under consideration didn't pay attention to the government and didn't pay the tax.

It happened that the government official came one night to investigate the matter. He seized one barrel and sealed it with the government seal to be evidence during the trial. For now they arrested the partners. Only one partner remained not arrested. He came to R. Pinchas Michael, of blessed memory, to ask him advice. At first, the saintly man didn't wish to answer him because it is forbidden to try to get out of paying government taxes. However, after the Jew insisted of the saintly man, the rabbi advised him that all the Jews should say during the trial that they made vinegar and not brandy.

And thus during the trial, the judges had the sealed barrel brought. They checked it and found that it contained vinegar and not brandy, and the Jews went free.

"Medical Treatments." Sarah Zisl, the only daughter of the elementary religious school teacher, R. Lazar of Hotvah, became very sick. A Polish pharmacist was in Antopol at this time. A big doctor came to him from Warsaw. The wife of R. Lazar brought the visiting doctor to see her dangerously sick daughter. This was at 2 p.m. on a winter Friday afternoon. The doctor examined the sick person and gave up hope for her. He said, "Why have you brought me to see a dying person?"

However, the parents of the daughter didn't entirely despair. R. Lazar ran for help to R. Pinchas Michael, of blessed memory. The saintly man said: "Do you think that what the doctor said is true? Here are six cents from money given to redeem a first-born child. Go to the rabbis and buy olive oil. Rub the child with the olive oil and God, may He be blessed, will help her."

R. Lazar did what the righteous told him to do. And after he rubbed all her body, the blister, which was in her throat opened, and the puss flowed out. Then, the child opened her eyes and wanted something to eat. The child went on to get better.

There was a baker in the city of Kobrin and his name was Jacob. This Jacob had a son who was sick with epilepsy, God forbid. He was sick until the age of six with this disease. They brought him to R. Pinchas Michael, of blessed memory. The saintly man put a cube of sugar in his mouth and said to him: "Eat and be well." He said to call him Zaidel. From then on, he was healthy.

*[Page 204]*

Once, a father of five sons came with his son who had suddenly lost the ability to speak. R. Pinchas Michael asked if he were a first born and if the ceremony to redeem the son had been done. The father remembered that he hadn't redeemed his son. Then, the rabbi summoned Yaakov the doctor, who was a Kohen, and another Kohen. They made the redemption ceremony as prescribed. After the ceremony, the mute boy began to speak.

Once, a bone was stuck in the butcher, Shual of Antopol. The righteous man advised that he be given a glass of milk to drink. His reason and point was that since meat and milk are forbidden together, this Shual would spit out the milk together with the bone.

# Personalities and Surroundings
## By Mosheh b. R. Akiva Yeruham Lifshits

Hillel Rozentsvaig, the grandfather of Barukh Yahalom, studied and taught a lot. He was a member of the old generation, that between the enlighteners and spiritual people keeping the Torah and commandments. However, they didn't ignore secular knowledge and science. He studied together with Hayyim Zelig Slonimski, the editor of the newspaper ha--Tsefirah, a newspaper for secular knowledge and science.

Hillel came to live in Antopol. He took for a wife Bailah, daughter of Shemuel Tsevi and sister of Tehilah Leah, wife of Efrayim Lifshits, and sister of Hayah Etil, wife of Yehezkel Saharov.

He had a house on Pinsk Street and an inn for travelers going from Brisk to Pinsk by way of Antopol. In addition to this, he made wine to sanctify the Sabbath and to welcome the end of the Sabbath for the inhabitants of the town and the surrounding area.

Hillel's house was open to acquaintances and friends. They would gather in the evenings to drink tea. A samovar stood on the table. His wife would distribute the drinks. She would give everyone a glass of tea. They would discuss what happened in town and in the country. Yekutiel the blacksmith and his brother Hirshl would come to events like this.

Yekutiel was a blacksmith by trade. All day he would strike the hammer to the anvil. However, during the evening after the afternoon and night prayer in the study hall, he would gather a group around the table and study with them a page of Talmud. This he did daily. His brother Hershl studied in the yeshivah and was renowned in Torah. Yaakov ben Aharon Shemuel, a person who rented farm land (about six dunam's of it), would also be among those who came.

The farmers rented about 1,200 dunams and paid a tax for this to the German estate owner, Voitash. They would till and fertilize the land and sow cucumbers and other vegetables. When it was a dry summer and there was no rain to water the earth, they would fill barrels from well water and bring it to irrigate the land. For harvesting the cucumbers, they would hire workers from a nearby village and prepare small barrels. After they filled the barrels and closed them with corks, they would ship them to Warsaw.

Henikh the wagoner had a big wagon covered in felt to protect from rain. Every Sunday he would make a list from the storekeepers about goods needed by them and also of travelers who had business in Brisk. He would travel on Monday. He would return on Wednesday with travelers and with goods. He would bring tied packages full of raisins for making wine. They would tread it until liquid came out. They would put it in barrels for three weeks. They would strain it with saccules hanging on top of the barrels until the wine came out clear and fit for drinking.

*[Page 205]*

The cucumber season was over. The month of Elul arrived. It was time to say the penitential prayers and they began to repent. Speeches were given. Preachers gave public sermons calling for repenting, doing good deeds, and leaving sin. Behold, Rabbi Naftali Tsevi Berlin of Volozin, called ha-Natsiv, was going to come to the city on the next Sabbath to give a speech in the synagogue. There was a lot of preparation to receive the well-known and praiseworthy rabbi. Everyone knew that the German estate owner Voitash liked the Jews in town because he would open the gate of his courtyard for the Jews, as if to say: "Open the gates and a righteous gentile will come to say the Tashlikh prayer by way of Shloss Street because there is a pool of water with live fish." Therefore, some Jews came to him and said that the famous rabbi R. Naftali Tsevi was coming to our town and would he please give us his carriage to bring the rabbi to us. "Jawohl," he answered. "If the great rabbi comes to you, I will put at your service my carriage and driver."

When Natsiv came, the town's important people went out to meet him on the intersection between Horodets and Antopol. When he came to the synagogue to give his speech, Abrahmel, the sexton, struck the wooden hammer on the platform and announced: "Let every living being be quiet out of respect for the rabbi. Silence is good!" And the Natsiv spoke for one hour. The rabbinical judge, Rabbi Tsevi Hirsh ha-Kohen Rabinovits, the son-inlaw of R. David Yosef the religious school teacher, gave a sermon on the Sabbath between Rosh ha- Shanah and Yom-Kippur, Shabat Shuvah, in the synagogue about the survival of the soul after death and on other things.

The houses in town were mainly small, poor, in bad condition, and old. The stores were made of wood and mostly rotten. Only the hotels were different. They were big and good. There was under one roof the house and a big stable for the big wagon with its horses and its goods because people went from Brisk di-Lita to Pinsk through Antopol. Hotels like these were in Kobrin Street next to the study hall and Pinsk Street.

One summer afternoon, a big fire broke out in town. All the wooden stores in the town's center, the houses on one side, the wooden study hall, and all the houses around the row of stores in the street, and a big part of the houses on Pinsk Street were eaten up by fire in the course of a few hours.

The harvest and summer were over. And everyone thought how to rebuild his house. They prepared all the days of the winter, whosoever with money and whosoever with materials. Spring came. Then, some people built a wooden house and some a brick house. Little by little people began to come out of their lethargic winter sleep. They built anew out of brick a women's section above the wooden study hall, whose walls were bent with age and which were threatening to collapse. In the summer they also built a beautiful house with pretty rooms, which could be praised as said before. The big room was for important guests. There were dining rooms and sleeping rooms with a pretty balcony to the street. Hayyim Zelig the carpenter made pretty designs, wooden engravings around the doors and windows. Everything was made in contemporary style. Life began to return to its old and usual course.

This is how life went on in Antopol. A generation came and a generation went. The kids became goats and new winds began to blow in town. Some people left town and scattered themselves in the big world. Some people remained in town and continued under the yoke and carried out the deeds of their ancestors until the great and bitter day when World War I broke out. Then, things became a mess for those people who remained in Antopol, and they didn't know what to do. Many years of disruptions and confusions passed over our brethren in Antopol and the last great one, that is the great enemy of the world Hitler, may his name and memory be blotted out, realized his plans. He completely destroyed our beloved ones and didn't leave a remnant from them. Jewish Antopol of four hundred years does not exist. However, we will endlessly remember it!

*[Page 206]*

# Lifshits Family
## By Aryeh Eliav

The head of this extensive family was R. Efrayim Halitsitsir. The dates of his birth and death are not precisely known. However, we can assume that he was born about 1750. R. Efrayim lived in the village of Halitsits, not far from Antopol in the Pinsk region. Halitsits was itself a big village farm and Efrayim was a tenant (orendator) of one of the gentile landlords in the region. He was a rabbinical scholar and considered learning more important than money. They said about him that a marriage broker came to engage one of R. Efrayim's sons with a rich Jew. When R. Efrayim met with his proposed relative by marriage, the latter told him about his wealth and emphasized that he didn't lose any money all his life, that is to say, he never helped anyone. R. Efrayim broke off the engagement immediately.

A son was born to R. Efrayim. R. Shemuel Lifshits was born about 1170. He was the first to have the family name, whose source is not clear. However, it seems that he was named after a place in the region. Already R. Shemuel didn't rent land from gentile land owners as a tenant. He was a poor man, a craftsman. He specialized in building windmills. R. Shemuel changed his home to the town of Antopol, which was from that time the place where the family would dwell for the coming four generations.

A son was born to R. Shemuel. R. Yoel Ber- Lifshits was born in Antopol about 1800 and died in it about 1880. He was a tall and handsome man. The name of his wife was Itke and she died before him.

R. Efrayim was the first born. Rabbi Eliezer was the child born after him. However, he met with misfortune. On one of his travels, he traveled over a frozen pond. The ice broke under the wagon and he fell into the water. As a result of that, he became very ill and died. Efrayim, his elder brother, named one of his sons Eliezer after him.

Rabbi Eliezer left after him a son by the name of Mordechai, who lived in the town of Homsk, near Antopol. He was a quiet person and a rabbinical scholar. A son was born to Mordechai by the name of David-Yaakov, who in the course of time became a clerk in the forestry business of R. Efrayim Lifshits.

Hanah-Shifrah was the daughter. She married Yoel Hershkah Reines, who was a tanner and a Torah scholar. They had boys and girls. One branch of this family immigrated to the United States and their name is Rozentsvaig. Hanah-Shifrah had a son who married into the Mintsberg family. They had relatives in Israel (Dr. Esther Mintsberg from Kupat Holim Tel Aviv and her husband Mr. Haruzi from the Post Office in Tel Aviv).

R. Efrayim Lifshits was born in Antopol in 1833 and died in it on the third day of Tamuz in the year 1906 (666), at the age of 73. He excelled still in his youth in his studies. His teacher was the saintly R. Pinchas Michael, of blessed memory. Efrayim and Mordekhleh were distinguished among his pupils. They say about them that they made an agreement in their youth that if Efrayim would be a rich merchant and Mordekhleh would continue his Torah studies, they would share their wealth fifty-fifty, that of this world and that of the world to come. And so it was. Efrayim became a rich merchant and R. Mordekhleh was a rabbinical judge. For many years Efrayim would give fitting financial support and would receive from him receipts for his share in the world to come.

R. Efrayim began to do business successfully and as a young and successful man married Tehilah Leah of the family of Roshovski. Tehilah Leah was born in the village of Roshovah, near Antopol, in 1832 and died in old age at 84 in 1916. The name of her father was R. Tsevi of Roshovah and from her their family name Roshovski. The name of her mother was Tovah-Hanah. They were poor people and they had a small tavern (kretsmah). Tehilah had brothers and sisters. The name of her elder brother was Yaakov Meir.

This branch of the family immigrated to the United States. Some of them are called Roshovski and some of them Gershtein. The name of the younger sister was Hayah Etel, who married R. Yehezkel Saharov. This couple had sons and daughters. One of them was R. Yitshak Mordekhai Saharov. He was the father of Yehezkel Sahar (named after his grandfather R. Yehezkel). The rest of the brothers of Tehilah Leah were Avraham- Yitshak, Mosheh, Hayyim, and Akiva. The family of Roshovski traces its descent to the descendants of R. Yom-Tov Lipman, who wrote Tosofot Yom Tov. And this is the order of the generations: R. Shemuel Tsevi, the son of R. Akiva, the son of Rivkah, the daughter of Devorah, the daughter of R. Mosheh Zeev Volf, the son of R. Yoel Bukhaver, the son-inlaw of R. Shemuel, the son of the. luminary R. Yom Tov Lipman.

*[Page 207]*

Now we will return to the marriage of R. Efrayim Lifshits with Tehilah Leah. They married, as was the custom in those days, very young. He was 17 and she was 16. While Efrayim expanded and increased his business deals with renting fields and forests in the region, Tehilah tried her hand at commerce. She had a tavern (shenk) in their house. She sold the gentiles brandy. Her goal in that was to help her family and charitable goals. Thus, she had her own source of income, without depending on her husband. All the money she earned she gave to the poor and needy in town.

In the course of years, R. Efrayim became still wealthier. He bought real estate. And since it was forbidden to a Jew to own in his own name fields and estates, he bought the estate called Poloshin in the name of the priest from Asmolovits. Poloshin was a big estate. It was not far from Antopol. It had about 16,000 dunams of land, and about 400 were fields and the rest in forest. Likewise, the estate had a big house and many farm workers. Poloshin was a big source of income and made R. Efrayim rich. Tehilah Leah tried and was successful in appointing her brothers and relatives as clerks in her husband's wide-ranging businesses.

Tehilah and Efrayim raised a big family. During the first years of her marriage, Tehilah Leah gave birth to five children. However, they died at birth or in their first year. And only after that did she give birth to ten sons and daughters who lived, and these are Akiva Fishel, Yitshak David, Frumah, Hayyim Yehudah, Yosef Eliezer, Mosheh Yaakov, Shelomoh, Yehoshua, and Avraham.

The Lifshits's house was the richest in Antopol. This was a house of Torah and great wisdom in one place. The children received a general and Jewish education. (The father Efrayim also knew how to speak but not write Russian and Polish).

The holidays and especially Purim were the peak days of the year. The mistress of the house gave money on Purim to all the needy and she gave liquor for a toast to every poor person, to Jews and gentiles. Their Purim table was set for tens of people. The actors in the Purim plays would stream to the house because they were well paid. They would bake homentaschen the whole day, and the joy was great. Thus, in this traditional and rich home, between a precise and severe father and a gracious and good-hearted mother, the children grew and became adults who were prepared to continue in the ways of their ancestors.

# People and Families of Antopol

## Sarah Itah Lifshits, The Baker
### By Peshe Ben-Tovim

Sarah Itah came to live in Antopol after her first husband didn't return from serving in the Czar's army. There she married her second husband, who was an elementary school teacher. Both in the period of her widowhood from her first husband and also after she married her second husband, she was an active and diligent woman who led household as an expert in baking different types of bakery products for happy occasions and different events in the town.

She was a righteous woman and did a lot of

*[Page 208]*

commandments and acts of charity. In addition to giving her money for charity, she would also have guests of needy people in her house. And when agents to collect money would come to town, she would give broadly also to them. When refugees and persecuted people would arrive in town, Sarah-Itah would be among the first to receive them, to support and take care of them. All her life she was modest and shy.

Sarah Itah's daughter went to Israel and after that also her son, but she remained alone in town when she desired to immigrate to Israel. However, she didn't achieve that and she died outside of Israel. Many of the inhabitants of Antopol followed her hearse.

May her memory be blessed!

# R. Avigdor Sirotah, of Blessed Memory
## By Dr. Menuhah Gorvits

It is difficult to write about our dear martyrs when their tortured images are mixed in the memories of our youth, full of joy, hope, and love.

R. Avigdor Sirotah was a powerful spiritual personality, most of whose life was sacred for the Jewish community in Antopol in which he functioned as town elder. He was true and devoted to his task. He didn't know compromises and carried out all the public work voluntarily and with all his heart. When I write these lines, I know for sure that our love and high esteem for our father was not only as to a father but also as if to the fatherly Jewish patron of the community.

I will not forget his sense of humor, which sustained us in difficult times until his grown sons came to his help. Even though he was religious, he was not extreme and also appreciated those who were not so religious.

Every year when the High Holidays approach, I remember how our children would go to hear my father in the prayer of Kol Nidre, the Additional Service, and the Concluding Service. I especially remember the prayer "Behold, I am poor in deeds". When my father would begin, his voice coming from his heart would pass trembling to the hearts of his listeners. And he himself praying would break out in tears. Was this a prophetic cry about what would happen to himself leading in prayer and to the congregation of prayers?

The man who was a father to his family and to every person who needed encouragement and help, the small like the adult, shared his fate with all the community. They say that the Germans, may their name be blotted out, gathered the Jews of Antopol in the marketplace and among them was my father, of blessed memory. One of the murderous officers called out: "Who is the most important Jew?" It is understood that all of them pointed to my father. And then the German took out his gun and killed him.

From the depths of my heart, I call out: God of vengeance, appear!

# R. Avraham Klorfin
## By Eliyahu Klorfin

Even with all his business concerns, he always devoted from his time to study a page of Talmud. He lived the Old Testament and knew all of it perfectly. His home was a traditional Jewish home, and in this spirit he also educated his children. He also didn't withhold from them secular education. From time to time he also loved to read secular literature in Hebrew and Yiddish, and he was among the constant readers of ha-Tsefirah. However, in his old age, he stopped reading secular literature and devoted all of his time only to religious studies. He got along with people. As treasurer of the big synagogue (the stone study hall), he was honored and accepted by all the prayers.

*[Page 209]*

He was recognized in business circles as being honest and of clear conscience and also for his logical and clear judgment. Merchants would frequently come to him to mediate their commercial disputes, and they would always leave satisfied with his mediation. His house stood in the market square, opposite the concentration of stores. I remembered that many of the storekeepers would come to him for charity and that he would always answer them pleasantly. He supported lovingly those studying Torah and generously gave to rabbinical seminaries. He would send his contributions in Israel to the Graduate Seminary of Horodnah in Jerusalem yearly. When the Jewish National and Basic Fund were established, he was among the first and continual contributors.

He preached to his children always good qualities and conscience, to be precisely just in business and to understand one's fellow man. And all of his acquaintances and those who held him in esteem remembered him as one of the noble types in town.

# Yosef and Esther Glashtein
## By Eliyahu Klorfin

R. Yosef Glashtein, of blessed memory, was a religious scholar and one of the esteemed people in the town. He would spend almost all of his time swimming in the sea of the Talmud. He studied and taught. After the morning prayer in the study hall, he would recite a page of Talmud before some Jews. Between the afternoon and evening service, he would explain a chapter of Mishnah, and he would preach from En Yaakov on the Sabbaths before a large crowd in one of the study halls.

He was gifted in interpreting. Pearls would go out from his mouth. He was pious and respectful of all of God's word. Together with this, he got along well with people. He would react calmly to what someone told him, even if he didn't agree with him. He was interested in worldly matters, and especially in what was going on in the Jewish world in all its Diasporas. Therefore, he would permit himself to spare a little time off from his studies and read daily the ha-Tsefirah.

As a philanthropist to every cause of charity, he took into account the deed and the person doing it. I remember that the preacher from Kovno would come yearly to our town to collect donations for the rabbinical seminary in Kovno. He would lodge all the time of his stay in town in the house of R. Yosef. R. Yosef would accompany him when he went to collect donations to the houses of the contributors. Likewise, he would help the religious scholars, who would come to our town to sell their books.

He gave his children a traditional religious education full of love for the Jewish people and the Land of Israel.

R. Yosef died in 1914 at the beginning of World War I. The women in town would come to spread themselves out on his grave and to tell their troubles. The local people considered him to be a saint and so it was thought.

Esther, his wife, was not well thought of just because of her distinguished husband. Rather, she earned her merit herself. She was a modest person. It is especially remembered that she founded the society to clothe the needy for the poor children of the Jewish religious elementary schools. She would prepare warm clothes and shoes for the winter for the needy children. She would visit the houses of rich people, and under her influence, they took responsibility to give donations for this purpose. Under her devoted supervision, this institution existed for many years until the outbreak of World War I.

May their memory be blessed.

# R. David'*l*
## The Rabbi's Wife, Lifshah Shahor, of blessed memory

R. David'l was known as an outstanding personality among the rabbis of the town. And indeed he was known as a very active spreader of the Torah. After the prayer, there would come to him the young pupils, and after them would come the adults to learn the Torah from him.

*[Page 210]*

His day was devoted to study and writing. However, he always found time to listen to bitter people coming to ask his advice. He would say: "Even if it is impossible to help a bitter person, the very fact of listening to his troubles is a great commandment." He was also experienced in making peace between husband and wife. Despite the criticism of the community that had concern for respect for the rabbi, he instituted Friday evening for the study of the Pentateuch in his house and used to say: "Jews come from all over town to study Torah, and who am I to prevent them from having this pleasure!" When the Sabbath was over, he would continue the lesson, and the public would take in with thirst his words.

The house was a type of inn for important guests: rabbis, preachers, professors of Talmud from rabbinical seminaries, or emissaries. Likewise, people would come from the surrounding towns to settle a dispute before him.

When, we went from Antopol to Semitits, all the people in town accompanied him. They walked by foot to the railroad station, and they frequently continued to visit him in Semitits. However, after a few years of serving in Semitits, R. David'l became sick and returned his soul to his Creator. May his soul be bound in the bond of eternal life!

# A Daily Page for the Soul of My Father, My Teacher, R. Lazar, of Blessed Memory
## By Mosheh Polak

If there were once 36 righteous people, they certainly were in Antopol, and my father, of blessed memory, was one of them. He was an honest and modest person. All his concerns were given always to serve God faithfully and devotedly without any limits. And all his inner feelings were always for the sake of the public, without a desire to be rewarded. He even acted to us children with great understanding. He didn't once ask us to do anything above our ability, and he would refrain from giving us orders so that we wouldn't sin, God forbid, and transgress against the commandment of honoring the father.

The great principle "And you should love your neighbor as yourself " was always taken by my father, and in this spirit, he educated also us children. He would always repeat to us the biblical sentence "Give him a helping hand" and he would add: "If you help your fellow man, then you should do it with all your heart and your wealth."

Father was gifted with the exalted quality of loving man, who was created in God's image. However, his main concern was for the weak and failing. Nothing would hold him back from coming to their help and encouraging and supporting them.

He gave the best education to us children according to the concepts of those days. He got for us the best teachers and he was very interested in our going forward in our studies. And he took care that his work would not be for nothing and he would be able to give us a good and religious education.

He devoted all his life to good deeds, to Torah, to prayer, and to work for himself, for us, and for everyone. He was trained in many crafts, and he would willingly and happily help every needy person in fixing his home or other help. And he did everything out of loving kindness and without taking any money.

He would visit Jewish scholars and those studying Torah for its own sake. He would help them in everything that he was able. His main care was given to people of work and deed, who were also people of the Torah.

He would first of all teach reading and book learning to those working with him in book binding, and after that he would teach the trade. He didn't act to his workers as an employer. Rather, he treated them as equals. He would also stop the work of the workers for the afternoon and evening prayers, and he would also teach them a lesson in the Talmud.

*[Page 211]*

He would not even collect the money for binding the book. He would give the bound book to its owners and add: "Take it and go it peace." Mostly, my sisters and I would collect the bill.

Father would give all his life and work for the study hall. And he would always be the first and always remain the last when prayers were over. Very often he would return home from the study hall together with guests passing through, whom he would invite to the evening meal. It was customary for him to invite two guests for the Friday night meal so that it would be possible to have three people to say grace after the meal. There would be no end to his happiness if he would chance upon a religious scholar passing through. He would serve him and not leave him all the Sabbath. Mother, of blessed memory, would give father challahs and a pot of cooked food every Friday night before the meal, and my father would rush to distribute these among needy people. At almost every meal, he would leave a part of it and say, "Perhaps there will still come someone who will eat."

Father took upon himself with happiness and enthusiasm the arrangement of celebrating the finishing of a talmudic tractate and the preparation of the festive meal. However, before all, he had concern for the needy, and he would invite them to participate in the 250 celebration and the meal. He also didn't forget those whom it was impossible for them to participate in the meal, and he would run to also give them.

When I read Y. L. Peretz's story, "If not above this," there stood before me the image of my father, of blessed memory. Didn't he also act for a long period like that saintly man? And he would get up early at night, at 3 a.m., and distribute bundles of wood in front of the houses of the needy.

In the winter evenings, my father would bring from home potatoes to the study hall and he would bake them in the oven of the study hall. He would distribute them to those remaining there to study and spend the night. Likewise, he would bring blankets from home for those remaining to sleep in the study hall so that they would be warm.

Father would also be involved in the youth, and he liked to be in the company of those gathering in our house to read books. And he would stir them to the idea of "the Return to Zion." He would always preach to us to do good deeds and not to waste our time, that we should not take time out from study of Torah and worship. How happy he was that his dream and desire was realized, and in his old age he was able to go to live in our Holy Land.

May his memory be blessed!

# R. Shelomoh B. R. Henakh (Greenberg) and His Wife Heniah Hadas, Daughter of R. Mosheh Shemuel, of Blessed Memory

### By Mosheh Polak

R. Shelomoh Henakh was a man who had a place in his people. His trade was selling wood for heating. He was very pious and he would give a tenth of the wood for sale to the poor. Besides acts of charity, he would be charitable in his speech. He would give good advice to all who needed it. He would also give a lesson in the new study hall.

His wife Heniah- was called by everyone "Aunt Heniah." She herself didn't have children of her own. However, many orphaned boys and girls called her "mother." This is because she was a mother to them. Certainly she was our mother's sister. However, she also acted like a mother to me. I spent a lot of time in their house, and she took care of me and spoiled me. I was always happy to help her in acts of charity for which she was known. She had a grocery store in her house. And whoever had not money to buy the necessities for the Sabbath, to that person she would give generously flour, salt, sugar, and oil.

Every Friday night before the lighting of the candles, she would run to the ends of the town, with a basket in her hand, and distribute the Sabbath delicacies to the needy. Likewise, she had the pleasant tradition of the commandment of helping new brides. And many orphan girls were helped by her at their weddings.

*[Page 212]*

The son of her husband was Rabbi Yaakov Greenberg, of blessed memory, who was the head of the Chicago Rabbinical Seminary.

It is sad for those lost who shall not be forgotten!

# R. Yaakov Fridman (Yenkel the Person from Oblie)
## By A. Antopolski

Who didn't know Yenkel, the person from Oblie? He was a fish merchant, whose place of origin was from the village Oblie. He was a pleasant Jew with a pretty beard. His house was near the church. There was always to be found in his courtyard "Tiralke", a well-treated cow, and "Shpan", a young horse, and a wagon. He would travel each week in the wagon to bring fish for the Sabbath for the Jews in town. All the days of the week when he was on the road, his wife would bake bagels for sale. R. Yaakov began to do public service when because of his age he already didn't need to travel so much on the roads. And his son Leizer, who got married, meanwhile inherited from him the fish business.

He entered the life of the community in a storm.

First of all, he initiated refurbishing the bathhouse.

To everyone's amazement, he became familiar with all the innovations known in the big cities. He fixed ovens to heat water that would not give off smoke, hot and cold water in every section, and more and more. When money was lacking to finance the project, he stopped the reading of the Torah until the needed amounts were donated. And behold, one Friday arrived when the new bathhouse was ready for the use of the community. And where was the person who initiated the project? He was sitting in a corner washing and not standing out.

Another initiative, which would bring blessing, of Yenkel the person from Oblie was to erect a local hospital in which permanent doctors and nurses would serve. One of the biggest supporters was Avraham Eliyah Kitshin, the son-in-law of Eliyah the bookseller, who was the treasurer in the Gentile Squire's Study Hall. People were still doing this and a new initiative was born and carried out-supplying ice publicly for sick people.

In the summer of 1914, the cornerstone was laid for the hospital. The walls were erected up to the roof before the outbreak of World War I and then work was stopped. The war broke out. The men were drafted, and behind the front lines there remained the women and children. And when the front passed through, town was burned and plagues killed people. Yenkel and Lipa Novogrodski the doctor received permission from the German commandant to turn the priest's house into a hospital. Beds, sheets, and instruments were supplied and a hospital was erected in which many lives were saved. Yenkel gathered together a medical team. Sarah Raizl, the daughter of Shaye the butcher, was a nurse; the wife of

Mordekhai Toker was a cook for the sick; and Yenkel himself was busy with the rest of the work in administering the place.

Meanwhile, Yenkel organized a society to visit the sick and a Free Loan society, and other public activities. In the difficult days of the summer of 1920 when the town needed him more than usual, Yenkel fell asleep forever and died in the month of Elul (August). May his memory be blessed!

*[Page 213]*

# In Memory of My Dear Parents, Brothers, and Sister, Who Shall Not Be Forgotten
**By Rinah Asif**

My parents were religious and observant and that is how they educated their children. My brother David studied in a rabbinical seminary until he got married. My father was once of the first of the Zionist youths still in the days of the Czar in town. In our house, they spoke a lot about the Land of Israel and Zionism, and followed after all news from the Land. Their desire was to go to live in the Land. The box of the Jewish National Fund stood out among the rest of the charity boxes of the rabbinical seminaries and orphanages. Among the books about the Torah, there were found the books of Herzl, the monthly ha-Shiloah, and the newspaper ha-Tsefirah. The boys studied in the Jewish religious elementary school and the rabbinical seminary. The girls were sent to the Tarbut school just as the tuition impacted the budget and despite the fact that the Polish government's school charged no tuition.

My father, of blessed memory, was absent from the house most of the days of the week for his business work. And when he would return to his family tired and worn out from his weekly work, he didn't rest but took care of the failing and needy, of the widow and the orphans. The doors of our house were open to family members needing help, advice, a n d encouragement and to orphans in World War I, who found support and guidance, and for giving help secretly. This was done really by savings on the part of the family members because livelihood was limited for most of the time.

The days of the festivals and the holidays left a great impression when all of the family was seated around a set table. My father would return from synagogue accompanied by a guest and a permanent guest from the town's inhabitants, Avraham Leb (called Di Maydl Keshene) who would eat with us on Friday nights. And if a guest remained in the synagogue, my father would hint to my mother to prepare a package that included a roll, a piece of fish, and more. After he brought it to the guest in the synagogue, he would return to sit with us at the table. We would sing songs and listen to words of the Torah. The Sabbath gave us inspiration and the physical and spiritual strength to continue a difficult life under bad economic conditions and to hope for better days.

I remember those eating our daily meals, Jewish children from the villages and settlements around our town, who came to study the Torah. And my mother would take care of them. She would feed them and take care of all their needs as to members of the family. In the course of time, we moved from our small house in which we lived together with the family of Aharon Shemuel Kaplan, and we went to live in a bigger house on Mitsrayim (Egypt) Street, facing the house of R. Yaakov Hayyim the ritual slaughterer. Youths studying in the rabbinical seminary would turn to him for help and arrangements. And our house served for the youths of the rabbinical seminary as a place to sleep and to get a hot meal. My saintly mother would wash with her own hands all the bed coverings and sheets for the youths of the rabbinical seminary. She would not give them to a Christian woman helper lest she miss doing the good deed. In our house, there also found refuge a poor woman who had gone crazy when she lost all her family in World War I. Here is not the place to list all the good deeds that they did for others.

From the lips of Elhanan Lifshits, of blessed memory, I heard that the rabbi of the city, Rabbi Walkin, gave my father and him a mission that endangered their lives. It was learned in town that in the village Demidivtsinah the gentiles killed the only Jewish inhabitant, a person who had no family, Arkah. This happened in the year 1940 at the time of the Russian conquest. The mission was to bring the dead man for Jewish burial in our town. My father and Elhanan accepted the mission and went on the way without telling their wives. When they returned after many dangers to town with the body of the murder victim and the matter was known to my mother, she fainted. When she regained consciousness she said, "Thank God that you carried out the commandment of the rabbi."

My father desired to immigrate to Israel with all his family. He became more hopeful when I immigrated to Israel. However, World War II took place first. My dear parents, my brothers and sisters, my sister-in-law and their children, my mother's big family, my friends, and all the people of my town perished at the hands of the great enemy. From all of them, I remain alone with a broken heart, with deep wounds that do not heal and will never heal while their memory and good deeds accompany me as I continue on.

*[Page 214]*

# R. Yaakov Hayyim Kotler,
# the Ritual Slaughterer and Examiner
## By Rinah Asif

We lived as neighbors to the family of R. Yaakov Hayyim and we were very tied to the Kotler family.

R. Yaakov Hayyim was a good-looking religious scholar. He always smiled and was full of grace, wisdom, and a good heart. He had a place among people and knew everyone. As the only ritual circumciser in town and the region, he would enter all the males born into the covenant of Abraham, our father.

He was active in the community and willingly took on himself its burdens. He was concerned for the public and the individual. And our town did not lack for cares and problems. The sources for employment and earning a living were limited. The Polish government gave little support or none at all, and the community took care for its needs in education, welfare, and health. It was like a state in a state.

The influence of the rabbi and the important people in town was great, and R Yaakov Hayyim was the driving force among the active people. Especially after World War I when most of the houses in town were burnt and there remained widows and orphans, they turned to people from Antopol in the United States. And these answered with a big heart and an open hand. With this support many inhabitants were saved from famine.

The doors of R. Yaakov Hayyim's house were open to poor guests begging, who went from town to town to gather donations. Likewise, there came people seeking dowries for brides, preachers, and youths of the rabbinical seminary, who studied in town. They received in the house of the slaughterer a hot meal, a place to stay, and also advice and instruction.

The Rebbe from Kobrin, who came to visit his group of hasidim in town, would stay once a year in his house. Certainly, he didn't belong to the hasidic community. However, he was happy to have the rebbe as a guest and he respected him. On the Sabbath in which the rebbe would visit, there was a stirring and emotion in town. The inhabitants would enter Mitsrayim Street and crowd before the house of the slaughterer. Tunes, songs, and dances filled the space. And deep happiness flowed over those seated and those standing outside.

I can still hear the tune of the closing prayer of the Day of Atonement that he would pray at the prayer stand in the new study hall, together with the Kol nidre prayer of R. Avigdor with his children as choir, and the additional service of R. David Grishevski. Their tunes would unite the community of praying people and make their hearts tremble, cast fear and awe, and make hopes rise for better days, which to our sadness didn't come.

R. Yaakov Hayyim died in 1932 from typhus. The local doctor made a mistake in the diagnosis. When they brought in haste a famous doctor from Brisk, it was already too late.

The daughter of the ritual slaughterer and her two children came to our house. Even though there were small children and an infant in our family, my parents didn't hesitate to help the family of the ritual slaughterer. My father helped at the bed of R. Hayyim. Meanwhile, the daughter and small son also got sick, and they were brought to the hospital in Kobrin. The doctor from Brisk did the best he could. However, R. Yaakov Hayyim died on Friday night. Great mourning fell down on the town. All the inhabitants from small to adults, rabbis from the region and youths from the rabbinical seminary in Kobrin participated in the funeral.

*[Page 215]*

After two days, the daughter also died. There remained two small orphans. The saintly grandmother Hayah Bernshtein came to take care of her grandchildren. When her son R. Eliezer married a second time with Pitsah Krum, the daughter of the sister of R. Yaakov Hayyim Shohet, she left Poland and immigrated to Israel to her two daughters. Her husband was among the 36 martyrs of Pinsk in World War I. Fate was also cruel to her in Israel and her daughter died at a young age. She cried about the bitterness of her fate because all her family also died in the Holocaust.

She died in a good old age in a nursing home in Bene Berak, may her memory be blessed!

There should also be mentioned the second ritual slaughterer, Menahem Perlmuter, who married Hayah Rahel, the daughter of the distinguished Rabbi Hirsh Rabinowits. He was invited to serve as an additional ritual slaughterer after the death of R. Hayyim, of blessed memory. He was beloved by the people in town for his honesty and good deeds.

# Shelomoh'ke Menahem of the Family Gershtein
### By Rinah Asif

Shelomoh'ke was the first teacher for Hebrew and mathematics. He raised up a generation of people knowing Hebrew. He would give lessons in Old Testament to the glory of youths in the study hall, and many of the youth would come to hear Torah from him.

He was very devoted to his mother, who had become blind, and would lead her by hand to every place until the end of her days.

When he was an older person, he established a family and had two children on the threshhold of World War II. All of them perished at the hands of the enemy, may his name be blotted out, with the rest of the people in town.

May their memory be blessed!

# The Family of Hayah and Aharon Shemuel Kaplan
### By Avraham Kaplan

Hayah Raizl, daughter of Mordekhai Slonimski, was born in Antopol, and Aharon Shemuel, son of R. David Kaplan, was born in the village of Tarikan, close to Antopol. Their children were Mordekhai (Motiah), David, Hanah, and Avraham (Yaakov).

Of the family's children, only the youngest, Avraham, immigrated to Israel in 1935 and established a family in Israel. All the rest were murdered by the Germans, they and their young children- two children of David and his wife Rahel from the Hirshenhorn family and three children, Rahel, Avraham and Mindl of Motiah and his wife Pashah of the The Czerniak family.

The family was supplied, like other families, with established traditional Jewish values and emphasized relations with their fellow men no less than their relations with God. It was known in town that their house was always open to the poor and needy. And never was a person turned away with nothing.

The source of income was in commerce (the grain trade). However, their business was conducted without deceit, and in this, no distinction was made between a Jew and non-Jew.

The trends of the time that appeared in town also didn't pass over this family. The parents' hand was always open to contribute to any national fund, and the children also gave their share to all the cultural, public, and national activities. The other children also dreamed in different periods of immigrating to Israel. How sad it is that they were not able to immigrate and all of them were killed and only one of them realized his dream and remained alive to perpetuate their memory in the memorial book.

*[Page 216]*

# Itse Sarah-Menies Berkovits
## By Mosheh Polak

His father, Yaakov Hayyim the elementary school teacher, was a Jew who was learned in Torah and whose origin is from Kartuz-Berezeh. His mother, Sarah-Menie, was from a big family in Antopol with seven brothers and two sisters.

As the son of an elementary school teacher, Itse was also learned in the Torah. He married the daughter of Yaakov-Zavel and earned a living from a store for ready-to-wear clothing. After the fire in 1911, his store also burned down and he suffered a lot from that. However afterwards, he was fortunate and built a store made of bricks and his condition improved a lot. His wife ran the business and he dealt with community matters. As a Jew who was a religious scholar, he would study with other Jews in the old study hall the book Hayye Adam and Gemara. There many would listen to him. He was also the treasurer of the Talmud Torah and other public institutions. Itse also led in saying the prayers and would share the Additional Services with Avigdor the town elder in the old study hall. Itse had an only son, who was called Yaakov-Hayyim, and died together with all the Jews of Antopol.

Two uncles of Itse, the Barkai brothers, were among the founders of Yavneel in the Galilee.

# R. Yisakhar-Dov Rovashavski (Berish the Leaseman), Notes on his personality

## By Rayah Kliman-Rovashavski

My grandfather, peace be upon him, is etched in my memory and in my heart as one of the most wonderful personalities. There was in him nobility together with love for his fellow men and love of the Torah.

I was sure in my childhood that my grandfather was one of the thirty-six righteous men for whose sake the world exists. To my sorrow, he died while I was still a child and I wasn't able to spend a lot of time with him. In the period that I knew him, he was already not healthy. However, he refused to lie in bed. He would always sit at the table and study Talmud.

My father, Menahem, may God revenge his blood, used to tell a lot about Grandfather, his deeds and his righteousness. My grandfather had a poetic soul, and I was always impressed by his ability to express himself. I remember that once on the intermediate days of the holiday of Passover he said: "Late at night, after the second Seder, when all the people of Antopol were already asleep, I went out to the balcony. In the silence of the night, it was as if I put a hearing tube to my ear and heard the sound of the Shofar blown from afar." And it is really too bad, that my righteous grandfather wasn't able to hear the blowing of the Shofar on the Temple Mount in 1967 (727).

# In Memory of Artsak and Sarah Gelershtein
## By Rayah Kliman-Rovashavski

R. Artsak, son of Lazar Mikhal Gelershtein, was an honest man, humble and capable. He worked with his brother Yaakov Hersh in the function of expediters in Horodets, whose railway station also served Antopol. He stayed in his brother's house all week and only on the Sabbaths would he come to his house in Antopol. He died in the 1930's.

His wife Sarah was born in Zambrov, near Bialystok. After the death of her husband, she immigrated to Israel with her daughter Sheindl, son-in-law Shemuel Neidus, and their children Tsiporah and Avraham'leh. To their misfortune, they returned to Antopol before World War II, and they perished in the Holocaust together with all the members of the community, may God avenge their blood.

*[Page 217]*

# R. Zalman Ben Shelomoh Shayah
## By Yehudah, Nadel, and Tovah Altberg

R. Zalman, son of Shelomoh Shayah, was known by his nickname R. Zalman the tailor. He was a refined person, whose desire was to help his fellow man. When it was cold weather, he took care so that the poor, the widows, and orphans of the town would have heating wood. Friday night he didn't return to his home without two guests being invited to join him. After World War I when the economic conditions in Poland were at their worst, R. Zalman came and took charge of all the grain supply so that it would be divided among all the people in town.

In 1921, he was paralyzed in half his body. And despite this, he continued, to help his fellow man. When his father-in-law died, he gave his room to poor people so that he could fulfill the commandment of having guests. During the period of a year in which poor guests stayed with him, he took care of all their needs. It happened not just once that when he sat in his house to eat, someone knocked at his door. Then, he immediately seated him and gave him his own meal. He himself was very poor and lived from the support of his family in America. His modest wife, Hodel, daughter of Mosheh Yosef, accompanied him with devotion all his life. He lived his last years in the United States in the company of his children and grandchildren. He died in 1933. May his memory be blessed.

# Memories
## By Shemuel Lifshits

It is in deep pain and sadness that we remember that terrible period when men, women, and children were innocently killed. Their pure blood was spilled like water and their bodies were spread like manure on the ground. Towns and settlements became a killing field. And this was done in the light of day, before the eyes of the big world. And there was no one to protest. Certainly, this was a great disaster, and a voice of wailing comes out, like the words of the prophet: "How we have been plundered-we are very ashamed."

The memories of the events that happened are terrible, and we are not able to grasp the depth of the tragedy. From the recesses of the past, we remember different people from the inhabitants of our town, who were distinguished by their character and spirit, despite the simplicity of their lives. Most of these people lived from the work of their hands. Despite their difficulty in earning a living, they would set times to study the Torah. They were religious in their faith and went on the straight path. They lived their Jewish lives full of the heritage of their fathers of ancient days, lives of a holy and pure family, with love and devotion, parents to their children and as the children of their parents. They carried on households without luxuries and waste, even those who were rich. And above all, they devoted their time to matters of the spirit. They were like this and thus is etched their image in our memory.

Still from my early youth, I felt myself mixed with all the people in town like one family, without difference in condition and station. And despite my station, as the son of a wealthy and honored family, I didn't feel any pride or distance myself from the others. And I was always wrapped in feelings of closeness and warmth when I came home from my studies in Vilna on vacation.

I remember how my parents, of blessed memory, would try to give loans to storekeepers before the big fairs so that they would be able to buy goods and participate in the fair. Giving help and support to their fellow man was one of the signs of how they all were recognized. They always kept: "Help your fellow man-and tell your brother to take courage."

Finally, I want to describe some of the images of one of the inhabitants of our town, Gedaliah Weinstein, of blessed memory, or as he was called by people Gedaliah der Polushiner. He was a clerk of my grandfather R. Efrayim Lifshits, of blessed memory, or more correctly as he was called in his time, a trusted one. And certainly, Gedaliah Weinstein was trustworthy and honest in all his deeds. He would sell trees in the forests of R. Efrayim Lifshits, of blessed memory. Once a week, on Sunday, all the clerks would gather to give reports about their sales, etc. However, Gedaliah would not keep accounts and things written down like all the others. Rather, he would empty out his pockets and say, "This is what I earned this week." His statements and deed were more trustworthy than all the witnesses and accounts.

*[Page 218]*

They say about him that once he bought for R. Efrayim oxen in the big fair from one gentile and after he paid the gentile and brought the merchandise home, it became clear that the gentile had made a mistake in the account for some hundreds of rubles, from what was set down in the price. Gedaliah didn't hesitate much. After some time he traveled to the village to give back the money and to make the gentile understand his mistake.

It is possible to tell more stories like this about these dear people, who were killed as martyrs and for their people.

May their memory be blessed and tied up in the bond of the soul of the nation.

# R. Yaakov Meir of Osmolovits

R. Yaakov was the brother of Tehilah Leah Lifshits. He lived in the village of Osmolovits. He was an honest person. His wife Yenteh took care of all his matters. She would travel to town to bring a barrel of brandy and what the farmers of the region had ordered: herring, tabacco-mahorkah, matches, and the like. He, R. Yaakov Mir, would come with a book of Mishnah in his hand, pour a glass for the farmer, sell him mahorkah and matches and return to the book of Mishnah. His wife would also take merchandise to town to sell.

During the High Holidays, R. Yaakov Meir would come to town with his son, David, to lead the prayers and his son David would lead in chanting. His praying brought many admirers to hear him, both in the old and new study hall.

# Meir Shub, of Blessed Memory
## By Maniah Volodovski (Kefar Saba)

Meir Shub was the son of the town elder in Antopol, and both his brother and son filled this task. Meir spent his time in Warsaw. However during World War I, he went to the Ukraine to Krementshug, where all of the horrors of the war passed over him and his family. The Bolshevik government took all his property and he remained penniless.

In 1921 he returned to Antopol, where he devoted himself to Zionism and culture. He collected monies for Zionist funds. Frequently, he went personally to collect the donations in homes. He made himself a contributor and contributed a lot himself. He was the authorized representative of the General Zionists and did a lot for the Jewish National Fund and Foundation Fund of the Zionist Organization. He did not only take care of public and national institutions, he also took care of plain needy people. He got loans for them and gave security for them.

He was an intellectual person, cultured and aware of everything that could bring advancement for the lives of the townspeople. He took care to found a secular school and tried to influence parents to send their children to this school. He tried to receive certificates for young people in Antopol in many trips to Warsaw to the Erets Yisrael Office. He also tried to get exit permits from the Polish government, which were mainly connected with sizeable monetary expenditures. Thanks to him, many youths immigrated to Israel.

He was friendly with young and old. He was a good person in his character and had a warm Jewish heart. His house was a place to go for Zionist activists and for all Jews needing advice or financial support. His youngest daughter, Anyutah, and his wife helped him in the Zionist work. His eldest daughter Miriam and her husband, Tsevi, of blessed memory, immigrated to Israel in 1925 as pioneers.

Both of them were artists.

[Page 219]

# R. Alter Zisuk (Alter Shelomoh the Housepainter)

## By A. Antopolski

R. Alter was born in the village of Barshevits. Since he was very young when he came to learn his trade from Shelomoh, the town adopted him and he adopted the S town. However, it was not without reason that the entire town saw him as Shelomoh's son. First, he was similar in appearance to the family of Shelomoh, and second he inherited from R. Shelomoh some good qualities, like helping the needy, giving charity anonymously, and the like.

At home, R. Alter did every kind of work to earn a living for his family. After the war when Poland annexed the region, he began to deal in trade. In 1925 his sister brought him to America in Chicago. There he worked for a building contractor, who was a family member. When the first Sabbath came, R. Alter went to pray with the group "Society of People from Antopol." There he met with people from the town, and he had a truly enjoyable Sabbath. However, the pleasure of his Sabbath didn't last long. Those relatives who gave him a job began to argue with him on the topic of observing the Sabbath. And R. Alter told me himself that on the next Sabbath he prayed early and began to go to work but on the way to work went back again to the synagogue.

Those who wanted to help him loved him afterwards for his honesty and treated him with respect. At the same time, he was one of the important people in the Antopol organizations in Chicago, not only in word but also in deed. He had a great influence on his children, who also became known in Chicago, and especially in the organizations of people from Antopol. May his soul be bound up in the bond of life.

# In Memory of the Family Zonshein
## By Esther Gamerman

There was a small house on the north side. The sun never penetrated this house. However, the house was clean and polished. In a corner of the room, there stood the worktable of R. Yitshak the watchmaker, who sat bent over the table all day long. It was quiet in the house. People heard only the ticking of the clocks from all different directions. Even watches belonging room to Shalom Aleichen were brought here to fix. In the middle of the stood an eating table on which was always spread a white cloth, with a ceiling lamp above it. R. Yitshak was pale and also crippled. However, he was a clever and modest Jew The eldest daughter in this family with many children managed to immigrate to Argentina. The mother, thin and diligent, was always busy with her housework, taking care of all its needs as a devoted wife. She always smiled and always waited for better days.

The daughter, Sarah, was thin, refined, and delicate, with flaxen hair and blue eyes. She was intelligent, trustworthy, and quiet. Together we underwent preparation for immigration to Israel in Lublin in 1933. She didn't manage to immigrate to Israel even though this was her dream in the ha-Shomer ha-Tsair Movement. She was active and worked as the head of the group, a member of the group leadership. Honestly and in a refined manner, she devotedly carried out her tasks.

In the last years before I immigrated to Israel, I visited her house, which was for me like a second home. There will accompany me in my memory all my life Sarah's house together with my house and the panorama of the town.

*[Page 220]*

# Segal family
## By Esther Gamerman

The house of my parents was full of sun and much light. Its windows faced south and east. There was a courtyard behind the house. It was a traditional but not fanatical house, When, as a result of the organization of the Youth Movement, there began to arrive to us the children, all types of pamphlets and newspapers, father also began to read them. He would examine them but not oppose them even if sometimes they were not according to his spirit.

My parents, who were always concerned with earning a living, dealt in merchandise. My mother as well as my two brothers helped to earn a living. When I left home, my brother Zaidl was only 16 and my brother Shemuel was 21.

I remember my father traveling to fairs, and in days when the weather was bad, we would wait with concern for him to return home. My mother, whose health was weak in the last years because of her difficulty in earning a living, always mourned for two of her sons, who died when they were still young.

My father had a sense of humor, knew Hebrew, and read a lot of Hebrew at the source, like Mapu, Shneur, Bialik, and Tchernihovski. He also read translations into Hebrew from Russian and French. On the Sabbath days of the summer, he loved to rise early to go outdoors and to read a book. When he returned from a stroll like this, he would immediately go to the synagogue for the morning prayer. This was a personality with a special mixture in its type, the love of nature and devotion to the synagogue.

The holidays were kept according to tradition. In addition to the High Holidays, the holiday most loved by all of us was the Holiday of Pentecost. The house was full of lilac and jasmine flowers. My mother prepared milk dishes in honor of the holiday. And most of the time, Uncle David would come to be a guest with us. He was my father's brother from the town of Selets.

During the High Holidays, my father would pray in front of the ark, and my brothers Shemuel and Zaidel helped him in the role of a choir. They had pleasant voices, and I loved to hear their repetitions and understandably also their prayers in the study hall.

On one morning of the month of July 1939, I left my father's house, accompanied by my parents, brothers, my uncle Tuviyah and members of his family to the railway station in Horodets. There we parted. My departure was difficult. I felt that something was going to happen.

You will look in vain in the window where they shined. The Jewish town is no more. There remain only a pile of ruins. May their memory be blessed.

Shoshanah Edri (of the Garblovski family): Memories from my Immigrating to Israel.

When I was a young person, I joined the youth movement Freyheyt. This was the working class youth. At an older age, I joined he-Haluts. In he-Haluts, I received a pioneering and Zionist education and preparation for life in the kibbuts.

One evening there came to us in the movement a person born in our town, our friend Hayyim Osip, may he continue to be with us in life, and he gave me the push to leave home and go to preparatory work. I accepted his advice and contacted the central organization in Warsaw. After a short time,

I received an answer to go to the Dombrovitsah group or to the Klosov group. I immediately packed my suitcases. I said goodbye to my parents and to my friends. And I traveled. By the fact that I immigrated to Israel, I saved another two of my family members: my mother, of blessed memory, and my sister Hayah of blessed memory.

On the way to the preparatory kibbuts, we met more members, who sat and sang pioneering songs. I thought in my heart that they were also traveling the same way. I asked them where they were going. They answered me at once: to the group of Klosov or Dombrovitsah. I remember as if it happened now how the railway conductor entered and shouted, "What happened? What is your great happiness?"

*[Page 221]*

I answered him: "These are the builders of the homeland of the State of Israel, pioneers, who will realize their goal!"

He let out a curse in Polish and left.

We reached the railway station in Dombrovitsah. There they waited for us members of the group with a list in hand and called out the names of those who would get off and those who would continue to Kolosov. I was chosen to get off at Dombrovitseh.

The members of the preparatory kibbuts received us very well, and we were like brothers and sisters. The condition in the preparatory kibbuts was then very difficult. 270 However, the desire to realize the pioneering dream and to immigrate to Israel broke up the difficulty and I continued to work. Our work was in the saw mill. And after four months of devoted work, I was permitted to travel home to prepare the papers and passport so that I could immigrate.

It was to my bad luck that immigration was closed for an unknown time in 1929. And I didn't have already any place to live as an individual alone since I had gotten used to the collective life in a collective. Therefore, I returned to the preparatory kibbutz. I was another year in preparation until to our good luck, the immigration began again. I immigrated to Israel in March 1930. Then, we traveled, 1500 of us pioneers, in fourth class, like cattle. We suffered a lot from sea sickness, but we passed through all the difficulties with our strong pioneering spirit. After five days at sea, we came to the port of Jaffe. From the port we went straight to the immigrants' house on Aliyah Street.

After a week of rest in the immigrants' house, people came from the central organization of Kibuts ha-meuhad to greet us. Part of us went to Yagur and part went to Ramat Rahel in Jerusalem. My heart prophesied to me that Jerusalem would be capital of the Second State of Israel and I traveled to Ramat Rahel. The life was difficult: there was no farm, no water, and no home. However, we continued our daily life when around us our unpleasant neighbors didn't give us rest for a moment. Nevertheless, we continued to work in the day and to keep watch at night. And we came here to realize the dreams that we wove in our town of Antopol.

# In Memory of My Family
## By Shoshanah Edre, of the Garblovski family

My father, of blessed memory, was a first-grade teacher in town. Many children studied with him the Torah. He was an educated Jew. He studied all his days, as is written: "And you should study it day and night." After a severe illness, he needed an operation, from which he died before the World War.

My mother, of blessed memory, was able to come to Israel a few months before the outbreak of the war. And she realized her desire to live and die in Israel.

My sister Hayah, of blessed memory, was a pioneer and achiever. She was able to immigrate to and live in Israel. We were together thirty-three years until cruel death took her In her 68th year. May their memory be blessed!

# In Memory of My Mother Elke Rahel and My Sister Mirah'leh
## By Sefulah Sosnik, of the Erlikh family

My mother, of blessed memory, born in Zafrud was and grew up as an orphan. Her father, my grandfather, of blessed memory, died at an early age.

*[Page 222]*

He was a religious scholar. He sat and studied day and night. After his death the job of earning a living fell on the shoulders of my grandmother, of blessed memory.

As they grew up in a village, they brought home a teacher, who taught the sons and daughters. My mother was fluent in Russian and Polish. She was also fluent in Yiddish literature. My grandmother raised the orphans for Torah, marriage, and good deeds. A part of her children immigrated to the United States and arranged themselves well there. And afterwards, they brought her to them. My mother and her brothers remained in Poland.

When my mother came to Antopol, she was beloved by all her acquaintances. My father's family esteemed her especially for her warm and honest relations with people. She always had a good and soft word for the needy. Even the young people who came to our house loved to spend time in her company and appreciated her intelligence and knowledge of life.

After our father became sick and was not able to work, the situation became difficult. We were still children and Mother was not able to share work with us.We went from a new and spacious house to an old apartment. The burden of earning a living was lightened a little with help from the family in the United States. Mother continued to give us an education in the Tarbut school, explaining to us that she was doing it to prepare us for life. She didn't complain once on the bitterness of her fate. She had us acquire the approach to accept everything with love.

She was proud of her children, and in her last years, she was encouraged in life by receiving letters from her children. She was unable to join her children because of the cruel war.

May her memory be blessed!

My young sister Mirah'leh, of blessed memory, was beloved by all of us. She was a pretty girl with blue eyes. She was always happy and joyful. When I immigrated to Israel, she was a pupil in school. As was usual in the Tarbut school, she absorbed love for the people and the land and she was proud to have a sister in Israel. In all her letters to me, she asked me to write to her about the life in Israel and hoped that when she grew up, she would also immigrate to Israel and build her life there.

# In Israel: Mosheh Stavi -- Abu Naman
## By Prof. P. Czerniak

Mosheh Stavi was born in Antopol in the 1880s. His father was Yitshak-Shemuel Stavski and his mother was Rivkah, from the Lifshits family. The family had still two more sisters and five brothers. When the flour mill for flax oil went up in flames, his father took the six children and Mosheh and went to Krementsuk.

In the many travels that he took on behalf of his father's produce business, the young Mosheh came to Warsaw and became friends with a group of young poets, who opened a period of renaissance in Hebrew Yiddish literature. There he began to publish his first works. Finally, he left his father's house and moved to Warsaw. And so did his brother Berl, who left home and studied to be a rabbi, and so did his sister Geniah, who studied gynecological medicine. The other two brothers also dispersed.

Mosheh would visit Antopol from Warsaw. Among his biographical stories is one from that period. It is told there: "In the years 1908/10, I would sometimes visit Antopol, and my family's home, and especially the home of my sister, Tsiviyah Feldshtein. In 1908, I came at the end of the summer to spend t h e holidays and remained until after Sukkot. Around me there would gather the youth, who sought literature and carried their heart to Zion. I also had then a family person in the underground, young Fradil, the daughter of Efrayim, my brother. She was a socialist. My group would sing songs of Zion and longing for the Land of Israel, and her group would sing songs of liberation of the Russian homeland. When the government planned to arrest her, I hid her in a wagon. I brought her to Drohitsin and through the fields and forests eastward to Krementsuk.

*[Page 223]*

Mosheh returned to Warsaw and continued his struggles. He preferred a life of deprivation as a young writer over a life of plenty in the house of rich parents. Here he met his marriage partner and decided not only to sing and long for the Land of our Fathers but also to live and work in it. In 1911 the couple took a primitive Russian boat from 0dessa to Jaffe-after a harsh struggle with the sea, the Turks, and lack of drinking water and food. When they came to Jaffe, there was not waiting for them an easy time. There began a long period of hard work. Mosheh, who from his youth so loved nature, saw it neglected in the land of his dreams and decided to change things.

He began to recognize the new milieu, the Arab neighbors. He became an expert in their way of life and friend of the tenant farmers and landowners, of the donkeys and the camels. He began to deal with barley and the vineyard and with citrus and subtropical fruits. He transformed himself from a Yiddish writer into someone with unusual knowledge of Hebrew in which he began to publish wonderful new stories and to adapt the earlier ones from Yiddish. When the first years in which he was a crusading writer became to difficult too bear (years about which he would tell me with tears of emotion in his eyes, the eyes of a hard person, obscure to any observation)-when he suffered hunger and his literary wages would arrive in miserly payment and with delay, despite his excellent social ties with Bialik, Frishman, and the other greats of the literary generation, Mosheh Stavi was forced to abandon literature for some years and passed to work with the plow and in places of employment.

And again he struggled hard, both as a coordinator for employment in Hebrew Petah Tikvah and as a worker and afterwards as a landowner in Beer Tuviyah. Here he learned well on his skin, back, and head all the difficulties and surprises of nature. However, he would tell with especial pleasure his war with the wind, the rain, the heat, and the hot dry weather in order to insure a good harvest and good sheep shearing, about the lack of roads and about travels during days and nights in wagons and on camels from Petah Tikvah or Beer Tuviyah south and north in his travels in the length and breadth of the land.

Finally, he decided to go to the city, which would perhaps allow him to return to Olympus. One fine day the author appeared on Mendele Street in Tel Aviv with a number of cows and in the face of many snobs, he dealt with love towards his household animals and sold their produce among the consumers. The agricultural writer again acted not like a regular farmer. He grew the treasures of nature. However, he also studied what was happening and examined the soul of the fields, the plants, and animals. Thus, he became an expert, a researcher for the encyclopedia of life in nature in Israel.

At the first opportunity, he slowly returned to his status and began again to write, lecture and teach. The man, who would not be still, began to think in this period about his future and set for himself a goal to set up an enterprise that would allow him the possibility of literary work without disturbances, out of need for worry about the most limited income with which he made due all his life, out of fear that he would again be forced to leave his pen as before. Almost with empty hands he began to build a house, which he erected by his own strength, with loans and great efforts from when he made savings from the food budget for himself and his small family. This is when his son Naaman not only studied but also worked.

In addition to that he continued at every opportunity to be a helper and adviser to others and among them to people from Antopol and his family members, who came to Israel in his steps. And he would say, "In those days, when after work, I would go to town. I had in files many problems to arrange and had plans for many meetings. And for what purpose? In order to give help to my fellow man, to the weak, and to the needy." He never forgot Antopol forever. With great effort, he would make trips from Israel to Poland and visit the town. All remember his visits from 1930-1938, when the schoolchildren and the organized national pioneering youth would come to the railway station to welcome him, a poet from the Land of Israel, to have the honor of conversing with him and to hear his lectures about Israel and Hebrew literature. After every visit, Mosheh Stavi left much material for the thought and feelings of the Antopol youth as well as to the youth of all the towns and cities where he visited and spoke, material that gave education and depth to Zionism in that period of renewal.

*[Page 224]*

When we arrived in Israel in 1950, we found Mosheh Stavi at the height of his literary, public, societal, and personal health when he wrote without stop, correcting and teaching Bible and Mishnah, and traveling to different settlements for lectures, plays, and presentations on how to work well in agriculture and how to take care of domestic animals. After some years, he began to struggle in a new arena. The difficult years that passed over him strengthened him and made him into a strong person. However, they destroyed him physically. His joints began to hurt and he had to struggle with pains and difficulties in walking. His eyes began to betray him and he had to struggle with losing his sight. This slowly began to cause much suffering to a person who was entirely tied to the written and printed word. Finally the loneliness of the life of a person alone became more pressing. However, Mosheh Stavi ignored the difficult condition and fought strongly and consistently with his nature. Under no circumstances did he allow a thought of pity and commiseration to appear in his many old and new friends, faithful friends who enjoyed his wide knowledge and special ideas.

On July 23, 1964, the dear person Mosheh Stavi, of blessed memory, left us forever. He departed after a strong and continued battle with the Angel of Death. The best medical fighters were mobilized for the battle. They didn't spare any effort that seemed useful. We used the best means we had but didn't succeed. We attested towards him, a person more diligent than all of us: "A person comes from dust and his end is in dust." Thus finished the last struggle of the man whose entire life was one chain of struggles with all that stood in his way in life. He was not a regular man. He rose above all his milieu.

During the last 14 years, I had the privilege of knowing the personality of the writer Stavi, of blessed memory. And I myself had the privilege of serving him in different tasks, and especially medical ones, to come close to him and to get the trust of my talented, difficult, and complex uncle. He was combative but beloved and precious. I observed and felt that under his iron chest there beat a generous heart that was sensitive, romantic, and profound. Under his skull bone there worked a thinking mind, learned, sharp, and incisive. Under the layer of hard skin, there was an abundant soul, stubborn but healthy and active from morning to evening and from evening to morning.

In summation, he was a man who in the course of eight decades worked hard, very hard, fought hard, and built a lot of physical and spiritual building. Thus, he established for himself a great, eternal monument stretching from the Jewish district in Warsaw, by way of Antopol, up to Lvov, up to Beer Tuviyah and Gedera, and from New York up to Tel Aviv. He was a man, who spread his house from 38 King Solomon Street to every agricultural settlement, kibbutz, and village, from his writing table, which was always full, to all the tables of his many friends.

The library of Stavski-Stavi was not wealthy in quantity of books but important in its quality. It included books on nature and labor, fauna and flora, and the legends of oriental peoples and of our nation, for children and adults, for the Biblical Hebrew language and agriculture and Arab life. His book The Arab Village (Ha-Kefar Ha-Arvi) was the crowning achievement of his social researches and one of the original and most important books to study the problem. This library was not only an eternal monument to the deceased writer but also an important national resource.

*[Page 225]*

He didn't finish his work. He prepared a lot of material for additional publications. For a long time, he began to work on memorial books. He participated in memorial books for Brisk and Koval and fought for a book on Antopol. In 1962, he was at the head of the Israeli committee for a book on Antopol. We spent many evenings working on the reading of the material sent to this committee before it was sent to the New York committee. Suddenly we had to part from him. With concern and fear, we fought hard to preserve his health, but we didn't succeed. However, the memory of the man remained preserved in our heart, as if it were hovering over us. And when the door bell rings stronger than usual, the first thought passing in my mind is: "Here the uncle comes."

A spiritually strong man seems to live forever. We quickly learned our mistake. However, we must establish a project to keep his memory alive in the future and to comfort us with his spiritual presence. We must establish a research institute with the method that he was so recently interested in. When he saw me working in the new field of atomic research, he also became interested in the details. He read several of our research works and wanted to know how to use nuclear knowledge in agricultural work. Thus, a fitting memorial for his name would be a radioactive-agricultural research laboratory, which would continue his ideas of research and improvement of natural resources in our country, which he loved so much and which now embraces him forever.

*[Page 225]*

# Points About Mosheh Stavi's Writing
## By Daniel Ben Nahum

A person always remembers to tell how good his youth was. And more than that, how good his childhood was. I still remember how my heart trembled when I met up with Mosheh Stavi's work Friends of Dumb Creatures (Yedide Ha-ilmim). They were thin yellow booklets published by Moriyah in Odessa. I remember the tears I shed about the cruel fate of Lagan the Aramaite. He was a rebellious and noble horse, which didn't want his owners to shoe him under any conditions. This is a hint to the kind of freedom that rejects the injustice of the Diaspora and to what happened in the Jewish Pale of Settlement. These stories look well when you meet them after many decades. You get a new taste from them and reveal images that have disappeared from the eyes of the child. Some of our great writers have had a lot of love for animals and made good descriptions of them. However, Mosheh Stavi is unique in our literature. He listened so as to speak the language of animals, both domesticated and wild, and to birds and put them at the front of his work. And precisely his stories about animals are very human.

The animals of Stavi have a place of honor in the house, pen, and fenced courtyard. In the stories of what happens to them, there are reflected as if in a mirror clearly the lives of the simple Jews and their gentile neighbors. And on all of them is the image of a blessed childhood, which was poor in events but rich in experiences and adventures. Its spiritual meaning is very out of place of the boundaries in which it occurs and forms a kind of protected corner, from which a person is fed all his life. And the mischievous and wide-eyed child is none other than our author, Mosheh, himself, the son of the owner of the flour mill in the center of Antopol, a small town in Polesia, full of gardens and lawns, whose streets and courtyards open to the wide fields around.

*[Page 226]*

Mosheh Stavi is a realist at his roots, gifted with sharp powers of observation and a penetrating glance, taking in every point and variation in nature, every movement and grimace in the animal and human world. And here are examples: "A small weaned calf lay down spreading out its legs. We don't know if it did this because it was taken off to slaughter, or if it did this because it was strong and happy, or if it did this because it was mischievous and lightheaded. Only young animals know to spread out like this." Or "A pair of young mules pushed at their bits with their lips as if they pulled the wagon not by their chests but by their lips and they impatiently moved their rumps as if one of the straps of their harnesses had become wrapped beneath their tail, and they were prepared to kick with their legs…" Only someone near to the animal world would know to appreciate all the preciseness and vitality in these descriptions.

As one of the classical school writers remaining from Mendele in our literature, Stavi was tied with all his feelings to the ground of reality and his creative imagination was not free forever from its authority. Bialik commented well to him in a letter when he tried as a youth his strength at a modernistic symbolistic style: "You don't have power to get into the secrets of the Law. My friend, your foot is a straight foot. And God created you and your skill straight. Why should you look for crooked ways? With love for your healthy ability. H.N.B."

And surely, Stavi's stories are full of health and earthiness, which are rare in our literature. And with this there was a lyrical romantic tone characteristic to Stavi, which raised reality to a symbolic level. Perhaps there is unintentionally recognizable in his way of writing the influence of Perets, Zeitlin, and Frishman, authors from Warsaw in whose company he spent the years of his youth. Some of his first stories excel in poetical sharpness and dramatic plot, in which there was the confrontation with fate just like the grace of love that did not distinguish between higher and lower levels of creation. And between what happens to man and his animal is drawn open and hidden feelings in the secrets and mysteries of life revealed, "In the Heat of Summer" ("Be-hom Kayits") and "In the Courtyard of Trees" ("Be-hatsar Ha-etsim").

Certainly, the permanent foundation in his work with many corners and fronts is the tie and love for the soil. Devotion to the earth, the foundation of the world is the profound line passing in all his literary work like the way he lived. He not only sings hymns in its honor but also is really woven into the life of the earth. The best pages in his works, both those written in the Diaspora and in Israel, are those that are poetically full of the strength and smell of the mother earth up to the point that the senses are drunk and the personality of the author is obliterated: "A new sun, fresh and red, as if coming out of the bath, is seen in the firmament of the heavens; from the earth, which just now returns to life, there rises the smell of grass, grass and flowers perfume the air.

There hung from the trees the last pieces of big and clear icicles. They fell to the ground some loudly and some softly. Somewhere, there remained the splinters hanging on the top of a stalk in the hiding place of a leaf and in the cyathium of a flower. They appeared to be pure silver tears in the eyes of an innocent child. The last rays of the sun sinking in the lower parts of the heaven penetrated diagonally from among the branches of the trees and were reflected in the fine silver splinter in a purple red." ("Be-Yom Kayits," or "On a Summer Day").

It is a well known truth that everyone brings up that we were uprooted from the earth. Certainly, we are missing a wide layer of real farmers, who earn their living from the earth. However, the foundation of the earth was not entirely missing from the lives of our people and their occupations. This was especially true in the case of the inhabitants of the suburbs, who were known to be poor. They needed the produce of their gardens and animals. They kept the backbone of attachment to the earth. They were never cut off in their conversation and in all their innocent surrounding from the life of the village. And even the high spirits of the Sabbath and holidays, the milieu of the study hall surrounded by the scent of the Torah and holiness of tradition didn't weaken the scent of the field and the stable. Many of the Jewish writers devoted their pen to the simple and their sufferings. However, few brought up the connection to the earth in their lives like Mosheh Stavi. He saw in the love of the simple Jew for his animal ("Parah ba-dir-berakahah ba-bayit," or "Cow in the pen-blessing in the home") "Hu ve-hi" [he and it] the tie to the hub of existence, to the origins of language from above and below.

*[Page 227]*

The love or the land is what Mosheh Stavi stood for. After his first stories were published and got him a reputation, he was on his way to Israel to find a place as a worker on one of the distant settlements on the border of the Negev, in Beer Tuviyah. It was there that his life and work were interwoven. Precisely, he, who was so rooted in the earth of the exile and in the rich folk language of the quintessential Jew, accepted for himself the judgment of the Israeli revolution more severely and consistently than other Hebrew writers who arrived in Israel during the Second Aliyah and were more spiritual and ethereal. The nature of the country and its land are not acquired only by intuition and frame of mind. Rather, wholeheartedly by the direct contact of the person struggling with nature as Jacob did with the angel in order to get out of him the strength of his blessing.

The stories of the Israeli village by Stavi breathe the air of the fields in which the plough moves like a candle that won't be extinguished, sweating, moving, above and below, from horizon to horizon ("Zaranu be-dimah", or "We planted with a tear"). The working hand is felt that sows, the body being relaxed and desiring rest. All the acts of creation, the changes of day and night, do not exist for themselves but are connected and united with the work of men. The night is for dreams and watching. The dew is for pasturing cattle. The silence before morning is to bring in from the fields. The wind of morning is to take out the beginning of the soft straw. The clear day is for plowing. The heat of the afternoon is for threshing. The wind at twilight is to plant crops ("Le-ahoti Beer Tuviyah", or "To my sister, Beer Tuviyah"). All the changes of existence here seem to be mirrored in the processes of work: "The thick fog begins to retreat, as if they turned it by the work of sowing and dispersed it with hands. Afterwards, when one of the loaded carts brought with it from the field to the threshing floor the gold of the young morning, together with the gold of blessing wrapped between the racks" ("ha-boker" or "Early in the morning").

Stavi was the first of Israeli writers who understood with sharp comprehension the vitality and reality of the uniqueness of the country's landscape without transmitting images and memories of other landscapes. His descriptions are apparently realistic and precise to the point of naturalistic exaggeration ("Somewhere a cow stirred and loudly urinated water. And immediately, its waste water surrounded all the village"). Nevertheless, there is an explanation in all its precision of a living past: "The light silk and grey mists, which sent their webs with the beginning of the evening from beneath the heaven sown with stars made the air fragrant with something wet and fresh, fell at midnight to the ground like a thick material, close and full of blessing...The moon of the end of the month came down now red from behind the mountains of Judea, as if ashamed by its late appearance. It looked at the ground with the pre-morning gaze, from behind silver fog, as if full of blood, and for a small moment increased the darkness."

Stavi is the poet of the beginning phase of Hebrew agriculture in Israel, before the all-powerful machine pushed away the labor of the animal and the human hand in milking and shearing, in planting and harvesting. This is a period from which we are separated by only a few decades. Nevertheless, it seems to us distant and forgotten. And not once does Stavi appear as a chronicler of a dear honey moon, a fresh honey moon with the first steps of the pioneers and settlers. His statements, despite their outer simplicity, are festive like a hymn or prayer: grass, sun and rain, and land and heaven and God.

*[Page 228]*

Even in his stories of the Arab village and its "legends, which were written from a deep and penetrating knowledge above and below, there beats the feeling of participation in a covenant of bread and salt for all this family, which gets its bread by its own sweat, a type of peasant cooperation. This is a happiness of rain in its time and the blessing of abundance, and their opposite, the pain of drought and the fear of famine, surround all the living and creeping existence on the face of the earth, without difference of sex and type, family and rank, race and nation, religion and class. Stavi's book ha-Kefar ha-aravi, or The Arab Village, is a basic contribution unique in its type in our literature in the field of Arab folklore before the British conquest and the penetration of modern influences. Stavi's insight into the patriarchal environment of his neighbors, which does not cover up the inner contradictions and deep social rot, is cruel and sober. However the description of the village struck by drought, waiting for the coming of the hot wands, is entirely full of the spirit of revolt and human pride trampled underfoot. These stories and writings are excellent for observing the substance of things, with a farmer's intelligence, rooted in the existence of the world, full of humor, and with a poetic vitality coming from the lines.

Not many guess how difficult are the pains of uprooting and planting anew from one language to another for the author, whose language is not only the instrument of his work but also the oxygen for his creation and the hapr for his inspiration. For a long time the Israeli stories of Stavi were translated from one language to another, from Yiddish to Hebrew (the excellent translation of A. Shlonski and also M. Tyumkin and Y. Kikhtnboim) until it took root in the soil of the Hebrew language. However, even here Stavi digs to roots with the help of his closeness to nature and agriculture, to the conversation of animals and birds, to the milieu of the Arab village, and to ways of agriculture in which ancient ways and customs were kept.

Our author learned about the early life of our language as it grew out of the nature of the land and its landscape and from the lives and work of our ancestors. In "Akhilat kurtsa" ("Eating bread = Slander"), kurtsa is the bread of the shepherds baked on cinders of the fire and eaten together and accompanied with slander, obscenity, plots, and gossip (for example, the story of the selling of Joseph). In "Hutra" ("Club"), throw a club in the air and it lands on its head (Tanuuma to Balak 17); the reference is to the Nabot, the Arab club, and the shepherd's staff, which has a heavy top, serving as a weapon and always falling on its head because of the weight. After Stavi gave a bill of divorce to the Diaspora, to its landscape, which made a big impression on his soul, he wiped away strongly its impression so that he would be able fully to give life to the land of Israel, to cleave to it completely without other visions and experiences separating him from it and mixing him up. And in this matter that he was severe on himself, he was also severe with others and prepared to rebuke them fully in long and detailed articles stating that our best writers and poets had a baggage of visions of other places and skies and if you this duality is stamped on all our national literature since our nation went into exile. The visions of an early landscape and foreign country are mixed up together.

There was no other writer among our contemporary authors like Mosheh Stavi, who was able to make the beginning of our history come out of the past, taking up the plow for the first time and opening the first furrow in the earth of the homeland after a separation of thousands of years. He is a person of the Second Aliyah, who went like a brother and friend with the Bilyyim in Gedarah and with the farmers of Ekron and Beer Tuviyah, simple people from the old generation.

He was always ready to listen, to learn and teach agronomy, linguistics, and literature, to help and share a burden according to the best of his strength and knowledge, as one of the family, as an insider, continuing a chain, which was not cut off from then, the chain of pioneering work. This was in spite of the contradictions between generations a heartfelt distance, despite the hard struggles taking place then between the farmers and workers in the centers of the settlement, in Petah Tikvah, Rishon le-Tsiyon and Rehovot. And when he was older, this would happen with the youth of the groups in the valleys and the Falilee. Who still knew, like him, to glean from the sands of difficult life the gold of the vision and from the thorns to gather the refined honey nectar of love. This was just like Rabbi Meir, who revealed from under the peel that was rough and tough the seeds of the inside.

*[Page 229]*

The book "First Ones" reveals the scroll of the life of our author, who testified about himself: "I never knew a greater happiness than this time when one's hands didn't listen to your wish of serving the food to the mouth after a day of vigorous work...And when the day will come and my hand will not be able to shear more than one ewe a day, I will not give up shearing one...Let one innocent ewe, who is compared to the Congregation of Israel, walk after being sheared by my hand, which when I was a youth tied itself with all the strands of its soul to these clumps of earth and to this land, the land of the country of birth" (from a letter).

Mosheh Stavi (Stavski) was rooted in the town of his birth Antopol, which was the source of his inspiration in its workers, simple people, and their customs in which he saw and fixed his world. He gathered from this source a full handful of statements about the Jewish milieu that he melted into the melting pot of his literary work. From it went out shining pearls of the soul of the people, which he engraved on fine silk strings. Antopol was sanctified to him. He saw in it the reflection of the Jew in the Exile and he devoted the best of his works to it (from the introduction to "Be-arov Yom", or "As the Day Goes on to Evening")

The memories of Antopol accompanied him until his last day and he wanted to memorialize them in a memorial for the town. Therefore, he worked and got people from the town to work in Israel and abroad to put out a memorial book for Antopol. And he himself wrote some chapters for the book from the history of his life and literary work.

Mosheh Stavi (originally Stavski) was born 1884 (1 Adar 644) in the town of Antopol (Polesia). In the late 1890s, he went to live with his father in Kremtsug to help in the grain business. In doing business, he went through most of the Russian cities in the south, and finally he came in 1904 to Aleksandrov, near the German border. It was in this place that he began to write his first stories in Yiddish. From 1907, he lived and wrote in Warsaw. There he met his wife and in 1911 they went together to Israel.

Until the outbreak of World War I, he lived in Tel Aviv and was active in literature, journalism, and also office work (in the Herzelia Gymnasium).

With the outbreak of war, he went to work as a farmer and watchman in Beer Tuviyah, Ben Shemen, and Petah Tikvah. In 1922 he returned to Tel Aviv and set up a milk farm on Mendele Street until 1929. In 1930-1932, he made a trip to cities and towns in Poland to promote the Hebrew book. When he returned from the trip, he lived in Tel Aviv until his death in 1964 at the age of 80. He was buried in Binyaminah.

Stavi began to write in Yiddish and continued in it for many years. He only passed over to Hebrew slowly in Israel. His first stories were translated from Yiddish into Hebrew. Among them is his famous story "Lavan ha-Arami", or "Laban the Aramean".

He increased more strongly and expanded the scope of the animal and nature stories that he began to write in the Exile in a foreign landscape in the landscape of Israel that he loved. The collections of his famous stories include Ha-Boker (At Dawn), Sefer ha-Behemot (Animal Book), Yedidim Ilmim (Mute Friends), Ha-Kefar ha-Aravi (The Arab Village), Be-Derekh le-Erets ha-Osher (On the Way to the Happy Land), Be-Arov Yom (As the Day Went on to Evening), and Ha-Zorim be-Dimah (Those that Plant with Tears). When he was around all his days in a village and working environment, he worked in his old age on linguistic research and terminology for nature and work. As a result of this research, he published his books: Pirke Teva ve-Lashon (Chapters on Nature and Language) and Geluyot ve-Setumot be-Lashon (Visible and Hidden Things in Language).

*[Page 230]*

Stavi loved three things with all his soul and power: Antopol, his hometown, his dumb animal friends, and the Land of Israel, which was for him his natural homeland. Stavi put down roots in this land. From it, there grew the author, Mosheh Stavi, who gave expression to us of its crop, and fed us from its fruits, and made us full of its goodness.


# The Land of Nature and Animal Life in the Exile

Antopol from which Stavi got his types at the beginning of his way in the Exile, was one of the few Jewish towns in the Diaspora in which the Jews were agricultural workers and raised domestic and other animals. It was from this town of birth that he got the inspiration to describe and set up the domestic animals, the household implements and everything concerning village life at home and in the field. Stavi loved animals, specifically, the cow; the horse, the dog, and the chicken are always found in the center of the picture. This is while other types from the world of the wilderness are subordinate to them. As is known, Mendele already put in "Susati" ["My horse"] and other animals to our literature.

However, Stavi did great things by opening for us a window to understand what goes on in the soul of the animals and he made the reader participate in the milieu of their lives and experiences, from which we see clearly that the relations of animals among themselves are just like the relations of humans among themselves.

# The Animal and Natural World in Israel

Stavi's power is not only to describe spiritual conditions that excite. He also describes peaceful pastoral conditions. Here is a description of a night in Israel in one of the days of harvest:

"Somewhere, a cow-finished its second meal, sat down heavily and groaned. Somewhere a horse scratched his hide with his teeth while sleeping standing. And the chains on his neck gave out a ringing sound. Somewhere there was heard the sound of sheep diligently and pleasantly chewing their cud and white foam appeared on their tongues. A big mouse passed by and frightened the chickens. Somewhere at the end of the village a lizard sleepily climbed the fence, moved onto a roof, stirred over the shingles for a moment, passed over the roof, and disappeared on the other side.

Then, there was silence. The dogs had already gotten their first sleep and spread out over the village. One dog went outside the village to listen to what was happening in G-d's world and to see if a wild animal had not sneaked up to the water trough of the well. One dog passed through the courtyard looking at leftovers from today's meal. Another dog joined the watchman making his rounds in the village, following secretly sometimes in front and sometimes behind him. And together with him, he listened silently to the night ("ha-Boker or" E "Before dawn").

" Stavi loved the earth, everything that grew from the earth, the wheat, barley, cauliflower, turnip, and carrot and all that it yielded to its workers. He especially loved the land of Israel. And because of this love, he forecast an abundant crop – the calves who would die until the end of the summer from a lack of pasture in the fields, will not die anymore. Their hides will almost burst from an abundance of fat. Thus, he describes the great abundance, which the work of the Hebrew worker brought forth. However, there is still a long way to go between "the dream of abundance" in the future and the present condition. Stavi was not happy about this and writes:

"In those days, it was before the Jewish settlement was able to raise sheep. The "Valley" didn't exist yet. The isolated attempts to raise sheep in Judah didn't work out well. When I went to work in a group that existed then in Beer Tuviya, the dream of having sheep here was also one of the golden dreams that we would dream in the group. We would dream, consult, speak and argue about in at the evening meal. However, the group split and dispersed and that was the end of the dreams."

*[Page 231]*

Even with the end of the public dream, Stavi didn't give up. He continued to dream his own dream. Certainly, it would not take long to realize it. Meanwhile, he passed a lot of hard changes and moves. From the pruning hook in Petah Tikvah, he became a watchman with a rifle and revolver in Beer Tuviyah. The main thing was to be near to the mother earth, to fulfill in it the commandment of loving one's mother and to diligently guard it until the dream of abundance would take place and become reality.

# The Arab Village

Just as he knew how to describe abundance in the Hebrew village, so Stavi knew to describe the life of want in the Arab village and "the fear of hunger and terror which hovered over the village. The mothers baked bread to use it sparingly over a day or two. In order to save the bread, they put into it excellent and nourishing grasses. They would also divide the bread into quarters, in order to save it. Then, they would give it to their hungry children.

Stavi knew the Arab village well. He knew its people, customs, and manner of speech. He put his knowledge of the Arab way of life and legends into the 2198 book "ha-Kefar ha-Aravi"("The Arab village"). This book tears open a window into the lives of the male Arab and the female Arabs with their many veils. He put down into writing again the legends of the Arabs in his book "Be-derekh lei- Erets ha-osher" ("On the shy to the happy land").

This book is not only a collection of Arab stories and legends for the child. Rather, it for young and old to share together. The stories contain the wisdom of life with an addition of light humor. They are a kind of "Thousand and One Nights" formulated by Stavi. He writes in his introduction to "ha- Kefar ha-Aravi":

"In the Land of the Patriarchs, to which I devoted the best days of my youth, I tasted a second childhood. I absorbed the impressions of this childhood together with the landscape and the nature of life described in it here, from the relations of good neighbors, side by side, furrow next to furrow and plough following plough ... I had to make a comprehensive description of the life of the Arab village in a country very similar to the lives of our ancestors in ancient times. We know still, from the days of the Jewish elementary religious school, about the quarrels of the shepherds of Abraham and Isaac with the shepherds of the foundation of the Arab village. There is no peace and plenty, no life and no fruitfulness without a well.

# Linguistic Research

The linguistic research of Stavi into all that concerns the concepts of the field and everything tied to it is a blessing in itself. Stavi does not come to this area of research as a researcher and linguist, but as one who has contact with the earth and knows and recognizes the land. He explained from his clear understanding of the life of the village and the field some vague sentences. or Biblical and Talmudic expressions, which the commentators had a hard time to explain. In his explanation of "Hatsir gagot"(Grass of the roof) he says:

"The top of the roof is covered with loam and plastered with mud. The thin material is mixed with straw and chaff. All this includes different seeds, which sprout with the first rain and cover the roof with a green covering. This is "Hatsir gagog" ["Grass of the roofs"]. Since the layer of loam and mud plaster is really thin and there is no earth under it to feed the grass, it quickly dries and withers. Psalms compares the wicked to this grass, which withers before the stalk and the stem come out." ("Pirke tevave-lashon," "Chapters from nature and language").

*[Page 232]*

This is the way he does it in his last book "Geluyot u-setumot be-lasaon" ("Things that are clear and obscure in language"). He digs to the source of a saying until he clarifies and explains it appropriately. He does this with articulate observations from the reality of Israeli life. He is so sure of his observations that he takes to task the great people of Hebrew literature and shows their mistakes in nature, animal life, and the processes of work.

Stavi does not respect even our best writers if they didn't pick up what is true to life. He certainly comes and refutes them if he finds a word or expression which is not according to the spirit of the Hebrew language. However, he especially corrected many mistakes in knowledge about the true feelings of animals, which he knew intimately.

This was written according to the article of Akiva Ben-Ezra in the Hadoar, issue 33 from 15 Av 724 (August 1964) and other sources.

# For the Memory of Manan Lifshits Fihanan

## By Rinah Asif

Elhanan Lifshits, the son of Judah and Kiarinah, comes up in my memory from my childhood days as a patron of the youth, as a representative of Hashomer ha-tsair Organization to the Polish government, and as a devoted friend and adviser to all who turned to him. He was an abundantly good-hearted person, a friend and companion to young and old. He would be the first to greet a person and was prepared to help every deprived and poor person. He stood guard and risked his life for the good of the community. It happened more than once that he saved the town from the Petlurav and Belchov rioters during World War I. All the people in the town, both Jews and Christians, respected him.

In World War II when the Russians conquered the region, he was appointed to head the town council. As was always his way, he acted for the public good without getting tired or being afraid. When the conquerors appointed him to divide parts of the forest for the cutting of trees, the gentiles accused him of giving the Jews the best part and that he was a bourgeoisie class and a kulak. They obtained the signatures of the inhabitants of the surrounding villages.

The authorities took him out at night and sent him to Siberia. He passed all the seven departments of Hell: hunger, disease, bodily and spiritual degeneration. He made this passage as a person alone, with all of his family remaining in Antopol. His stories about that period cause the hairs of one's head to stand up. He held himself up and passed all the sufferings, which gave their signs on his body and health, but not his spirit.

He arrived in Israel in 1951. The people from his town, his family in Israel, and especially his sister, Hadasah, received him with love. His sister took care of him like a mother, and he began to return to his strength.

He didn't want to be a burden to anyone. He searched and found work fit for his being an elderly person as a guard in the Alskor factory in Tel Aviv. He recovered and his will to live returned to him. When people visited him at work, which was not according to his previous status, he was proud that he was working and useful. He took care of himself and met with the people of the town, friends and relatives who respected him. As he was accustomed to doing, he became interested in community service. The first assembly of the community in which he lived and worked was held at his initiative. People founded the Organization of the former inhabitants of Antopol, now living in Israel, at this meeting.

There were accepted at the first meeting proposals and decisions to memorialize our martyrs, to publish a memorial book, and to erect a synagogue in their memory. There were divisions of opinion regarding erecting a synagogue or other institution. It was decided under the influence of Elhanan, of blessed memory, to erect a synagogue in memory of the martyrs. His points were that all the days of the people of the community were spent in the synagogue, in which they poured their soul and bitterness of their heart. The synagogue was their fortress and refuge. They drew comfort and strength to continue to live and to hope for a better fixture.

*[Page 233]*

The organization had ties with former inhabitants of Antopol abroad, especially, in the United States. Elhanan sent letters, answered replies, gave reasons until he received promises that they would give us aid. He took care and worked during the heat and rain. He ran about, influenced and directed. They laid the corner stone for the synagogue in 1956. How his face shone! Such happiness and joy filled him that his desires were going to be realized. On that occasion, he said to us, "If G-d wills and we will be able to erect this monument and I will see the synagogue established with my own eyes, then I will be able to die in peace.

The synagogue was magnificently built. However, Elhanan, of blessed memory, wasn't able to dedicate it. He fell down and expired in purity on the anniversary of the death of his mother Karinah, a distinguished woman, a patron, of the orphanage, as he was saying the kaddish for her.

We continued and carried out his will. The years of effort and struggle continued. We are happy in what we were able to accomplish. The magnificent building is standing on its foundation as an honor, glory, and memorial to the names of our dear ones.

We would not fulfill our responsibility if we didn't mention his sister, Hadasah Glazer, of the Lifshits family. The fact is that she and her husband received their brother with boundless love and devotion. Their care returned to him the will live and to feel important again.

Life was cruel to Hadasah and Noah. They had two children die and they remained childless. All of their life in Israel was a continual struggle for a hard existence with weak health. Despite everything, she didn't complain about the bitterness of her fate and was active and interested in all the activities of the organization. She didn't miss a meeting or memorial. She was interested in the welfare of the members of the organization and gave contributions beyond her ability.

# R. Avraham Yitshak Weinstein, of Blessed Memory,
## the Man from Poloshin
### By Yaakov Rimon

He was born in Antopol and was a farmer all his life. However, he longed for the day when he could immigrate to Israel and participate himself in bringing to life its desolate land. This desire was realized when he and his wife immigrated from Antopol to the Sheinkin neighborhood near Tel Aviv, with the help of his children in the United States. They settled on land that was prepared for them ahead of time. The inhabitants of the neighborhood remember until this day the cabin that stood at the top of the hill and the piece of land around It planted with vegetables. It was exciting to see the old couple working their farm, in the stable and the chicken coop when their eyes shone from happiness that they were able to settle in their old age on the land of their ancestors.

R. Avraham Yitshak used to walk on the Sabbaths to the nearest neighborhood to complete a prayer quorum. It was a pleasure to him to help establish a prayer quorum in the Jewish neighborhood. At the end of his life he was able to move to Kefar ha-roeh. There his happiness was complete, because he was able to live in a village of pious people. When his modest wife died, he became increasingly lonely. His children put him into an old age home in Jerusalem. He was happy again to live out his last days in the eternal city. The deceased was the son-in-law of Rabbi Shelomoh Fridman, of blessed memory. He left behind two children. One of them, Mr. Joseph Barukh Weinstein, was the secretary of the municipal department of health of Tel Aviv.

*[Page 234]*

The memory of this capable and innocent man, who served G-d in the Holy Land will remain engraved in the hearts of all who knew and cherished him. R. Barukh Yosef Weinstein from Poloshin was the head of the family. R. Avraham Yitshak and his wife Sarah Hindah lived in Israel during their last years and took care of a farm. They died in a good old age in the Sheinkin neighborhood near Tel Aviv.

# R. Avigdor B. R. Yosef, the Mason
## By Shmuel Dov Hayyim Kris

The town of Antopol did not only issue scholars, rabbis and luminaries who enlightened the world with Torah, both in the town and also in other cities. It also put forth honest merchants and laborers who were Jewish. They were simple and innocent in a period when many families related to physical work with contempt. These laborers were also pious with all their heart and full of love for the Creator of the world and for His people Israel.

One of these laborers was R. Avigdor b. R. Yosef, of blessed memory, who was the mason. He was an oven builder who was the son of an oven builder. He chose this work, because in Russia it is possible to devote oneself to it half a year and spend the other half a year with G-d. He would work in the summer and support himself. When the building season was over in the winter, he would sit in the study hall and study with the righteous person of the generation, R. Pinchas Michael. However, he would also not pass up the midnight prayer in the summer and the shedding of tears for the destruction of the Temple and Jerusalem.

He would always make due with little. He would save from his salary to buy a farm in Israel, where he could walk on the land that Abraham, Isaac, and Jacob walked. Meanwhile, he raised a family and educated two sons and three daughters. He built himself his own house and lived in honor among his brethren in Antopol.

However, he packed all his belongings and moved with the whole family in 1910 to Israel. Here he bought a plot of land near Tel Aviv. He built a house on it. He and his son Nahum would go out every day to work in the small town of Tel Aviv. Testimonies to their work remain today in the porches and fences from that time.

His wife Lenah Feigel was a proper daughter of Israel and a woman of valor. She did not rely on the acts of charity of her husband and would also donate according to all her means. She would pray three times a day from the prayer book, Korban Minhah Gadol, with the translation from Hebrew into Yiddish.

She would get up early in the morning to bake bread in the oven, which her husband built. She worked with her weak strength and with the small income which her husband brought home to maintain the household. They were a symbol to the honest and faithful people of Antopol.

During World War I, Avigdor and his son Nahum worked for the contractor Wolfson to build fortifications for the Turkish government in Beersheba. When Beersheba was bombed, R. Avigdor was wounded. He died two days later in the Hebrew month of Tevet (1917). His wife Lenah Feigel died a year afterwards.

# Tsevi Volodovski, of Blessed Memory
## By Miriam Volodovski

I lost my husband, friend of my youth, the man dearest to me of all. He was an exalted person. He fled honor and hated ill-gotten gains. He was humble and modest, pure in spirit and innocent. He loved nature, the land, and art.

Tsevi Volodovski was born in Homsk, Grodno province. His father sent him to business school in Brest-Litovsk, with the hope that after finishing his studies he would devote himself to business. However, he was an artist in all his soul and devoted himself more to painting. When he finished his studies in school, he sent his paintings to the Academy of Art in Cracow. He was accepted there as a student.

*[Page 235]*

In 1914, when World War I broke out and the Germans conquered Poland, he immigrated to the Ukraine with his family. The Revolution and the pogroms, which he put on canvas in his paintings, passed over him there.

In 1921, after he was already married, he returned to Poland and worked as a teacher in schools in Pinsk. In 1925, he immigrated to Israel and entered to study in the Art school Retsalel in Jerusalem. In 1931 he went to Kefar Saba.

He had a wonderful mix of a multi-talented artist – he played music, painted, sculpted, put on plays, and wrote songs, some of which became folk songs outside Israel. He didn't skip work, even when he was sick, even on the last day before he died. May his memory be blessed!

# In Memory of Frumah Ben Tsevi of the Fridman Family
## By Yosef Pen Tsevi

Frumah was born in Antopol to her parents Feigl and Joseph Fridman. They belonged to a large, broad, and honorable family. The children Ezra and Leibl live in the United States while the parents and their children Sheinah, Yentah, Shemuel, Eanah and their families were destroyed in the Holocaust.

Frumah immigrated to Israel in 1936. She married Yosef Ben Tsevi, gave birth to a son and daughter and was an exemplary wife and mother to them. She was beloved and honored by her family, the people from Antopol, and all her acquaintances and people, who esteemed her. She died in 1951 but her blessed memory will live in our midst forever.

# Zaidel (Yehudah) Barshavitski, of Blessed Memory
## (1908-1963)
## By Rinah Osip

Zaidel grew up in a house of Jewish workers, honest and good-hearted people. He helped his father from a young age in the blacksmith shop. However, his heart drew him more to agriculture and he would farm himself their piece of land. He joined the ranks of Freyheyt and he-Halhuts. He became an activist. He always wore an embroidered Russian shirt. There was always a laugh on his face. His eyes showed good heartedness and devotion to his fellow man.

He came to Israel in 1934, after he passed his training in Poland. He was distinguished as one of the best workers. He had a Jewish heart and gentle hands. He was accepted as a worker in a flourmill. He worked patiently and he would put on his shoulders very heavy sacks of flour that were for him the weight of a feather. He added honor and respect to the Jewish worker.

In Israel, he joined the deeply devoted members of Kibbutz Dafnah. No work was difficult for Zaidel who was always healthy and in love with life. His kibbutz was on the Syrian Lebanese border. He would plow on the tractor always with a rifle at his side. He didn't complain even once. He would always care for his fellow man and was tirelessly devoted to his wife and two daughters.

When we last met at Kibbutz Givat ha-sheloshah at the bar mitzvah of his sister's son, he said, "I didn't sleep one night without the rifle at my side."

We left him with the idea of meeting at the wedding of his eldest daughter Sarah. He died one week before the wedding. He, who may be compared to a strong tree, died on his watch, the dear son of our town and agricultural worker, at the side of the tractor which he loved so much.

Esteemed Zaidel, your memory will be kept with us forever.

[Page 236]

# My Wife Vardah, of Blessed Memory
## By Mikhael Kusht

I knew her from her youth in our town of Antopol. She was a daughter in a family that knew want and need. However, her parents knew to give their four daughters an excellent education in the Tarbut and Polish schools in town. The sisters were also active in the youth movement of those days.

When I went to Israel, Vardah was a girl, a student in school. When years passed and I visited town again, I already met her as a young adult. We decided to get married and raise a family. Vardah succeeded in leaving Poland for Israel a few days before the German invasion in 1939.

We built our family during a stormy period followed by one full of action. First we began with the fear of World War II and the Holocaust. This was followed by the struggle against the Mandate Government and the Var for Independence. I was absent a lot from home. The children were little. Vardah, like a typical Jewish mother, devoted her life with great love and continual worry over their health and success.

She stood at my side faithfully during all the changes and struggles in the daily reality of our farming community. This was especially true even in the worst of times. When things improved, we made a determined cooperative effort to build a new farm and group in Kibbutz Yifat.

Vardah was devoted to the cooperative effort. She instinctively loved children and found great satisfaction and substance in her life by continually working with the young. She was full of energy and love for life.

She knew how to have sincere relations and friendships. She took an active part in social events especially in readings. Her life was full and complete, especially with the marriages of our daughters (Nitsah and Leah) and the birth of grandchildren. Such contentment is all that simple people wish.

Fate wanted something else. During the Six Day War, perhaps from a desperate jump into a shelter ditch during an alert, she began to suffer from back and leg pains. There followed a long chapter of examinations and hospitalization until she suffered an unsuccessful operation on her spine. Despite her suffering, she continued to struggle with great effort and strength of spirit.

May her memory be blessed!

# Belah Libenfroind – Kletski
## By G. Nahmani

She died in the middle of her life when she was still thirsty for life, knowledge and activity. All her life was a chain of bettering herself. She didn't make due with her high education and sought to deepen her knowledge and to expand her horizons. She was born into an esteemed Zionist family in Antopol, in Polish Polesia. While she was still young she excelled in her studies and after she finished the gymnasium, she completed a course in pharmacy and attained good results despite difficulties. This was the anti-Semitism that Jewish graduates faced in Poland.

When World War II broke out, her family was broken and split up seeking to save itself. And she, Belah Kletski, wound up alone in Russia. She struggled with the difficult life that was prevalent then in Russian. However, thanks to her profession, she managed to overcome the obstacles and to find a place for herself. When the war ended, she hoped still to find her family or survivors from it. However, all of them died in the Holocaust and she was alone. She left the tragic place and wanted to go to Israel where her only brother lived as a teacher. After difficult attempts to reach Israel in the days of the Bevin government, she managed to come to Israel a little before the establishment of the State. After struggles to find a place and get used to things, she came to peace and established a family of her own. As she was a wise and sociable person, many people liked her and she had a big circle of friends.

*[Page 237]*

However when she was at the high point of her life, occupation and achievements, she got a mortal disease and passed away to the sadness of her family, friends, and many people who esteemed her.

# Naftali Volinots, of Blessed Memory
## By Ester Ton (Volinots)

Just like in the children's legend of a person who goes to the bottom of a well and finds there a different world of wonders, so I sink into the recesses of my childhood to find a world of innocence, purity, love, happiness, and beauty. This legend is not topped by a crown. There is only the yellow sand around a big wooden cabin divided in two. The first part has two rooms with a concrete floor. The second part is bigger and lacks a floor. A carpenter's table stands there and doors and windows, which have not been finished are set against the walls. I see my father standing by the carpenter's table and the sound of the saw seems like a choir singing.

There were mornings when I woke up and the carpentry shop had become a dormitory. The doors that stood against the wall had become beds. Mattresses were put on them and guests were sleeping there. These were guests, newly arrived to Israel from Antopol, who had come for the night. They found lodging in the cabin that was our home. It became their house until they made arrangements for themselves. It was natural for my father to find them work although it was hard to get work and housing in those days.

It always seemed that the door of the wooden cabin was waiting for people to enter it. They brought happiness and hope to the house. Their shared conversation them filled the cabin with the clear air of faith and hope for the nation and the individual, which their spirit of pioneering brought and then blew into our hearts.

Not only the carpentry served as a hotel for guests. When I came home, I would also find that the furniture in our small living room had been moved. And in a corner stood an infant's bed. What good fortune! A child was born to a couple from Antopol. However, they had no living quarter to which to bring their infant. So a room was made and their was a place for both the young parents and their infant. The infant brought much joy to the cabin.

There was no time when the living space was too small for the people in the household , the parents, their five children, and the guests, who were considered like members of the family.

My father was full of love for every living creature. He built a birdhouse for doves near our cabin. Once a cat sneaked into the birdhouse and killed a dove. My father was angry and threw a rock at it to chase it away. The cat collapsed and my father's face became immediately pale. And he said to my mother, "Who should be separated from a long life? Go to see if the cat is still alive?!"

I remember the Sabbaths of the summer. Clean sand was spread on the floor of the carpentry shop. We children sat on the floor. Our fingers drew pictures in the yellow sand and our ears listened to father read from the weekly portion of the Torah.

At the Sabbath table when the newspaper was in his hand, father and his friend Alter would talk about the big problems of the world. Alter was like a member of the family until he went to live in Jerusalem after his marriage.

The ideals of returning to Zion and deep faith in our destiny lived in the innocence of my father's soul. I remember how happy my father was when the wharf in Tel Aviv was erected during the Arab riots of 1936. Then, he prophesized that there was still for us a great future ahead in Israel. My father was attached with love for Israel. He didn't want to leave it, even in the difficult times. When he was first in Israel, his sisters in the United States sent him all the necessary documents with money, so that it would be possible for him to immigrate to the United States.

*[Page 238]*

He returned to them everything that they had sent and informed them that he would never leave Israel. When our brother, Nahum, of blessed memory, fell in the Arab riots of 1939, he told me, "Don't cry; he fell for the motherland!" I saw my father many months later holding a child's tooth that had fallen from Nahum in his childhood. He was looking at it and crying.

After all this, the innocence, faith, and optimism that were fundamental to his nature, didn't end. Even when he was in the sickbed in the Hadasah hospital, about a year and a half after Nahum fell, father said, "There is a great future in Israel. Medicine in Israel will some day be the best in the world and bring healing to the world.

Father dealt straightforwardly with others, "And you should love your neighbor as yourself with all your might and all your soul." Where did my father get his innocence and purity? Is it not the same source from which also drew those good people from Antopol, the friends of our family?

Purity, love and the warmth of eternal life, these things continue to flourish in the legends that feed the soul of mankind and all life. The source of the legend grew in the distant mists of the town of Antopol. The legend is in the personality of my father's mother, Goldah, who died early in life. At that time my father was a small child and his sister Tsirel was younger than him. My father had a marvelous love for his sister Tsirel, who immigrated to the United States. This was based on the longings of love for his mother and the softness of mercy for an orphaned sister without her mother's love. And his sister Tsirel knew how to return this love.

All this became a legend of a distant tune, lost in the mists of the horizon, when they were to be seen orphaned, lost, and confused in Antopol and lost and confused. They held each other hand in hand and supported one another.

A seven-fold wonder was revealed to me in my first meeting with Goldah, the daughter of Tsirel, the sister of our father, who was born in the United States and named after my grandmother Goldah. Despite the distance of our countries, a different education and a different culture, despite the fact that we didn't know her mother and she didn't know our father, we shared the stories about the depths of love that the brother and sister drew out from themselves. And we shared the legend of the innocence, love for every creature, love for life and modesty that grew up in distant times and land, when the seed was implanted in the place called Antopol. Goldah even painted this legend. She called the picture Antopol.

# In Memory of Our Sons, Who Fell in Combat
## By Vardah Koshet

In memory of our sons,
whom we will not meet more,
in any place.
Because their life has stopped,And all their beauty has been hidden, And the bereaved remain.
We remember the young springs,the shining growth, the happiness that makes the heart rejoiceand hopes that soar to the heavensNow there remains the glory of death and destruction.
Tell, why do we need to smile

*[Page 239]*

When our heart inside is exploding?
Why do we need to be silent
When everything is shouting until the end of our strength?
It is necessary to swallowTo swallow until the end of the cup of poison.
It is necessary to stop speaking about the pastAnd the present is foggy and unclear.
Something great has disappeared and its name is life.In it there is an unknown substance,Something not anticipated.
This is what life compelsTo walk further on the plowed path.
To continue, so that you may press olives And to hope for a better daythat will follow.
Because after the night A new morning breaks outFor the creation that awakes.

# To Our Son, Mezer Shahor,
# of Blessed Memory,
## Who Fell With Bravery in the War for Independence,
## at Shaar ha-gai, in Defense of the Old City of Jerusalem
## By his mother, Fridah Shahor

My dear son Eliezer,

I took upon myself the very difficult goal of writing some lines about you after your death. May you rest in paradise. We should not complain. The Creator of the world leads His world and we should not ask questions.

My dear son! You are my right hand, my teacher and rabbi for good qualities and deeds. You were taken from us at the time when you hurried to give First Aid to a soldier at the time of the Battle of Shaar ha-Gai in May of 1948 (4 Iyar 708).

In the act of doing this humanitarian deed, the arrow of the enemy struck your pure heart and ended your life forever. This good heart of yours, which always beat and worried only to act good towards your fellow man, has stopped.

When you were five and your brother David, may he live, was three and a half, he would be wild and I would want to punish him. Then, you protected him with your body and said to me, "Mother, strike me.

When you strike him, I feel hurt. And when you strike me, I don't feel hurt..."

When you were about six and your brother David was about four, you used to go with him to the beach and watch carefully and not let him put his hand out of the bus window. When our old relative Mrs. Rozenblum saw what you did, she was so astonished that she came up to you and asked who you were. This was before she recognized you. And when she heard your name, she came to us and proudly told us what sort of a child you were.

When you were seven , you went by yourself to the dentist, because your mother was busy. When you came and saw that no patients were waiting in line, you spoke your heart to the dentist and said to her, "Don't worry, today is Friday and no one has the time to go to the dentist. You will still get work."

At about the same age, you once came home from the Bilu School and came up to me with tears in your eyes saying, "Mother! Do you know that my teacher apparently doesn't earn enough money and it is necessary to take care that he receives a raise." "Why," I asked. You told me that you paid attention during the break and when all the teachers were eating a rich meal of rolls with butter, your teacher was just eating a roll without any spread. This was because he didn't have enough money to live. Thus from your childhood you cared only for your fellow man.

*[Page 240]*

# The Dear and Unforgettable Frumah Ben Tsevi
## By Rinah and Hayyim Osip

It has been twenty years since she died. However, it is just as if she stands alive in front of us, goodhearted, with her house open to all those coming from Antopol and Kobrin, the city, where your husband was born.

The day in which Tel Aviv was bombed is unforgettable. The cabins around us in the Nordiyah neighborhood were hit. You put your life in danger when you were in the young days of your life. You visited the burning cabins to see whether or not we had been hit. It was as if an angel from heaven came to visit us. The moment in which you entered will not leave our minds.

You died young and left an orphaned family, a loving and devoted husband, young children, friends, and everything dear to you. And you loved life so much. We will not forget ,you, our dear friend, Frumah. May your memory be blessed!

# Berish Dov Matolski, of Blessed Memory:
## Sketches of the Mother of the Family
## By Malkah Yentah Shvarts, her daughter

Our mother was born in Antopol, in the year of 1880 (the third candle lighting of Hanukah), to her mother Raizl and her father R . Berish Dov. She died in Tel Aviv on Wednesday, 7th of Iyyar 730. She lived 89 years.

Her father R. Berish Dov was a Torah scholar, knowledgeable in books, wise, with an analytical mind, religious in his faith and just In his actions. Many people rose early to his door to ask advice and help. The grandmother of our mother was also famous for her wisdom and knowledge. She had a religious elementary school for girls in which they studied Torah, writing, laws, and prayers.

The family had a lot of children and lived poorly. Despite this, R. Berish was always ready to give. Our mother continued in this manner as those who preceded her from her glorious lineage. She had a hard childhood. When she was still young, her mother died and she was forced to go to work to help her family. She married our father R. Yaakov- Yosef Shvarts, of blessed memory, when she was very young. His place of origin was from the small village of Osah near to Divin (the forests of Polesia). This region was mainly Christian, with only a few isolated Jewish families.

Our father was the scion of a family of rabbis, scholars, and honorable Hasidim. After the wedding, they went to Warsaw. There were born to them seven sons (today four sons remain alive: Yitshak, , Yerahmiel, and Avraham). After living in Warsaw nearly 40 years, the family went to live in Israel in 1925.

It took a long time until we settled in and got a place to live worthy of its name. After wandering from. one place to another to live: a room rented from an Arab on the border of Tel Aviv, a cabin with the first settlers on the dunes of Bat-Yam. Meanwhile, during the struggle for existence and the struggles of the bloody events of 1925, 1929, 1930, our father died. We moved to an apartment in Yad Eliyahu and finally to a big apartment on 1 King Solomon St., Tel Aviv.

However, to our disappointment, our mother was not able to benefit from this apartment for a long time. Our father died at a relatively young age of 59. He was a clever and good-hearted person, very honest, loving people and also animals. However, his love for his children didn't know any boundaries. Our mother became a widow when she was still 55. She overcame the bitter disaster and continued to run the house and educate the children in a good way. She was a widow for about thirty-four years of her life. And even though she received honorable proposals for marriage, she rejected them, because she wanted to keep her connection with her children. She never bothered with matters that didn't concern her and she never expressed an opinion that was out of place. She had the understanding to adjust herself to a new period and to understand the new wind blowing. This didn't prevent her from being deeply religious with the commandments of the Torah lighting up her way. These two poles were mixed in her personality. Our mother was a diligent woman, wise and pleasant. She took care to be clean wear clean clothes. She was tall and her face expressed understanding and authority.

*[Page 241]*

The house was warm and open to every needy person. Our mother was respected by all the family and by her friends and acquaintances. During the bad times and disasters, which visited her (first the death of her husband and then of her first-born son Mosheh Dov, of blessed memory) she stood strong and didn't surrender.

People say that our mother died in good old age. However, a vacuum entered the house when she died. Everything which we absorbed and swallowed in the light of her image remained forever within us. Her will to live was strong and she continued to fight with the Angel of Death with all her strength until the last moment. She commanded and instructed how to act after her death with clarity and astonishing logic. We honored her. However, her friends and acquaintances honored her more. They saw the wonderful thing in her, her wisdom, her glory, and her cleverness. Both the old and new generations were folded into her life.

A big crowd attended both her funeral and the ceremony of the unveiling of her monument on the thirtieth day after her death. They remembered during these two times her generous qualities and her personality. Rabbi Yedidyah Frankel, Rabbi Isar Frankel, and Mr. Zalman Shahor gave the eulogies. Binyamin Unger, the head cantor said the prayer.

# Nahum Volinets, of Blessed Memory

Nahum, of blessed memory, died before he was very old. He was tall like a pine tree and his spirit wanted to grow. It hadn't finished its development. He was handsome, good-natured, full of humor, and full of the happiness of youth. He was generous and loved to help with the housework. When he was a child, he would run towards his mother and take the basket that she was carrying from the market.

His generosity and love to help his fellow man pushed him to fill a required position in the defense. Who knows if he was then active in the Haganah? Who knows that he was a guard in Ramat ha- Kovesh, which was a point of attack by Arab gangs?

And on the last night, the night of the 24th of January 1940 (Tevet 699) when the took the place of a friend to guard a neighborhood on the edge of Tel Aviv, who knew this?

He died at his post in defense of the nation. This happened before he was fully-grown. Who is able to utter and enumerate the praiseworthy results of his generous soul which should have had the fortune to grow up and have a long life? He was good hearted, honest, and generous beyond all measure. How much happiness could he have poured out on his fellow men as a son, brother, husband, and father?

And he sacrificed all this on the altar of defense of his homeland. His sacrifice was accepted like the sacrifices of many others, whose memory is in our lives, which grew out of their sacrifice and the pain over the victim, who and did not have a chance to live. It is always tied up in the knot of our life. May his memory be blessed in the blessed life for which he gave his life.

*[Page 242]*

# Yehudah Slonimski

He was the son of Alter-Binyamln Tsevi and Ahuvah. He was born in January 1927 in Tel Aviv. When he was one year old, his parents moved to Jerusalem. He was educated in an elementary Jewish religious school and continued his studies in a rabbinical seminary in Rehovot. He began to seek work at a young age, so that he could ease up a little the poverty at home. He learned to polish diamonds in Netanyah. He worked in Peri-mazon (Fruit and Food). He served a year in the Palmah in Givat Brener. He returned to Jerusalem, where he worked in construction and gave all his salary to his parents. He joined the underground movement, Etsel. He participated in actions and was jailed in Latrun. When he was absent, the poverty increased at home. He was aware that his duty was to his homeland, which took precedence to that towards his parents. He returned immediately to underground actions after being freed. However, he asked for and received some small support for his mother.

When the War for Independence broke out, he participated in Tsahal in the framework of Etsel and participated in the battles for Sheikh-Jarah, Har Tsiyon, and in the well-known battle to defend Ramat Rahel. As a saboteur, he marched at the head of the conquerors of the village of Malhah. He was also the first to fall in conquering the village on July 14, 1948. His fiance, Pat Sheva Yom Tov, also a member of Etsel was killed two days after he died on guard in the north of Jerusalem. He was buried in Sheikh on Adar 1, then reburied on September 10, 1950 on Mt. Herzl in Jerusalem.

# Avraham Kotler

He was born in Argentina on December 21, 1931.

He entered the service of ha- Shomer ha-Tsair at a very young age. He received there his first pioneering education. He immigrated to Israel in 1954 together with his group. They were immediately absorbed into the Kibutz Revadim in the northern Negev.

After a short time, he was drafted into Tsahal and served the Nahal. He was killed by Egyptians in an incident on the border at Kisufim on April 4, 1956, two weeks before his release from service. Avraham Kotler was the grandchild of Aryeh Osipovits, who was born to his father Tsevi and to his mother Esther Kotler, who was born in Antopol. May his memory be blessed!

# The United States, Dr. Fabius Feitil Berman
## By A. Ben-Ezra

Dr. Fabius (Feitil) Berman was one of the shining stars in the skies of America. He was born in Antopol and was full of the spirit of Antopol until his death. Dr. Berman, who was called Feitil in our town, was born in 1890 in Antopol and died in 1967 in the United States.

His father was Rabbi Mosheh Berman. As fitting to the son of a rabbi, he received a rigorous religious education from the best teachers in Antopol. At a young age, Feitil went to Ruzshini, his fathers' place of birth, to study in its well-known rabbinical seminary. After that, he studied two years in Yanove in a seminary, not far from Antopol.

The young man was not satisfied with Talmud and rabbinical legal authorities. He began to look at books in Hebrew and Russian. He traveled to Pinsk as a result of his great thirst for education. There he studied in the local gymnasium. He finished his studies with excellence and returned to his city of Antopol. He began to study Russian and general sciences.

Feitil was active in the socialist movement, which was well organized in Antopol, together with his profession of teaching. His stormy nature and his thirst for learning brought him to the United States in 1913.

He already entered to study in the University of Southern California in Los Arigales in 1916. He was also excellent in his studies there. He received a gold medal and a stipend to cover his tuition.

*[Page 243]*

He received the title of Doctor of Medicine in 1919. He fully devoted himself to his subject. He was appointed in 1929 as administrator of the regional hospital in Los Angeles, one of the biggest hospitals in the United States. He continued to lecture in the university in which he had studied, together with his appointment as hospital administrator. The hospital grew under his leadership from 1,000 to 3,800 beds and more than 100,000 patients a year.

He saved the hospital a lot of money with his effective leadership. Some of his discoveries and inventions are used in the field of medicine throughout the world. He retired in 1956 and devoted himself to various activities. However, he continued to be connected with the medical staff and also with everything concerning Judaism and Hebrew.

Dr. Berman was one of the most active when the idea was born to put out a memorial book as a literary monument to our community. He devoted himself to the work with youthful energy. He himself also made a big contribution and also got others to contribute to publish the book. His literary contribution, in the form of articles to the memorial book, is full of deep love for the town of his birth. His wife Mashe (the daughter of Yudel the writer), had a big part in his success in everything which he did. The poet, Pintshe Berman, was his brother, and cooperated with Feitil in communal work. Unfortunately, he didn't live to see the publication of the memorial book. However, his memory will accompany us forever.

# Leibl Valovalski
## By P. Czerniak

The family Valovalski left their house in Antopol on Grushvah Street in 1927, after World War I. The parents with two daughters and two sons came to New York. The elder of the sons was Leibl. He was then in his twenties. He was full of life and plans and memories from the town and people who he had left.

Leibl was a young intellectual, well educated, organized, and very devoted to these things in his life: his family, his town, Judaism, Zionism in general, and the State of Israel after its establishment.

Leibl was especially able to serve as an example to the youth of Antopol, with his goals for advancement and wanting to rise on the ladder of life in the United States. In the process of this, others also grew up as representatives of Antopol, acting on its behalf and for its sake in every place of their dispersion.

As he was the oldest brother, Leibl took care to set up the family in the United States. The family arrived without any experience on how to establish in the United States and, after his parents died, he took over these duties himself. He helped his sisters and younger brother arrange themselves in life and set up families. However, he didn't have time for himself and he left taking care of his own matters to last. Thus, he remained alone all his life. When his sisters and brother left home, Leibl got himself his own apartment. He dealt in business, so that he could work for himself and help, according to his ability, to establish those goals that were important to him.

The second goal in his life was the city of Antopol and its problems. Before World War II, his parent's house was a center for actions on behalf of the orphanage, the Tarbut school, the Library in the name of Perets, the bathhouse, the ice storage and similar institutions of the town. He kept an ear open to listen to the individual requests of people from Antopol, who saw in the United States a financial power able to spread out dollars to needy people. Libel's house was the address for a widow, who didn't have a place to live, and for an old man who didn't have money to live.'

After World War II and the destruction, he began to work to memorialize the community and its people. He was active in setting up monuments to the murdered people in cemeteries in New York and beginning in 1954 this monument in writing to the town and its inhabitants.

*[Page 244]*

At the beginning of 1953, a group of people from Antopol gathered in a Tel Aviv coffee house on the corner of Frishman and King Solomon streets, with Mr. Stavi, Osip, Elfandshtein, Lifshits, and Tserikover.

They decided to begin the work of gathering material and support to publish a memorial book for Antopol. With the help of Mr. Akiva ben Ezra, who published the book on Horodets, we turned to the United States and there organized the committee for the memorial book. Leibl headed the committee. Being steadfast, energetic, and stubborn, the committee began to collect money and the appointed editor began to collect literary material. Then, we sat and wrote a constitution and chapter headings for this book. In 1966 when I returned from a trip to the Far East, I stopped in New York for a number of days. There took place a discussion and arrangement of the literary material with Leibl and the rest of the members of the book committee. Leibl didn't agree then to spend more than necessary to publish the book. He took good care of the money and trembled at spending every penny of the public money. Each penny was as precious to him as if it were double. Certainly, this approach, perhaps too miserly, interfered with getting on in summarizing the effort.

In 1968, they passed over to Israel the material and the money for the final publication of the book. When I visited Leibl in New York for the last time, I found him old and weak. He still wanted to continue to devote much of his thoughts and his time to the history of Antopol and cared for what happened to the money and material that he had sent over. I always felt him to be a true person of Jewish culture, an honest man, faithful to the beautiful ideals of the Lithuanians from his time.

He had a third goal in his life. This was his activity on behalf of Judaism, Zionism, and Israel. He cooperated with and helped many philanthropic organizations of Jewry in the United States, beginning with the Joint and finishing with local organizations of mutual help. He was a contact person and collected money for the Jewish Foundation Fund and the Jewish National Fund. In later years, he gave money and got others to give money for Israel Bonds. In recognition of his help, he received a number of excellence awards and letters of esteem from the administrators of the philanthropic organizations. However, Leibl didn't take them out of the drawer to show them or use them to boast with. He didn't buy this world with them but kept them for the next world. Similarly with other activists, devoted in heart and soul, Jewish citizens from Antopol and similar towns, Leibl did his work to satisfy his soul, for its own sake. He died in the spring of 1971 leaving an interesting spiritual heritage to those that remained behind. May his memor y be blessed.

# May They Be Separated for Long Life
# Avraham Varsha's Book:
# Years of Blood and Fire.
## By Avraham Barbau

There were thousands of Jewish towns on the map of destroyed European Jewry. However, only a few found someone to memorialize them and to establish for them a spiritual, memorial in writing. The memorial books, which according to their number, leave us with the impression as if they encompass all the towns that were destroyed in the Holocaust, really reflect only those towns that had the good fortune to have a part of their Jewish inhabitants miraculously saved. And among them, there were capable people, who could record the story of their towns. Hundreds, and perhaps even thousands, of Jewish towns were completely wiped out from the map of the living and don't leave after them, to our great sorrow, any remnant.

*[Page 245]*

It is a known fact that as the Nazis approached more to the East in their conquest of Europe, their cruelty to Jews increased. This fact mainly touched Polesia, White Russia, Ukraine, and part of Lithuania. In those territories, the German Angel of Death took bloody account with the Jews, publicly, in front of every one, without any mask. The unfortunate Jews were commanded to dig their own grave pits, and with the help o f the gentile population, hungry for blood and Jewish property, they destroyed them on the spot. This was the fate of the warm Jewish town Antopol.

However, Antopol, the small Jewish town in the district of Polesia (near to Kobrin and about 70 kilometers from the capital of the district Pinsk) was lucky in that many years before the Holocaust, it had youth who maintained a strong nationalist Zionist connection. And fortunate people from its midst were able to immigrate to Israel at the right time – before the terrible retribution, and to be among the pioneers who built the land under the difficult conditions of those days and kept the memory of the town in their hearts.

For the sake of the truth, it was not only to Israel that the Jewish youth of Antopol streamed. In its time, many immigrated to overseas lands, and especially to the United States. However, also there they kept in close contact with the town of their origin, with its Jewish milieu, and proudly carried the name of Antopol.

Two gifted people who left Antopol, among the many in the United States, are known to me from reading their books. One of them is Pintshe Berman, a popular lyric poet, about whose books I have published reviews in Israel and abroad. The second author is Avraham Varsha, now a resident of Miami Beach, about whose book, "Years of Fire and Blood" (published by the Jewish National Farband of Chicago). From his modest introduction, we learn that the skill of a writer took twenty years to come to fruition. During that long period of time, he wrote his stories of Antopol. However, his modesty was so great that he didn't at all think of publishing them in a book and he didn't even think they were worthy of that. He writes thus in his book about that matter, "The stories that are published in my book were written during twenty years. The pictures and types come without pretense. The writing was for me a kind of grace, a temporary gift and personal liberation, which immediately compensated me. I never dreamed about publishing a book and was not attracted to the crown of thorns of a writer and nor to the kingdom of Yiddish literature in the United States."

However, people in authority and precisely those at the top of Yiddish literature in the United States, like Dr. A. Mokdoni, and the great popular poet, Avraham Reizen, and also A. Kravits (editor of the Jewish Way) appreciated the literary skill of A. Varsha. They urged him, together with people from Antopol, to publish his big book in the knowledge that with the publication of the book, they were erecting a modest spiritual monument to the holy community of Antopol, whose end was so tragic.

And truly when we read the book, we reveal in it two things: the prose writer, Avraham Varsha, who was refined in spirit and expression, and Antopol, the town and its people. We learn of the simple Jews, who knew how to recite Psalms and the learned Jews, locals and guests, craftsmen and merchants. Sublime rabbis and religious functionaries who could not boast about their genealogy. There were the Lovers of Zion, youth and adults, and on the other hand there were the socialists of different varieties, and even orthodox communities. To make a point, Antopol was alive and busy, before it was destroyed.

The ability of A. Varsha belongs to the type of writers who saw their hometowns with the warmth of their hearts and judged them positively. They described them lyrically. Therefore, there is a sad, poetic tone in all the stories of A. Varsha, although the events themselves are full of shocks and tragedies. For example, in 1920, when Antopol was caught between Poland and Russia under the attacks and counterattacks of the opposing sides, A. Varsha truly describes the fear and trembling of the Jews of the town:

*[Page 246]*

"Day and night the cannons of the enemy thundered, making frightening whistles, and painting the heavens red and blue. Clouds of a green-white color spread throughout the sky. The forest sparkled with its golden yellow leaves in the Fall sun, and answered with an echo to the explosions of bombs that shook up all creation. On the ground that soaked up blood, people crawled frightened in green uniforms like the grass of the field. By way of hidden paths people sneaked into the forest to hide from the eyes of the enemy and his huge airplanes that rained fire and human limbs. Hundreds of human beings in green uniforms like grass were swallowed into the forest, in which there was the echo of steel, fire, and tin, which extinguished tens of souls in a minute."

The Jews of Antopol didn't want either the Russian or the Polish forces. They didn't want the Poles with their poisonous anti-Semitism, who killed and plundered, and they didn't want the Bolsheviks, who also caused fear. Didn't they rise against the Jewish tradition to make it pass from the world, and against religion in general? And they were also against private property. However, it is better that they would come than the Poles. One living Jew is worth twenty murdered ones, G-d forbid.

At first, they were happy for the new Bolshevik rule that temporarily triumphed. However, almost immediately, on the eve of the Day of Atonement, the Jews of the town felt that the Bolsheviks were driving out the Jewish soul and the Jewish G-d. This was the first act that went against their will, followed by other similar and even worse acts. Today we know that was the beginning of the end of the national Jewish life in Russia, with the help of the antireligious phraseology and brutal force.

"In the market on a platform-built , for the occasion, speakers stormed against G-d, and ancient customs and practices that covered, in their words, the eyes of the masses, who carried an unjust burden. The voices of the speakers echoed loudly in the evening and broke into the houses of worship as, 'There is a light sown for the righteous and happiness for the innocent' was being said. The people praying looked at each other in astonishment as if they wanted to ask, "What is happening here? Are they not publicly desecrating G-d's name?"

A. Varsha drew his inspiration directly from the source of love he felt for his town of Antopol. "We as small children of Israel listened attentively to the stories of our elders about the greatness of our town. Certainly, these were not just empty words. And where is the list of rabbis that the ancient rabbinical seminary gave to all of Israel and the world? And where are the number of scholars found in one town? All of this poured out over us a feeling of joy and honor."

# Akiva Ben Ezra
## By Eliezer Leidiger

A young man came to the United States in 1914. He was 17 years old. It took him some years to find his way. He was a peddler and had different factory jobs. He found what he wanted, his way of life, in 1917. Since than, he has devoted himself to Jewish education. He taught in some schools and acquired much experience in teaching the Hebrew language and religious studies in general. His students liked him. He was a successful teacher and had grace in teaching.

When he was still teaching young kids, he researched methods of teaching and published some articles in this field. As he was faithful to everything pertaining to Jewish tradition, he taught his students the laws and customs of Jewish life. In the course of his teaching, he wrote instruction manuals for the students about the laws of Sabbath and Festivals. He came to recognize the value of prayer while teaching and reading Hebrew. He also researched deeply in this field and brought up in his research principles to teach the prayer book, which he published in articles in the educational press in the United States.

*[Page 247]*

He taught in those years in the Yeshivah Ohel Mosheh in Brooklyn, a position he held for 30 years. He increased his literary activity. He participated in the Yiddish press in the United States on daily tonics and in the Hebrew press in research on language in the Hadoar, Tsiyon, Shevile ha-hinukh, ha-Tsofeh, and other literary venues. He also wrote book reviews. He was also interested in the history of Hasidism and published a book on the Yanuka of Stolin.

His monographs are: R. Pinchas Michael, of blessed memory, R L. Mordekhai-Li of Slonim , and others. Additionally, he wrote information on the literary world. He did not stop publishing his articles on the customs of the Jewish holidays. He summarized these researches and published an important work, "Customs of the Holidays."

Ben Ezra writes in the introduction to his book, "I gathered into this book the different customs from the earliest times until recent years, inclusively. Likewise, I took time to explain the customs prevalent in different communities. As much as possible, I cast light on them." This book was scientifically written. It is a treasury of notes and bibliographical references. Ben Ezra writes not only for grownups but also for children. He gives them benefit from light stories that draw the attention of the reader. His book, "Stories for Children" demonstrates his ability.

Ben Ezra had a great deal of love in his heart for the Hebrew book. He loved books. His private book collection numbered in the thousands. From this love, his bibliographical knowledge, he arranged and published bibliographies for a number of authors, like Professor Zevi Scharfstein, Dr. Shelomoh Rubin, and others. He also wrote the bibliography for Shevile ha-hinukh and edited the Hebrew writings of Dr. Morris Robinson.

Ben Ezra was a zealot for the Hebrew language. His friends and acquaintances know this. He does not speak another language except if he is forced to do so. He educated his children to speak Hebrew. The Ben Ezra family is known as one of the first families in the United States, whose children spoke this language. Ben Ezra was able to give his son and daughter a national religious education. They were students of the Flatbush Yeshivah. When they graduated, the son went to study in the Teachers College of the Jewish Theological Seminary. He is now a chemical engineer and active in the community of Binghamton, New York. His diligent and capable daughter Miriam studied in the Teachers College Herzeliyah in New York and graduated with honors. She married Professor Hayyim Denburg of Montreal, Canada.

Two years ago, Ben Ezra retired from teaching. He immediately visited Israel in the company of his wife. Here, he made the decision to settle in Israel.

They realized their wish this year (~1972).

# Avigdor Varsha

Avigdor Varsha was born in Antopol to one of the oldest families in the community. In 1929, he immigrated with his four brothers and parents to Israel. He was then ten years old. He was forced to go to work at the age of 13. First, he worked as a messenger in a law office. He paid for his education with the money that he earned. He was the only member of his family who chose an academic profession. He would visit the court of law during the day and study for his matriculation at night. He began to work at the end of his military service as a clerk in the office of the lawyer, Akiva Persits. He completed his studies in the evening at the College for Law and Economics in Tel Aviv. He completed his specialization in the office of Akiva Persits and afterwards became his assistant lawyer.

*[Page 248]*

When he traveled to the United States, in connection with his business, he was active there in the World Committee for the sake of Israel linked to the Center of Bnai Brith. He also met there his future wife, Avivah, of the Kiev family. He returned with her to Israel, to Kiryat Ono. He began public service in Kiryat Ono together with his professional work as a lawyer. His public service brought him much esteem and support. When he presented himself as a candidate to the city council, he got the support of the majority of the voters and was elected head of the council.

# Avraham Leaf (Lifshits)

Avraham b. R. Dov Leaf (Lifshits), born in Antopol, immigrated in 1904 to Canada. He received from his parents both a Jewish education and a wide basic general education. When he grew up, he went to work and studied law at the University of Toronto. He graduated successfully in 1926 and began to work as a lawyer.

When he became known as a successful lawyer, he was appointed Justice of the Peace and finally a Supreme Court Judge.

He inherited from his home a big love for Zionism and Israel. He visited Israel, took part in congresses and was active on behalf of various appeals for Israel. He served for many years, beginning in 1947, as the President of Temple Agudat Israel. When he retired and gave this task to his successor, he received a festive reception in which his excellent public service was stressed. There was established at this gathering a fund in the name of A.F. Leaf to bring scholars to Ottawa to lecture on matters of Torah and the Science of Judaism.

Avraham Leaf is the brother of the philanthropist, Louis Leaf, who gave recognizable sums for fellowships to descendants of Antopol, living in Canada, to continue their college studios. He is the son of the uncle of Yisrael Lifshits the well-known teacher in Canada. He is the son of the aunt of Rinah Osip of Tel Aviv. His brother, Morris Leaf, is a Professor at the University in Washington.

# By Vardah Kusht

The lilac blooms opposite my rooms
Its color Is bright blue
It captivates the eye with its beauty
and makes the heart rejoice.
Why have you bloomed so differently this yearWith so pale a color?My heart trembles Is astonished and amazed!
In the evening when everything is quiet I hear a whisper among the branchesDo you remember past days? I will reveal to you the explanation of the secret.
You had another house and gardenA big lilac treeThere in my shade You spun your dreams.
You passed boundaries and countriesYears have passed since thenThe thin mist that covers your eyes Has mad my flower pale.
I understand the hintI answered, You are correct! The lilac is as beautiful as alwaysYou have not changed The secret is trapped in me.

*[Page 249]*

# Holocaust and Destruction
## Testimony on the Destruction of the Jews of Antopol from a rescued person

### By Gitl Tserniak, one of the seven survivors

Until the outbreak of the war, there were 3,000 people in the town of my birth. A quarter of the population was White Russian. There were about 2,300 Jews. There was almost no anti-Semitism before World War I. The Jews felt themselves to be free. They dealt in different occupations like tailoring, carpentry, and shoemaking. Many of them dealt in agriculture and commerce. The businesses frequently passed in inheritance from father to son.

There were Zionist youth movements in town, he-Haluts, ha-Shomer ha-Tsair, and other social political movements. The children studied in Jewish religious elementary schools including the Tarbut school, with its language in Hebrew. When they finished elementary school, they went to other centers: rabbinical seminaries, trade schools, gymnasiums, and universities. I went to high school in Pinsk in 1931 and continued to study pharmacy in Warsaw until 1935. Then I returned to the town of my birth and was there until the outbreak of war. I worked as a pharmacist in the only pharmacy in the area, which was owned by Mr. Neidits.

## The Outbreak of War

At the end of 1939, the clouds darkened over Polish Jewry. This was as a result of the agreement between the governments of Russia – Germany, known as the Ribbentrop-Moltov agreement, according to which the great part of Polish Jewry was conquered and divided, passing under Nazi rule. It was the fate of my town, Antopol, in the province of Brest-Litovsk, to be included in the Soviet part, with the Bug River, as the border between conquering armies.

Thus, the Soviets entered our town. They nationalized all institutions. Among them was also the drugstore. Commerce stopped. Agriculture became limited. There was a lack in necessities and food. The Jewish inhabitants of the town, who dealt mainly as the makers of goods, as craftsmen, and particularly as farmers who supplied their produce to the big cities, were hurt from the new arrangements imposed upon them. In place of the freedom of the individual and initiative in all areas of economic and social life, there came the method of planning imposed from the top and dependence on the good will of government representatives. This regime was forced on all the inhabitants.

One of its methods was to uproot inhabitants from the sources of their income and to transfer them to other places. So it was set for Mr. Neidits, the owner of the pharmacy in town, for whom I worked for four years. He was commanded one day to leave and work as pharmacist in the city of Zabinkah. I had to fill his place as director of the pharmacy (which in the meantime was moved from Mr. Neidit's house to that of Mr. Lifshits in the marketplace). In addition, I received orders to open branches in the nearby town of Horodets and some surrounding villages, so as to make it easier to distribute medicines to the population.

Mr. Neidits was known to be sickly. If he had to move to another place, it would hurt his well-being. Therefore, I intervened with the authorities in Brisk, so that they leave him in his place. I was asked to sign being responsible in full for any sabotage that the former owner, Mr. Neidits, would do. I signed. In addition, Mrs. Rozah Ozernitski-Rozenbaun, the daughter of Henia Ozernitski who owned the cosmetics store, began to work with us.

In the course of time, life returned to normal. People got used to the new way of life and accepted it. The Russian authorities established in Antopol their civil and public institutions: schools, regional hospital, court, police, bank, cartels of craftsmen, government houses of commerce, etc. Some of these different functions were fulfilled by officials brought from Russia. There was a need to solve for them the problem of housing. For that purpose, the houses of property owners were expropriated. Some Jews were forced to then crowd into the apartments of their neighbors. Some passed to distant places in Russia. The owner of an estate, Yankovits, was also forced into a similar exile. His estate on the eastern boundary of Antopol became government property. A hospital was built on it. My husband, the doctor, directed in that period the regional clinic, established in the house of Mr. Lifshits, at the beginning of Pinsk St. The authorities put upon him the planning and direction of the hospital.

*[Page 250]*

This condition continued until June 21, 1941, the day of the sudden attach of the Nazi army on the Soviet army. The Germans invaded the Russian zone of conquest. The army retreated, taking with it citizens and institutions. This retreat continued for three days until the Germans took control of the region from Brest-Litovsk until they reached Antopol and from there continued there conquest.

The Soviet period was over. It was a time in which the Jewish inhabitants had security for their lives. Suddenly, they were faced with the bitter reality of the coming of the Nazis, which opened the terrible period of the Holocaust, which came after the Russian rule.

A few days after the Nazi conquest, when the front was far away, the Germans set up a civilian rule. They placed at its head, the former mailman, who was a German, a Folksdeitsch, as a mayor. Until then, this man had lived in friendship with the Jews and hid his anti-Semitism. His name was Khrominski. Later he was the man who set the life and death of the inhabitants. He collaborated immediately upon the entry of the Nazi army and began to undertake with great trustworthiness, as mayor, the instructions from the Nazi civilians. Their head was Kreiz- Landvirt.

The transfer of the Jews to the left side of the street created in actuality an open Jewish ghetto. There were about 2,500 Jews in the open ghetto, since in addition to the Jews of Antopol, the Jews of Horodets, Sharshuv and Zabinkah were brought there.

The ghetto remained open only for two months. According to the order of the authorities, which was given in August 1941, the ghetto was divided into ghetto A and ghetto B. All those who had any occupation and were productive in the eyes of the Nazis and their helpers, entered into Ghetto A. These people had the right to join their family members and parents. The remainder were gathered into ghetto B. This included the remnants of families, who heads were no longer alive, old people, weak and the like. All the inhabitants of ghetto A had special documents, which they received from the Judenrat. My husband the physician, and I, the pharmacist, were transferred to ghetto A. At that time, ghetto A was declared to be closed. It was surrounded by a high fence of boards and wire, so that to enter or leave, one needed to pass the entrance gate. This was guarded from the outside by the police or gendarmes. Among the pro-German police (the Greens or Zielonowcy) who guarded the ghetto gate, were a number of Russian communists and Kosmosol members who had remained in place after the German conquest and volunteered for the police. They wanted to prove a high degree of loyalty, therefore they were the worst police. They used to make strict searches when the inhabitants of the ghetto would return from work. Besides the Russians, local White Russians joined this militia.

The gendarmes were only Germans or Volks-Deutsche. There were about 850 people in ghetto A. Jewish life took place only in the ghetto. Yiddish was the language of speech. I and my husband had the right to register our mothers and transfer them to ghetto A. There was the feeling that ghetto A would last longer in the future and ghetto B was judged for destruction. Therefore, there were cases when a youth in ghetto A would bring over a young woman in a fictitious marriage in order to save her life.

Life in the ghetto. In the ghetto, and especially after the action before the last, families and individuals were torn apart. Family, social, and cultural life had ended. The people knew or felt in the depth of their heart what awaited them. They awaited without any choice their death and for the decree to be carried out. They were human shadows, without any will to live and any hope. They were hungry not only for bread but also for a good word, for any comfort, for a spark of hope, for information about what was happening in the world, on the front, in the Land of Israel and the Zionist movement, in the welfare and work of their relatives in the Free World. They did not receive daily newspapers and it was forbidden to receive them, either local or German. Their radio sets were taken away, according to order, from the ghetto

*[Page 251]*

Outside of frightening rumors and exaggerations about the victories of the Germans, which the gentiles would tell them and would cause even greater depression, they had no other source of information. Professional, industrial, and commercial life had ceased. Craftsmen did not work. There was no one to work for and no reason to work. The secret commerce was limited to an exchange of food for all sorts of goods that remained with someone. In the morning they would take out the men to work outside the ghetto according to an examined list. The men would work mainly on digging and fixing roads. The women would work as housekeepers to clean German residences. There were also those, who worked for Russian citizens and local gentiles in agricultural work. The latter and the women that cleaned succeeded in sneaking in a little food to the ghetto. There were cases when White Russian citizens would bring food to the ghetto gate and succeeded in passing it to a Jewish acquaintance or to throw it to him through the fence. Understandably, this depended on the circumstance of the guard and the strictness of the search by the police at the ghetto gate. The inhabitants of the ghetto would give from their poor possessions that they still had to these "humanitarian neighbors."

Jewish Antopol went into decline. The terrible Holocaust began. The Holocaust has 3 periods: Before the ghetto; the ghetto; and the final annihilation.

In the first period of Nazi occupation, before arranging the ghetto, the harm done by the murderers took place in the center of the town, in the market. The market had a square. Around it were concentrated the Provoslav Church, the police, the pharmacy, the post office, the radio station which the Russians established, the hotel, the bank, and other institutions. The SS murderers, with the black sign of death on their helmets, known for their cruelty, would come to this square in cars from Kobrin. When they arrived, everyone knew that there would be trouble. This is how it was the first time in the ease of two Jewish soldiers, who fled from

German captivity. The hateful Khrominski than out as if they had spread upon their return Atrocity Propaganda about acts of terror against the Jews which they had witnessed. As a result of this information and as a punishment for this, the youths were cruelly beaten until they lost consciousness and they were finally shot to death.

Another time a young Jew went to visit family members. He passed the square in the market. The SS soldiers, who saw him on his way, forced him to run back and forth to their car until he lost strength and consciousness and fainted. Then, they threw water over him and returned to their abuse. I remember another time the SS called some Jewish children and forced them to lick their car until it shone. In payment, they received kicks and shouts, "Away with you, accursed Jews."

More than once, they brought Jews who they had caught to the police station. They beat them unconscious, left them until they revived, then continued to mistreat them while they screamed aloud in great pain. I heard and saw this while I stood by the window of the pharmacy, which was in Lifshits's house (in which I continued to work). This house was in the market square, which was opposite the police station in Weinstein's house. The cars generally came to there. I received a hysteria of crying and pain in all my body, out of fear for the fate of them, from the shouts and cries of those being beaten. All my life I hear them, and among them Weisman from the Sirota family and the father of Tsertok.

*[Page 252]*

On another day, a closed military car of SS people appeared. They came with the excuse that they saw someone parachute into the region. They arranged a precise search in the town from house to house until they finally found Grinman, one of the Pinsk St. farmers, who had married before the war. They decided that he was the one, who had parachuted. They shot him just like that on the spot without any investigation, discussion, or judgment. They apparently returned to Kobrin with a report in them hands on the capture of an important Jewish spy, who had parachuted in and was judged to death. Thus, there began a period of decrees, humiliations that were morally and physically horrible and the spilling of the blood of the Jews, innocent of crime, of my town of Antopol.

## The Period in the Ghetto

In the beginning there was isolation or a moral, ideological ghetto. Some days after the conquest the Germans gathered the gentile population into the church. They decreed contempt and distance from the Zhids, ugly and dirty, the enemies of the Christians, the worse than gypsies and with similar appetites. After that an order was given to the Christian inhabitants and to the farmers in the villages, that they were forbidden to sell agricultural products to Jews and to have commercial, or any other contact with them. Big announcements were printed and glued to the walls of houses and on the fences of the market.

At, the order of Khrominski, the former letter carrier, a Judenrat was established, which represented the Jews and served mainly as an instrument of the enemy to carry out the orders and decrees which arrived from the Gestapo in Kobrin to the person in charge of the district. Rozenberg, the head of Judenrat, was a member of the Judenrat. He was the son in law of the merchant Paltsuk,Pinyamin Volf, Zalman Altvarg (his nickname was Zalman Kolbe), Rubinstein, and Rabbi Wolkin, the memory of the righteous for blessing.

Vulf was the most active. He came to Antopol from the nearby town of Yanovah and set up in our town the electric station. The rabbi of the town, Wolkin, may the memory of the righteous be blessed, avoided collaborating. However, he was forced to have the sessions of the Judenrat in his house, The members of the Judenrat were the most respected people in town and the richest, having established positions, merchants, and the like, who knew well the town and its people. They were required to carry out the orders and decrees that came from the Gestapo in Kobrin. Here are examples of the first orders that they carried out: to put on the yellow patch, go to forced labor, gather money and things of value, as they were required by the Germans (the Judenrat determined who paid and how much), the prohibition to assemble and agitate, the prohibition to do commerce or have connection with the Aryans, who were of blue blood; the organization of a Jewish police.

The head of the militia was Barukh Hersh Rabinowits. His assistants were the policeman David Kaplan, Shertok, Epstein, and the eldest son of Vulf. Among the functions of the police was to maintain general order, to make sure that no one would leave the ghetto, that they would wear the yellow patch, that they would not escape, and that they would go to work. They would also bring the food to the ghetto and distribute it. This food included bread and milk. In the beginning they made the bread from wheat and barley. Afterwards, only from barley. It would break up and was difficult to eat. However, people also fought over it, because there was not enough for everyone. The milk was without fat, It was the remains that came out of the centrifuge.

Among the functions of the police and the Judenrat was also to help the Germans carry out their raids. This participation was generally very weak. The main streets of Antopol, Kobrin and Pinsk St. had a sidewalk only on the right side. One day the order of the mayor came out that all the Jews, who wore the yellow star and lived on the right side of these main streets need to leave their houses. They had to gather on the left side only and they were forbidden to use the side walk. Who would not do this would be killed.

During the first days, people were terribly embarrassed to appear in the street with the stigma of humiliation, with the yellow patch and only on the left side in the sand and mud of the streets. However, there was no choice. Certainly, I needed to get to the pharmacy and my husband needed to get to the clinic.

*[Page 253]*

An event that happened was while my husband worked in the clinic outside the ghetto. The mayor gave him a special permit for that. A policeman would daily take him out to work and return him. The Russian farmers that came for examinations in the clinic loved him and secretly brought him food. As a pharmacist, I was able to leave the ghetto only in the company of a local citizen. Once I decided to go to visit the clinic. My husband gave me the little food that he had received. I hid it under my coat and took it home. One of the Russian volunteers (Zelinovits) saw at the gate that I had hidden food. He brought me to the police station. However, when I came there, I asked for the chief of police. The chief knew me and agreed to free me despite my having food. This was because he remembered that I was the wife of the doctor, who had given help to his sick wife.

The synagogues stopped serving as a center of Jewish spiritual life, as was the case in the past. The Russians had turned the old synagogue (of wood) into a storage for grain. The Germans continued to do this. The new synagogue (of brick) was empty. There only prayed there those who still believed in Mosheh. Most felt despaired and paralyzed. Even though they fervently prayed on Sabbaths and holidays, their eyes were dry and the voices of those leading the prayers were without life. I especially remember the prayers on the last High Holidays in the ghetto, about two weeks before the final liquidation. They prayed silently and fervently to the Creator of the World, "Why are you silent? Give a sign and a wonder!"

The memorial prayers were so long, each person thought, "Who will remember me in the future? No one, unless there will be a miracle and lightning from the heavens to wipe out the enemies of Israel."

The state of health in the ghetto was very low. This was mainly due to the lack of food and the results of hard work. Dr. Czerniak, my husband, would treat the inhabitants after he returned from work in the evening from the clinic. He was tired and depressed. He was helped by medicines, which he would sneak in from the clinic. And in the same fashion, I would bring in medicine from the pharmacy.

He would receive an order to leave the ghetto to take care of severely ill gentiles. This was similar to the regional hospital, which the Russians established in their time. Once when he went to the village of Novosilulki, he brought medicines for the Jewish workers in the work camp of Zafrud. He went through the first gate of the camp. However, he was arrested at the second gate. Only the pleas of the farmer, who was bringing him to the sick person and who had accompanied him to the camp, saved him from execution on the spot. He was take another time to a farm in the village of Yaroshvi. It became clear that the sick person was Philip, the leader of the partisans, who had begun to organize at that time. He took care to treat him without telling the secret to anyone. In that fashion, there began the connection between us and the fighters of the anti-German underground. About a month before the last action in which all of the Jews still remaining in the ghetto would be killed, along with myself, my husband and 5-month-old baby girl, we traveled late at night to care for a sick person outside of Antopol. We did this without the required permission, because the town was locked under curfew.

We were in danger of losing our lives if caught. However, the value of human life then was very low, so that we didn't object to carrying out the request of Ivan Baidok, who came in a hurry to my husband and begged him to come quickly to save the life of his wife. On the contrary, we thought that they should catch us and put an end to our lives and suffering that was inhumane, a life in the ghetto with 300 shadows, 300 bodies walking without any sign of being human in heart and mind.

*[Page 254]*

However, they did not catch us. We returned late at night to the ghetto. Our baby was already not at home in the room. This is because three days before we had given her to a patient, Vera Okhrits, with the goal of saving her. When the last action came, we were saved thanks to the many patients we had treated before and during the cruel war.

We heard the steps of people searching, who took out people from a hiding place near to our room and told them to take money, since they were all going to a work camp outside the ghetto. After that, a German entered our room and saw my husband, with a Red Cross on a background of white, as they ordered him. This was a sign that he was a doctor (There was still in force an order not to take doctors). The German saw the cradle for the infant. He asked about the woman and the infant. My husband answered they had already took them. I was in the clothes closet, almost choking. When the German left, my husband opened the closet, so that I could breathe. My mother Tsiviah hid under the bed (All the elderly were on that list). My mother-in-law, Shifrah, was in a hiding space under the floor boards in that place. However, the Nazi accepted what my husband said and loft. Opposite us in the house of Markiter, there lived the Kaplan family, my sister-inlaw Pashah, with her two children. They made a double wall in the entrance way. They painted it and there was no sign that behind it was a space. When the action began, the Kaplan family with the two children said also Pashah's sister, Rodyah, entered the hiding place. The Germans discovered to my sadness the hidden wall and the hiding place behind it. The farmers who accompanied the Germans were ordered to destroy the wall with axes. We saw how they took out all they found there, how Pashah took her two children with her two hands, mid after her were Motyah, her husband, and Rodyah, her sister. The Germans were drinking at the ghetto gate from a barrel of alcohol, so that they would be drunk and dull of all human feeling.

Our room was in the third house to the left (after the house of Halabnah) from the gate of the ghetto. Thus, we were able to hear the orders of the Germans. Since there will still not enough people and the list was not full, there came the order to take us all, even doctors and people in other protected occupations. My husband hurried to hide n the hiding spot on the roof.

An infant was asleep after being drugged. We covered her with a sheet and left her lying in the cradle The mothers remained under the bed and boards. During the hours that people were being gathered, there were shouts that tore the heart and made a person crazy. Even now, I hear the echo in my ears and I tremble. The quiet of death took over the ghetto in the afternoon. The hunters had left. People, like mice, began to crawl out of their holes and saw that the sun was not ashamed to shine and to spread warmth and light on almost empty ghetto. Only about 300 people remained. New final lists were made. The elderly, who were intended to be shipped to death and were able to hide, were already not thought to be among the living and were not listed. They were torn apart spiritually, saw no hope, and prayed that their end would be swift and short. Their life was too hard to bear.

## The Fourth Final Action

On October 15, 1942, the Gestapo entered the ghetto and arrested the police and Judenrat. Their function was finished. They locked them in a store in the marketplace. This was a clear sign that the ghetto was set to be destroyed. However, no one knew what was happening, because we were all asleep. The prisoners in the store were taken out early as the first ones to die. I woke up early in the morning to hear the cries of my brother, Abramtsik.

*[Page 255]*

He opened the outside shutters and called to me that the ghetto was surrounded by Germans and then he fled. His voice still echoes in my ears. I did not see him anymore. My husband and I dressed quickly. We went to the room where my mother-in-law and mother were hiding. They looked at us with eyes full of fear and anticipated our reaction at what to do.

The infant was already not with us. We had luck a month before that I threw her at the entrance of the door of the Okhrits family according to agreement that my husband had made with his patient Vera. She agreed to take the child, to save her, because as she said simply, "You will all be killed." My husband decided to leave the house to see what was being done. I shouted after him that perhaps we would not see one another again. However, he returned immediately and said that the ghetto was surrounded.

We left the house and my husband led me to Shmerl's house, near the new synagogue. This house was on the border of the ghetto and behind it was the street of the gentiles. The windows of the house were covered with boards. My husband took off a number of boards, so that he could jump through the window. The hour was about 5:30 a.m. It was still dark and people couldn't see a few steps ahead. My husband jumped quickly before I was able to stop him. And behold, I heard a Nazi on the other side of the street shout, "Stop." He arrested my husband and took him away. I immediately returned in the direction of our house. Opposite our house was the house of Joseph Sirotah.

In his house, there was a big hiding place under the floor. A number of people, my brother among them, had hid there in an earlier action. I saw a number of families running to hide in the house of Sirotah. Since they had taken my husband, I stood frozen with no will to hide. My mother began to go away from me toward the people calling us to join them. She did not call me. She only turned to me, looked and didn't say a word. Once, my mother told me that in the time of an action it is forbidden to call to one another. That everyone should do what they want. Thanks to that I remained alive.

I stood like this for some time until it came to my attention that the gate would open and the action would soon begin. There was a need to hide. I entered our house with my mother-in-law and we hid in the hiding place in the entrance that was under the floor. The hiding place was part of a block cellar. Meanwhile, the hunt began. We heard a German enter the house and shout, "Get out." He seized an infant from the Zaidl family, whose unfortunate parents had left behind. The action lasted all the day. We heard isolated shouts and pleas of women that they should leave them alive, because they are able to work.

The action continued also at night. We heard then the gentile farmers going around into the houses and plundering the property that remained. They also entered our house, rooms, and attic. They threw from there items onto the floor, which was at the entrance to our hiding place. The next morning, we heard the voice of the Volks-Deutsch enemy, Khrominski and the Russian doctor, Troshnikovah, who inherited my husband's position. The two came to steal all the medical equipment that remained in our apartment.

We remained in our hiding place all day and night. We decided to leave the next day before morning. I thought that we would remain buried and die from hunger. I attempted to make an opening and succeeded. My mother-in-law and I went out. Suddenly, we heard the steps of a man, who immediately spotted us and said, "Get out." I saw that he was not a German but a Polish policeman from the area. I knew him. I asked him if he knew me and he said, "Yes, from the pharmacy." I asked the mother of the doctor him to get us out of the ghetto. He said that it was not possible during the day. I asked him to come at night. I gave him my marriage ring and said that he should come at night and I would give him more. I said this despite that I knew that I had no more to give him. I told him that we would remain in the hiding place until he would come. Otherwise, they would kill us. We went down to the cellar of our last apartment in the ghetto with a piece of dry bread and some water. I was worried if it was the policeman or someone else with every knock on the window and every step in the house I heard during that very long day. We knew that it was very late that night when the moon set. The gentile still had not come.

*[Page 256]*

We decided to leave the hiding place. In the process, we made a noise and suddenly someone entered and lit us up with a flash light. This was the Polish policeman. However, he was drunk and stood on his feet with difficulty. He apologized that he was at a party in the police station. Apparently they celebrated the victory over 300 Jews from the ghetto, whose only weapons were hiding places, prayers and curses. He told us that the ghetto was already empty of Jews.

He thought everyone had been killed. The work was finished. His voice didn't even have a sentiment of pain, fear, shame, or sadness. It was a dry story and understandably one of murder, killing, plunder, destruction and death to everyone.

The gentiles were freed of the Jewish plague according to the guidance, organization, commands, and undertaking of the German occupants. Thus, we heard his few words and understood that our dear ones had given up their lives for eternity.

## Fleeing the Ghetto

The drunken policeman, the gentile from the village of Demidovshtsinah, said that we should take off our shoes and not make a sound, because there was still a strong guard around the ghetto. This guard remained in its place one week. Shots were heard outside so he went ahead of us to scout. He checked the area and after that he called to us. We came to a break in the fence. The break was made by the gentiles, who came to plunder the ghetto. We left the ghetto. We crossed the street, Zaniviyah, and went by way of the alley to an uncultivated field. When we were in the field, a thin rain came down. The skies were dark. The policeman asked from more money. I took out a number of bills of money called Korbvanetsi (money that was in use then). However, that was not enough for him and he wanted more jewelry. I didn't have anything. I distanced from him some steps. I said that I had something in my stocking. Meanwhile, my mother-in-law took advantage of this opportunity and began to go away in the direction of the village of Haroshav.

After I moved farther away in the dark, I began to run and he began to shout that he would shoot. It was the same to me. I continued to run but he didn't shoot. He was afraid to make noise lest harm come to him. Thus, I escaped to the right in the direction of the village, Zaniviyah and Frishikhvost. I crawled on my stomach. I wanted to go around the mill, because I thought that they had a watch dog. The house of Ivan Paiduk was not far from the mill. I remembered that some weeks before, this man came to the ghetto to take my husband to treat his wife, who had a serious flow of blood. He did this despite that he knew that my husband did not have a permit to leave the ghetto. I thought then that something would happen to my husband, therefore I joined him. The farmer peacefully returned us that night to the ghetto and he promised that if we were in trouble he would accept us.

I directed my steps to the house of Ivan Baiduk. Nevertheless, I was afraid to enter, lest a stranger was there. I decided to enter the granary in which they kept the cows. I hid under sheaves of grain and waited for the morning. I imagined that the farm lady would come to milk the cows and then I would come out to her. I hoped that perhaps my husband was hiding with this farmer.

In the morning, the farm lady came to the barn and observed that the gate was open. She was frightened and looked around. When she saw me, she became more frightened and her tongue clove to her palate from excitement. She was afraid that I was being followed. I calmed her by saying that it was not my intention to stay with her and that I had only come to ask if my husband was with her. She told me that he was hiding on a pile of straw above.

*[Page 257]*

It is hard to describe the meeting with my husband. He told me how he had managed to escape from the ghetto after the German caught him and how in the two days that he was here, they had treated him nicely. He got food and even a newspaper. When I joined him, it was Sunday. Ivan and his wife left the house. They went to church. They did not give us food. They left food for the cows and returned only in the evening. Then, they told us that they would have kept my husband but now that I came, they were afraid.

We had to leave. My husband asked for a coat, since it was very cold. The farmer directed us to another sick person, the wife of Nastrok, who lived in the village of Frishikvost, about two kilometers away. His wife had heart disease and was one of my husband's patients.

We left that night in the direction of the village of Frishikhvost. We entered the village but didn't know which barn belonged to the farmer named Nastrok. Therefore, we hid behind sheaves of straw, near the wall of one of the granaries. We decided to wait until the morning, to see where the farmer would go. In the evening, we went from behind the straw and entered his barn. My husband identified himself, and this time we didn't reveal that there were two of us. The farmer was afraid to keep my husband. He told him of the apartments of two other sick people, Tanyah and Zusyah.

We decided at once that I would try my luck with the patient Zusyah, and that my husband would go to Tanyah. After I identified myself, Zusyah screamed loudly. I began to run from her in the darkness of the night. Meanwhile, my husband was transferred to Tanyah's aunt, who lived near the railway. She was a widow with two sons. He was relatively safe with her. After I was cast away by Zusyah, I decided to go to Tanyah to look for my husband. She told me that he was already transferred to another place and that she was prepared to take me to her aunt. Thus, my husband and I met again.

The winter had already begun. My husband dug a hiding place under the floor, whose entrance was in the wall of the stokehold, under the big oven in the kitchen. We spent the winter months there.

In the summer of 1943, the partisans began to put mines under the railway. The Germans ordered the removal of the trees by the railway and also all the isolated houses up to a distance of 500 meters. Tanyah and her young son took advice on how to get rid of us. The older son was a drunk and didn't even know that we were in the house. They decided to poison us. We heard this under the floor of the kitchen while listening to the conversations. They decided to buy mouse poison or fox poison from merchants who went around the village. However, to our luck they did not succeed in buying this poison. Then, they decided to tell the matter to Tanyah's lover, the policeman, Kostak, so that he wand take us to the forest and shoot us. We made preparations to escape before the execution. However, we did not have shoes. One day when the aunt left the house, my husband prepared rags in place of shoes and a skeleton key for the outside door. That evening, Tanyah told her aunt that when she told the policeman of the dilemma and how Dr Tserniak had saved her when she was sick, he promised to get in contact with the Director of the Employment Office, Mr. Artsishevski, who had hidden a Jewish girl. When the employment director heard the story, he agreed to accept us, as he remembered the medical help that his family had received.

During these days, there was still a curfew beginning at 7:00 p.m. We had to go before this time from the aunt's house to Artsishevski's. "We were weak as we left from under the floor. The aunt took me under the arm and the director of employment took my husband, while we were disguised as farmers and returned to Antopol by way of the Shlus Alley. We came to the house of the Director of the Employment Office. We entered again into an attic in the barn. His house was in the boundaries of the ghetto on the left side of Kobrin St. Thus, we returned to the ghetto and were, to our great sorrow, two isolated Jews, abandoned and unfortunate, awaiting the daily visit of the good servant lady of Mr. Artsishevski. She would bring us food and cry from excitement at seeing the apartment of the doctor and pharmacist from Antopol. Mr. Artsishevski would sneak into the barn in the evening. He would climb a ladder and silently tell about the war and the Nazis, whom he hated both as a Polish patriot and as an intellectual, intelligent and humane. He gave us encouragement to suffer only until the redemption would come.

[Page 258]

# I Cry Over These
## By Rabbi Yaakov Pester

I cry over these, over the great in Torah, the cedars of the Lebanon, holy to G-d, who did not stop reciting text all their lives and gave their soul, for martyrdom, for the holy Torah, the holiness of our people, and the holiness of our land!

Our small town of Antopol was like all the towns in the Kobrin district, small in numbers and great in quality. Of the inhabitants of the town, some were craftsmen, some farmers, and some dealt in commerce. The local Jews were simple in their nature and image. However, they were great in their spirit and soul. They were strict in Torah and commandments. They were ready in their simple faith to give up their life for our holy Torah. All their desire in life was to increase and glorify the Torah. They loved Torah and respected rabbis. Everyone who was able to raise their sons to the study of the Torah was considered to be very rich. Everyone who did not see the happiness of the father upon his son arriving from the rabbinical seminary for the Passover Tabernacles vacation, did not see happiness. Our small town also raised great rabbis, whose fame was known over the width of the country. We will say something about the rabbinical graduates of our town, who fell at the hands of the murderers, may their names be blotted out. We must raise up a monument in memory to those who died without leaving out a name or memory. However, we do not have to recruit for the memory of the righteous. Their words are their memory.

In Antopol, there were more than twenty youths who had studied in graduate rabbinical seminaries. Eleven of them fell as martyrs.

The first martyr was the rabbi R. Mosheh Nudel, of blessed memory, who was ordained by great rabbis in Poland. He studied in the rabbinical seminary of Branovits and afterwards studied in the rabbinical seminary of Kamkfets. He was one of the most diligent students in the rabbinical seminary. He was very studious and had a wonderful memory. He studied all his days with great diligence and with faithful love for the Torah.

His father was a very poor shoemaker. However, he was rich in the way that he merited to raise a great son in Torah. R. Mosheh Nudel married a woman from Damatsheve, the daughter of one of the important people in the town. R. Nudel dealt in Torah and commerce and these were tied together until his last day when he gave up his pure soul to his Creator.

I remember for eternity Rabbi. Klug of blessed memory. His father was a baker. R. Yitshak Klug studied all his days in rabbinical seminaries, primarily the rabbinical seminary of Kamiriets in which he received ordination from important rabbis. He was very diligent and invested all his strength to the study of Torah. He was very successful in his study and especially in Codes. He had a good nature and was endowed with good qualities. He vas beloved to people acid G-d. He married a woman from Pinsk and dealt in commerce until his last day, when he returned his pure soul to its Creator.

One of his friends was R. Yosef Kisilov, of blessed memory. He studied in the seminaries of Kletsk and Brisk. Even in his youth, he was recognized for his skills. He made wonderful innovations in Torah with his sharp mind. He married a woman from Shashev and dealt in commerce until his last day. May his memory be blessed!

*[Page 259]*

The truth must be said. I admit and am not ashamed that I do not have words to express the value and greatness of one of the people of Antopol, Rabbi Shemuel Varsha, of blessed memory.

R. Shemuel Varsha studied in the seminaries of Kobrin and Kaminets. He was known by the name, "Genius of Antopol." And it is known that in the rabbinical seminaries of Poland and Lithuania, people were precise in giving such praise. He had a marvelous memory and was very diligent. He spent his nights like his days, in the study of our holy Torah. He had a marvelous ability to express himself and left after him many written innovations in Torah. He also dealt with public affairs in Antopol. He was one of the founders of the society, Glory of Youth. He organized the religious youth for the Mizrahi to prepare for pioneering. His father, R. Benjamin Varsha, was known to be a scholar and to do good deeds. Their house was open to travelers. May their memory be blessed.

With a painful heart, I raise some words about the Rabbi R. Hayim Sirotah, of blessed memory. He was one of those individuals distinguished in the rabbinical seminaries. He studied in the rabbinical seminaries of Kobrin and Mir. Even as a young man, his sharp mind caused excitement in town. All the people in town loved him very much. He married the daughter of our rabbi, R. Mosheh Vulfson, of blessed memory and he dealt in commerce until his last day. May their memory be blessed.

I write to memorialize the young rabbinical students. One of them was R. Tsevi Erlikh, of blessed memory, who studied in the seminaries of Pruznah and Kaminets. He never stopped studying. He was righteous in his deeds and humble in his manner. He was meant for greatness but was cut off very young.

R. Yehial Vulfson, of blessed memory, the son of our town rabbi was very great in Torah when he was young. He studied in Branovits and Kaminets. They said about him that the Torah came to its inn.

And I memorialize the dear pleasant youths: David Fridman, R. Leib Goldberg, R. Alter Goldberg, R. Yisrafil Mikhael Volinets, his brother Yitshak Volinets, and R. Pinchas Postol, who studied in the rabbinical seminaries of Branovits and Kobrin. They were strict in Torah and commandments until their last day when their light was extinguished by cursed murderers.

We stand with bent head on the grave of the members of our town, which is etched in our heart. They fell at the hands of murderers, who killed our infants having been just weaned from their mothers breasts. They killed them and had no mercy.

The voice of the blood of our people cries from the ground, "Earth do not cover our blood!"

The heart is sad and drips blood and a cry breaks out, "How long, G-d, will the enemy desecrate your name? G-d of vengeance appear!"

We believe and we are the children of believers. The decree went from Him and we cannot think about it. However we also believe in the promise, "I will revenge and repay." And near is the day of their suffering when their evil will come upon them. They will drink from the cup of poison and receive their reward. They will recognize and know that all on earth have a day of Judgment and a judge and His kingdom is over all.

# My life of Terror in the Ghetto of Antopol and My Salvation
## By Shoshanah Kats

There were some Germans who lived in town with their families and fulfilled various administrative functions. They employed Jewish girls from the ghetto for household work. I was among them. On one of the days when I returned from work, I went to visit a friend. However, I was not able to return home to my mother. The confusion was terrible, and the mother of my friend did not let me leave the house that evening. Action number 2 began at 6:30 that morning. When I returned home, I did not find my mother. My uncle and aunt, who hid in the garden of our house, told me that she was taken to Bronnah Gura together with all of them.

*[Page 260]*

The local German with whom I worked came to the Judenrat and asked about me, since I did not come to work. They showed him where I was. However, I was afraid to go with him. I began to cry bitterly. The German began to calm me. Also the Judenrat person said that I should go with the German to my house and not be afraid because the Action was already finished. The German came to accompany me to my house.

It was already written on the entrance on the door of our house: "Entrance forbidden." I entered with the help of the German inside. I began to search the rooms and to call: "Mother! Mother!" However, all was in vain. She already was not among the living. My uncle Yaakov Leib and my aunt Stirah answered my call from the courtyard and garden. The German permitted them to enter our house and wrote on the entrance that with his permission Jews live here.

I went with the German to work. There was no boundary to my anguish. The German acted humanely with me. He offered me food and when I finished the work, he suggested to me that I sleep in his house since he knew that I was afraid. However, I returned home.

My uncle, my aunt, their daughter and her child also came out from their hiding place and assured me the best they could. Life returned to its path and thus passed three months. There appeared the covered cars again in the market place on one clear day. I felt toward evening in the house of my employer the preparation of the SS. Preparations were again made for the eventuality. I returned together with all of them that evening to a hiding place.

Before morning, we heard steps in the house and the voices of the SS, who went around the rooms and searched the hiding places of their victims. The entrance to our hiding place was masked by a bed that stood on the entrance to the tunnel. One of the SS moved the bed with a blow of his boots. He opened the entrance of the tunnel and understandably found all of us. There were in one room my uncle and aunt, their daughter Lifshah with her child Lailah, their second daughter, Itkah, her husband, and daughter Rivkah, age 12, and son, age 9, and I together with them. The SS ordered us to follow them through the courtyard, one after the other, as one SS went in front with a whip in his hand, and the second, who looked like a monster, closed the procession.

There was found together with the SS, a representative of the Judenrat, a youth my age named Hayim Epstein. When we went, he whispered to the SS behind us that I was his girlfriend, and the German whispered to me to go away. I obeyed him and slipped away to the side of the house. I entered quick as lightning again the tunnel. The house was empty from any living being. I remained alone.

I heard in the hours of the afternoon sudden crying and recognized the voice of the daughter of my uncle, Itkah. I went above and saw Itkah and her husband (I forget his name) and their daughter Esterkah, her sister, Lifshah, and her daughter Lili. Their parents, my uncle and aunt, and their nine-year old son were taken to the place of execution. Lifshah and Lili, who were also together with me when our house was searched also succeeded in escaping from the line and hid, without my knowledge, between two closets that stood in the vestibule. I had passed by them in my flight without noticing them. They only left their hiding place when her sister and her husband came.

Again about four months passed. People were again taken to work. It was fall, the time of the potato harvest in the fields. There a total of about 300 people left in the ghetto.

Before dawn, when we were still asleep, we heard cries of terror outside. When we opened the window, there was revealed the known picture of the crowd of SS, the police, armed from foot to head, and their faithful police helpers from among the Christian population, as they pursued their victims. I jumped outside into the courtyard of our house dressed only in my nightgown and from there I entered the garden of my Christian neighbor. I ran down the narrow path when suddenly I noticed a pile of empty bean sacks. I dug into the pile and held my breath. The hunters passed me, but they did not notice me. There, I remained the whole day.

*[Page 261]*

I left my hiding place in the evening and began to seek an exit from the ghetto. On my way by one of the houses I noticed the elderly Grinman, aged

80, and her grandson, aged 7, embracing in death. I slowly approached the ghetto fence and began to dig at the frozen ground with my hand. After superhuman efforts, I was able to pass to the other side of the fence.While taking care that the Christian inhabitants did not notice me, I left by an alley to outside the area of town. I began to walk in the direction of the nearest farm, in which I knew one of the daughters of the Christian family. I entered the house and asked for my acquaintance, Ginyah, to give me some old dress. She said that I should go in the direction of the nearest grove. More Jewish escapees were there and tomorrow she would bring me a dress if I would now give her the ring on my finger. She did not offer me food and not even water to drink. Therefore, I understood her intentions and left the house.

When I went a little distance from the place, I heard voices of people speaking Yiddish. When I came near, I. found the wife of David Kaplan, her daughter, Hadassah, and her infant daughter, about a year old. Hadassah's mother began to insist that her daughter follow me. Perhaps, we would be saved. She should leave the infant at the entrance of the house of a farm of Christians. Perhaps, they would adopt it. She convinced with difficulty her daughter to take the desperate act of abandoning her infant daughter. She left the fruit of her womb under a window. When we left, we heard the shrieking of the infant, who awoke from her sleep.

Hadassah did not stop crying all the way. The crying of her daughter echoing in our ears did not give her rest. When we wandered that night, we were sure that we arrived at a settlement distant from Antopol. However, we found ourselves near again to the town. We began in haste to run in the opposite direction and we arrived at a farm before dawn.

Hadassah was not calm. She left me and returned to the place where she left her mother and infant. I managed to hide inside a pile of straw that was laid against the wall of the stable. I heard steps coming close after some hours. I held my breath from fear. Someone approached, raised slowly the corners of the pile, and whispered: "Don't be afraid. I saw you hide here. Remain until evening and then you can enter the house." The man returned in the evening and invited me to his house. They fed me and gave me drink. The woman gave me a dress, boots, a blouse, and overcoat. These were used clothes. However, they were in sufficiently good condition. They were members of the Vitovits family, about whose humane actions to save Jews many know to tell.

Mr. Vitovits instructed me how to act in case I was caught by Nazis or local police. I was to say in this case that I did not know the people and I did not enter the attic of their barn with their permission and he, understandably, did not know that I existed. Thus, I remained with this family, in which all of them cooperated, the children and the wife, to save Jews, whom they hid in different places on their farm and for whose needs they undertook to supply.

I heard that night the whispering of people, who were also dwelling in an attic, near me. They were Shayke Neidus and his friend, who fled from a camp of arrestees in Kobrin and arrived at the family Vitovits. Mr. Vitovits passed us from the attic in the barn to the pit in a nearby forest, which was prepared as a hiding place during times of attacks. We remained here about two weeks.

*[Page 262]*

Finally, Mr. Vitovits decided that we could not continue to stay with him since the Germans had advanced up to Moscow and the prospects seemed hopeless, especially since the neighbors began to follow after the preparation on the farm. Vitovits equipped all of us with food for some days and accompanied us until past the farm of Grushvah so that we would not stumble upon Germans, who were camping in the place, and advised us to reach the ghetto Pruzni, in which still no harm was done to the Jews. He also attempted to provide me with an identity card (passport) of a young Christian girl who had died at this time. However, he was not able to execute this for different reasons.

The three of us went to Pruzni and we reached the village of Zafrod at 2 p.m. on our way. The inhabitants observed us (as apparently, the village guard alerted them by ringing bells). Immediately, panic arose. We began to run in order to escape the village and were able to reach a grove at the end of the village. And here we separated in the dark of night.

I remained alone until dawn and saw that paths pass the grove in which cattle went to graze. I went farther into the midst of the forest so that no one would come upon me in it. I passed all day there. Before the evening when I was entirely wet from the rain that fell, I decided to approach the village and try my luck again. I knocked on the house of one of the farmers. He went out and asked who I was. When he recognized that I was not one of the women of the place, he shut the door. I drew a little water from the well in the courtyard. I took down from the fence a wet sack in which I covered my head with it and walked the length of the village until its other end. When I left the village, I met to my astonishment again with Shayke Neidus and his friend, and the three of us walked together upon the advice of Shayke to a nearby farm. Shayke suggested that for the ten dollars that he had he would ask the farmer to lodge them one night.

To be sure, one farmer agreed. He opened the barn and put us in it. However, before one hour was up, the police appeared, whom he invited, and they took us outside. We received murderous blows. I was separated from my friends and the police brought us to the station. The commander, who spoke Polish, began to examine me for my place of origin and other details. During the examination, I began to implore him to let me off and allow me to go to the ghetto of Pruzni as if in it were found my relatives. I succeeded in influencing his humane feelings and even tears were seen in his eyes upon hearing all that had passed over me and he agreed to free me. He advised me to wait until before dawn and together with the farmers bringing fodder to their farms to go towards Pruzni.

When I left the police station, rain was falling. I didn't know where to go in the dark. I saw a pile of fodder under an awning especially set up. I penetrated under a layer of fodder and fell asleep. When it became day, I saw farmers' wagons loaded with fodder going in the direction of the border that the Germans set up for some reason near Pruzni. I joined one of the wagons without the farmer paying attention to me and walked after him. Suddenly, the farmer turned aside and I found myself facing the boundary. A farm woman, who was bringing a wagon full of cabbage, came towards me and to my question if she saw Germans on the way said to me that I could go forward without fear. The Germans remained at home because of the rain and were busy playing cards. I passed the boundary and when I went two kilometers, Shayke and his friend came out from the side of the forest. They told me that they were able to bribe the police with some dollars and thus were saved.

We decided to go separately with me going before them as a scout. Suddenly, there appeared three people in front of me. All of them were wearing German uniforms. One of them spoke Polish and two of them spoke German. When they saw me, they shouted to me, "Stop!" I pretended that I did not understand and continued to walk. However, the Pole caught up with me and angrily stopped me, shouting: "Why didn't you pay attention to the order? Tell me, who you are, Russian, Jewish, or Polish?"

*[Page 263]*

I said that I am Russian. "I was working in the potato harvest in a nearby village and I am returning now to a second village near Pruzni."

"Show me your documents," again ordered the Pole.

I said that in our village we still didn't receive any documents. One of the Germans confirmed that it was truly still before documents were given and thus they allowed me to continue on my way.

My two friends, who were walking after me, saw what was happening and had fled into the forest.

I continued to walk and near Pruzni met a cart. In it there were two youths with the identity sign of the yellow patch on their breasts. They recognized that I am Jewish and advised me to hide during the day in the nearby brick factory and in the evening they would enter me into the ghetto together with the women working in the field on the potato harvest and thus it was.

When I came to the ghetto of Pruzni, I went to the house of Yasha Lifshits, an inhabitant of Antopol. He came here before there was a ghetto when the Christians slandered him that he was a Communist. And after he received murderous blows, he left Antopol with his family and went to Pruzni. The meeting with the family was full of tension. They asked me a lot of what happened to Antopol, the town of their birth, and about the destruction of the ghetto. Mr. Lifshits returned home in the company of some men and among them, as was known to me afterwards, a Christian. All of them were dressed as Jews living in the ghetto with a patch on their breasts. However, these were partisans, who had already begun to act in the region.

On one winter night when there was a snowstorm taking place outside, the wires of the fence were cut and we passed to the concentration of the partisans in the region, who were armed with light weapons of all sorts and ammunition. I acted in the ranks of the partisans until the day of liberation in the month of August. It was the period of the grain harvest.

I decided to visit Antopol, the place of my birth. Alone and with the certain knowledge that I would not find one of my family alive, I walked to the place where the house had stood in which I was born and raised. I stood on the hill where our house had stood and I caused to come into existence in my imagination the house, its rooms, and exits. The good days of my youth passed quickly before my eyes. All this was no more. I was choked with tears and left the place.

This is my incomplete story because truthfully a person could not exhaust the description of the disaster that passed over all the House of Israel and the community of Antopol in it.

# The Action of an Underground Doctor from Antopol
## By P. Czerniak

In 1941 when the Einsatz Kommando of Himmler and Kaltenbruner arrived in the countries of Eastern Europe, their goal was to destroy people who were not similar or not necessary to their goals: Jews, gypsies, communists, intellectuals, nationalists, sick people, babies, and aged parents (who could not work making war materials). A Jewish doctor and partisan was to them a threefold criminal, most dangerous for the Third Reich.

Four years passed. With great delay, justice returned to the world and also after a delay began the judgment of the murderers, who were professionals with diplomas, after they managed to spill 24 million liters of

Jewish blood from among the 52 million liters that they spilled like water. And they likewise produced tons of soap from the remains of fat left on the bodies of the starved Jews, who were destroyed. The wind blew the ashes of the chief murderer. As to his assistant hangmen, some of them were sentenced, and some of them still compete with the "genius" of the accursed Jews so that they can find holes under the earth to keep justice from reaching them. The threefold criminal (Jew plus doctor plus partisan), who was judged to death by Hitler, returned from the forest, from the underground to the city, so that he could fulfill his function as doctor. He summarized and compared the action of the murderers, the super-men, on the one hand, and his, the persecuted animal, the accursed Jew, the gypsy, the Zhid, on the other hand.

*[Page 264]*

He began the search for his colleague doctors and was informed: one from Brisk (A. H.) poured sulfuric acid on his murderers, who came to take him to execution, and jumped from a high story in his house. Thus, he preferred to end his young life rather than by being pierced by German bullets. One from Kobrin (A. G.) prepared two hand grenades and threw them on his enemies and himself. The third in Horodets (Z. A.) was forced by them to dig a pit near the stable in the courtyard. They threw him dying into there together with his wife, who held in her arms their two-year-old child. The fourth in the nearby city of Drohitsin injected into his veins a sufficient dose of morphine while he still had time. The fifth and sixth, may their memory be blessed, did not leave the community that they treated before they were killed like tens of thousands of their brothers and sisters and thrown into a common grave. There were killed by the Nazis in two and a half years in my Lithuanian town: two young doctors, a dentist, two pharmacists and three assistant pharmacists, two barber-surgeons, two midwives, three nurses and other assistant medical help.

I remained alone, abandoned and wretched. I heard questions not just once: "Did many Jews not succeed to save themselves and stood organized in line to be killed?" I will answer with a question: What were the possibilities to be saved? The answer: 1) To hide with goodhearted people, not Jews; 2) to join the partisans in the forests; 3) to move to a strange place with the forged identity of a non-Jew. However, then the question to ask is When to carry this out? 1) To flee early while there is still time or 2) to flee in a time of the Action, partial or final destruction of the ghetto. The first way was connected with severe repressions by the occupants. If a person disappeared from the ghetto, they took out in his place for execution 50 or 100 others, relatives and town notables. And who wanted to try to save himself at so frightening a price? The second way demanded from the person undertaking it much inner strength and strong desire to live, despite the psychological disease of psychological totoplegy, which took hold of those who lived in the ghettos. From the medical viewpoint, this paralyzing disease is the reason chiefly for the ease by which the homicidal people destroyed millions.

How were they able to cause totoplegy? Please imagine the following. They took people, who until then had been free, cultured, intellectual, active in science, commerce and industry, active in the free professions, children of parents, brothers, and friends. They humiliated them according to plan slowly, continually, indifferently, with mockery and contempt, laughter and cruelty that were inhuman for people lacking defense or even supporters, for people not necessary to anyone, no value, for whom anyone in a green uniform, having a problem, could at any time, at any place, as he being intoxicated, wanted to kill them for a made up pretext. They locked these people in ghettos, crowded, poor, primitive, hungry, and dirty. They cut off all connection with the world; near and distant. They put on them a regime of prisoners, orders, contributions, theft, and forced labor without payment and without any satisfaction in addition to continual fear of death, concentration camp, and destruction without judgment and reason, without argument, with the natural fear of their hiding place being revealed and the removal of adults and children, like mice from their holes, and bringing them to mass graves or killing them on the spot, after murderous blows. In addition to living like that, without any hope for a change for the better and thus during a year and another year: 360-720 days.

*[Page 265]*

What becomes of the psyche of people in these conditions? What value does their life have for themselves? Why live, for whom and for what? This is a condition so severe that I heard young and strong people in the past, with whom I waited in one group for a van to come to take them to pits where they would be made to undress and get a bullet in the neck, and I heard them say: "May the end come quickly, but quickly! We do not want to live and suffer any more." Death was like freedom from a burden. When I turned there to the young doctor V.P., who had graduated a year ago from the Faculty in Vilna and requested: "Rafi, come let us escape." I received the answer: "There is no value and I will not leave my mother here." This is a psychiatric disease and its name is totoplegy, a self condemnation to death. This is self degradation to zero, with resignation from life. This is what helped the homicidal people. Only a remnant of much inner strength that was superhuman, beyond normal, and a weak hope drove individuals to try their luck. And when the first stop, running away, succeeded, there remained still a long way to remain in life, after the escape.

This way from the ghetto under siege, from the square awaiting expulsion to a place of refuge was very difficult. It was dangerous and the chances for success rare. Those who passed through it did this not according to a single rule. Each one had his or her own odyssey. Here is one of them from Antopol. It is April 1942. A farmer appears before the

Jewish doctor with a pass from the German gendarmes in this language: "We approve for the Zhid doctor P. Ts. to leave the ghetto for twelve hours and to visit the sick person in the village H." The cart brings the doctor to a house at the edge of the village. A sick person with jaundice enters the room. His dress, his gun, a machine gun on his shoulder and hand grenades in his belt testify who he is, which he says: "You and I are persecuted We have faith in you. Act and be silent There will come a time and we will help you." Similar episodes occur. It is October 1942. The Einsatz kommando had surrounded the ghetto for final liquidation of its last 300 or so inhabitants.

The doctor decided: "I will not go to undress at the edge of the pit, to receive a bullet in the head, and to fall on a pile of bodies that preceded me." He succeeded on his third try to escape the Umzatsplatz. The places and addresses of the Jewish academic were these places: fields, stables, ruins, piles of straw, under the floor in those days. This was until he made contact with the people in the forest, and the Jewish doctor, who escaped from human hunters, began to act as a person needed to someone. He began to devote himself heart and soul to his saviors. He found in the Yokhni forest, near the village of Odrinkah in the district of Antopol, a group of about thirty people in the underground. They dwelled in tents or on the grass under a tree, near the swamps. They still had only a few weapons. They were in one place today and in another place the next day. This was because the Germans ambushed them and sent spies. It was always an emergency situation. However, you were breathing freely. You had a weapon in your hand to fight and hope in your heart. It was not important that exclusive of your professional knowledge in your brain that you had nothing. There were no medicine, instruments, professional help, work place, light, and the like. Work goes on even under these conditions. This is especially the case since there is a great desire and volunteering without bounds. Behold, you are free and equal among equals. You have absolute responsibility in matters of health in the camp and for those who believe in you. The Jewish doctor began to act.

The first examination of the fighters was done behind a sheet between trees, on a blanket spread on the grass. There was a handkerchief in place of a stethoscope. It became clear that half the people suffered from scabies. Treatment was immediately begun. They brought sulfur and pig fat (Adepssuilli). The pharmacist, G. Ts., the wife of the doctor, who also escaped from the ghetto under siege, prepared an ointment of twenty percent sulfur. During a number of days the odor of sulfur spread among the trees of the forest. They washed their bodies in the nearby swamp. They boiled part of the clothes and threw away the rest, burning them. The people in the forest said after about two weeks: "How good it is for us; we can rest and sleep." The ointment doctor, of the threefold criminal – doctor, Jew, and partisan – was given without payment to people in contact, to sympathizers, to the village population. There were among them many sick with scabies. This helped. The Jewish couple who escaped the hunters became blessed people.

*[Page 266]*

At the same time history tells according to document no. 94 of the Nuremburg trial for Nazi criminals that a German doctor, with blue blood in his veins, belonging to Einsatz Kommando A found among the Jews of Newel and Janowiczc cases of scabies. (No one knows if it were really scabies. The diagnoses of the blue blood were wrong more than once). As a diligent epidemiologist, the doctor sought to eradicate the disease so that it would not spread. The deed was done in an original, contemptible Hitlerian fashion. They killed 640 Jews in Newel and 1,025 Jews in Janowiczc and burned their houses. So, here you have the method of public medicine for dermatology as done by Jews and as done by Nazis. The odor of sulfur and healing of the disease without any fatality in the case of thousands of people in the district of Antopol and the smell of burning and piles of ashes of houses plus the smell of lime from the mass grave; of 1,665 Jews, the 1,665 victims in the district of Newel. Light versus darkness, blacker than darkness.

# The End of 1943 to the Beginning of 1944

The working conditions of the doctor, Pyotr Aronovits, the threefold criminal, improved. The scope of his work increased. We were already 700 people in two camps: the fighting group (about 400 soldiers) and the family camp hidden in a safe place in the region of the Sporowo swamps. I sent there the doctor, Trushnikovah, whom the Germans brought to Antopol in my place and had fled to us in the beginning of 1944 when the condition of the front worsened for the Germans. The Jew and his wife remained in the operative camp. The number of victims went up and also the number of wounded and sick. The partisan unit took on itself to supply medical help to the population of the villages in which it camped. Since it was forbidden to us to travel to the district city of Antopol, we had a lot of work.

1. A partisan infirmary was set up. In the beginning it was a tent and after that one of the houses in the village to which the group entered. An adjutant soldier was assigned to the authority of the doctor, a horse and wagon, and equipment for packing. We worked out a plan according to which we could quickly pack up the infirmary and leave the place together with the bed in times of emergency. This infirmary worked all hours of the day and night because there was constant movement in the camp. The groups of fighters would constantly go out to fight, sabotage, scout, make contact, and other things. Partisans from other groups would come or pass on the way to their goals, and among them there were not a few needing medical help. Sick people from the population would knock on the door after they received permission to enter our area from people whom we trusted.

A partisan pharmacy was set up and instruments assembled. The soldiers were asked in a general assembly to bring medicine left behind in village houses. The action was successful. There quickly appeared a pile of packets and boxes with pills, injections, ointments, and powders. The pharmacist counted the property. The Nazi pharmacies were a secondary source of medicines. People of the Third Reich would sell for pig fat to our contact people medicines according to the lists of the Jewish doctor. Also, the central medical service of the partisan unit was also sent from time to time a certain supply. Finally, there served as a blood bank after sterilization in a barrel for homemade vodka bottles with physiological water. There was also organized a clinical laboratory for chemical examinations of urine.

*[Page 267]*

The collection of medical instruments was done in a similar way, including local inventions. For example, we invaded the village of Demidovshtsinah. In about a half hour, there appeared a local inhabitant, who was crying: "Help, my wife is going to die." It became clear that she had a miscarriage in the third month. There were no instruments for scraping. We mobilized a village blacksmith, who worked for two hours. We made tongues from iron rods which had been used to clean rifles. There were joined pieces of tin from the copper of a battery to another iron rod. Another tool was made from an aluminum tube of different size, which had been used in the village to distill homemade vodka. Similarly, a speculum was made, which completed the gynecological tools. A pot served as a sterilizer and the kitchen table became a gynecological one. The scraping was done and the bleeding stopped. The woman got better. Her future pregnancy would be better. In another village (Drobnoyah) a pregnant woman began to give birth and she had triplets. To my good fortune, everything went well. I tied the umbilical cords and made a massage of the area of the womb so that the placenta, which was late in coming out, would come out.

At that same time, Nazi doctors stopped the natural bleeding of Jewish women in concentration camps, with completely different methods, with a goal that the women would never be pregnant again. And here again you have the contrast of the gynecological and birthing methods of the Jewish doctor in comparison with the Nazis: treatment of a woman's bleeding with the human goal of her getting better and to save her future fertility as opposed to the method of castration by those, whose names should be blotted out, of young Jewish women to sterilize them and destroy their fertility.

The special worry of the Jewish doctor was the sanitary condition in the fighters' camp, liquidating and preventing epidemics. An epidemic of typhus broke out in our area at the beginning of 1944. The soldiers would sometimes remain to sleep in the villages and have lice attach themselves.

They brought the epidemic in this way to the camp. The number of sick people was ten. We began to act. We built at the entrance of the camp in the ground a room for preventive disinfection with steam. There we hung all the clothing and bed utensils for two hours. Hair was cut and all bathed in a bathhouse in the field. The orders were carried out. The soldiers were freed from the third plague of Egypt. The sick were separated for treatment. The results were good. We reached the number of 22 sick and all of them recovered. There was not one death. This was in spite of the fact that the Nazis attacked us during that time with the help of the Hungarian cavalry. We were forced to leave the place and drag four very sick people on stretchers made from the branches of trees and cloth.

At that time, the history of the criminal of blue blood tells: the commander of Einsatz Gruppe B, Nebe, sent on October 10 a proud report to Berlin. He informs in it that there was typhus in Vitbesk. There was suspicion that its source was the ghetto that was crowded. Therefore, 4,090 Jews were taken for execution and the ghetto liquidated. The sanitary authorities found in Radomysl that the ghetto was, so to speak, filthy. They suspected that this was likely to cause an epidemic of typhus. Therefore, 1,668 Jews were killed and the fear of the potential epidemic passed.

It is possible to distinguish the difference in the methods of epidemiological work. The Jewish doctor (the: anti-Nazi criminal) effectively fought in the forest under the conditions of partisans against lice that spread the disease and the pseudo scholar doctors of the group of criminals that thought itself to be at the height of humanity fought the epidemic by killing the sick. Didn't they show to their contempt both their bravery and their skill what is Nazism?

*[Page 268]*

We were concerned for the wounded and sick who needed hospitalization. It was the ambition of the Jewish doctor in the case of the wounded to return them to the front as soon as possible. Small operations, bandages, and taking care of breaks were done in place. We had in our possession a large amount of plaster from a captured van with some things necessary for us. We would transfer the severely wounded to behind the front lines with the help of planes, which would come at night from time to time to the partisan airfield in the forests.

And here is an episode. Behold, there was a small boat with the adjutant and wounded soldier. It was scouting. It came upon a German unit and there was a battle. The person wounded in his foot fell to the ground. A German soldier came up. He gave him a kick with the foot and said "dead". However, he shot a bullet to the region of the jaw neck to be more sure and left. The bullet passed the jaw and the mouth. The jaw was paralyzed and the lungs got gangrene from swallowing. We traveled with this wounded person in the canals between the swamps many kilometers and many hours to the partisan airfield. A Piper plane came at night and took the wounded person and brought him to a hospital where the Germans were not in power.

Another image appears before my eyes. I am brought to a corner of the ghetto for final liquidation on a Sunday. We are waiting for the van. An excellent young carpenter is brought to the area. The Nazi found him in a hole and shot him because he did not hurry to leave. The bullet struck the stomach, through which opening the small intestine came out. The young man was suffering from terrible pains. He held his head in his hands. What help could I give him? With the help of a handkerchief with traces of blood from a blow which I received on my forehead in my first attempt to flee, behold I put back his intestine and closed the opening. The pains became quieter and that is all. I knew that in 10-20 minutes they would come to take us and also the youth to there for execution. And I made the third attempt to flee before the van came and I succeeded.

And again the comparison of the two methods of medical surgical help: the help to him from the free Jewish doctor, traveling with him to distances while risking life with the goal to save the wounded, and the German method without any concern to give medical help to wounded, without any humane feeling to do something for the wounded. Just throwing him on the ground in a camp to kill the wounded. Is this thing believable?

As said, the partisan doctor was also a doctor for the village population in which we temporarily dwelled. However, sick people from the distant region, who heard about the Jewish partisan doctor working with the partisans, would make efforts to reach him. They sought help from our contact people and the end result was the need to give them medical aid. It was also necessary to travel to villages where the sick were lying, according to recommendation of our staff. The underground medical help was maximal and free.

And, behold, there was an event about which I knew later. A child from a family in the service of the occupying authorities received lengthy treatment from the Russian doctor in Antopol, who took the place of the Jewish doctor, whom they wanted to kill and who had fled. The treatment of the child did not succeed. Then, the authorities of the district gave this advice: "Go the village of Haroshvo, seek protection from the partisan doctor, and we will hear what he says." The thing was done. The medical treatment was successful.

And at that time history tells of Nazi horrors against Jewish children. A German doctor found in Shimiatitsi sixteen retarded Jewish children in a medical institute. According to him, they were not receiving the necessary supervision. It is for that reason that he shot them in the head and killed them with great German precision. And in those days in another place, the representatives of the Hitler youth would take Jewish children from the Lemberg ghetto and use them as targets for good shooting. Is it necessary to compare the pediatrics of the Jewish criminal doctor and the medicine of the super-humans?

*[Page 269]*

Yes, the methods of work and medical and human ethics of the Jewish partisan were entirely different than those of the Germans. Even then in the case of the Jewish doctor there were no differences in the treatment of the sick whether they were Jews or not Jews. Jewish partisans received treatment similar to that of non-Jews and also all the non-Jewish population, in which perhaps more than one of them showed Anti-Semitism in other circumstances received similar treatment. However, when they needed the medical help of a Jewish doctor, there was professional knowledge verbally and actively, objectivity and similar devotion day and night.

There will testify to that some figures that were gathered by the Jewish doctor in the forests: in the course of 18 months, he saw 7,320 walk-in patients of partisan sick and 2,400 sick from among the population, which lived in the region of action of the partisans. There received treatment 58 wounded partisans and 6 citizens. There were made 35 small operations, there were 213 sick people put into the hospital, and there were 152 visits to the sick who lived in about 46 points of settlement. He participated in 9 big military actions.

In order to carry out the great amount of work and to take care to provide quick first aid, which is certainly known to be frequently the determining factor in the fate of the wounded, it was necessary to have a staff to help during military engagements. There were no qualified people or very few qualified people among the fighters. Certainly, the Jewish doctors, barber-surgeons, nurses, and sanitary workers had been killed. Therefore, the doctor in the forests had to teach practical nurses and sanitary workers among those present. In the course of a number of months, sixteen young girls received lessons and examples in first aid. Every one of them was attached afterwards to a certain unit of fighters. In cases when the staff and most fighters would go on a big action, the Jewish doctor was also permitted to join and see with his eyes acts of vengeance and actions taken for freedom, as he was considered a member of the staff. The practical nurses and combat sanitary workers, who were instructed, filled their task faithfully, devotedly, and professionally in a way worthy of distinction.

It is unnecessary to emphasize the differences in approach and instruction in giving first aid, including the staff treating the sick, which on the one hand the accursed Jew showed and which on the other hand the hunters of humans showed. The former attracted medical staff, taught the art of medicine to assistants, and increased their number in order to offer medical assistance to the needy. And the Nazis killed in that region and at the time of occupation doctors, dentists, pharmacists, midwives, nurses, and sanitary workers and destroyed clinics and the regional hospital. In doing so, they destroyed most of the existing medical help.

# The Last Battle with the Germans

At the beginning of June 1944 our contact people informed us that a group of German soldiers were dug in the forest in front of the alcohol factory. All of us went to attack from the side. They were frightened and fled. There was fire seen in the horizon from Brezah-Kartuzkah. Evening came. The skies were red from the fires that the Germans lighted before they retreated. However, there were no Germans. We were free. There was the light of redemption before us. We came to it and it came to us. There was made on the afternoon of the second day the first contact with the shock troops 373 of the army that fought, like us, against criminals, frightened people, small and sad, who fled in such great haste and who on the 22nd of June, 1941, with the sound of orders and spark of the sword invaded a country not theirs, to our Antopol, and turned it into a pile of ruins.

Exactly after three years, on June 22, 1944, we entered Antopol again with a group of fighting partisans. There was quiet, an empty vacuum – no Jews – all lost. There remained one comfort for a Jewish doctor, who returned to this place – to devote all his strength and time to the restitution of medical service and to find comfort in that. And in that time, to realize his dream, from the time of his youth, to seek all possible ways in order to reach the homeland that he was lacking and to those like him in the course of a dark and long exile, to live in it free and to work for its good and greatness.

*[Page 270]*

There ended a chapter that was not forgotten in the lives of Jews and in the lives of Jewish doctors. Many enemies had surrounded us and caused great harm. Much blood had been shed from our bodies. However, there were those who wept bitterly with us. Their anguish was deep when they killed us and also deep then when the remnant that was saved began to leave for goals it had. And here are the words in parting of one of these Polish friends:

Smoke goes up from the chimney of the crematoria –
We are with you when it goes up from your bodies.
Know, your souls were not burned –
They remain in life forever and instruct us
With their understanding, emotions and greatness
How we should act in order that the German beast
Does not arise forever Brother Jews – we are with you always
To wherever you turn and go.

*[Page 270]*

# Our Being Saved from Destruction
## By Gitl Feldshtein-Czerniak

It was Thursday, October 15, 1942 at 5 a.m. when the frightened shout of my brother Avraham wakened me from sleep: "Gitl, the ghetto is surrounded!" He opened from outside the shutters and disappeared. With him also his voice became silent. His excited shout accompanied me for many years. I did not see him anymore.

My husband and I dressed quickly and entered the nearby room in which we found my mother, Tseviyah, of blessed memory, and the mother of my husband, Shifrah, of blessed memory. They were standing as if frozen by fear and their glances asked: "What should we do? Where should we go?" My mother-in-law gave me a warm wool kerchief. It was a cold and rainy fall morning. The cold was felt in full strength. The potato harvest in the fields was then at its peak.

I remember that the day before then there appeared in the ghetto the German inspector for the agricultural harvest (Kreislandwirt) and he announced that everyone would be able to dig in the field and to harvest three pood of potatoes (a pood is 16 kg). My brother, Avraham, prepared to go to the field, assuming if they allowed us to harvest the potatoes that the winter would pass peacefully and they would not harm the inhabitants of the ghetto. I was not so optimistic. Oppositely, I feared that who knows if we will benefit to taste from them. And thus it was. The Judenrat was arrested by the police on the night after the declaration of the Kreislandwirt. The ghetto was surrounded by the Nazis before morning. Thus, the Nazis and their helpers would trick the inhabitants of the ghetto each time before a criminal action, in order to put to sleep their watchfulness, organization, or opposition. The fact that this time the Judenrat was arrested was severe and gave witness that the intention was to liquidate all of us.

The moments passed. We had to decide on steps to save ourselves. However, no one knew what to do. My husband said, "I will go out and see what is going on." He quickly returned excited and said that he suspected there was no chance to be saved since the guard around the ghetto was very strong. And then came the thought: "Perhaps, we will succeed to go out by way of the house of the family, which is on the border with the Christian street." When we got there running, we saw that many people had the same idea. We got there and filled the house. The windows were covered by wooden boards and no one dared to remove them and make an opening to escape.

*[Page 271]*

My husband succeeded in removing some boards and was about to jump outside. I took hold of a corner of his coat and warned him to look if there was no guard. However, the thick mist of that fall morning prevented him from seeing anything. When he jumped and went ahead a few steps, we heard the order of a German: "Stop!"

I was able to see the armed Nazi seize my husband by his shoulder and take him away from the place. Those who remained hurried again to close the opening and leave the house. There passed after a few seconds a group of people going toward the house of Joseph Sirotah, in which dwelt Peltsuk's son-in-law, who was arrested with the Judenrat. They called us to join them. As it seems, however, I did not hear their call because my eyes were turned toward the near fence in the hope that perhaps my husband would see me. However, my mother began to walk in the direction of the group, which was going away, as her look full of despair and sadness rested on me. I will forget the expression of her face in that moment, her frightened eyes, pale face, and embroidered kerchief on her head.

I remember her words after we were saved from the previous Action: "Children, in the future in the time of an Action, do not call and encourage one another. Let each one go her way, as fit to him and may good fortune accompany him." And thanks to that I was saved and remained alive.

I remained with my mother-in-law, of blessed memory, who, full of mourning and despair, kept on murmuring: "They took Pinchas. Pinchas is no more!" And her voice was full of tears. We felt it dangerous to remain outside at a time when at any moment the gate was going to be opened and the Action begun. We entered a house that was near the fence and hid in the small cellar. The criminal Action began after a short time in the ghetto. We heard in the rooms the steps and shouts of a German: "Out!" We heard in a nearby apartment the crying of an infant. Its parents, the family of Avraham Zaidl, were not able to give it to Christians as we did a month before then. This time the parents left the infant as they fled since there was no other choice for the unfortunates.

The crying of the infant stopped because the Nazi that walked into the house and shouted "Out" took it with him. Immediately after this the cry of a woman outside broke the silence. She tried to convince some Nazi that she could still work and bring value and because of this he should let her remain alive. A shot put an end to her entreaties and life.

Thus, the hours of the day passed that seemed like an eternity. The evening came and with it darkness. The Christian inhabitants began to break into the houses to plunder. The entrance to the attic was found above the cellar in which we hid. We feared that perhaps one of the plunderers would direct to us a flashlight through the opening and reveal our hiding place. In addition to this there were isolated shots that sounded through the air from time to time. They increased the terror that surrounded us. We sat together on the floor and were silent.

Slowly there came the morning light of Friday. We heard the creaking of a board from a nearby hiding place. From it came out our neighbor Rachel Kaplan, from the Hirshenhorn family, with her two children, a son of six or seven and another of about two. To my question through the boards where was her husband and what she intended to do, she answered to me, that her husband was not with her and that she was going to get water and some kerosene for the lamp. When she returned after some minutes, the small child did not want to return to the hiding place after he saw that it was light outside. However, Rachel put him in by force, as the child was crying. When they just managed to get into the hiding place, a strong knocking was heard and the police burst into the house upon hearing the crying of the child.

*[Page 272]*

One of the police went to the cellar that was in the second part behind the partition of boards, where I was hiding with my mother-in-law. He began to feel the boards. We huddled in these moments in a corner and held our breath.

It is possible that there is not a heavy guard in the boundary of the ghetto and the market place, where there is the police station and the police dormitory (Paltsuk and Sirota's house) because there they secure. And so, it was. By crawling on his stomach between these two aforementioned houses, Pinchas succeeded in leaving. He passed the market place, the rows of stores, reached Visotski's house and from there to the side streets in the direction of the Pinsker farmlands. The streets were dark and abandoned. A light rain fell. Suddenly, he heard the order: "Stop." Pinchas recognized that the one shouting was York, a local policeman. This policeman wanted to avoid participating in actions against the villagers, who would refuse to collaborate with the Germans. He had come to me and received an ointment to cause an allergic reaction, which he put between the toes of his foot. They swelled up and he was not able to put on his shoes. Therefore, he remained on local guard duty. When Pinchas recognized York's voice, he said, "Don't shoot me. It is I, the doctor Tcherniak." The policeman put down the gun. He said where the German guard was and left. Pinchas continued on his way beyond the house of the inhabitants and reached the farm of Ivan Raiduk.

We did not speak much at our meeting, Pinchas and I, in our conversation about what happened to us. We were dazed. And to the degree that we were able to concentrate our thought, we were given to plan for our flight because there was not a place to assume that the danger was behind us. And what was the situation at Vera Okhrits? How could we be informed?

We felt that Ivan and his wife disappeared from the farm. They did not take care even to feed their animals. That Sunday passed on us standing guard, looking through the cracks if the police or SS were not appearing. Ivan and his wife returned at night and informed us because of fear that they would be revealed and in this endanger their lives that they could not continue to hide us.

We left about 12 a.m. in the direction of the village of Frishikhvust that was near Antopol. Ivan explained to us exactly the way to the farmer Nastruk, who was one of our patients. We arrived there. We found a place to hide among the pile of clover against the wall of the barn. We spent all the day standing up. We saw early in the morning how Nastruk harnessed his horse to the wagon and went with his wife. When it became dark, we entered the barn and when Nastruk returned my husband approached him and asked for refuge. After advice with his wife, he returned and brought us milk, eggs, and bread. However, he informed us that he could not hide us because his wife had heart trouble and this would endanger her health being in constant fear. We left in the evening.

It was clear that it would be difficult for two people to hide together. Therefore, we decided to split. I would go to Zusyah and my husband would go to Tanyah, two patients of my husband for whom he did a lot. Tanyah agreed and did the best she could She gave food to Pinchas and sought a refuge. She talked things over with her aunt, who lived in an isolated house nearby, not far from the railway tracks to Pinsk. She persuaded her to put up my husband. Likewise, she took it upon herself to provide the food since her aunt was poor. This did not happen for me with Zusyah. When she saw me, she was afraid and began with her old mother to ask that I leave her house. My pleas did not help. Her husband appeared. He explained that the Germans employed him in burying the dead. They were killing all the Jews in the ghetto. And the meaning: what was I doing here? They intentionally raised up the flame of the light in the room and Zusyah opened the door. My condition was very bad. I had to act quickly: I left the house and immediately changed my direction in order to disappear from the sight of Zusyah and her husband. I also went to Tanyah. I saw from the window inside her house that she was with a man. I knocked on the door and a man came out, whom I did not recognize. I asked him to tell Tanyah that her friend wanted to see her. She went out, immediately recognized me, and informed me that my husband was with her a short while ago and she hid him with her aunt. At my request, she brought me also to the hiding place of Pinchas.

*[Page 273]*

We spent a few days and nights in the potato cellar and again a few days in the attic of the barn until it became too cold. We persuaded the aunt to let us dig a hiding place under the floor of the house in the entrance beneath the stoke-hold of the oven. There we remained all the months of the winter under inhuman conditions. Even Tanyah's visits became few and the portions of food became more miserable. We had to take care from the oldest son of our host, who would frequently get drunk, and we feared that in his drunkenness, he would reveal us.

Groups of partisans began to operate in the region. From time to time, they mined the railway tracks. The Germans ordered to cut down the forests and to destroy the houses near to the tracks so that they would not serve as a hiding place for those doing demolition. The house in which we were was a distance of about 200 meters from the railway. They were ordered to leave it by May 15 because it would be destroyed by the Germans.

The question arose about what to do with us. If they let us leave, then the Nazis could catch us and then they would hang the participants who had helped the Jews. They began to make plans in the kitchen between Tanyah and her aunt. Pinchas heard the sessions of advice above. He would crawl to the stoke-bold each time that Tanyah would come to the sessions. One evening it was decided to poison us. They put on Kolik to bring mouse poison. The next day Kolik informed that he would not get it since the sale of poison was forbidden by the Germans for security reasons. They came up with a second plan, to kill us by shooting. It was decided it would be carried out by the lover of Tanyah, the policeman Kostik.

We prepared for the developments. My husband got a key to the door and got a hold of clubs so that we would be able to escape in case it was finally decided to execute us. All this was done when the mistress of the house and her small son, a shepherd, were out. In those hours we would go out of our hiding place like mice to get fresh air, to wash, etc. We continued to listen to the sessions of planning that were held from evening to evening in the kitchen. We listened with excitement to the report of Tanyah, who gave the answer of her lover, Kostik. He was shocked at the suggestion of his beloved, and he remembered the help that Dr. Tcherniak gave to her and to him when he was still in the ghetto. Finally, he refused to carry out the plan and suggested to take advice with the Director of the Office of Employment in Antopol, the Pole Artsishevski, who as he knew had saved a Jewish girl during the killing and he assured them that he would agree to help Dr. Tserniak and his wife.

Our hostess told us the next day of the order to leave (she understandably did not know we had heard everything) and gave the good news that Artsishevski was about to visit us and that we should prepare for this visit. She made it possible for us to wash and to go away. He appeared at dark and broke out crying at our poor appearance. Leaving the place was carefully planned. Artsishevski came a second time before evening. I was accompanied by him and my husband was in the company of the aunt. Holding arms, we went in the direction of Antopol by the Pinsk farmland in the evening hours. On the way Mr. Artsishevski greeted acquaintances passing by with a good evening. Understandably, they did not recognize us. We arrived at his house. Artsishevski took care to prepare for us a hiding place in the attic of his granary. His servant took care of our needs.

The activities of the partisans became more frequent in the region. Artsishevski brought us news from time to time about that. He also made contact with them. My husband requested him to take from us to the partisans, who were active in the region of Grusheva, the news that we were alive. My husband made contact with this group when he was still in the ghetto when he gave it medical help. It did not take long and we received the news that we were to prepare ourselves for the way to join them.

*[Page 274]*

When the supplies ran out that we brought with us, we began raids on the surrounding farms in order to get food and information about what was happening in the region. In the beginning there visited us at set times contacts from other groups in the region and they instructed us about what was going to happen. They brought us news about organization in a broad scope and promised to give us aid with supplies and arms in the approaching spring. Meanwhile, we sat in the bunker and waited.

A deep snow covered the ground, and from fear of leaving signs from steps that could reveal us, we sat for five days straight without food. On one of these nights when I stood outside on my watch, I heard steps coming close. I entered the bunker and alerted the people of the group. And indeed these were steps but not of people. Rather they were of a horse that lost its way and reached us. Since we were hungry like wolves in the winter, we killed the horse and ate its flesh that was cooked without salt and was tasteless and caused us nausea despite our hunger. From fear of being revealed, we tried to do as little as possible in the search for food from farmers in the region. However, not just once we were forced to endanger ourselves in the search for food from the farmers in the region when we were very oppressed by hunger. Then our youth would raid the nearby farms and bring us some food. We held out all the winter months under these conditions.

From time to time our people would carry out different actions under their own initiative. One of them was carried out by seven youths of the bravest in our group. They attacked on one night the residence of the Gebiets-Kommissar in Pruzani and took him prisoner without firing a shot, so as not to make noise. They covered his mouth, bound him, and managed to take with them all the office equipment with the military documents, all the arms that included a submachine gun and a Mauser, and also all the ceremonial dress of the Gebiets-Kommissar. The documents included very important information, as was revealed afterwards. When they returned from this action, the youth succeeded in disarming a unit of German soldiers that happened upon their way.

Because I could not rest after what happened with the young men, he agreed to my request. When I told him what happened in our group and I asked him to explain the matter, he answered me that certainly a sad incident had happened, that innocent people had died, and those that falsely accused them would be examined when the time came and would get punished. However, I was to be silent until then, or I would endanger my life. In the first weeks when I was in the new camp, I could not relieve myself because of the depression from the tragedy. I would take every opportunity to tell my sadness to people, who came up to me. Those who were guilty of committing the crime did not like this and to get rid of doubts about themselves, they decided to get rid of me so that I would not testify against them when the day came.

There was a Jewish man of middle age, by the name of Misha Moitigski, in the group to which I belonged. One night we were sent out to mine the railway tracks. On the way I felt that Misha was really following my tracks and watching that the distance between me and him would not widen. The matter bothered me and I asked him why he was following me. He answered me in Russian: "It is not your business; it is necessary." After some time, when I calmed down a bit, the danger passed and the commanders began to relate to me as an active partisan for everything, Misha told me, because on that night the partisan murderers had decided to kill me also, and he decided to frustrate their plan.

*[Page 275]*

The fate of Misha and another young man from Minsk Sanyah (Shimon) was decided when they returned with their unit from a military operation against the Germans. The house to which they entered to rest was surrounded by Germans. There remained no way out for them to save themselves. They burst outside, threw a grenade against their attackers, and killed some of them. However, this did not save them. The chain around them tightened more. They threw another grenade at the Germans and killed some more. They kept the last grenade for themselves. When the Nazis approached shouting revenge to capture them, they lit the fuse of the grenade that took away the thread of their life. Misha and Sanyah also kept the slogan of the hero Samson – "Let-my soul die with the Philistines" – and their blood was mixed with that of their attackers.

Those who were investigated returned to the group warned not to say anything to their colleagues. They began the preparations for the road before evening. Each of us went out in groups of five with some space to the nearby village. When we were sent away from the place, I remarked to Galyah in whose group I went that for reason we cannot see our youth. She reacted to that with a lack of patience and advised that I should not make a fuss about it because it could be dangerous for me. She also promised to speak with me about it afterwards. Suddenly, I heard shots from a submachine gun and I was very frightened. And as I found out later these were the shots of execution killing our seven brave young men.

When we came to the village, we found in the houses of the farmers a warm meal, which the contact people had prepared for us in advance. And after a light rest, we were called to the gathering point, where wagons harnessed to horses waited to take us to the partisans' camp. Into the house, where I was staying with Galyah, the wife of Yosl Untershtraus, there entered one of the partisans, who had visited our group to mobilize us. He was wearing a man's jacket, which I recognized as belonging to Maitsek. He had the submachine gun and Mauser of Maitsek. When he took off the leather man's jacket because the room was hot, I saw that he had Maitsek's shirt and gold watch from the spoils of the Nazi from Pruzani. I understood at once that a tragedy had happened to our young men and I burst out crying bitterly. All the night on the way to the partisans' camp, I sat in the wagon next to Galyah and cried about the bitterness of the fate of our brave youth, who had been murdered for no reason.

Towards morning we arrived in the partisans' camp in the name of Tseklov, which was camped in the thick forests of Bilovzaskiyah Potshtsah (formerly the estate of the Russian Czars). The camp had tents and different buildings. It was properly equipped. We divided into the tents and after a short while we were called to a census. Each one of us was put into a certain group. At the end of the counting and registration we were freed to rest. Among the people from headquarters who took the count, I saw one man from the underground, Afanasiev, whom I recognized from his many visits to our group. When we were freed, I approached him and asked him for some minutes to speak with me.

There was found an abandoned bunker about 20 km from our partisans' camp. Units used to visit it on their return way from night raids to rest. Once one of those who participated in an action and visited the bunker informed me that he saw there four people, among them a girl that resembled me. He asked me if it were my sister. These were a husband and wife by the name of Shapira, a youth by the name of Roitkopf, and a girl named Nina, whose similarity in appearance to me moved the man to think that she were my sister.

When I was informed that the finding of the people saved was brought to the knowledge of the commander, I asked him to permit me to visit them and bring them to the camp. The commander hesitated and tried to make me change my mind from doing this by saying that he did not have in his possession the weapons needed to outfit them.

*[Page 276]*

However, he did not stand my great pleading and the next day we went to the place. We didn't find any one in the bunker. Its inhabitants hid in the nearby thickets during the day and would return to it only at night. It was permitted for me to call to them in Yiddish in order to gain their trust and lessen the fear of those hiding. I called to them not to fear and that I am a Jewish partisan. Certainly, they were calmed and came out to us from their hiding place. Their appearance was frightening. They were wearing rags, their hair was not cut, and they were worn out and pale. They told us that one of the farmers from the nearby farm supplied them with some food for the last money that they had. Shapira, whose profession was a carpenter, managed to make the model of a rifle out of a tree. He used it to frighten the farmers to get food.

The appearance of the saved people and my pleadings influenced the commander. He decided to bring them to the nearby civilian camp that benefited from his protection. There were many civilian families in it. Since in one of our successful battles, we got a large spoil of weapons, we outfitted the four and added all of them our partisan camp. All of them are living now in Israel.

The battles became more frequent. Understandably, the Germans opened an action against us and our men had to wander from place to place. During these days one of the units of our group received the order to mine the railway tracks and did not return at the set time. This situation forced all the group to remain in place as much time was possible. The farmers, who came to harvest their crop and were warned not to reveal our place to the Germans, were not able to keep their promise and informed on us. Our camp was found in the cave of a forest surrounded by deep swamps. Suddenly, the man on watch, who sat in a high tree, informed of people approaching. At first, we thought that these were our men from the unit, who were missing from last night and being led by Yashah. However, it was revealed that these were Germans, who were scouting the place, as a result of the information of the farmers.

The commander ordered us to take position and not to fire without command. The group of German scouts had eighteen people. We let them approach to a good range and the submachine gun wiped all of them out before they were able to use their weapons. Three of them, who were wounded, were taken to camp for interrogation. They were also killed when we had to leave. I was chosen to kill one of them. I listened to the laconic comment of my commander, "too bad to waste a bullet", and I was happy to put an end to one of the monsters in the form of a human with my knife.

The main force of the group approached following the German scouts and the noise of the shots. The commander, Pioter Ivanovits, went together with some partisans towards those keeping watch in order to prepare the battle against the German army that was advancing towards us. The battle developed so that they were able to kill about forty German officers and soldiers. However, they found themselves cut off from us. We thought them to be lost and the subcommander took over command. Pioter Ivanovits and his men returned to us; about after a month, worn out, hungry, and with no weapons. Our happiness knew no boundary.

When the battle was over with the Germans in our victory, we know that additional units of the German army with much more weapons would reach our place in order to gather the bodies of their dead. And certainly it happened like that. Our now commander organized a successful ambush by the dead bodies. When the additional Germans came, we killed about one hundred of them and retreated to another place.

Despite the fact that I had held a weapon, participated in all the daring battles of the unit to which I belonged, and placed my life in danger with them wherever they went, I was severely deprived at the end of the war by my commanders, who wrote on my partisan's document that I was a cook. This burning humiliation was the part of many, very many of our boys and girls, who served in the ranks of the partisans. They were motivated by vengeance to endanger their lives. They did not avoid the most dangerous actions. They were always the first to volunteer to carry out dangerous tasks. They put on them false charges with their liberation at the end of the war with the goal of lessening the many merits that they deserved on the field of battle.

*[Page 277]*

# Mosheh Dor Ber Pomerants, Poet of the Holocaust
## Remarks in Evaluating his Poetry

The collection of poems of Ber Pomerants, the new book of poems, which appeared in the framework of the series called Nefesh of the Association of Writers (this time through the means of Masadah – and what a difference to the good in contrast to the two previous books of this type, the collections of David Fogel and Noah Shtern), is almost entirely in the force of a revelation.

I knew until now a total of three poems of the poet (who died at the hands of the Germans in 1942 after his hiding place in a Polish forest was discovered). These poems were included in Mivhar ha- Shirah ha-Ivrit ha-Hadashah edited by Asher Barash, which was published in 698 (1939). Those poems were able to attract attention and more than this: the uniqueness of their author stood out without any possibility of denying it. However now, when we are presented with the complete poetry that he left behind, that is, what he was able to publish in his lifetime, we do not stop to be astonished. The guesses as to what any poet would be able to produce if he had remained alive is an old issue in the history of literature. However, what force it has in the present circumstance. The ability of Pomerants has already come to exciting proof in his poems that were published. Precisely this proof gives a place for exciting speculations. The style, which is the seal of the personality of the poet, is stamped in it to such an extent. It is a sincere, convincing, authentic modernism. At the same time, it is without pretension, because of the modesty of the author, which pours out onto the lines of Polish Hebrew poetry of the 1920s and 1930s. And this is even the poetry of the Land of Israel on its own merit.

And first of all, what is modernism? This is the new cut of speech in faith, the clearly independent point of view, and the wisdom of absolutely individualistic combinations. These are all because they are necessary for the inner development of the poet. Certainly, there are also influences on Pomerants from either poets writing in foreign languages or in Hebrew. However, these influences were forged on the anvil of personal creativity, which is the gland and its seed, originality. It is interesting to compare the poem of Pomerants, "Galshah av agulah adamdemet" ("A round, reddish cloud glided down") to that of "Mi-tokh viduyav shel huligan" ("From the Confessions of a Hooligan" by Sergei Yesenin). There are some close elements in them.

According to the testimony of those who knew, Pomerants read a lot of Russian literature. However, come and see to what degree each of these two poets have their own clear identity. Yesenin says in the translation of Shlonsky,

Poor, poor farmers!
Certainly, you have become ugly
And you also feared my master and the mud of every swamp
Ha, if you only understood that among you in Russia he is the greatest of poets.
While, Pomerants is above all a Jew: The world?

And I got up in clean cloth with a portion of kosher milk, the gift of an alert mother.

The mother loved her son  who had an ugly nose and ordered the sun to watch his steps,  even if he disobeyed her with the guilt of his beauty beneath his flesh; If he even would go out to move above thorns, Perhaps, he will be once to justly spread out love.

*[Page 278]*

The poetry of Pomerants is clearly autobiographical. It is possible to reconstruct it according to what is made to speak from it even without the order of a formal life. This is great praise. You learn from it about the personal history of a Jewish youth, born in a village in the depths of a region of forests. He was formerly a Russian and Polish after the change of government. The material condition of his family was difficult. His father died. He had deep emotional ties with his mother. This is a chapter in the study of the poetry of Pomerants, which is worthy of a separate and comprehensive discussion. The displacement makes a comment on everything that is understood from it, whether from the standpoint of the struggle with the new urban landscape or from the standpoint of the longing for the pastoral landscape from which he was taken from its bosom. This is a poem with expressionist resonance. However, it does not shout it but turns it inward.

How nice is the small poem "Hithamek ha kokhav ha-maadim" ("The red star disappeared"). How much of an original point of view there is in it. To what a degree are the images taken from the material world so that it is possible to feel it with one's hands. The star is compared to a debtor, who has lost his wealth. There is no hint here of an abstract typed romanticism. And also the description and the passage in the street in front of it. It is a scene likely to glide into excitement, captivating and noble, quiet inside itself. The milieu of the forest and village, like that of the city, with its drunkards and whores and the cruelty basic to it, both of them real and living.

The poems about the father, whose background is the beloved region of his birth are not an idyll with all the warmth of feeling that comes out of them.

Take, for example the poem, "Al ha-hadom" ("On the footstool"):

And when you return
And a heavy cloud rose above the house
and filled the house with a spirit of great happiness
because beside the joy of life that sang forth
and the goodness of heart promising
Did you not bring a sack of potatoes
and a jug of honey.

There are in the poems of Pomerants, which are mainly written in blank verse out of a refusal to be bound by an ensnaring framework, great gentility but never femininity. They have great pride but are not haughty. They are not arrogant in closed . Rather, they have humane pride, which gathers its strength from the honor of man in the image of God. This is without turning a back to the distortion of this in a cruel, brutal, and inhumane world. They have Jewish pride but clean from a suspicion of chauvinism, which is startling, not just once, in the works of other poets, who needed nationalistic and aggressiveness in order to take a stand in the face of a hateful external milieu and desirous of revenge.

This is pure Jewish pride, which was cleansed by great historical and personal suffering altogether. In his poem, "ha-Sharif ":

I am judged to hate by those, who inherited the forest desiring to breathe in absolute despair, but proud while the light of day destroys in me innocent trust and I am even without weapons a Semitic hero.

It seems to me that in the case of Pomerants, it is definitely possible to come across the prophecy of a heart growing heavy, of the catastrophe waiting at the gate. This is even if one should be very cautious in distinguishing "prophecies of destruction" in the area of poetry of Jewish writers before the Second World War. It is so astonishing for this reason to read the last poem that he was able to publish before the depth opened its jaw. It is apparently the summer of 699 (1939), and in it are the very joyful words of Pomerants to his only young son:

[Page 279]

"Sleep, my dear, and be charming to yourself and your mother.

The soft leaves of a tree have gone out from the forest to cover your crib."

It is really not pleasant in conclusion to comment on the superficiality of the Academy to this wonderful book, to which it had erred in routine language and concept. However, its shallowness cannot cast a cloud over a project worthy of praise, which the Association of Writers did in putting together the work of Pomerants. In the same way, nothing in it can lessen the feeling of happiness, tragic as it is, that Hebrew literature has a unique poet like this.

# About the Graves of our Dear Ones, Sons of Antopol
## Two Invitations in Memory of the Destruction

### By P. Czerniak

Being brought to Jewish burial is the holy duty of the one remaining yet alive towards the Jew who died. Thus, the sons of Antopol acted in the time of the 400 years of their existence until the years 1940/41. During that time, there took control of the town beasts of prey and carried out the barbaric executions of infant, women, and unarmed men, innocent of crime. In the sands that face Frishikhvust at the side of the highway to Pinsk, there were dug pits, mass graves, by the gentiles from the nearby village at the request of those who carried out the crime of genocide.

We returned to Antopol on June 22, 1944. The beasts of prey left in haste. The heroes of the murders of unarmed victims feared the terror of death of those returning with arms.

The first invitation. On September 17, 1944, the Isfolkom of the town of Antopol organized a ceremony of opening the mass graves. I received an invitation from Mr. Pastoshenko, the chairman. It was written in it: "We ask you to participate in the sub-committee for 394 opening the graves of the victims, whom the Germans, ravaging Fascists, killed in a bestial manner during the time of occupation." It was very hard for me to give a positive answer.

I sent in my place the Jewish doctor from Moscow, who was sent to help me. She told me: "It was a terrible scene. Huge amounts of tears fell from our eyes when in the open field, between mountains of sand, they showed the place of burial, dug a little, and there began to appear bones and the poor remains of which were once living beings. It was impossible to identify any individuals. Among those killed from the ghetto, there were also the bodies of a number of gentiles who were killed by the Nazis, who suspected them of treason. Those present heard words of eulogy in Russian, brought up memories, and cursed the accursed Germans. Then they covered with sand the 394 remains of the dear ones, put wire around, and with pain held in that closed the throat from speaking, returned in silence to Antopol.

Second invitation. Twenty-seven years after that there was sent an invitation at the request of the Organization of People from Antopol in Israel to the dear people from our town. This is its content: "By this you are invited to a ceremony of memorial and burial of pieces of soil from the mass grave of our dear martyrs of Antopol, may God revenge their blood, in the cellar of the Holocaust on Mt. Zion in Jerusalem, which will take place on Monday, 21 Sivan, June 14, 1971 at 17 hours (5 p.m.) A member of our town Leibl London, who had recently immigrated to Israel with his family from Russia was a messenger for a good deed, and at our request traveled especially to visit the mass grave of our dear martyrs in Antopol, whose grave remained open to beasts of the field and humans, so that when he immigrated to Israel, he would bring from their grave soil to the Land of Israel.

*[Page 280]*

In burying the remains of our martyrs in the cellar of the Holocaust on Mt. Zion in holy Jerusalem, there was filled the duty and holy deed to bring them in this form to bring them to Jewish burial.

Rabbi Blau, may he live along and good life, will lead the ceremony of memorial and burial of the remains in the cellar of the Holocaust. Professor Pinchas Tserniak will speak in the name of the Organization of People from Antopol. The participants after the ceremony will all say Kaddish.

We turn to and ask by this of the people from our town to come to participate in the ceremony in the set place and time and to give the last honor by this to our dear martyrs from Antopol, may God revenge their blood."

Rabbi Blau, may he live along and good life, showed in his words of eulogy that he already knew the good deeds of the Jews of Antopol before the outbreak of World War II. Under the black marble tablet of the black monument that symbolizes the graves of many brethren from the camps of destruction and the ghettos, we put a small bag of remains, of which each grain in it symbolizes a dear person from among so many that are missing now among us, sunk in pain, praying and saying chapters of Psalms. May their memory be holy. The sad and deep voice of the cantor says out the prayer of El male rahamim for them, and those present say aloud Kaddish.

At the symbolic grave in the Land of our ancestors, we take leave from the martyrs of the town, we who remain alive. And here are the words of one of those saved, Pinchas Tserniak: The dear and silent remains of thousands of parents, brothers, and sisters, who were buried on the altar of the nation 30 years ago. The surviving remnant, which fled from the graves prepared to swallow them. The people from Antopol who in their good fortune had left while there was still a chance!

All of us are again united here. Before our eyes are more than two thousand people from the dear town that was and is no more. Behold, in front of us there hover the spirits of the youth and old, pupils and teachers, fathers, and their infants, as the remains of their bodies are laid in front of us, here in the cellar of the terrible Holocaust, the deed of German murderers.

In the years 1940/41, we walked in the streets of the ghetto of Antopol with the sign of a yellow Star of David on our breast and back, just like robots, whose sign of humanity had been stolen from them, the warmth of the heart and the power to think. We listened there day and night to the absurd gentiles, who ruled over us, to their absurd justice. The (accursed) judge Hitler had decreed a death sentence without possibility to appeal over all the people of the Jewish nation. And behold, they were innocent of any crime, except one. That they were born, grew up, and uplifted in their spirit in the times of his Germans, Hitler's before they had been allowed to see the light of day and to be warmed in the Holy spirit. In addition to this, these Jews were always, despite everything, an example for other nations, who learned law and good deeds from them, and not from the hated superman of the executioner.

About these years 1940/42 that came on us in the ghettos and the camps, Ezekiel the prophet has said in chapter 37:11: "Behold, they say: Our bones are dried up, and our hope is lost; we are clean cut off." And so it was.

We did not have then in the ghetto of Antopol any hope to live. There was no hope to live again. We were cut off, cut up without any hope that we could again return to our whole state.

The Nazi decree was carried out with a cruelty without example. And we, who are still alive, ask, and ask again: Why, how did this happen? What will be, what to do, how to suffer? How to act? How can we make it easier for the spirits of the dead that hover here after life were cast out from their bodies in the spring of their life?

*[Page 281]*

And here is the answer of the prophet (the following is from Ezekiel 37:1-14). The valley about which the prophet spoke is the cellar of the Holocaust in which we are standing and around us the dead bones, the holy remains from the Nazi Hell that was in all Europe, the remains of 6 million people.

We return to the question asked of Ezekiel: "Son of man, will these bones live?" Is it possible to put the spirit of life into these remains? And the answer that was received: "Behold, I will cause breath to enter into you and you will live. Behold, I will open your graves and bring you to the Land of Israel, my people, and you will live."

There rises the hope in us. Perhaps our deeds and thoughts will succeed in making live the dry bones seeking mercy for themselves, to continue in their lives, in their thoughts, in their desires, to carry out the plans of their own and children's lives.

Catastrophes similar to ours there were also in other times and places. Tens of thousands were killed, and the only comfort that remained was for the people that the souls of the murdered remained in life. The soul is something that a weapon cannot destroy. It is not of flesh and blood. Therefore, we set up graves and monuments for remains. We dedicate houses of worship and places to come together with the soul.

People who remain alive keep watch on one side over the remains, the dry bones, and on the other side the hovering spirits. They raise their hand and take an oath to do everything to continue the lives and desires of the murdered after the sword has taken the soul from the body.

We swear here that we will give birth to a new generation in a new land, that the dry bones will get skin, that spirit of life will enter people to bring a regeneration and rebirth of this people. In the words of the prophets: "We will come out of the grave and be a very great people."

Know, our remains and dear souls, that your sacrifice was not in vain, that your dreams fashioned in the Diaspora are being realized. We will do everything to advance them more and more. Rest in peace in Paradise.

Mr. Lifshits, as representative of the people from Antopol in Israel, concluded the day of memory for the martyrs of Antopol in the cellar of the Holocaust, with an instructive story on their greatness, qualities, and adherence to Torah, worship and good deeds by those who are no more.

We left full of sadness with the decision to realize the oath.

# Activities of the Organization in Israel
## The Organization of Former Residents of Antopol in Israel

## By H. Osip

The organization was founded in 1951 with the arrival in Israel of the first survivors, who brought the bad news of what happened and the fate of our parents, relatives, and all the community of the martyrs of Antopol.

A deep feeling of being orphaned and loss surrounded us. An inner drive instructed us to establish an organization of Holocaust survivors, the few families, which remained from a community of hundreds of families so that we could have meetings, memorials to mourn together, and to establish an annual memorial meeting in memory of our martyrs. The organization of former residents of Antopol in Israel numbers 70-80 families, who know one another from their days of living in the town of their birth and going back two or three generations.

We maintain connections with the committees of organizations of Landsmanshaftn in the United States and with many families in other countries. We succeeded with the help of these organizations in erecting a beautiful synagogue in Tel Aviv to memorialize the memory of our community and our martyrs. The synagogue is called The Synagogue in the Name of the Martyrs of Antopol. It has a memorial hall for meetings and memorials that we make yearly on 4 Heshvan.

*[Page 282]*

The organization established a Free Loan Society in the name of the martyrs of Antopol, which is called The Fund of Harry and Fanny Osipovits, of New York. This fund grew with their help and activity. The fund distributes loans to members of the organization to be paid back in small payments and without interest.

The name of the community was memorialized in the Holocaust Cellar in Jerusalem by the family of Max and Rebecca Futerman of New York during their visit to Israel in 1964. There were also brought to it in 1971 ashes from the mass grave of our martyrs.

Recently there was founded a fund for scholarships in the name of Louis and Jean Leaf. The philanthropist was born in Canada and his parents are from Antopol. The interest, which will build up in the fund will be distributed as scholarships to students of members of the organization.

Understandably, the biggest success is the publication of the memorial book for the martyrs of Antopol, which we were able to see published due to the initiative of the committee of the organization in Israel.

# Synagogue in Memory of the Martyrs of Antopol in Tel Aviv
### By Z. Z. Shahor

R. Zalman Shahor established a temporary synagogue at the end of Elul 697 (August 1937) in the old Lodz Factory on Nahmani Street, which was called afterwards synagogue in the heart of Tel Aviv. The attempt succeeded and the synagogue developed. Some prayer quorums prayed in it on the weekdays and the synagogue was noisy with a throng of worshippers on the Sabbath and festivals. The founder of the synagogue looked forward from the day of its founding to a permanent synagogue on a fitting plot nearby. He called for that purpose to an assembly the congregants and residents nearby. A committee was elected and an association established to build a synagogue in the heart of Tel Aviv. Some years passed and despite the applications of the committee to the Tel Aviv Municipality, no fitting plot to build a synagogue was found. Zalman Shahor applied in 699 (1939) to an inhabitant of Sharonah (which bordered on the streets Yehudah ha-Levi-Koresh, Mazeh). His name was Ginter. He asked him to sell a plot belonging to him and facing the streets, Yehuda ha-Levi on one side and Koresh on another side. A cabin stood on this spot and in it were a grocery and butcher. The German agreed after lengthy negotiation to sell the plot, whose price would be set by an estimator. Zalman Shahor gave him fifty lira as an advance.

At this time, World War II broke and all the inhabitants of Sharonah were arrested, including the abovementioned Ginter. Zalman Shahor did not give up his plan. He applied to the mayor, Yisrael Rokeah, with the suggestion to ask the Mandatory Government to expropriate the piece of land bordering with the streets Yehudah ha-Levi-Koresh, Mazeh so that a central synagogue would be built since there was no synagogue in the neighborhood. Mr. Rokeah asked the Mandatory Government about this, and it expropriated an area of 24 dunams from the land of Sharonah. After lengthy negotiation with the mayor and the director of municipal property, there was agreed to set aside one dunam to build a synagogue in the heart of Tel Aviv.

People from the Antopol community applied in 714 (1954) to the chairman of the association to build a synagogue in the heart of Tel Aviv.

He was the son of the luminary Rabbi Yosef David, of blessed memory, the rabbi of Antopol. They suggested to him that since they had a certain sum of money to build a synagogue in memory of the martyrs of Antopol and since a plot had been received from the municipality to build a synagogue that they enter in a partnership with the association and build together a synagogue in memory of the martyrs of Antopol. After a series of meetings with the committee of the association, it was decided to accept the suggestion of the people of Antopol. On the 23rd day of Shevat 714 (January 1954), there was signed with good will an agreement to build a synagogue in the heart of Tel Aviv. On the day after the signing of the agreement, there began fervent activity by the united committee to create the conditions that would make it possible to lay the foundation stone for the new synagogue. We approached some known architects and requested suggested plans. After precise examination and consultation with the director of municipal property at that time, Dr. Kaduri, the plans of the architect Mohilever and Koifman of Tel Aviv were chosen as the most appropriate.

*[Page 283]*

There took place on 4 Marheshvan 716 (October 1955), which is the memorial day for the martyrs of Antopol, the festive laying of the foundation stone. This took place in the presence of the Chief Rabbi of Israel, Y. A. Herzog, may he be spared for long life; the Chief Rabbis of Tel Aviv, Rabbi Unterman, may he be spared for long life, and Rabbi Toledano, may he be spared for long life; Hasidic Rebbes, city rabbis, the mayor, Mr. Hayyim Levanon, his assistants, Rabbi Abramowitz and R. Avraham Boyer, Director of the Section for Municipal Property, representatives of the engineering division, citizens of Tel Aviv, people from Antopol from all over the country and the congregants from the synagogue in the heart of Tel Aviv. Chief among them was their rabbi, the luminary, R. Dov Rozntal, may he be spared for long life, Rav Ezor Lev, Tel Aviv, and rabbi of the synagogue.

The laying of the foundation stone was celebrated with much glory and dignity. Immediately, we approached the building. We contacted the contractors of the Company Hartsovah. We began to build the first part, the foundations, the shelter and the supporting pillars to a height of 12 meters. We received 9,000 dollars from people from Antopol in Chicago. Mr. Zalman Shahor received confirmation from the minister, R. Mosheh Shapira, to receive a loan from the Ministry of Religions for 10,000 lira. We approached the municipality and Mr. Boyer promised to pay the loan from the Ministry of Religions on the condition that we return to him 4,000 lira that he lacked for the yearly budget of little synagogues, which do not have the possibility of finishing their buildings. In order not to delay the building, we agreed and the Municipality of Tel Aviv paid the loan. We began to raise money from the congregants of the synagogue in the heart of Tel Aviv and also from the few in number of the people from Antopol in Tel Aviv. A member of the committee, Mr. Hayim Osip, who traveled to the United States to visit his family, arranged a meeting of people from Antopol in New York and on his return brought some cash and much enthusiasm, which he planted in people's hearts. We finished with God's help the first stage and were forced to make an interruption since we had no more money.

Since the synagogue building was next to the Yehudah ha-Levi School, its supporting pillars served as a good goal for children to climb and jump from them. This fact forced the principal to come and warn us that if we did not complete the building or at least build a barbed wire fence, we would be responsible for what happened, God forbid, to any child. We faced the choice of completing the building or building a fence around it. Since we didn't have money, the committee decided after some stormy sessions to build a barbed wire fence. This would cost more than 1,000 lira. Zalman Shahor could not sleep that night. He thought that if we fenced the building that we would have peace from the principal of the school and the municipality. However, who knows when we would begin to build again?

We needed to begin building and God would help! In the morning he contacted some members of the committee and informed them that he had made up his mind. He replied in answer to the question of from where they would get money: "God will help!" He asked Shemuel Lifshits and Hayim Osip if they were prepared to sing on notes due to the contractors. When he received a positive answer, he called the contractors, new agreements were signed, and building was begun. There began intensive work to get sources of money in Israel and in the United States. Slowly, there began to stream some money from the Untied States through the devotion of Mr. and Mrs. Harry and Fanny Osipovits-Osip, people from Antopol, who themselves gave sizable sums and raised small and big sums from people from Antopol in the United States.

*[Page 284]*

With diligent work by the committee of the association to build a synagogue in memory of the martyrs of Antopol, it was already possible to gather and pray in the new synagogue even though it was not completed. They prayed in the new synagogue during the High Holidays of 719 (1958). They also had prayers in the old synagogue in the heart of Tel Aviv. In 720 (1959), they moved to the new synagogue, whose building was completed, although there was still some work to be done. They continued working on the glorious building all these years and are still doing so up to this day. A monumental Holy Ark was built by the architects Nisim Shtrik and Shelomoh Bernstein. The Holy Ark is composed of marble, wood, and artistic glass. The woodwork was a gift of a congregant of the synagogue, the owner of a carpentry shop, Mr. Pesah Angel, in memory of his son Dan, of blessed memory, an air force pilot who died in the Six Day War.

There prayed in the synagogue daily one prayer quorum after another in the morning and evening. Impressive prayers were led on Sabbaths and festivals by well-known cantors. Spiritual activities of the study of the Torah were led by the rabbi, may he be spared for long life, who taught a daily lesson in Talmud. He gave lectures in ethics of the Fathers and midrashim. Also Rabbi Yekutiel, may he be spared for long life, gave daily lessons in Mishnah between the afternoon and evening prayers. Parties were made for the third Sabbath meal in which Rabbi Yekutiel said words of the Torah. The chairman of the synagogue, R. Zalman Shahor, taught a class in Talmud and the weekly portion of the Talmud. Lessons for young people and youth took place. Thus the synagogue served as a spiritual center for all the neighborhood.

This year we were able to put an advanced seminar of about ten adults completing their rabbinical courses and studying in the synagogue from morning to afternoon. The sound of Torah is heard in the synagogue all day and the doors are open to everyone seeking to quench their thirst for Torah. The people of Antopol managed to memorialize their loved ones' memory in a most sublime memorial by creating a big and beautiful synagogue in a quiet neighborhood in the center of Tel Aviv. The synagogue is surrounded by a beautiful garden and pretty trees, which add to the glory of this holy place.

# Translation of a Letter

## By Isar Yehudah b. R. A. Unterman, Chief Rabbi of Tel Aviv – Yafo and District.

With the help of God, Tel Aviv 2 Marheshvan, 721 (October 1960):

In honor of our dear brethren, immigrants from Antopol, in Israel. Peace and blessing. I heard that you are making today a memorial day for the martyrs of your city, who fell victim by the murderers, may their name be blotted out, during the terrible Holocaust. On memorial days like these we unite with the memory of the martyrs and place in front of our eyes the greatness of the destruction and the depth of the tragedy of European Jewry, which was destroyed with such terrible cruelty.

I think it worthwhile to add some drops of comfort to you because concerning your city of Antopol, you have made a fitting memorial by your great participation in the building of a synagogue in the heart of Tel Aviv, in memory of the martyrs of the city, of blessed memory, God will revenge their blood.

*[Page 285]*

I don't know of a more fitting memorial to your city, in which there lived great and famous rabbis and which had a good name for its residents distinguished in Torah, generosity, and devotion to Judaism than the building of a synagogue like this in the Holy Land. It serves not only as a place for prayer but also for permanent Torah lessons to develop the youth spirituality and to strengthen good deeds in the Hebrew city of Tel Aviv.

I have no doubt that this will bring contentment to the souls of the martyrs whose memory will rise up before the public because of this sanctuary.

I cannot refrain from mentioning in this that I had family ties in Antopol because my relatives, the luminary Rabbi Mosheh Tsevi Unterman, of blessed memory, lived there with his dear family. Likewise, when I was a rabbi in Horodna, my friend, the luminary, Rabbi Mosheh Volfson, of blessed memory, was accepted there as rabbi. It is a pity that this tree was cut in the middle of its growth.

I hope your action will serve as a good example to many to show that a memorial to a holy community needs to be tied to the building of a sanctuary, which makes hearts come near to our Father in Heaven and to cling to His holy Torah.

May God cause you together with all our brethren or Israel to merit the complete redemption through the merit of all those who gave their lives to sanctify His name and to see the building of Zion and Jerusalem soon in our days.

With much respect and wishes for comfort, Isar Yehuda Unterman, Chief Rabbi of Tel Aviv – Yafo and District

With the help of God – An Invitation

The addressed and his family are invited by this to participate in the celebration of laying the foundation stone for the building of the synagogue, which will take place, God willing, on Thursday, 4 Heshvan 716 (20.10.1955), at 3 p.m., with the participation of the Chief Rabbis of Israel, The Chief Rabbis of Tel Aviv – Yafo, government officials, mayor, and its representatives, rabbis of our city, and cities of our country.

We would like your attendance. Respectfully, the Committee.

There will be no collection. Buses: no. 20. get off at Mazeh Street, corner of Petah Tikvah Street; no. 12, get off at Yehuda ha-Levi Street, corner of Mazeh Street. Enter the campus: from Mazeh Street 77, by way of Petah Tikvah Street and from Olifant Street, corner of Yehuda ha-Levi Street, no. 64.

# Memories From Erecting the Synagogue
## By Shemuel Lifshits

It is my pleasant duty to bring up memories about erecting the synagogue in memory of the martyrs of Antopol.

The synagogue was erected to memorialize the memory of our dear martyrs, God revenge their blood, and to give a fitting expression to those who cling to faith in God and the endurance of the Jewish people. The beautiful building, which is distinguished by the beauty of its style, is located in the center of Tel Aviv. The name "In Memory of the Martyrs of Antopol" was put up at its entrance.

I want to present a shore review on who things developed as one of the many who helped this project and as a person who was always involved in the building work.

R. Elhanan Lifshits, of blessed memory, thought the idea of a synagogue in memory of the martyrs of Antopol and made the basic assumption. R. Elhanan was the son of my uncle, R. Yehuda, son of R. Efrayim Lifshits, of blessed memory, who was murdered together with the rest of the martyrs of Antopol in the Holocaust.

*[Page 286]*

R. Elhanan was a refugee from Russia. He arrived in Israel crushed and broken. He began to preach for the idea and to spread it among members of the town in Israel. However, there were also people who didn't accept the suggestion and inclined to other suggestions. Nevertheless, he didn't give up and remained committed to his suggestion and opinion. He directed letters to people from Antopol in the United States and other places. He strongly pushed for the good of the matter until the idea slowly penetrated people's hearts.

Meanwhile, he became weak and one day when he went to pray in his synagogue in Givat Shmuel, he collapsed and died.

May his memory be blessed!

We received the first big sum of money, approximately 9,000 dollars from people from Antopol in Chicago and this was the push to begin the project.

We decided after a lot of struggles and debates to get in contact with the synagogue, Heart of Tel Aviv. The municipality had promised it a big plot in the center of the city. However, they did not have the money to begin building. We agreed after negotiation that we would build the building and that it would be devoted to the memory of the martyrs of our town and would be named after them.

The well-known communal worker R. Zalman Shahor, who was born in Antopol, the son of the luminary, Rabbi David, of blessed memory, who acted as rabbi of Antopol, was the chairman of the committee of the synagogue, Heart of Tel Aviv.

R. Zalman Shahor was the living spirit behind the whole project. He devoted himself wholeheartedly and gave much of his spirit and energy to this matter. The erection of the building was inseparably tied to him. Every matter and action was done with his alert and active participation. People undertook works and decision that it is difficult to imagine would have been carried out without his participation. The project during its erection and afterward under his management became a reason to live for him. His blessed work has continued until this time.

I want to quickly note the alert and diligent participation of my brother-in-law R Avraham, son of R. Efrayim Lifshits. He was intricate with the details of the project and took an active part in it. He devoted much of his time and diligence. He was able to raise money and make the project go forward thanks to his many connections.

We came across different difficulties and delays in the long process of erecting the building despite all the many efforts. We had to stop building from time to time. After the foundation was laid and the walls were raised, no building went on for a long time and this caused a part of the walls to be ruined.

We managed to overcome all the obstacles after a sufficient period of time. It seemed to us sometimes that higher hidden forces helped us to reach the stage of completion.

I would not be fulfilling my responsibility if I would not take care to point out the fruitful activity of the family of Hayim and Rinah Osip. They took an active part from the beginning of dealing with the suggestion of building the synagogue and until its final phase. Their house was the center of activity. Every meeting and gathering of friends and brethren took place in their house. They did everything in a quiet and modest way while the difficult work pressed on them. They also influenced their good spirit on all our friends and acquaintances to participate in this work. When they visited the United States they brought a lot of people over to the project and raised recognizable sums of money. I am not able to describe the great and fruitful work, which they invested and the great value they brought to this matter. It is only possible to mention some of the praise, which they deserve. Their reward will be in their work.

I also mention the activity and devotion to this matter of Mr. Yehoshua Varsha. He devoted from his time and energy to the benefit of the project. I mention with blessing the great activity of the family of Harry and Fanny Osip from New York, who gave a lot of money themselves and got others to give money. Likewise, there gave a lot to the good of this matter the families of Max Puterman and his wife Rivkah, Goldman and Aharonski, of blessed memory, who gave a lot money, and also Mirkah Zaidel, the Leaf family from Canada and others.

*[Page 287]*

I want to especially point out the people from Chicago, who helped us a lot, Radil Postol, Pashah Novik, and the families of Zisuk, Vernik, and many others. It is worthwhile to mention here also the Torah scroll, a gift received from Chicago.

All these should be blessed who took part and gave help in this holy project, this synagogue, which is a glory to people from our town and the memory our dear holy martyrs who died in the Holocaust.

# The Free Loan Association in Memory of the Martyrs of Antopol
### By Mosheh Polak

This is the Fund of Harry and Fanny Osipovits and the Fund in the Name of R. Aharon Asher and Tamar Volinets, of blessed memory.

I repeatedly requested my proposal to the members of the committee of the organization of people from Antopol in Israel in our many sessions to be entered into the agenda of the general meetings of people from Antopol taking place every year on the 4th of Heshvan at the time of the evening memorial for the martyrs of our town Antopol. The suggestion was to set up a fund for a Free Loan Association in Memory of the Martyrs of Antopol in order to be able to help people, especially needy people from Antopol in Israel, and to help new immigrants who came to Israel after the Holocaust from Antopol with nothing. However, my suggestion was postponed from year to year so as not to damage our collection to build the synagogue in memory of the martyrs from Antopol, which we built.

When the Sabbath was over in the evening before the coming day of 25 Tishre 721 (October 1960), I brought up my demand again after the synagogue was already completed in our meeting in the committee of the organization that it was already possible to establish a fund for a Free Loan Association.

This time all the members of the committee, Shemual Lifshits, Rinah Osip, Hayim Osip, and myself decided to bring my suggestion to the agenda of the general meeting. On memorial evening on the night before the day of the 4th of Heshvan (October 24, 1960), I brought my proposal to the general meeting of people from Antopol. All the participants at the meeting voted unanimously in favor my suggestion. The fund for a Free Loan Association in the Name of the Martyrs of Antopol was established that evening. Likewise, the assembly suggested and chose me to be the manager and treasurer of the fund. All the participants donated that evening the sum of 1,000 lira. They voted again on a committee for the Free Loan Association according to my suggestion, Rinah Osip, Esther Gamerman, Shemuel Turninski, and Mosheh Alpenshtein. They chose me chairman and fund manager.

The fund began to work in that week. It gave five loans in the sum of 200 lira per family. At the end of 1961 the fund grew by seven times. This was thanks to our honored guests, Harry and Fanny Osipovits from the United States. They visited Israel and gave 3,000 lira to the fund. In addition to this they brought for the fund an additional 3,500 lira, which was donated by their family, relatives, and friends, who were from Antopol and by organization of people from Antopol in the United States. We decided to name a special fund in their name together with that of the Fund for the Free Loan Association for the Martyrs of Antopol because of their good-heartedness and their great activity.

*[Page 288]*

Likewise, we decided to register a fund in the name of R. Aharon Asher and Tamar Volinets, of blessed memory. When he was still alive in the United States, he sent me his manuscript from his twelfth book Ve-da mah she-Tashiv (And Know What to Answer). He asked me to devote myself and take care of all the work of printing and binding and to publish it. He devoted all the income from the aforementioned book to the benefit of the Fund of the Free Loan Association in the Name of the Martyrs of Antopol. His son Eliezer Volinets and his family from the United States asked me to continue after their father died and to take care of the printing and binding. They sent 800 dollars for the publication of the aforementioned title. After I sold all the books, this entered into the Free Loan Association a sum of more than 4,000 lira.

When we look and examine the general balance of the fund upon the completion of ten years since its founding, we esteem and value all the people from Antopol wherever they are for their great accomplishment, interest, and contribution on behalf of the Free Loan Fund. This is for the benefit of people from Antopol in Israel who are helped by the aforementioned fun with interest-free loans and with an attitude of friendship and respect, which is fitting for the name of people from Antopol, who contributed to our glory and for the memory of continuing the goodness and beauty of the past when Antopol existed.

When I take a general account now from all the period of my work for this glorious project, I have great satisfaction. I was able by devoting my time and energy to realize and continue a chain to benefit the honor of people from our town of Antopol and in memory of the martyrs of Antopol who perished and in whose name is called the Fund of the Free Loan Association.

Likewise, there is a special fund for urgent help for the needy from our town, which is managed by the managers of the Free Loan Association. This special fund was founded in 1965 upon the suggestion of the friends from our town, Sarah Krum, from the Bronx. When she visited Israel in 1965, she saw a family from people from our town of five to six people living in one room with no toilet and with a leaky roof. Since then, I took an interest in fixing their living quarters. First of all, we collected a goodly sum of money from people from Antopol in Israel, and also Sarah Krum sent a sum of money from the United States, which was enough to add a toilet and fix their living quarters and roof. Since then we continue to give needy a gift of money on the eve of holidays. We have also sent gift packages to Russia for the isolated people from our town, who remain there.

I thank here those individual from our town, who live in the United States. They will be blessed for their generosity and donation to help the needy. Today we have in this fund for help, the sum of 250 lira.

## Document of Registration of Fund of Free Loan Association
## State of Israel.
## Administrative Offices of the Tel Aviv District no. 2926/99, 14.3.63

Addressed to Mr. Mosheh Polak, Society Chairman and Manager of the Fund of the Free Loan Association in Memory of the Martyrs of Antopol, The Harry and Fanny Osipovits Fund, and the R. Aharon Asher and Tamar Volinets Fund, Holon 13 Feierberg Street.

I have the honor of confirming receipt of your letter from 25.12.62, with the addition of an announcement of paragraph six of the Ottoman Law for Association of 1909 regarding the following association:

Name of the Association: Fund of the Free Loan Association in the Name of the Martyrs of Antopol, and the Funds in the Name of Harry and Fanny Osipovits, and R. Aharon Asher and Tamar Volinets, of blessed memory

*[Page 289]*

The address of the Association: Holon, 13 Feierberg Street, at Polak, Mosheh, aforementioned office.

The goal of the Association: to help and aid members in the case of a disaster, illness, and in every condition needing help and to develop every form of aid for members, and mutual help to every needy person, who are from the town

All these activities done without expenses.

Sincerely, Y. Kuperman, Officer for the Tel Aviv District

# Antopol Martyrs of the Holocaust

| Surname | First Name(s) |
| --- | --- |
| ADREZSHINSKI | Eliezer, and Beilah and the children, Pesiah and Mordekhai |
| AIZENBERG | Hilbni, Moshkah and 2 children |
| AIZENBERG | Itkah, the children, Hershil, Tsadok |
| ALPER | Laizer and the children, Shainah, Yisrael, and another daughter |
| ALPER | Shaye, Esther, and the children Motl, Avraham, Rishke, Devorah, and another child |
| ALTER | Nunis, his wife and 3 children |
| ALTVARG | Bailah and Libah. Yehudah and his wife |
| ALTVARG | Zalman, Hayah and the children, Eliah, David, Yaakov, Bailah and Shabtai |
| ARTSIK | Hinpah and members of his household, 8 people |
| ASH | Yosef, Bailah, the children, Akiva and Eliezer |
| ASOVSKI | Bodiah, and the children, Asher, Nahum, and Hanah-Gishah |
| ASOVSKI | Pinchas-Eliah, Goldah, and child |
| ATNOVSKI | Leib, Itke and the children, Meir, and three more children |
| AVERBUKH | His wife and child |
| AVRAHAM | Mordekhai, his wife, son, daughter, son-in-law and child |
| AZERNITSKI | Beril, his wife and 3 children |
| AZERNITSKI | Brinah |
| AZERNITSKI | Heniah |
| AZERNITSKI | Libah and the children, Yisrael and Esther |
| AZERNITSKI | Motl, Moshkah and the children, Migdal and Hanah |
| AZERNITSKI | Shimon and Shaindl and 3 children |
| AZERNITSKI | Zalman and Moshke and the girls, Mikhalah and Rozah |
| AZERNITSKI | Menasheh and the people of his household |
| BAKALTSUK | Yirmiyahu, Yente, the children, Mosheh, Hayim, and 2 more children |
| BALMAT | Laizer, his wife, and 3 children |
| BALMAT | Yaakov and his household members |
| BANIUK | Yonah |
| BARNBOIM | Leibl, Rahel-Leah, and the children, Zundl and Zaidl |
| BARNBOIM | Pinchas, his wife and child |
| BAYER | Tsirl |
| BAYUK | Berakhah |
| BAYUK | Ekiah |
| BAYUK | Hayim-Mikhal, Libe, and their household members |
| BAYUK | Laibil and their household members |
| BAYUK | Yitshak-Hirsh and their household members |
| BEDER | Avraham-Yitshak |
| BEDER | Laizer, Rahel-Libah, the children, Ester, Simah |
| BEDER | Raitsah |
| BEDER | Yitshak |
| BEKHER | Mosheh and their household members |
| BEKHER | Shemuel and their household members |
| BERKOVITS | Eliah |

| | |
|---|---|
| BERKOVITS | Yaakov-Hayim, Minah and their 2 children |
| BERKOVITS | Yitshak and Sarah |
| BERMAN | Peshah-Hodes |
| BERNSTEIN | Eliezer, Paitsah, the children, Aryeh, Yisrael and Hayah |
| BERSHNOTES | Hershil and Hayah-Bailah |
| BLAT | Shemuel, Rahel, and 2 children |
| BRASHEVITSKI | Raizl, the children, Maitah, Efrayim and Hanah |
| BRASHEVITSKI | Shelomoh and Esther-Bailah |
| BRASHEVITSKI | Yosef, Leah, and the son Yaakov, Gedalyah |
| DAIKSEL | David-Hirsh and members of his household |
| DAIKSEL | Ezra, his wife and child |
| DAIKSEL | Libe and the children, Shemuel and Ribah |
| DAIKSEL | Miraim-Raizel and the children, Gindel and Hayim |
| DAIKSEL | Yisrael, Devorah and his mother |
| DAZOK | Shemuel |
| DOMSKI | Leah |
| DUBINER | Beril, Leah and the children, Yitshak and Yaakov |
| DUBINER | Mosheh and Sarah-Maitah |
| DUBINER | Velvil and Bailah-Libe |
| DUBOVSKI | Yosl-David, Faigah, and the children Mosheh, Yaakov-Meir and Yisrael |
| DVINETS | Avraham, his wife and 5 children |
| DVINETS | Eliah, his wife and 4 children |
| DVINETS | Raishah and 4 children |
| EPEL | Mikhal |
| EPEL | Pinchas and the children Yitshak and Yaakov |
| EPELBOIM | Akiva and his family |
| EPELBOIM | Bailah and the girls Faigah and Brainah |
| EPELBOIM | Mordekhai and Bashah |
| EPSTEIN | Akiva and Tsiporah |
| EPSTEIN | David, Yente and the children Hayim and Mosheh Epstein Yaakov and Hayah and the daughter Rivkah |
| EPSTEIN | Fraidl and the children |
| EPSTEIN | Reuven, his wife and the children Shelomoh, Hanah and Mikhal |
| EPSTEIN | Yitshak Leib and members of his household |
| EPSTEIN | Yitshak Meir, his wife, his daughter and her husband and two grandchildren |
| ERLIKH | Elke and her daughter Miriam |
| ERLIKH | Mordekhai, Haikah, the children Avraham, Hershil, Velvel, Laibl and Peshe |
| FAKHPAH | Yaakov and his wife |
| FALMAT | Shelomoh, Minah, the children Tsiviyah, Yosef, and two more children |
| FANTSHUKH | Avraham-Eliah |
| FANTSHUKH | Meir |
| FANTSHUKH | Reuven, his wife and seven children |
| FANTSHUKH | Shimon and Moshkah |
| FANTSHUKH | Yekutiel, his wife and six children |
| FARBER | Meir |
| FARBER | Yosef Laib and the children Zlatah and Shelomoh |
| FELDMAN | Mosheh, Sarah and two children |
| FELDSTEIN | Avraham |
| FELDSTEIN | Ben-Tsiyon, Sarah and the daughter Rahel |

| | |
|---|---|
| FELDSTEIN | Tseviah |
| FERNIK | Motl, Bailah, and the daughters Bubl, Fridl, and Hinkah |
| FESTER | Shainah, the children Miriam, Hilel, Hayah-Leah and another girl |
| FINKELSTEIN | Katriel, his wife and daughter Bubl |
| FINKELSTEIN | Leah and two children |
| FISH | Hayah and the daughters, Mirl, Libe and Teme |
| FISHER | Pesah, his wife and two children |
| FISHER | Yaakov, his wife and two daughters |
| FISHMAN | Laizer, Bubl and the children Efrayim, Itke, Mosheh and Tsirl |
| FLOMBOIM | Zalman, Perl and the child Nehemiah |
| FRIDMAN | Berl and the daughter Zlate |
| FRIDMAN | David, Krainah and the daughter Sarah |
| FRIDMAN | David-Aizik, Zlatah and child |
| FRIDMAN | Eliezer, Leah and the children Yaakov, Yehudit+B186 |
| FRIDMAN | Havah |
| FRIDMAN | Hirshl, his wife and child |
| FRIDMAN | Mosheh, his wife and the children. Rahel, Mosheh, and three more sons |
| FRIDMAN | Mosheh, Shainah and two children |
| FRIDMAN | Yosef, Faigl and the son Shemuel |
| FRIDMAN | Yosl, Shainah and the daughter Hayah |
| FROIM-ELOMHIS | Eliah, His wife and 3 children |
| FUKS | Aharon and his son |
| FUTERMAN | Beril, Hanah and the child |
| FUTERMAN | Hayim Zalman and Pashah |
| FUTERMAN | Tsadok, Bailah and the children Mosheh and Yaakov |
| GALOBTSHIK | Hershil, his wife and 2 children |
| GALOBTSHIK | Laizer, Sarah, the children, Shainah, Hayah, Vikhnah, Rodiyah, and Faigl |
| GALOBTSHIK | Mosheh, Bubl, the children, Heniah, Shelomoh, and David |
| GARBER | Zekharyah, his wife and the children, Leah, Avraham, and Rahel |
| GARFINKL | Eliah-Leib, Goldah and the children, Gedaliah and Motiah |
| GARFINKL | Faigah-Rahel |
| GARFINKL | Sarah and the children, Mosheh-Velvil and another child |
| GARFINKL | Shmerl, his wife and the children, Yosef and Brainah |
| GARFINKL | Yoshkah |
| GARFINKL | Zaidl and his daughter Heniah-Rahel |
| GARGLIKHES | Her son-in-law, his brother, and their families |
| GELERSTEIN | Hayah and her household members |
| GELERSTEIN | Sarah |
| GERSTEIN | Gavriel, his wife and child |
| GERSTEIN | Mendl |
| GERSTEIN | Mordekhai, his wife, the daughter Frumah and another child |
| GERSTEIN | Noah, Pesil, the children Esther-Malkah, Reshah, Fraidl, Akiva, Mosheh, Yisrael and Yosef and Menahem |
| GERSTEIN | Rivkah, the children, Mosheh and Mindl |
| GERSTEIN | Shelomoh, Mosheh, the children, Menahem and another child |
| GERSTEIN | Shimon, Sarah and a child |
| GERSTEIN | Yitshak-Hersh and his wife |
| GLATSER | Itse, Bailah and the children, Yentah and Minah |
| GLATSER | Shaie, Hanah and the children, Shimon, Zelig, Zlatah, Haitsah and Bailah |
| GLIK | Avraham |
| GLIK | Hershil, his wife and the children |
| GLIK | Shemuel-Yitshak, Sarah, and the children Rahel, Hershel, and 3 more children |

| | |
|---|---|
| GOLDBERG | Aharon and Esther |
| GOLDBERG | Avraham Yitshak, Heniah and their daughter Bashah |
| GOLDBERG | Dinkah |
| GOLDBERG | Frumah |
| GOLDBERG | Gedaliah, Hentsah and the children, Hinkah and Mordekhai |
| GOLDBERG | Goldah and the children Note and Meir |
| GOLDBERG | Lipman |
| GOLDBERG | Mordekhai, Miriam, and the children, Aryeh and Bubl |
| GOLDBERG | Moseh-Eliah, his wife and daughter, Frumah |
| GOLDBERG | Mosheh and Rahel-Malkah |
| GOLDBERG | Mosheh, Bailah, and 4 children |
| GOLDBERG | Nahum, his wife and the children, Alter, Sarah, and 4 more children |
| GOLDBERG | Pashah |
| GOLDBERG | Shelomoh, his wife and child |
| GOLDBERG | Shimon, his wife and three children |
| GOLDBERG | Yaakov, Hashah and the girls, Hinkah, Heniah, Blumah and Tseviah |
| GOLDBERG | Yaakov-Hirsh and his household |
| GOLDBERG | Yaakov-Mosheh and his household members |
| GOLDBERG | Yehudah and his wife |
| GOLDBERG | Yisrael and Frumah |
| GOLDBERG | Yitshak and his wife and his household members |
| GOLDBERG | Yudl, Raizl, and the children, Leah and Bashke |
| GOLDFARB | Meir and his wife |
| GOLDFARB | Toibah, the children, Meir, Pinchas-Eliah, Yaakov |
| GOLDFARB | Zelig |
| GOLDSHUL | Bailah and Libah |
| GOLDSHUL | Yitshak, Rainah and 2 children |
| GOLDSMID | Yaakov, his wife, and 7 children |
| GOLDSTEIN | Yisrael, Bailah-Goldah, the children Pinchas, Leah, and Yaakov |
| GOPER | Avraham, Alte and the children, Miriam, Bashke, Goldah and Gedaliah |
| GOPER | Hayim, Rivkah, and the children Hanah, Eliah, Yehiel, Yosef, Sarah and Faigah |
| GOPER | Yitshak, his wife and their daughter |
| GORDON | Binyamin, Heniah-Gutke and the son, Motiah |
| GORDON | Yeshayah, Nehamah and child |
| GORNIK | Yeshayah, his wife and 4 children |
| GOZALTNI | Faivl, his wife and 4 children |
| GRINBERG | Asher, Mosheh and 2 children |
| GRINBERG | Hayim |
| GRINBERG | Raizl |
| GRINBERG | Sarah |
| GRINBERG | Yaakov, Leah and the children, Yosef, Fraidl |
| GRINMAN | Getsil |
| GRINMAN | Hershil |
| GRINMAN | Laizer |
| GRINMAN | Rahel |
| GRINMAN | Sarah |
| GRINSPAN | Yosef and his mother |
| GROSMAN | Gershon, Rahel and the daughters Hashah and Ilke |
| GROSMAN | Hayah |
| GROSMAN | Mosheh, and his household members |
| GUNSK | Hershil, his wife, and 5 children |

| GURSKI | Mosheh, his wife, and the children |
| GUTER | David |
| GUTER | Itsl, Hanah, the son and grandchild |
| GUTER | Libe |
| GUTER | Yosef and Itke |
| GVIRTSMAN | Eliah and the son, Avraham |
| GVIRTSMAN | Laibl, Libe, and 2 children |
| GVIRTSMAN | Yeruham and Leahkah |
| HERSHENHORN | Faigl |
| HERSHENHORN | Lifshah and her daughter Lailah |
| HERSHENHORN | Rivkah, the children, Mosheh and Mindl |
| HERSHENHORN | Shelomoh, Ester and the children |
| KADINER | Laibl, Pashah and the children Blumah, Vikhne and Gitl |
| KADINER | Mosheh, his wife and 2 children |
| KADINER | Pesil |
| KAGAN | Eliah, his wife, their son and their married daughters |
| KAGAN | Lipman and his wife |
| KAGAN | Reuben and members of his household |
| KAGAN | Shelomoh, Goldah, the children Yaakov, Mosheh, Sarah, Nehamah, Brainah, Motl and Rozah |
| KAGAN | Shemuel, his wife and daughter |
| KAGAN | Yaakov, Hayah Hodes and the children, Itkah, Genshah, Yitshak |
| KALABELSKI | Hayah and the children Perl and Shelomoh |
| KALADNER | Yisrael |
| KALDANER | Meir-Yosl, his wife, the son Getsil, the daughter Rahel, her husband and 2 children |
| KAMENETSKI | Aharon-Asher, Goldah and the children Avraham, Yisrael and Fridah |
| KAMENETSKI | Berl, Zlate and the children |
| KAMENETSKI | Gershon, Tseviah and the children Raishah and Shemuel |
| KAMENETSKI | Mordekhai, Tsiporah and the children Ester, Pashah, Devorah, Goldah, Shainah, Daboshah |
| KAMENETSKI | Mosheh and Sarah, Hershl, Yoel and Shifrah |
| KANTSIPER | Abba, Tsaitl, and the children Yudl, Yosef and another daughter |
| KAPELUSHNIK | Laibl and Fridah |
| KAPELUSHNIK | Mordekhai |
| KAPELUSHNIK | Velvil and members of his household |
| KAPELUSHNIK | Yitshak |
| KAPLAN | Aharon and members of his household |
| KAPLAN | Aharon Shemuel, Hayah and the daughter, Hanah |
| KAPLAN | Aharon-Asher, Leah and the children Ester and Ben-Tsiyon |
| KAPLAN | David and Malkah |
| KAPLAN | David, Rahel and 2 children |
| KAPLAN | David-Yosl, Rodiah and the children Libe, Laibl , Rivkah and 2 more children |
| KAPLAN | Gedaliah |
| KAPLAN | Gershon, Berakhah and the child |
| KAPLAN | Hayim |
| KAPLAN | Henekh |
| KAPLAN | Hodes, and members of their household |
| KAPLAN | Laizer and members of his household |
| KAPLAN | Mosheh, his wife and 2 children |

| | |
|---|---|
| KAPLAN | Motl, Pashah, the children Rahel, Avraham and Mindl |
| KAPLAN | Sarah and members of her household |
| KAPLAN | Yitshak and members of his household |
| KARLINSKI | Shelomoh, his wife and the children Hanah, Note, and another child |
| KARLINSKI | Zaidl, his wife and the child |
| KATS | Shimon, Bailah and the child Laib |
| KAZAN | Avraham and members of his household |
| KAZAN | Ezra and Bodiah |
| KAZAN | Pinchas, his wife and 2 children |
| KAZAN | Yitshak and members of his household |
| KAZUKH | Laib |
| KIPL | Sarah and 7 children |
| KISELOV | Bailah and the children Hayim, Yosef and Mirelah |
| KITSHIN | Hayah and her daughter Mindl |
| KLUG | and his family |
| KLUG | Hershil and his family |
| KLUG | Miriam |
| KLUG | Shemuel, Shainah-Rivkah, and the girl Devorah |
| KLUG | Yitshak |
| KLUG | Yosl, his son, Avigdor, his wife and 6 children |
| KOHON | Avigdor |
| KOHON | Hershl |
| KOHON | Lipman and his wife |
| KOHON | Mosheh, his wife and their son, Nehemiah |
| KOIPERMAN | and member of his household |
| KOPL | Avraham-Yitshak, his wife and the children Gershon, Bailah, and three more children |
| KOPL | (Der Kotlar) |
| KOTLIAR | Ber-Laib |
| KOTLIAR | Sarah and the children Taibah and 3 more sons |
| | Laibl and his wife |
| KOVOL | Avraham-Yitshak and Heniah-Rivkah |
| KOVOL | Beril, Etil, and the children Yaakov, Sarah, Haninah, Hayim-Getsil |
| KOVOL | Beril, his wife and children |
| KOVOL | Yisrael, Breine and the children Mosheh-Laid, Shemuel, Yaakov, Yosef, Hanah, Perl and Haninah |
| KRINSKI | Pintsah and members of her household |
| KROKHMALNIK | Yosef and members of his household |
| KRONENBERG | Mates, his wife and children |
| KRONENBERG | Pinchas, Hayah and the children |
| KRUM | Laibl, his wife and 3 children |
| KUPERMAN | Arieh and members of his household |
| KUPETSKI | Beril and members of his household |
| MARENBLAT | Mosheh, his wife and children |
| MARKITER | Reuven, Sarah-Vitah and son, David |
| MELAMED | Nehemiah and his wife |
| MELAMED | Yitshak and members of his household |
| MELAMED | Zerah and members of his household |
| MELIS | Eliah, Pashah and the child Laibkah |
| MIKHAEL | Yoel-Leibs and members of his household |
| MILSHLTEIN | Binyamin, Plate and two children |
| MILSHTEIN | Mosheh and members of his household |
| MILSHTEIN | Rivkah and members of her household |

| | |
|---|---|
| MILSHTEIN | Yehudah |
| MILSHTEIN | Yisrael, Rivkah and the children, Yaakov-Hayim and three more children |
| MILSHTEIN | Yosef, Hayah and child |
| MOLIAR | Pinchas, his wife and 4 children |
| MOLIAR | Shemuel and members of his household |
| MOLIAR | Tamah and the children, Hayah and another child |
| MOLIAR | Tsipah and the children, Brainah, Yosef and another child |
| MOLIAR | Yitshak-Aharon, his wife and the daughters, Rahel and Yente |
| MORGENSHTER | Hayim, Taamah and the children, Eliezer, Elimelekh, Zerah and Yitshak |
| NADELMAN | Reuven, Hayah and 2 children |
| NADL | Eliah, his wife and the children Boniah, Mosheh and one more child |
| NADL | Ezra and members of his household |
| NADL | Mosheh |
| NADL | Nahah, Bailah-Golde and Pesil |
| NADL | Tsirl, Shelomoh and sons Yisrael-Mikhael, and Yitshak-Hersh |
| NAIDITSH | Mosheh, his wife and the children Zunik and Nunik |
| NEIDUS | Shaye, Goldah and daughter |
| NEIDUS | Shemuel, Shaindl, and the children Tsiporah and Avraham |
| NITSBERG | Hershl |
| NOVIDK | David-Yosl, his wife, daughter and grandchild |
| NOVIK | Devorah and members of her household |
| NOVIK | Faivl, Tamarah and four children |
| NOVIK | Mikhael, Teme and the children Hanah, Berakhah, Tsipah, Shemuel and Shaindl |
| NOVIK | Mordekhai, his wife, their daughter, their son-in-law, and 3 grandchildren |
| NOVIK | Mosheh, Martah and the children Gindil, Zusl, Leah and one more child |
| NOVIK | Shemuel and members of his household |
| NOVIK | Shimon and members of his household |
| NOVIK | Yaakov-David, his wife and 6 children |
| NUSBOIM | Avraham-Aharon, Faigl, Itsl, Yosl and Sarah |
| OLIKER | Hayim, Beilah, and the children, Heniah and Itsil |
| OSIPOVITS | Ber-Leib, his wife and 3 children |
| OSIPOVITS | Brainah and his son, Motiah |
| OSIPOVITS | Pesiah |
| PASHAH | Yaakov-Hayims |
| PERLMUTER | Menahem and Hayah-Rahel |
| PILTSHUK | Mordekhai and members of his household |
| PODOLEVSKI | Hayim-Yitshak, Ester and the children Hershl and Meir |
| PODOREVSKI | Avraham, Faniah and the children Rozah and one more child |
| POIMER | Leah and the children, Itsil, Shaindl, Shelomoh |
| POLEVSKI | Shmeril, his wife and daughter Sarah |
| POLIAK | Aharon, Miriam and the children Rivkah, Rahel and Asher |
| POLTSHUK | Yosef |
| | Beril, Itkah and child |
| | Fridah and her son Motil |
| POMERANETS | Gedaliah, his wife and four children |
| POMERANETS | Henakh, Brainah and the children Hershil, Yaakov-Meir, Hayah and Leah |
| POMERANETS | Hershl, Bashah-Yente, Bailah, Rahel and another brother |
| POMERANETS | Leah and the daughters, Gitl, Blumah |
| POMERANETS | Maniah and her son |
| POMERANETS | Meir and Hayah-Leah |

| | |
|---|---|
| POMERANETS | Meir-Hayim and Ester |
| POMERANETS | Mordekhai and his wife |
| POMERANETS | Mosheh, Shainah and the children |
| POMERANETS | Note, Dinah and child |
| POMERANETS | Pashah and members of his household |
| POSHTSANKER | Aharon and members of his household |
| POSHTSANKER | Laizer |
| POSTAL | Akiva, Toibah and four children |
| POSTAL | Devorah and the son Yisrael |
| POSTAL | Faigah-Pashah and the daughter Hayah |
| POSTAL | Goldah and the children Mosheh and Mirl |
| POSTAL | Hayah-Raizl, the daughter Ester, her husband Yosef and the children Minah and Faigl |
| POSTAL | Meir |
| POSTAL | Pinchas |
| POSTAL | Shainah-Faigl |
| POSTAL | Yehezkel and Goldah, Meir and Shaindl |
| POZNIAK | Beril, Sarah and members of their household |
| POZNIAK | Laib, Heniah and the children Avraham and three more sons |
| POZNIAK | Meir, his wife and 7 children |
| POZSHES | Hayim-Meir, Malkah and the children Zaidl, Yaakov, Lilbah |
| POZSHES | Yerahmiel, Etil and daughter Faigl |
| PRUZSHANSKI | Mendl, Rahel and the children Tsiporah, Yaakov, Perl and Nehemiah |
| PRUZSHANSKI | Mosheh, Yehoshua, Shainah and child |
| PRUZSHANSKI | Yaakov, Hanah and the daughter Rahel |
| **R**ABINOVITSH | Barukh-Hirsh, Hanah, and the girl, Goldah |
| RABINOVITSH | Hayim, his wife and 4 children |
| RABINOVITSH | Nahah (ha-Rabanit) |
| RAIZENFELD | Yaakov |
| RATNER | Mosheh, his wife and the son Beril |
| RAVINSKI | Avraham-Hirsh, Minah and the daughter Shoshanah |
| RAVINSKI | Miriam |
| RAVINSKI | Mosheh, his wife and the daughter Hentse |
| RAVINSKI | Rivkah |
| REZNIK | Pinchas, Nehamah and the son Shemuel |
| RIMLAND | Lifshah |
| ROTENBERG | Mordekhai, Tsipah and the children Hayim, Meir and the 2 daughters |
| ROZENBERG | Avraham |
| ROZENBOIM | Laizer, Rozah and the daughters Shulamit and Hayutah |
| ROZENBOIM | Yaakov-Shemuel and Lifshah |
| RUBINSTEIN | Efrayim |
| RUBINSTEIN | Gadie and his wife |
| RUBINSTEIN | Hayim |
| RUBINSTEIN | Heniah-Faigah |
| RUBINSTEIN | Shalvah and Rodiah |
| RUBINSTEIN | Shimon, Bertah, and the children Faniah, Poliah, Motl and 3 more children |
| RUBINSTEIN | Yosef, Malkah and the children Zelig, Motel and Rivkah |
| RUDETSKI | Devorah |

| | |
|---|---|
| RUDETSKI | Yirmiyahu, Faigl and child |
| RUSHEVSKI | Shelomoh, Dinkah and the child Elkanah |
| RUSHEVSKI | Zalman, Elke and the child Meir |
| SAHAROV | Avraham, Hamke, and the daughters Osnah, Hayah-Etil, Shainah and Bereleh |
| SAHAROV | Hanah-Rivkah and the daughter, Taibl |
| SAPIR | Binyamin and his wife |
| SAPIR | Yaakov and members of his household |
| SAPIR | Yosef and members of his household |
| SEGAL | Ever, Raizl, and the children Shemuel and Zaidl |
| SERKIN | ha-Moreh |
| SHAGAN | Aharon, Bashe, Yente and child |
| SHAGAN | ha-Rofe and his wife |
| SHAINBOIM | Mosheh |
| SHAINBOIM | Zaidl, Rivkahand the son Zelig |
| SHAPIRA | Avraham-Yitshak and Rahel and 3 children |
| SHAUL | ha-Nagar and his mother |
| SHEDROVITSKI | Fraidah and 3 daughters |
| SHERESHEVSKI | Eliezer, Heniah, and the daughters Faniah and Sarah |
| SHEVELEVITSH | Mikhlah |
| SHEVELEVITSH | Motl, Mirke and the children Hayah, Hayim and another child |
| SHPILKE | Tamah-Leah |
| SHTERMAN | Hanah and members of her household |
| SHTERMAN | Hershil, his wife and son Yisrael |
| SHTERMAN | Mosheh, Hanah-Malkah and the children Pashah, Sarah, and Rahel |
| SHTERMAN | Shimon |
| SHTERMAN | Zalman |
| SHUB | Eliah |
| SHUB | Hodes and members of her household |
| SHUB | Motl, Svitsah, and 2 children |
| SHUB | Shelomoh |
| SHUB | Yirmiyahu, his wife and members of their household |
| SHUB | Zaidl and members of his household |
| SHVARTSSTEIN | Eliah, his wife and 2 children |
| SHVARTSSTEIN | His wife and 10 children |
| SHVARTSSTEIN | Motl, his wife and 2 children |
| SHVARTSSTEIN | Shevtil and his wife |
| SIROTE | Avigdor and Hashah |
| SIROTE | Hayim, Hayah and child |
| SIROTE | Yosl, Bubl and the children Mirah and Mosheh |
| SKAKUN | David-Hersh |
| SKAKUN | Shakhna and Bailah |
| SLONIMSKI | Eliah, Hayah and the children Shaindl, Motiah, Asher, Hanah and Yente |
| SLONIMSKI | Shaye, Zlate and the children Hershil, Shaindl, Fridl and Asher |

| | |
|---|---|
| SOLOVAITSHIK | Yosef and his family |
| STARASELSKI | Meir, Ester and 2 children |
| STAVSKI | Bashkah |
| TENENBOIM | Devorah, her husband, mother and 2 children |
| TIMIANKER | Rahel-Bashah and the children Velvel, Laizer and one more child |
| TSIRULNIK | His wife Tsiporah and child |
| VAINSHTAIN | Efrayim |
| VAINSHTAIN | Ester |
| VAISMAN | Yosef, Raizl and the daughters, Bailah, Hanah, and Rahel |
| VAITSL | Hayim, his wife and 3 children |
| VAIZL | Mosheh, his wife and 7 children |
| VALDMAN | Barukh, Libe and the children Devorah, Shelomoh, and Mosheh |
| VALDMAN | David-Yosef and his household members |
| VARSHAVSKI | Bubkah |
| VARSHAVSKI | David, GItl, and child |
| VARSHE | Avraham-Yaakov, Gitl and daughter |
| VARSHE | Binyamin, Pesl, and the son, Shemuel |
| VARSHE | Eliah, Goldah and the son, Gershon |
| VARSHE | Ester, her husband, Berl, and 2 children |
| VARSHE | Laizer, Hayah-Sarah and the children, Mikhael, Rahel, and 2 more children |
| VARSHE | Motl |
| VARSHE | Shainah and the children, Avraham-Yaakov and Haikah |
| VARSHE | Shemuel and Brainah |
| VARSHE | Velvil, Ester-Leah, and the children, Raishah, Peshah, Barukh and Goldah |
| VARSHE | Yehudah and his household members |
| VARSHE | Yitshak, Shifrah, and 6 children |
| VARSHE | Yudl, Rahel and the 2 children |
| VEKSLER | Yitshak |
| VERNIK | Hayah and the son Laibl |
| VIGOTSKI | Pinah, Tsipah and the children |
| VINIK | Hashah and her grandson, Aharon |
| VINIK | Laibl and members of his household |
| VINIK | Shelomoh and members of his household |
| VISOTSKI | MeirPolah and the daughter Tsilah |
| VISOTSKI | Shemuel |
| VLADOVSKI | Hershl |
| VLADOVSKI | Kaitah |
| VLADOVSKI | Motl |
| VOLANSKI | Berl and his household members |
| VOLANSKI | David, his wife and the children Yente, Libe and still three more sons |
| VOLANSKI | Davidhis wife, the children, Yute, Libe and 3 more sons |
| VOLANSKI | Mosheh-Meir, Soniah, and the children, Libe, Haim, and Heniah |
| VOLANSKI | Shelomoh, Ester-Bailah, the children, Hayim, Maitah and Navah |
| VOLFZON | David |
| VOLFZON | Leah |
| VOLFZON | Malkah |
| VOLFZON | Mirelah |
| VOLFZON | Yehiel |
| VOLIAK | Libl, Sarah and 3 children |
| VOLILNETS | Asher, his wife and 2 daughters |

| | |
|---|---|
| VOLILNETS | Beril, Bashah and 2 children |
| VOLINETS | Avraham and his household members |
| VOLINETS | Avraham-Hirsh and his household members |
| VOLINETS | Beril, Faigl and child |
| VOLINETS | David, Itkah and 2 children |
| VOLINETS | Efrayim |
| VOLINETS | Ester-Raizl |
| VOLINETS | Fradel and her son Mosheh-Ber |
| VOLINETS | Hayah-Leah |
| VOLINETS | Hershl, Stishah and the children Ester, Tsaitl, and 1 more child |
| VOLINETS | Hersh-Laib, his wife and the children Laizer, Ester, Avraham, Heniah, and 2 more children |
| VOLINETS | Leibke and Rivkah |
| VOLINETS | Menahem and his household members |
| VOLINETS | Mindl and the children, BInyamin, Asher, Tsiril |
| VOLINETS | Mordekhai, Yokheved, and the children, Sarah, Tsadok, Itl-Heniah, Ruhamah, Berl, Avraham and Hayah |
| VOLINETS | Mosheh and his household members |
| VOLINETS | Mosheh Velvil and his household members |
| VOLINETS | Mosheh-Yitshak, Itkah and the children, Ester and Avraham |
| VOLINETS | Moshkah and the daughters Leah and Shainah |
| VOLINETS | Motil and his household members |
| VOLINETS | Naftali, Tsarne and the children, Yosef and Bailah |
| VOLINETS | Nahum and Heniah |
| VOLINETS | Ribah and her children, the Rabbi Shemuel and another son |
| VOLINETS | Shaindl |
| VOLINETS | Shelomoh and sarah and 3 children |
| VOLINETS | Tsevi-Leib, his wife, his son, his daughters and their families |
| VOLINETS | Tsiril, her husband and 2 children |
| VOLINETS | Tuviah, Rahel and the children, GItl and Pashah |
| VOLINETS | Velvil and the members of his household |
| VOLINETS | YItshak-Aharon and his household members |
| VOLINETS | Yosef and Bailah and the daughter Ester |
| VOLINETS | Yudl and 2 children |
| VOLINETS | Yudl, Rivkah-Leah and 2 daughters |
| VOLINETS | Zaidl, Ester-Leah, and the children Rodiah, Yeshayah, Shaindl, Yehudit and Yehoshua |
| VOLINETS | Zalman, Ester and the children Sarah-Leah |
| VOLKIN | The Rabbi, Yitshak-Elhanan, Shifrah, and the children, Mosheh and two more children |
| VOLLINETS | Hershl, Leah, and the children Samuel, Aidl, Berl and Nahum |
| VOLOVELSKI | Menahem, Malkah and the children, David and one more child |
| VOLOVELSKI | Sarah-Rivkah |
| VOLOVELSKI | Senkah, his wife and the children, Atiah and one more child |
| VOLOVELSKI | Yaakov-LeibSetirah and the son David |
| VUDENAS | Yaakov, Miriam and the daughters, Hayah and one more daughter |

## TABLE OF CONTENTS OF THE ORIGINAL YIZKOR BOOK

## Political, Social, Economic, and Fashion of Life

## Photographs

# Hebrew Messages

# People and Families of Antopol

## Antopol Martyrs of the Holocaust

# INDEX

www.ingramcontent.com/pod-product-compliance
Lightning Source LLC
Chambersburg PA
CBHW061833260326
41914CB00005B/982